Direct Effect

Europa Law Publishing, Groningen 2002

Direct Effect
Rethinking a Classic of EC Legal Doctrine

Jolande M. Prinssen & Annette Schrauwen (Editors)

The Hogendorp Papers (3)

Proceedings of the Annual Colloquium of the
G.K. van Hogendorp Centre for European Constitutional Studies

Europa Law Publishing is a publishing company
specializing in European Union Law.
For further information please contact Europa Law
Publishing via email: info@europalawpublishing.com
or visit our website at: www.europalawpublishing.com.

© Europa Law Publishing, G. Betlem, D. Edward, W.
Eijsbouts, J. Gerkrath, J. Jans, A. Nollkaemper, P.-J.
Kuijper, S. Prechal, J. Prinssen, D. Van Eeckhoutte, A.
Ward, J. Wouters, 2002

Typeset in Scala and Scala Sans, Graphic design by
G2K Designers, Groningen/Amsterdam

NUR 828; ISBN 90-76871-09-4

British Library Cataloguing-in-Publication Data
A catalogue record for this book is available from the
British Library

Preface

Direct effect, a concept and principle boldly launched by the ECJ in the Sixties, has proved successful to the point of threatening its own survival. As much was demonstrated when Sacha Prechal (Tilburg University) in her applauded inaugural lecture suggested that the time has come to take it out of business for want of self-containment.

The challenge by Prechal occasioned the Conference in Amsterdam, June 2001, which is at the basis of this book. The Conference's brochure claimed:

'Still, the old term [direct effect] is best kept as a symbol. There is a single, intelligible field of study concerning the normative cross-over from EC-law into domestic law. This is why we now suggest to use the term 'Direct Effect' in the widest sense, to cover all ways by which EC norms, on their own authority, exert legal force in the Member States, be it by way of simple normative substitution (Van Gend en Loos), *of exclusion* (CIA Security), *of interpretation requirements* (Marleasing), *of tort principles* (Francovich), *or additional standards of judicial process* (Comet).

The leading questions are if it is necessary, and if so, on whose authority, on what grounds and in what form to delimit such wide applicability'.

These questions the present book answers by cutting back overgrowth and over-ambitions of the doctrine of direct effect, to sober it up and recover its essentials, leaving it a proud yet not immodest tenet of EU Law. One may read each of the chapters as an attempt to correct, to emend, to simplify a single or a set of ramifications of the doctrine.

Judge David Edward (European Court of Justice) sets the tone of modesty for the doctrine as a whole, claiming its purpose is to help find 'acceptable legal solutions to practical legal problems'. This is a shift away from the emphasis on coherence of the doctrine and its actual set of tests. Sacha Prechal however, basically maintains her original claim that the concept has become 'too broad, imprecise and diluted'.

The founding stone, or 'the correct starting point for any analysis of direct effect', as Edward writes, is the obligation of result on the State. The driving impulse of its development, on the other hand, is its creation of 'individual rights', as is clearly shown by Angela Ward (University of Essex): '[The concept of 'individual rights'] has spearheaded liberalization of Article 288(2) damages liability, opened out the Article 234 avenue for validity challenge, and bound national judges to alter and enhance national sanctions and procedural rules in disputes concerning Community law'. With such multiple origins and functions, no wonder that coherence is not the first virtue of the concept.

It helps, however, to distinguish between a restricted, technical notion of direct effect and a wider, foundational sense. In the first meaning, direct effect is a test, used to tell certain entitling or empowering EC legal provisions from others. Gerrit Betlem (University of Exeter) discusses the rule of consistent interpretation or construction as an offshoot of direct effect in its technical sense. Its growth necessarily leads to problems of coherence and legal certainty, which Betlem counters by indicating of reducing legal uncertainty.

On the other hand, direct effect has a wider sense. It is a special quality of the EC Treaty, one might say a tool of communication with other legal systems. In the remaining six contributions to this volume, this is the notion to prevail.

Jan Jans and Jolande Prinssen (University of Amsterdam) deal with 'differences and similarities in the application of the doctrine of direct effect by the various national courts'. They show that direct effect does not call for uniformity in legal protection, turning to the question what differences are acceptable and which aren't. Differences between domestic conceptions and receptions of direct effect between French and German Courts is the subject for Jörg Gerkrath (Avignon University). Where the German legal order is open towards international law, the French Constitution is more closed, 'deeply marked by the classic concept of national sovereignty'. Still Gerkrath concludes that the German and the French constitutional courts, each in its own way, both accept the principle of direct effect of EC law.

The relationship between public international law, domestic law and EC law respectively, is subject of the next two contributions. André Nollkaemper (University of Amsterdam) compares direct effect in public international law and EC law. He qualifies direct effect as a concept needed to 'straddle the threshold of two legal systems and that indeed qualifies the relevance of that threshold'. Jan Wouters and Dries Van Eeckhoutte (Leuven University) raise the question 'whether and under which conditions the Community courts accept the invocability of customary international law'. Again, direct effect works as a communicative tool between legal systems, albeit 'on a case-by-case basis having regard to the nature of the rule of customary international law at hand'.

Finally we turn to the question: shall we be able to do without direct effect in EC Law? Tom Eijsbouts (University of Amsterdam) denies this, claiming direct effect to be a 'constitutional founding stone' of the EC. Pieter Jan Kuijper (University of Amsterdam and European Commission) in his epilogue would stress the practical side: 'there can be little doubt that notions such as direct effect and harmonious interpretation are now applied with added stringency in the international/national law relationship, even by some Member States' courts, because they have 'passed through' Community law'. Even if in the technical sense it will continue to intrigue legal practice and frustrate scholarship, for lack of system, coherence, logic, as a meeting ground between legal orders, it has become indispensable. It is here to stay.

The editors
July 2002

Contents

Preface   v

CHAPTER I   **Direct Effect: Myth, Mess or Mystery?**
               Judge David O.A. Edward

      I   Direct effect: myth, mess or mystery?   3

CHAPTER II   **Direct Effect Reconsidered, Redefined and Rejected**
               Prof. dr. Sacha Prechal

      I   Introduction   17
      2   The plea against direct effect   18
      2.1   The concept has become broad, diluted and leads to
               more confusion than assistance in addressing the
               relevant issues   18
      2.2   The traditional conditions for direct effect are of very limited
               value. What sense does it make to verify their existence? 21
      2.3   The context within which direct effect operates is
               changing   22
      3   Redefining direct effect   23
      4   Direct effect rejected ... what next?   25
      4.1   Impact on legal relationships   27
      4.2   The final character of the obligation   31
      4.3   Defining legal consequences   34
      5   Uniformity v. divergence   39

CHAPTER III   **More than an 'Infant Disease'; Individual Rights, EC
               Directives, and the Case for Uniform Remedies**
               Dr. Angela Ward

      I   Introduction   45
      2   Individual what? The parameters of Court of Justice
               discourse on 'rights'   49
      3   Ramifications of reliance on 'individual rights' for the
               development of effective sanctions against EC institutions 54

3.1	Liability of Community institutions under Article 288(2)	54
3.2	Article 230(4) nullity review	58
3.3	Article 234 validity review	60
4	Setting the boundaries: Court of Justice regulation of Member State remedies and procedural rules?	64
4.1	Uniform treatment?	66
4.1.1	Interim relief	66
4.1.2	Excusable error	68
4.1.3	The raising of new arguments on appeal	69
4.2	Payment of interest	70
4.3	Vacillating boundaries and the principle of non-discrimination	71
5	Procedural rules and remedies and non-directly effective directives	73
6	Conclusion	75

CHAPTER IV **The Doctrine of Consistent Interpretation; Managing Legal Uncertainty**
Dr. Gerrit Betlem

1	Introduction	79
2	The doctrine of consistent interpretation: the *Von Colson* principle	81
2.1	The time factor: is expiry of transposition period for directives relevant?	85
2.2	Limits to consistent interpretation: the ECJ's inconsistent *Arcaro* judgment	88
2.3	Disguised indirect effect and the communitarization of private international law	90
2.4	The 'incidental' effect of directives	92
2.5	Inverse vertical indirect effect of Community law: a bridge too far?	96
2.6	Comparative note: 'the English *Marleasing*' (Human Rights Act 1998, S. 3)	98
3	Direct effect and *Francovich* liability: independent but not unconnected	101
4	Conclusion	103

CHAPTER V	**Direct Effect: Convergence or Divergence? A Comparative Perspective**	
	Prof. dr. Jan H. Jans & Jolande M. Prinssen, LL.M	

I	Introduction	107
2	National case law and the direct effect doctrine 'as such'	107
2.1	Questioning the doctrine and its consequences; Dutch, French and Spanish case law	108
2.2	Formulating the conditions; the House of Lords in the *Three Rivers* case	111
2.3	Horizontal direct effect or not; Spanish and Italian approaches	114
2.4	Horizontal side-effects of vertical direct effect; examples of national (mainly English, German and Dutch) case law	116
2.5	Conclusions	119
3	National case law and the 'modalities' of applying the doctrine of direct effect; the *Berkeley* case	120
4	Direct effect from the perspective of minimum harmonization	122
5	Conclusions	125

CHAPTER VI	**Direct Effect in Germany and France; A Constitutional Comparison**	
	Prof. dr. Jörg Gerkrath	

I	Introductory remarks	129
I.I	The relevance of the constitutional law position	129
I.2	The appropriateness of the comparative approach	130
I.3	The convenience of the choice of Germany and France	133
2	What the Constitution says	135
2.1	General clauses on the domestic effect of international law	135
2.1.1	The German Basic Law	135
2.1.2	The French Constitution	137
2.2	Special provisions on European integration	138
2.2.1	Participation in the European Union	140
2.2.2	Transfer of powers	141
2.2.3	Association of national parliaments	142
3	What the judges say that the Constitution says	144
3.1	... interpreting the specific clauses on international and EC law	145

3.1.1   The principle of direct effect is generally accepted
         under the domestic Constitution   145
3.1.2   Both constitutional courts maintain limits to direct
         effect deriving from domestic constitutional law   149
3.2   ... interpreting other constitutional clauses related to the
         principle of direct effect   151
4   Conclusion   153

CHAPTER VII   **The Direct Effect of Public International Law**
               Prof. dr. André Nollkaemper

1   Introduction   157
2   The concept of direct effect   159
3   The conditional nature of direct effect   164
4   The voluntary acceptance of direct effect   167
5   The determinants of direct effect   169
6   Conclusion   179

CHAPTER VIII   **The Enforcement of Customary International Law
               Through EC Law**
               Prof. dr. Jan Wouters & Dries Van Eeckhoutte

1   Introduction   183
2   The position of customary international law in
         Community law   185
2.1   Customary international law as a limit on
         State/EC jurisdiction and powers   186
2.2   Customary international law as providing rules
         of interpretation   191
2.3   Customary international law as gap-filler   194
2.4   Reviewing the legality of EU acts based on customary
         international law?   196
3   An analysis of *Opel Austria* and *Racke*   200
3.1   The facts of both cases   200
3.2   An analysis of *Racke*   201
3.3   An analysis of *Opel Austria*   208
4   The invocability of international agreements *viz.*
         customary international law: consistent case law?   215
4.1   Introduction   215
4.2   International agreements in general   215

4.3	GATT and WTO	219
4.4	Comparing the case law on the invocability of international agreements *viz.* of customary international law	223
5	By way of conclusion: the nature of customary international law and its invocability	229
5.1	The nature of customary international law	229
5.2	The invocability of customary international law	232

CHAPTER IX **Direct Effect, the Test and the Terms; In Praise of a Capital Doctrine of EU Law**
Prof. dr. Tom Eijsbouts

1	Introduction	237
2	Logic, limit, law	238
3	The test and its saving flaws	239
4	The spirit	242
5	From rights to obligations	244
6	The terms	246
7	Conclusion	249

CHAPTER X **Epilogue: Symbiosis?**
Prof. dr. Pieter-Jan Kuijper

1	Introduction	253
2	International law background to direct effect	253
2.1	Direct effect in monist and dualist systems	255
2.2	State responsibility	256
3	International law, Community law and direct effect	257
3.1	Opening up the Community legal order to international law	257
3.2	Imposing supremacy and direct effect as a constitutional court	260
3.2.1	The Treaty itself and regulations	260
3.2.2	Directives	260
4	The doctrine of 'direct effect of directives'	262
4.1	Non-implemented directives	263
4.2	Directives and individuals	264
4.3	Uniform application and remedies	265
5	Concluding remarks	267

Bibliography 269

Table of Cases 291

Abbreviations 305

Index 309

Contributors 317

CHAPTER I

Direct Effect: Myth, Mess or Mystery?

Judge David O.A. Edward

1   Direct effect: myth, mess or mystery?

There are almost as many articles of *doctrine* as there are judicial decisions about direct effect. The comments range from enthusiastic approval to contemptuous dismissal of what the Court has done. For some, direct effect is an essential characteristic of the Community legal order and without it the Community legal order would not be the same. For others, direct effect is an infant disease[1] or, more depressingly, the Court has lost its way or, more ominously, the Court has mystified a simple problem in order to confer a special sanctity on the Community legal order and therefore on the Court.

I must say that I sometimes wonder whether I am on the same planet as some of the commentators. Taking part in the Court's deliberations, I see only a group of judges from different countries seeking to find acceptable legal solutions to practical legal problems.

My diagnosis is that direct effect is not a disease but that it is liable to become a virus infecting the correct analysis of what are in reality separate though related problems. Essentially, I suggest that there is a danger of falling into what philosophers call the nominalist fallacy. This is the belief that because we use a particular word or expression, there must exist, somewhere in the universe, something to which that word or expression refers. So when we use the expression 'direct effect', there must be somewhere outside Community law a concept (or as Plato would have called it an 'idea') of direct effect. That, and only that, *is* direct effect. Anything that does not correspond to that model is not direct effect and, to the extent that the Court uses or seems to use that expression in relation to other phenomena, it must be wrong.

Commentators have suggested a number of different ways of describing what direct effect is about. On one view, it is a package of criteria for selecting the norm to be applied or, in some cases, for rejecting a particular norm as the norm to be applied. On another view, it is a filter of judicial competence, designed to answer the question, 'is this particular norm one that a judge can apply in this particular fact situation, or has it not yet reached the province of the judiciary?' Put another way, direct effect is concerned with the separation of powers. That analysis was applied by Chief Justice Marshall of the United States in 1829 in a case raising the question whether a treaty had become 'self-executing'. After

---

* This paper is a revised version of a lecture delivered at the Court of Justice on 5th December 2001, developing the author's ideas in "Direct Effect, the Separation of Powers and the Judicial Enforcement of Obligations", in: *Scritti in onore di Giuseppe Federico Mancini* (1998, Vol. II, p. 423-443). Joxerramon Bengoetxea, Dieter Kraus, Marie Demetriou and Anneli Howard contributed many useful ideas and corrected several errors, but bear no responsibility for the end result.

1   Pescatore (1983).

affirming that by its nature a treaty is a contract between nations and not a legislative act, he said:

> 'Our constitution declares a treaty to be the law of the land. It is, consequently, to be regarded as equivalent to an act of the legislature, whenever it operates of itself without the aid of any legislative provision. But when the terms of the stipulation import a contract, when either of the parties engages to perform a particular act, the treaty addresses itself to the political, not to the judicial department; and the legislature must execute the contract before it can become a rule for the Court'.[2]

Another way of looking at the problem is that direct effect (or the techniques of direct effect) are closely related, and in some respects identical, to familiar problems of national law. How far can individuals rely on programmatic legislation to derive rights for themselves? For example, when the Parliament has set up a system of urban and environmental control, to what extent can an individual rely on those statutes to prevent a neighbour building a house in a particular way or in a particular place? If Parliament requires local authorities to make arrangements for housing homeless persons, can an individual rely on that legislation to insist that a particular local authority must provide him or her with a house?

Again, direct effect can be related to the distinction between remedies in public and private law and the question of *locus standi*. Is this dispute a matter for judicial review of executive action or for a private law remedy under the civil law? Does *this* individual have capacity, title and interest to sue for *this* remedy in *this* case? As Professor Winter said in the article which began the analysis of direct applicability and direct effect:

> 'In every Member State there exists quite a bit of law which is not enforceable in the courts because those rules were not meant to give the private individual enforceable rights, or because they are too vague or incomplete to admit of judicial application'.[3]

In order to bring some order into the discussion, it is useful to go back to the beginning with the Opinion of Advocate General Lagrange in *Fedechar*, the tenth case decided by the Court. There he said:

> 'One could, no doubt, make the point that our Court is not an international court but the court of a Community created by six States on a model which is more

---

[2] *Foster & Elam v. Neilson*, 27 US (Pet.) 253, 314 (1829), quoted by Winter (1972), at p.429.

[3] Winter (1972), at p. 436.

closely related to a federal than to an international organisation, and that although the treaty which the Court has the task of applying was concluded in the form of an international treaty, and although it unquestionably is one, it is nevertheless from a material point of view the charter of the Community, since the rules of law which derive from it constitute the internal law of that Community. As regards the sources of that law there is obviously nothing to prevent them being sought where appropriate in international law, but normally, and in most cases, they will be found in the internal law of the various Member States'.[4]

Taking that as the starting point, the problem for the Court in the 1950s and early 1960s was to define more precisely how the internal law of the Community was to be inserted between conventional international law and the domestic law of the Member States? There were, and still are, several different approaches to this. Of the original Member States, Belgium and Luxembourg were monist. They found it easy to accept that international norms, and therefore the norms of the Community Treaties, are as much part of the law to be applied by a national judge as any provision of national law. Germany and Italy were dualist. For them, it was far from evident that Community law had entered the realm of national law to be applied by a national judge. France and the Netherlands took an intermediate position. France accepted the binding nature of treaty obligations but insisted on reciprocity. The Netherlands amended its Constitution during the 1950s, first to increase the extent of internal application of treaty law and then, three years later, to limit it.

Logically, the first question to be decided was the question of primacy: in the event of conflict, does the law of the Treaty prevail over inconsistent national law? Under the EEC Treaty, that question arose one year after the question of direct effect. Under the ECSC Treaty, it arose in *Humblet* in 1960. There the Court said:

'[If] the Court rules in a judgment that a legislative or administrative measure adopted by the authorities of a Member State is contrary to Community law that Member State is obliged by virtue of Article 86 of the ECSC Treaty [Article 5, now Article 10 EC], to rescind the measure in question and to make reparation for any unlawful consequences which may have ensued. This obligation is evident from the Treaty and the Protocol which have the force of law in the Member States following their ratification and which take precedence over national law'.[5]

It is worth noting that, in that short quotation from 1960, we find enunciated two of the three basic principles of Community law, the principle of primacy and the obligation to make reparation for breach of treaty obligations.

---

4   Case 8/55 *Fedechar* [1956] ECR 245, at p. 277.
5   Case 6/60 *Humblet* [1960] ECR 559, at p. 569.

In the EEC context *Costa/ENEl*[6] dealt with the question of primacy but was preceded by *Van Gend en Loos.*[7] Nevertheless, it is important to note the reasoning in *Costa/ENEL*. Essentially it is this. Acceptance by all the Member States of the Community legal order on a basis of reciprocity is logically inconsistent with a unilateral power on the part of individual Member States to pass incompatible national legislation. Article 10 (ex 5) EC (the obligation to abstain from measures liable to jeopardize attainment of the objectives of the Treaty) would be unenforceable if Member States could derogate unilaterally. The unconditional contractual obligations undertaken under the Treaty would be merely contingent obligations if Member States were free to pass incompatible legislation.

The Court emphasized that the Treaties were contractual, that they created obligations for the Member States and that the action taken by them must not be such as to derogate from or nullify the obligations they have undertaken under the treaties. It is in that context (albeit expressed subsequently) that we should consider what the Court said in *Van Gend en Loos.*

The question put by the Dutch tribunal in *Van Gend en Loos* was whether Article 12 (now Article 25) EC has '*direct application* [in the original Dutch *interne werking*] within the territory of a Member State, in other words whether nationals of such a State can, on the basis of the article in question, lay claim to rights which the courts must protect'.

In its argument the Netherlands Government insisted on the distinction between internal effect (*interne werking*) which I think we would now call direct applicability, and direct effect (*directe werking*) the first being a condition of the second. The first question is, does the norm apply in internal national law at all? The next question is, can it be invoked by an individual?

The argument is clear, but the terminology is not. The confusion of terminology is worse when one examines the different language texts of the judgment. One expression is used in German (*unmittelbare Wirkungen*; plural), but two different expressions are used in French (*effets directs* and *effets immédiats*; plural) and in Dutch (*onmiddellijk effect* and *directe werking*; singular). The Italian text uses quite different terminology (*atto a produrre direttamente degli effetti sui rapporti* and [*avendo*] *valore precettivo*).

What this shows is that, when the Court decided *Van Gend en Loos*, it was not applying a pre-existing concept which had already been fully worked out in international law or in national law (except to some extent in Dutch law). The practical problem raised by the Dutch court, to which the Court had to give an answer, was whether Article 12 EC had, by virtue of the Treaty alone, entered the national law of the Member States and, if so, could it be invoked by Van Gend en Loos against the Dutch Government? Or, put another way, did enforcement of

---

[6]   Case 6/64 *Costa/ENEL* [1964] ECR 585.

[7]   Case 26/62 *Van Gend en Loos* [1963] ECR 1.

Article 12 remain solely within the province of the legislature and executive, or had it come within the province of the judiciary? The Court's answer, which is too well known to need repetition here, depends on an analysis of the obligations undertaken by the Member States towards each other and towards their citizens.

The problem of vocabulary disclosed by the different language texts of *Van Gend en Loos* persisted until Winter (significantly, a Dutch professor) wrote his article in 1972. It is worth noting, given some of the recent criticism of the Court's judgments, that having made the important distinction between direct applicability and direct effect, Winter wrote:

> '*It is not to be excluded … that provisions of regulations which are not suited to take direct effect may nevertheless have certain limited effects in the relationship between the Member States and persons under their jurisdiction. It is conceivable that a national judge declares inapplicable a State measure taken in violation of a regulation without going so far as to secure for the private individual the exact legal position which he would have had if the State had taken the correct positive measures for performance of this obligation'.*[8]

Thus, having established the distinction between direct applicability and direct effect, Winter warned that this would not be the only problem. The question would also arise whether a directly applicable provision of the Treaty or of a regulation may have certain 'direct' effects but nevertheless not go so far as to create positive rights for specific individuals.

In the light of *Van Gend en Loos*, the analysis is now relatively simple as regards provisions of the Treaties themselves and of regulations which are by their nature directly applicable. Following *Costa* (and Advocate General Lagrange in *Fedechar*) the Treaties and regulations are part of the corpus of law to be applied by the national judge. The question in any given case is, not whether the Treaty or a regulation has breached the firewall between international and national law, but rather whether the particular provision at issue has the necessary characteristics of clarity, precision and 'directness' to enable a judge to apply it at the instance of an individual.

In the early 1970s, two new problems arose which were treated as being problems of the same type, as indeed, in a sense, they were. The first concerned the direct effect of international agreements including the Association Agreements, and the second the direct effect of directives.

As regards international agreements, the question arose first in the *International Fruit* case:[9] was the GATT directly effective? The Court answered 'No'. The analysis was, once again, to ask first what obligations were undertaken

---

[8] Winter (1972), p. 436-7.

[9] Joined Cases 21-24/72 *International Fruit* [1972] ECR 1219.

under the GATT, and then to ask whether those obligations were judicially enforceable or not. The answer was that they were not because enforcement of the obligations left room for executive negotiation. That takes us back to Chief Justice Marshall and the separation of powers. The same analysis was adopted more recently in *Portugal v. Council*[10] as regards the direct effect of the WTO Agreement.

As regards the Association Agreements, the decision in *Haegeman*[11] seemed to solve the problem of direct applicability. The Court held that the Association Agreements entered national law because the agreements were concluded by directly applicable regulations. This somewhat forced analysis was replaced by a sounder analysis in *Kupferberg*,[12] repeated in *Demirel*.[13]

The question of direct effect was raised more acutely in *Polydor*.[14] The terms of the provision in question were identical in the EEC Treaty and the Association Agreement with Portugal. When the English Court of Appeal referred the case, it seemed obvious to Lord Justice Templeman that there must be direct effect. The terms of Article 30 (now Article 28) EC and Article 14(2) of the Agreement with Portugal were the same. Article 30 had direct effect, so Article 14(2) must also have direct effect.[15]

The answer of the Court, to the surprise of some, was that that was not so. In their arguments before the Court, the intervening governments and the Commission stressed that the obligations assumed under the Treaty were different in character from those assumed under the Association Agreements. The mechanisms for settling disputes between the contracting parties were also different, in that the Association Agreements left scope for negotiation.[16] Put another way, dispute settlement remained in the province of the 'political department'.

In its judgment, the Court adopted the same analysis as it had adopted in *Van Gend en Loos*, starting with the nature of the Association Agreement in which Article 14(2) appeared and the obligations undertaken by the contracting parties. Just because Article 30 had direct effect and Article 14(2) was in the same terms, it did not follow that Article 14(2) must have direct effect.[17]

---

[10] Case C-149/96 *Portugal v. Council* [1999] ECR I-8395.

[11] Case 181/73 *Haegeman* [1974] ECR 449.

[12] Case 104/81 *Kupferberg* [1982] ECR 3641.

[13] Case 12/86 *Demirel* [1987] ECR 3719.

[14] Case 270/80 *Polydor* [1982] ECR 329.

[15] See the judgment of the Court of Appeal, per Templeman (L.J.) in [1980] 2 CMLR 347, at p.421 (paras. 38-40).

[16] See the arguments reported at [1982] ECR, p. 340-341.

[17] See, most recently, the judgment of 29 January 2002, *Pokrzeptowicz-Meyer*, Case C-162/00, nyr, paras. 32 and 33.

Finally, as regards international agreements, we should mention the recent TRIPs cases, though the point at issue is of relatively marginal interest.[18] TRIPs (the Agreement on Trade-Related Aspects of Intellectual Property Rights) is Annex 1C of the (WTO) Multilateral Trade Agreements. It contains provisions relating to the conditions under which courts will grant interim measures in intellectual property disputes. The question raised by the Dutch court was whether these provisions have direct effect in the sense of conferring rights on individuals which the courts must protect.

Having said that the WTO Agreement does not have direct effect, the Court said that the same was true of TRIPs. But the question raised by the national court did not exhaust the problem and, indeed, was beside the real point. The real issue is, what are the courts of the Member States to do in circumstances where the procedural provisions of TRIPs apply?

The Court's answer depended again on an analysis of obligations. The Member States, individually and as Member States of the Community, have undertaken certain obligations as to what their courts will do when granting interim measures. These obligations are incumbent on the national courts as organs of the Member States as well as upon the Court of Justice as an organ of the Community. The obligation to comply does not depend on whether the obligation can be enforced at the instance of individuals. To put the point another way, the rule at issue is a rule of procedure binding on the courts irrespective of the wishes of the litigants (when we have to decide whether a rule of procedure should be applied, we do not normally ask whether litigants have a subjective right to require it to be applied, though it may be relevant to ask whether a particular litigant has a legitimate interest to do so).

As regards the direct effect of directives, the correct approach was identified by the English judge who referred *Van Duyn*, the first case that raised this question.[19] He was faced with the question whether the Directive 64/221 had direct effect.[20] Article 3(1) of that Directive provides : 'measures taken on grounds of public policy or public security shall be based exclusively on the personal conduct of the individual concerned'.

Was that a norm that a national judge could apply for the benefit of Mrs Van Duyn? Article 189 (now Article 249) EC provides that, unlike regulations which are directly applicable, directives are binding as to the result to be achieved, leaving to Member States the choice of form and method. The referring judge said:

---

[18] Case C-53/96 *Hermès* [1998] ECR I-3606; Joined Cases C-300/98 and C-392/98 *Dior* [2000] ECR I-11307; Case C-89/99 *Schieving-Nijstad* [2001] ECR I-5851.

[19] Case 41/74 *Van Duyn* [1974] ECR 1337.

[20] OJ 1964, p. 850.

'Article 3, paragraphs 1 and 2, in that directive clearly I think go to the 'result to be achieved' within the meaning of Article 189 of the Treaty and not to the 'form and methods', which are left to the national authorities'.[21]

The judge distinguished between the obligation to achieve a result and the possibility of choosing how you will arrive at it. The terms of Article 3(1) of the Directive ('measures taken on grounds of public policy and public security shall be based exclusively on the personal conduct of the individual concerned') left no room for Member States to choose between different forms and methods. They prescribed unequivocally the result to be achieved.

That seems to me to be the correct starting point for any analysis of direct effect in the context of directives. The cases following *Van Duyn*, or at least the discussion of them, has concentrated excessively on creating a parallelism between directives and regulations as legal instruments. This has led to a certain amount of intellectual acrobatics on the subject of vertical and horizontal direct effect, *estoppel*, and so on, as well as the proposal by more than one Advocate General that the distinction between vertical and horizontal direct effect is out of date and should be abandoned.

In order to understand the distinction between the vertical and horizontal direct effect of directives and the consequences that should be drawn from that distinction, the correct approach is, I suggest, again to start from the obligation of result. Many of the early cases were concerned with the directives on equal treatment of men and women in employment. As in the case of Directive 64/221 (at issue in *Van Duyn*), some provisions of these directives left no doubt as to the result to be achieved. In the case of private employers, national legislation was still necessary to impose the obligation of equal treatment on them. But where the Member States (or 'emanations of the state') were themselves the employer, the result to be achieved was already clear. The need to decide on form and methods in the case of private employers could not affect the obligation of the Member States to comply with the requirements of the directives in respect of their own employees.

By contrast, in *Faccini Dori*,[22] which concerned the 'doorstep-selling' Directive,[23] the dispute was between two private contracting parties. The Directive did not (and indeed could not) impose any obligation of result directly on them. Since Italy had failed to implement the Directive, Recreb (or rather Interdiffusion, from whom Recreb's rights were derived) were not bound by any norm applicable to them to give Mrs Faccini Dori the time for reflection prescribed by it.

---

[21] See [1974] 1 WLR 1107, at p. 1115(E) and [1974] 1 CMLR 347, at p. 357 (para. 15).

[22] Case C-91/92 *Faccini Dori* [1994] ECR I-3325.

[23] Council Directive 85/577/EEC, OJ 1985, L 372/31.

The distinction between vertical and horizontal direct effect may appear produce paradoxical results. It may or may not be desirable for other reasons that the distinction between regulations and directives should be eliminated. But, so long as it remains, the logic of the distinction between vertical and horizontal direct effect does not seem to me to be open to criticism.

The recent case of *Unilever*[24] has been severely criticized as blurring, or even breaching, the distinction between vertical and horizontal direct effect. But what was really the issue in *Unilever*? Unilever had undertaken to deliver a certain quantity of olive oil to Central Food. The oil was rejected by Central Food on the ground that between the time when the contract had been made and the time when the olive oil was delivered the Italian Government had introduced a new labelling requirement with which the oil did not comply. The Italian law had not, however, been notified under the terms of Directive 83/189.[25] In *CIA Security*,[26] the Court had held that national measures to which the Directive applied but which had not been notified in accordance with the Directive could not be applied. In *Unilever*, the Court simply said that, in those circumstances, the Italian law was inapplicable.

The difference between *Faccini Dori* and *Unilever* is that in *Faccini Dori* the doorstep-selling Directive introduced an exception to the long-standing, and in other respects still valid and subsisting, rule of private law that contracts are contracts and must be observed. The issue was whether Recreb could rely on that existing rule of law, or was bound to allow Mrs Faccini Dori the time for reflection prescribed by the Directive but not yet transposed into Italian law. In *Unilever* the issue was not whether Central Food could rely on a pre-existing, valid and subsisting rule of national law, but whether they could rely on a new law which was invalid and unenforceable *ab initio* because it had not been notified.

A different set of problems arose in *Grosskrotzenburg*,[27] *Kraaijeveld*[28] and *Inter-Environnement Wallonie*.[29]

The *Grosskrotzenburg* case was an infringement action by the Commission against Germany. The German Government was alleged to have failed to subject the extension of a power station to an environmental impact assessment as

---

[24] Case C-443/98 *Unilever Italia* [2000] ECR I-7535.

[25] Council Directive 83/189/EEC of 28 March 1983 laying down a procedure for the provision of informa-tion in the field of technical standards and regulations, OJ 1983, L 109/8, as amended by Directive 94/10/EC of the European Parliament and the Council, OJ 1994, L 100/30.

[26] Case C-194/94 *CIA Security* [1996] ECR I-2201.

[27] Case C-431/92 *Grosskrotzenburg* [1995] ECR I-2189.

[28] Case C-72/95 *Kraaijeveld* [1996] ECR I-5403.

[29] Case C-129/96 *Inter-Environnement Wallonie* [1997] ECR I-7411.

required by the Environmental Impact Assessment Directive.[30] The argument of the German Government was this:

> 'The basis of the case-law of the Court ... is that a Member State cannot plead its own failure to implement a directive or its own defective implementation thereof, as against citizens who may be able to base rights on it, and thus concerns exclusively situations in which individuals' rights against the State are at issue. On the other hand, if it is not that category of persons who are relying on the provisions, the authorities cannot be required to apply such provisions, them no matter how definite and precise they may be'.

This is the nominalist fallacy again. 'Direct effect' is about individual rights so, if we are not talking about individual rights, there is no norm to be applied and no obligation to be enforced.

The Court's reply was that the relevant question was whether the Directive imposed an obligation on Germany to assess the environmental impact of the project. 'That question is quite separate from the question whether individuals can rely as against the State on provisions of an unimplemented directive'.[31] In other words, the question is whether the provision at issue has entered the province of the judiciary and can be judicially enforced, irrespective of who is asking for it to be enforced.

In *Kraaijeveld*, the issue was slightly different, but the confusion about direct effect was the same. The issue was whether the claimants could rely on the Directive to ensure that, before a dyke was constructed which would prevent their access to the water, its environmental impact should be assessed. The consequence of the assessment might or might not be that the dyke would be constructed blocking their access to the water. What mattered was that the procedural obligation be complied with. Then, and only then, would the substantive question arise whether the dyke could be built or not.

The Court's answer goes back to the point made by Winter in relation to regulations that there may be circumstances in which a state measure may be declared inapplicable without going so far as to secure for the private individual the exact legal position which he would have had if the State had taken the correct positive measures for performance of its obligation.

The same analysis can be applied to *Inter-Environnement Wallonie*. The question was: what is the status of a directive and what obligations does it impose during the period between enactment and the time prescribed for transposition? The answer is that from the moment of enactment there is an obligation to

---

[30] Council Directive 85/337/EEC on the assessment of the effects of certain public and private projects on the environment; OJ 1985, L 175/40, amended by Council Directive 97/11/EC, OJ 1997, L 73/5.

[31] Para. 26.

achieve a result. The state may be allowed a period of time within which to choose the form and methods for achieving that result and putting them into effect. But, in the interim, the state may not act inconsistently with its obligation of result. Put another way, the period allowed for transposition (which, incidentally, is not a characteristic of all directives) does not put the obligation of result into cold storage till that period has expired.

In summary, the Court's position has been stated in *Linster*:[32]

> '[It] would be incompatible with the binding effect of directives to exclude as a matter of principle any possibility for those concerned to rely on the obligation which directives impose, particularly when the Community authorities have by directive imposed the obligation to pursue a particular course of conduct on the Member States. The effectiveness of such an act would be diminished if individuals were prevented from relying on it in legal proceedings and if national courts were prevented from taking it into consideration as a matter of Community law in determining whether the national legislator, in exercising its choice as to the form and methods, had kept within the limits of its discretion'.

The analysis should always start with the obligation, an obligation on whom, to do what and by when. If you start from there, you will arrive at a coherent result. But the questions then to be solved are not the same in each case. In some cases the question is, does the individual have the right to sue for performance of the obligation? In other cases the question is, does the Community have the right to enforce the obligation? And there may be a series of different problems to which the same apparent reasoning is applied.

As I have said, I do not think that, put in that way, the questions at issue are materially different in a great many cases from questions that arise in national law. 'Direct effect' (using that expression in a broad way) provides us with criteria for selecting or rejecting the norms to be applied and for clarifying the scope of judicial competence. In that respect, it seems to me that it is neither a myth nor a mystery, and I hope that it is not entirely a mess.

---

[32]   Case C-287/98 *Linster* [2000] ECR I-6917.

CHAPTER II

Direct Effect Reconsidered, Redefined and Rejected

Prof. dr. Sacha Prechal

1   Introduction

The present contribution is a new instalment of something which seems to be becoming a legal serial, the outcome of which is still far from certain. A publication in serial form has the important advantage that it permits the story to develop little by little, building upon what has happened in the previous instalments - and it can go on forever. The latter is certainly true for the discussion of a concept such as direct effect. Although it is not my intention to be occupied with 'direct effect' forever, I could not resist the temptation to participate in the Amsterdam Conference and, then, to write a contribution for the present volume.

After years of enthusiasm and almost unconditional support for the doctrine of direct effect, in the 1990s, when writing my PhD,[1] I started to question the doctrine's usefulness. Over the next few years, some of the ideas evolved and resulted in another publication.[2] In the present instalment of the serial I will, first, briefly summarize the main arguments which advocate against this doctrine, at least in a Community law context. Next, I will elaborate a number of issues which are still highly relevant even in situations where direct effect does not operate anymore. This latter discussion will also place the proposal to do away with the concept of direct effect in a proper perspective and will make plain that there is, in fact, nothing revolutionary about this idea.

There is also another, more practical perspective. A quick scan[3] of the preliminary judgments of the ECJ given during the period 1995-2000[4] reveals that direct effect as such was only a real issue in less then ten cases. By that, I refer to the traditional questions of whether such and such a provision is directly effective, may be relied upon before national courts etc. Moreover, quite a number of these few preliminary cases were concerned with direct effect of international agreements[5] or with questions linked to the denial of horizontal direct effect of directives. What does this say about direct effect as a central doctrine of EC law? Perhaps not so much. Many cases related to the application of Treaty provisions which are, according to well-established case law, directly effective. Cases concerning regulations are not very revealing either, since the presumption about their direct effect is well known and, as a rule, there is no need to ask questions to this effect. However, it is striking that many cases on directives[6]

---

[1]   Prechal (1995).

[2]   Prechal (2000).

[3]   Based on rough numbers, which, however, give sufficient indication.

[4]   Approximately 150 per year.

[5]   Or they concern decisions based on these agreements. See, for instance, Case C-65/98 *Eyüp* [2000] ECR I-4747.

[6]   Approximately 50 per year.

focus purely on their interpretation and not on the question of how the directive at issue should be given effect. Apparently, in many cases the ECJ simply interprets the directive and, if relevant, prescribes the result in terms that the directive precludes the application of national law. However, it is up to national court to figure out how to give effect to these findings in the concrete case before it. In this light one may wonder whether and to what extent direct effect is an issue that preoccupies national courts on a daily basis.

2 The plea against direct effect

Without denying the crucial role direct effect has played in the construction of the Community legal order thus far, and in the European integration process in general, the question is whether, at this stage of development of Community law, it still makes sense to maintain the doctrine, at least in the relationship between Community law[7] and national law of the Member States. The arguments which lead, in my view, to a negative answer to this question are based on considerations which may be divided into three groups: conceptual, technical-legal and contextual. The main lines of this triptych will be sketched in the next three paragraphs.[8]

2.1 The concept has become broad, diluted and leads to more confusion than assistance in addressing the relevant issues

Put in somewhat simplified terms, the conceptual problem in relation to direct effect boils down to the question what is covered by the concept and what not. Over the years, the concept has become broad, diluted and leads to more confusion than assistance in addressing the relevant issues. Four points may substantiate this proposition.

First, as is well known, the Court of Justice started to define direct effect in terms of creation of rights, but subsequently it broadened the concept to invocability, which means that Community law may be relied upon for a number of purposes. Not only to claim rights, or to establish a positive claim, but also in a negative way, for the purpose of reviewing the legality of national provisions, in order to have national provisions set aside in case of incompatibility. The most debated case in this respect is probably *Kraaijeveld*.[9] *Kraaijeveld* is the explicit

---

[7] 'Other' EU law needs perhaps also a more cautious approach.

[8] For a more detailed discussion see Prechal (2000).

[9] Case C-72/95 *Kraaijeveld* [1996] ECR I-5403. Note, however, that the 'figure' of relying on Community law in order to have contrary national law set aside is much older then this case.

recognition of legality review in which a Community law provision serves as a standard for this test and where Members States dispose of a (broad) margin of discretion. In *Kraaijeveld* no rights of Mr. Kraaijeveld were at stake. The Environmental Impact Assessment Directive (EIA Directive)[10] did not protect Mr. Kraaijeveld's rights. It did not even protect his particular interests, namely the access to his harbour. Probably for this reason it was argued in some quarters that *Kraaijeveld* is not about the direct effect at all.

Second, another - closely related - confusing factor is the case law on State liability. One of the requirements for State liability is that the provision which has been infringed intends to confer rights. The ECJ has up until now not indicated, at least not clearly, what it means by the term rights, and what parameters we should use for this purpose. In some cases we read that a previous finding that a provision has direct effect is already sufficient to satisfy this requirement. But since direct effect is a broader concept than the creation of rights - direct effect *may include* the creation of rights - such an approach does not really make sense.[11] The *Unilever* case - much debated for other reasons - can be understood as an explicit recognition that direct effect is not necessarily a matter of creation of rights.[12] This case was about Directive 83/189 on notification of technical standards[13] - a kind of *procedural* directive - which may be relied upon, and whose non-observance has as a consequence that the relevant piece of national legislation is not enforceable against individuals. *Unilever* was a 'horizontal case' in the sense that it concerned a contractual dispute between Unilever and Central Food about the delivery of olive oil. In this case the Italian and Danish governments argued, among other things, that the Directive can not of itself impose obligations on individuals, so it cannot be relied upon against an individual, following the well-known *Marshall* and *Faccini Dori* case law.[14] However, the Court responded, that this case law was not applicable in *Unilever*:

---

[10] Council Directive 85/337/EEC, OJ 1985, L 175/40, amended by Council Directive 97/11/EC, OJ 1997,
    L 73/5.

[11] In my opinion exactly this distinction has caused confusion in the *Three Rivers* case; House of Lords
    (18.5.2000), *Three Rivers District Council and Others* v. *Governor and Company of the Bank of England*,
    [2000] 2 WLR 1220, discussed by Jans & Prinssen in this volume's chapter V, paragraph 2.2.

[12] Case C-443/98 *Unilever Italia* [2000] ECR I-7535.

[13] Council Directive 83/189/EEC of 28 March 1983 laying down a procedure for the provision of informa-
    tion in the field of technical standards and regulations, OJ 1983, L 109/8, as amended by Directive
    94/10/EC of the European Parliament and the Council, OJ 1994, L 100/30.

[14] Case 152/84 *Marshall* [1986] ECR 723 and Case C-91/92 *Faccini Dori* [1994] ECR I-3325.

'...Directive 83/189 does not in any way define the substantive scope of the legal rule on the basis of which the national court must decide the case before it. It creates neither rights nor obligations for individuals'.[15]

Nevertheless, this finding did not prevent the Directive from being relied upon in order to have national legislation set aside.

Third, another source of confusion is what I have called the *national perceptions of direct effect*. By this term I refer to the phenomenon that in different countries, understanding of the concept, as defined by the ECJ, is influenced by national legal thinking. A somewhat simplified example may illustrate this.[16] Both in Germany and the UK, direct effect is considered as being a matter of protection of rights. Yet, in Germany the concept of rights has a specific meaning and a doctrinal test can be applied in cases where it is necessary to establish whether there is a right or not. English lawyers, at least as far as I know, use the concept of rights much more loosely. They quite easily label different types of legal relationships as being a matter of rights. In such circumstances, putting a German and an Englishman, or at least a German and an English lawyer, together will result in a tower of Babel. On the other hand, the French do not, in the first place, focus so much on whether the situation involves rights or not, but rather on the question whether the behaviour of the State or public authorities is compatible with Community law: a much more objective - legality-oriented - approach. The tragedy is that the French write for French, German for German, English for English, Dutch for Dutch, Italians for Italians etc. In this way, a kind of national sub-doctrines of direct effect emerge, a concept which was believed to be a Community concept *par excellence*. The core problem is that, on the one hand, it is very important to translate the consequences of EC law for the different national legal system, for the 'national law colleagues'. On the other hand, there is also a considerable danger of miscommunication and confusion. This may happen at a Community law level to some extent as well. All the actors on the Community legal scene, such as individual judges, Advocates General, representatives of the Commission, undoubtedly have excellent knowledge of EC law. However, they also come from a specific national background which implies that national legal traditions and divergent approaches also influence what is going on at Community level, and in relation to issues like direct effect in the Court of Justice in particular.

My last point - to be mentioned very briefly[17] - concerns the relationship between EC law and traditional international law. The ECJ's approach in this area of Community law is not really very helpful for understanding what direct

---

[15] Para. 51 of the judgment. On the problem of direct effect and creation of rights see also Prechal & Hancher (2002).

[16] For a more detailed discussion with further references see Prechal (2000), at p. 1052-1056.

[17] On the relationship between EC law and international law see the contributions of Nollkaemper, Wouters & Van Eeckhoutte and Kuijper in this volume's chapters VII, VIII and X.

effect is about. A review of the legality of Community acts in the light of the
GATT, for instance, is allowed under certain circumstances, but at the same
time, in some cases, it is also suggested that this is not a matter of direct effect.
In other cases, however, the Court seems to lump the two approaches together.

2.2 The traditional conditions for direct effect are of very limited value. What sense does it make to verify their existence?

The technical-legal considerations which cast doubts on the
usefulness of direct effect, relate to the traditional conditions for direct effect.
These have, in fact, very limited value and one may wonder what sense it still
makes to verify their existence, at least *as a precondition* for the application
of Community law provisions. Community law can be relied upon for several
purposes, in different contexts, in different types of proceedings. Depending
on this, the assessment of the conditions will also differ. For instance, for
positive application of Community law provisions as a fully-fledged alternative to
national law - Germans call it *'Alternativ-Normierung'*, French call it *'invocabilité
de substitution'* - the national court will need more and certainly different guidance from situations when the provisions at issue are relied upon for purposes of
review of legality of national measures.

In the ECJ's case law, there are a number of examples which clearly illustrate
that the question of what a party is seeking affects whether or not provisions
have direct effect. The most obvious example is still Article 6 of the Equal Treatment Directive.[18] In *Von Colson*,[19] Article 6 did not have direct effect in order to
get a contract of employment by way of sanction, but the same Article did have
direct effect in *Marshall II*[20] in order to have an upper limit to compensation set
aside. We see similar things happen in relation to the Habitat Directive.[21] Article
6 of this Directive does not contain a specific obligation to designate Special
Areas of Conservation, i.e. natural habitats or areas that should be protected
in accordance with the Directive. However, once an area has been designated
as such, review of the national measures in the light of Article 6(2) seems to
be possible.[22] The judgment in *Comitato*,[23] concerning Article 4 of the Waste
Directive,[24] is another example that can be mentioned. In this case the Court

---

[18] Council Directive 76/207/EEC, OJ 1976, L39/40.

[19] Case 14/83 *Von Colson and Kamann* [1984] ECR 1891.

[20] Case C-271/91 *Marshall II* [1993] ECR I-4367.

[21] Council Directive 92/43/EEC, OJ 1992, L 206/7.

[22] Cf. Jans (2000), p. 181 and p. 419.

[23] Case C-236/92 *Comitato* [1994] ECR I-438.

[24] Council Directive 75/442/EEC, OJ 1975, L 194/47.

held that this Article does not require in itself an adoption of a specific measure, of a particular method of waste disposal, such as recycling instead of building a tip for waste disposal. In this sense, the Article was not sufficiently precise and unconditional to have direct effect. However, at the same time, this finding certainly does not exclude the possibility that, once the authorities have done something, this could be reviewed in the light of the Directive.[25]

The very purpose of the conditions for direct effect is judicial application. A national court equipped with the provisions at issue must be able to deal with the problem before it, depending on what the party relying on Community law is seeking. In his Opinion in *Linster,* Advocate General Léger proposed no longer to examine whether the conditions for direct effect are satisfied in a situation when a directive is relied on for the purposes of review of legality of national provisions.[26] In his view, in such a situation it is not necessary to look at those conditions. The only thing that matters is to review whether the national measures at issue are compatible with the relevant provisions of Community law. I would like to go one step further, and submit that it makes no sense to look at the conditions *as preconditions* at all. Why should we not accept that national courts should handle Community law provisions in the same way as national law, i.e. without making this formalistic and obsolete preliminary inquiry into unconditionality and sufficient precision? I believe that national courts are very well equipped to do so.

2.3 The context within which direct effect operates is changing

The contextual considerations focus mainly on the constitutional setting in which direct effect functions. Put briefly, the argument is that this setting is changing. It follows clearly from the previous section, in particular, that direct effect is, in the first place, a matter of justiciability. Justiciability may be regarded as a technical-legal issue, but it is also intimately linked with the doctrine of separation of powers. In fact, this doctrine is one of the most important foundations for the concept of direct effect.

In relation to the separation of powers doctrine in general, there is a process going on in several Member States which results in the position of the judiciary vis-à-vis the legislature and vis-à-vis the executive being strengthened. In the specific area of foreign relations, traditional mechanisms which should exclude courts, such as the political question doctrine and the *'acte du gouvernement'*, are eroding. The effect of these trends is, *inter alia*, that acts of the State or

---

[25] Cf. Case C-365/97 *Commission v. Italy* [1999] ECR I-7773

[26] Case C-287/98 *Linster* [2000] ECR I-6917. On this 'French' approach and the somewhat ambiguous position of the Belgian Council of State see Gilliaux (1998), at p. 114-119.

State authorities concerning the conduct of foreign affairs are coming within
the jurisdiction of national courts. This also means that the courts then more
easily review the State's behaviour in the light of what has been internationally
agreed.

Apart from these general constitutional tendencies, the specific EC constitutional context implies that most of the traditional considerations behind the
doctrine can no longer be upheld.[27] It is a platitude to state that the European
integration process and EC law, in particular, cannot be equated to simple
co-operation between States, governed by traditional international law. Although
at Community, and indeed EU, level much can still be improved, in particular in
terms of legitimacy of the legal system, nevertheless it is exactly the 'different'
character of the Community legal order that provides arguments against the
traditional considerations and in favour of rather unhampered effect, on an
equal footing with national legal provisions.

In the Community context, a system of law-giving exists, which has a
number of procedural and substantive guarantees, an increasing democratic
input, and certainly does not amount anymore to traditional treaty negotiations.
In this perspective, instruments like directives should not be seen as a sort of
instruction to the Member States, but rather a specific type of legislation. By the
same token, European affairs are no longer a matter of fully sovereign States; for
that reason also, there is no justification for keeping courts out. On the contrary,
the Community is said to be a Community based on the Rule of Law. The
measures of both the Member States and the institutions cannot avoid review by
courts as to their conformity with Community law. This review is not only a task
for the Court of Justice, but also for national courts. This is clearly illustrated by
the system of decentralized judicial protection as it has developed over the years,
mainly on the basis of Article 10 EC Treaty, in the ECJ's case law. The same holds
true in fact for national administrations, insofar as the latter are responsible for
the application and enforcement of EC rules. In such a setting, national courts
and parts of the administration act as direct agents of the Community legal
order. All these factors - presented here in a very cursory way - considerably
weaken the traditional arguments relating to the need to filter the effects of
ambiguous, uncertain, legal provisions of doubtful legitimacy, as well as the
necessity to protect individuals against these provisions.

3 Redefining direct effect

Obviously, when a concept becomes too broad, imprecise and
diluted, an effort can be made to redefine it. Basically, there are two options:

---

[27] For the traditional considerations see the contribution of Nollkaemper in chapter VII.

narrow it down or broaden it. Whatever direction this may take, I have serious doubts about the usefulness of such an exercise.

If the concept is narrowed down, the somewhat pathological fixation on direct effect will not do justice to other possible effects of EC law. These effects include State liability in cases of non-directly effective provisions, the *Kraaijeveld* and *Unilever*-like approach, the implications of consistent interpretation and some innovative techniques developed by national courts, like that used by some Dutch administrative courts, where individual decisions may be annulled because the authority did not consider the question of compatibility with EC law. This amounts to a violation of *national* requirements that the reasoning behind a decision must be sufficient or that a decision must be prepared with due care.[28]

The still predominant fixation on 'direct effect' seems to make it extremely difficult to think in other categories. This is, for instance, witnessed by the efforts to find new catchwords for the legal effects Community law may produce. Terms like disguised, diagonal, mitigated, passive, indirect, incidental or whatever (direct) effect[29] seem, in the first place, to refine the concept further, making it increasingly complex, rather than providing an intelligible alternative. Similarly, other important implications of Community law are still too often coupled with 'direct effect', suggesting that they only occur in relation to direct effect but may be neglected otherwise. For instance, the role with which national courts are entrusted under Article 10 EC Treaty, namely to ensure legal protection, is often bracketed together with direct effect.[30] Yet, also in cases where direct effect does not play a role, like State liability or where the route of consistent interpretation is followed, the need for legal protection remains.[31] The same holds true for the limitations of national procedural autonomy. The principles of equivalence and effectiveness apply whether the rules at stake are directly effective or not.

On the other hand we may broaden the concept and even go so far that 'direct effect' will denote 'all ways by which EC norms, on their own authority, exert legal force in the Member States, be it by way of simple normative substitution (*Van Gend en Loos*), of exclusion (*CIA Security*), of interpretation requirements (*Marleasing*), of tort principles (*Francovich*), or additional standards of judicial

---

[28] Cf. Jans & de Jong (2002). In a recent case the Dutch Council of State coupled this requirement with Article 10 EC Treaty; Dutch Council of State (10.5.2001), *HMG*, JB 2001/152.

[29] Admittedly, these terms are often coupled with the problem of non-horizontal direct effect of directives.

[30] See for instance Case 45/76 *Comet* [1976] ECR 2043, or, more recently, Case C-242/95, *GT-Link* [1997] ECR I-4453.

[31] See Joined Cases C-6/90 and C-9/90 *Francovich* [1991] ECR I-5357 and Joined Cases C-178/94, C-179/94 and C-188-190/94 *Dillenkofer* [1996] ECR I-4845.

process (*Comet*)'.[32] Then the term is nothing more then an expression to refer
to 'the normative cross-over from EC law into domestic law'.[33] Although such a
meaning and 'descriptive' use of direct effect is rather extreme, I can live with it.
However, if direct effect is used to indicate these, or some of these, phenomena,
it should be once and for all disconnected from the technical legal connotation
it implies, namely the preliminary inquiry into the question whether the conditions for direct effect are satisfied. The problem is then, it is submitted, that
the link between direct effect, the inquiry into the conditions and the relevance
of the provisions in national legal order is so embedded in lawyers' habits of
thinking, that divorcing the two and stopping use of the concept direct effect in
this way will cause considerable confusion, to say the least. So, a broad definition
of the concept will not help to solve the problem that direct effect might become
an obstacle for the application of Community law in all the different modalities,
rather than a vehicle. Apart from that, it will not resolve a whole line of questions
which have to be addressed anyhow, irrespective of whether we choose such
a broad definition or decide to do away with the concept of direct effect all
together.

4   Direct effect rejected ... what next?

As was already submitted, Community law should be applied
without making the preliminary inquiry into the unconditional and sufficiently
precise character of the provisions at issue or, respectively, as to their direct
effect or not, as understood in traditional Community law. After all, Community
law is part of the national legal orders of the Member States: all Community
law, not just directly effective provisions. It is the law of the land and it should
be treated accordingly. In many quarters, this would probably require a mental
quantum leap, since it implies the negation of the alien origin of Community
law. In practical terms, however, it demands above all a change of perspective.
While regulations are by their very nature considered as being directly effective,[34] that does not necessarily imply that all their provisions can always be
applied in every case. Yet, as in relation to national law, a preliminary inquiry
as to their direct effect is refrained from. The same approach should also apply

---

[32]   Preface to the present volume; Case 26/62 *Van Gend en Loos* [1963] ECR 1; Case C-194/94 *CIA Security*
       [1996] ECR I-2201; Case C-106/89 *Marleasing* [1990] ECR I-4135; *Francovich* (as cited) and *Comet* (as
       cited).

[33]   Preface to the present volume.

[34]   As explained elsewhere, I do not make the distinction between direct applicability and direct effect. See
       Prechal (1995), p. 260-264.

in relation to directives and decisions.[35] This suggestion comes, in fact, very close to a proposal made elsewhere in this volume, namely that direct effect should be presumed and if a court wants to deny it, it must make a reference to the ECJ.[36]

Somewhat naturally, the focus of this contribution is on secondary Community law. Are there reasons to treat the EC Treaty differently? It is, after all, not a piece of Community legislation, but a Treaty. To a great extent such a discussion is irrelevant: over the years the direct effect of a whole line of Treaty articles has been established and an inquiry into their direct effect is obsolete. On the other hand, there are still several unclarified issues, old and new, such as the 'genuine' horizontal direct effect of Article 12 EC,[37] the direct effect of the full Article 10 EC, direct effect of new Treaty provisions and the principles enshrined therein, such as the principles of precaution and prevention, in Article 174 EC,[38] or direct effect of Article 18 EC.[39] When addressing these issues, one should not forget the main lessons from *Van Gend en Loos* and *Costa/ENEL*, which also hold true for Treaty provisions, namely that '[the] Treaty is more than an agreement which merely creates mutual obligations between contracting states'[40] and that '[b]y contrast with ordinary international treaties, the EEC Treaty has created its own legal system which ...became an integral part of the legal systems of the Member States and which their courts are bound to apply'.[41] The EC Treaty thus has a different status from other - 'normal' - treaties. Therefore, there is a case for approaching the question of the effects the Treaty provisions may produce in a different way; again, without posing the traditional question as to the direct effect first. Also EC Treaty articles should be considered as articles which *by definition* are to be applied, as soon as they are susceptible thereof in a particular concrete dispute. In the light of the ECJ's case law on the 'constitutional status' of the Treaty[42] a pertinent question might be: what does that mean for the issue of internal effects of the relevant provisions? To draw a comparison with the legal effects national constitutional provisions may produce could be a useful exercise.

---

[35] The effects decisions may produce have remained in the shadow of the direct effect of directives. On the complex and interesting issues which may rise see Greaves (1996).

[36] Cf. Jans & Prinssen in this volume's chapter V.

[37] Cf. Case C-281/98 *Angonese* [2000] ECR I-4139 on the one hand, but also Case C-411/98 *Ferlini* [2000] ECR I-8081 on the other.

[38] Cf. Prechal & Hancher (2002) and Doyle & Carney (1999).

[39] Cf. Case C-413/99 *Baumbast*, pending, opinion of AG Geelhoed of 5 July 2001.

[40] *Van Gend en Loos* (as cited), at p. 12.

[41] Case 6/64 *Costa/ENEL* [1964] ECR 585, at p. 593.

[42] Opinion 1/91 *EEA* [1991] ECR I-6079.

In my critique of the concept of direct effect I argued that it has become broad, diluted and leads to more confusion than assistance in addressing the relevant issues.[43] The question is indeed, what are the relevant issues then? And, more importantly, how should they be addressed?

What follows is certainly not an exhaustive discussion. I will address here a few of the issues, which are, in my view, important. First, there is the question of how to establish that a provision is relevant for a concrete dispute, in the sense that that provision must be, as any other binding legal rule, applied in order to resolve dispute. Obviously, there are a number of rather 'standard' requirements which must be satisfied in order to make a rule applicable, such as that the rule is binding, that it applies *ratione materiae, ratione temporis* etc. I am not going to discuss these broad issues. I will only concentrate on the questions when does a rule have an impact on a legal relationship and how concrete must the content of the provision be in order to allow judicial application. The second, main issue to be addressed is what are the legal consequences of the application of the Community law provision? Those familiar with problems of direct effect will immediately see that these are exactly the questions which often arise in relation to direct effect. I will try to discuss the issues abstracting from the doctrine of direct effect. The point is, however, that the questions mentioned play a role in the context of applying any norm, and they are not exclusively linked to direct effect. Moreover, it is a good thing to keep in mind that also in national law, depending on the provisions at issue, on the circumstances of the case or on other elements, legal acts can or cannot be relied upon and they may have limited and varying effects.

4.1   Impact on legal relationships

In order to find out whether a provision (or provisions) is relevant, one has to focus on the question whether the provision affects the legal relationship at issue. This is, in fact, a traditional issue of direct effect: does a rule, which is agreed between States, by its nature, also lend itself to producing legal effects in relations between the State and individual? In a Community law context, this perspective is, however, somewhat simplistic. While such a traditional approach could hold true in relation to Community Treaties, other instruments should be conceived more as pieces of legislation than agreements between States.[44] Yet, even in the case of Community legislation the question whether the provision affects the legal relationship at issue will arise. In some cases this may be relatively clear-cut, for instance in a situation where the addressees of the provision can be directly ascertained on the basis of the plain text of the provision. This will be the case in particular where the addressees coincide with the personal scope of the relevant rules. When Mr. P buys from a doorstep seller, Mr. X, a miracle ointment against baldness, we know that the 'trader' Mr. X is, *inter alia*, under an obligation vis-à-vis the 'consumer' Mr. P[45] to give the latter a written notice of the right of cancellation.[46]

In other cases it is more difficult to ascertain the addressees, the latter not being always explicitly mentioned. A considerable interpretative effort may be necessary to find out who the addressees are. Furthermore, a provision or a set of provisions may also affect the legal position of individuals (or other legal subjects), even where they are not the addressees of the norm. Nevertheless, the legal relationship they have with another legal subject may be influenced by the provisions.

When States agree to abolish quantitative restrictions on imports and all measures having equivalent effect, this may at the first sight seem to concern only the relationship between States. However, upon further consideration, this type of provision will necessarily produce effects *in* the States as they will affect the relationship between individual traders and state authorities. Another example of the problems which may arise is provided by Article 39 EC Treaty. While from the text and context it is relatively clear that employees are the parties entitled to rely on the prohibition of discrimination in Article 39, the parties against whom they might enforce the prohibition is less clear. That the State or a State authority is an addressee of this Article was never seriously disputed. However, it is only recently that the ECJ has made clear that an employee may rely on Article 39 against a private employer.[47] Even less obvious was the issue whether an employer may rely on the prohibition of discrimination of employees in his relationship with state authorities. This was one of the concerns of the referring court in *Clean Car Autoservice*,[48] in which a residence requirement precluded Clean Car, a Vienna-based company, from appointing Mr Henssen, a German national residing in Berlin, as manager. In proceedings before the *Verwaltungsgerichtshof* against a decision of the competent authorities rendering the appointment impossible, Car Clean relied, *inter alia*, on Article 48 (as it then was). As to the question whether an employer could rely on this provision, the ECJ found that there is nothing in the wording of Article 48 to indicate that parties other than workers - the 'direct addressees' - could not rely on it. The ECJ referred to the full effectiveness of that Article, which entails the employer's entitlement to engage workers in accordance with the rules governing freedom

---

[45] Both as defined in Article 2 of Council Directive 85/577/EEC, OJ 1985, L 372/31.

[46] Cf. Article 4 of Directive 85/577.

[47] Cf. *Angonese* (as cited).

[48] Case C-350/96 *Clean Car* [1998] ECR I-2521.

of movement for workers. In brief, both in the relationship 'employee - employer' and 'employer - district administrative authorities', Article 39 is of relevance.

The *Levy* case[49] provides a comparable example in the context of criminal proceedings against an employer who employed women in nightshifts. He relied on Directive 76/207 and the ECJ's case law according to which the prohibition of nightwork for women and not for men, was found incompatible with the principle of equal treatment of men and women. Levy was neither within the personal scope of the Directive nor within the category of persons protected under the Directive. Yet, nothing prevented the employer raising the prohibition of discrimination as defence in criminal proceedings. In other words, the obligation of the employer under the Directive not to discriminate between men and women in relation to night work[50] also has consequences for the relationship 'the accused - state' in criminal proceedings.

As these few examples already show, legal rules may regulate a relationship between legal subjects not only in a direct way. They may also have a more indirect impact, which ultimately alters it. This is, in particular, the case where the rules do not themselves regulate the relationship, but where they influence the application of a rule which does directly regulate a parties' relationship. Striking examples of this are, in fact and in more detail, discussed elsewhere in this volume by Betlem.[51] Both in *CIA Security* and *Unilever*[52] it was the status and validity of public law regulatory standards which determined the private law obligations between the parties, either non-contractual (*CIA Security*) or contractual (*Unilever*). The respective obligations were dependent on the lawfulness of national 'technical' standards, which were not notified or adopted, in violation of Article 8, respectively 9, of Directive 83/189. These standards then became unenforceable since they were contrary to a Community law rule.

In other words, although Directive 83/189 regulates the relationship between the Commission and the Member States (and the Member States *inter se*, since the latter may also make observations on proposed measures), it is nevertheless also found to be relevant for the regulation of the relationship between individuals, in the sense that the incompatibility of the applicable national rules with the Directive entails the disapplication of the former. The two examples discussed here concerned, in particular, public law incompatibility as a preliminary issue in the private law dispute.[53] In the first place, this issue must be situated in

---

[49] Case C-158/91 *Levy* [1993] ECR I-4287.

[50] At least this is the substance of the Equal Treatment Directive. Due to the denial of horizontal direct effect, the Directive as such cannot impose such an obligation directly upon her employer. Cf. however Lhernould (1999).

[51] In chapter IV, paragraph 2.4. His discussion focuses primarily on the issue of horizontal direct effect. For another interesting analysis of these cases see Gundel (2001).

[52] *CIA Security* and *Unilever Italia* (as cited).

[53] See Betlem in this volume's chapter IV.

the context of a much broader practical and academic debate, which tries to grasp the exact scope of (non-) horizontal direct effect of directives. Moreover, Directive 83/189 is, in a way, an unconventional Directive in the sense that it lays down a *procedure* for the notification etc. of technical standards. Its aim is not to regulate behaviour either between private individuals or between individuals and public authorities.

However, similar problems may arise in areas other than private law also. What about, for instance, a Member State which fixes certain limit values of nitrogen dioxide in a border region without having consulted the neighbouring Member State, as provided for in Directive 85/203 (air quality - nitrogen dioxide)?[54] May the persons who have to observe these limit values, or an environmental interest group, attack the limit values arguing that the prescribed consultation did not take place? The answer is probably yes, with the consequence that an obligation between Member States will have effects for the relationship between an individual and the state authorities.

A more unorthodox example is provided by cases where, before national courts, individuals present an argument that a measure is invalid because it has been adopted on a wrong legal basis. Although individuals have not yet fully discovered this road to contest Community legislation, a few cases have already reached the Court.[55] On the one hand, legal basis provisions have an important function in protecting individuals against measures which institutions are not competent to take. On the other hand, as such, they are not really intended to govern the position of individuals in the relationship with other individuals or with Member States. Yet, they may be relied upon by those individuals and produce legal effects in the relationship between individuals or between individuals and a Member State: the invalidity of, for instance, a directive will have consequences for national law implementing it.

Such indirect effects on legal relationships are certainly not limited to procedural safeguards only. Substantive law provisions may operate in the same way. The case of *Phil Collins*[56] provides a good example. Collins applied to the *Landgericht München* for an interim injunction prohibiting the marketing of a certain compact disk by *Imrat Handelsgesellschaft*. The compact disk contained the recording of a concert in the US and was made without Collins' consent. Under the German Copyright Act, artists of German nationality are protected. However, Collins, a British national, could not prohibit the distribution of the recordings at issue. The ECJ found that the relevant provisions of the Copyright Act were contrary to Article 7 of the EC Treaty (now Article 12). As to how

---

[54] OJ 1985, L 87/1.

[55] For instance, Case C-331/88 *Fedesa* [1990] ECR I-4023 and Case C-74/99 *Imperial Tobacco* [2000] ECR I-8599.

[56] Joined Cases C-92/92 and C-326/92 *Phil Collins* [1993] ECR I-5145.

the prohibition of discrimination had to be enforced, the Court held, first, that Article 7 precluded legislation of a Member State from making the grant of an exclusive right subject to the requirement that the person concerned be a national of that State. Second, it held that the principle of non- discrimination 'may ... be relied upon before a national court as the basis for a request that it disapply the discriminatory provisions of national law which denies to nationals of other Member States the protection which they accord to nationals of the State concerned'.[57] What is happening here is that, as in *CIA Security*, national legislation, in this case the Copyright Act, determines the non-contractual private law relationship between Collins and Imrat. An EC Treaty provision, which is couched by the ECJ in terms of an obligation of the Member State, is decisive for the outcome of a private law dispute. The incompatibility of the relevant provisions of the Copyright Act with Article 7 of the EC Treaty entails the disapplication of the former and this has, in turn, an impact on the application of a rule which directly regulates the private parties' relationship.[58]

Mainly - but not only - on the basis of the examples discussed here, it is submitted that the indirect consequences of certain rules for a legal relationship, occur in particular in cases where Community law rules are relied upon by way of an incidental plea/exception of illegality and the court proceeding focuses primarily on the legality of national rules. *CIA Security* and *Unilever* are, in fact, only two examples which fit into this broader category of cases. Some of the examples have similarly made clear that in this way even those rules which are not meant to regulate the relationship between the parties concerned, are nevertheless relevant for the resolution of dispute. When considered from the point of view of national law, we may discern an interesting parallel. In every Member State there exist many legal rules which are not meant to give individuals enforceable rights and which are primarily meant to regulate the public authorities behaviour, also *inter se*.[59] Yet, the same rules may often be relied upon in the context of a review of the legality of public authorities' action and the incidental plea of illegality is one of the vehicles for such a review.

4.2   The final character of the obligation

Some Community law rules may contain perfectly clear and well-defined obligations but, nevertheless, are not relevant for a dispute if they

---

[57]   Para. 34 of the judgment.

[58]   Another striking parallel between the *Phil Collins* case and *CIA Security* is that in both cases it is not clear whether a person is directly bound by EC law provisions at issue; the judgment in *Phil Collins* was rendered several years before *Angonese*. Cf. above, paragraph 4.

[59]   For instance certain guarantees or (programmatic) provisions, like a guarantee of a social minimum or the protection of environment as provided for in a constitution and, furthermore, all rules which regulate the relations between public authorities.

have no impact on the relationship at issue and are, in their effects only limited to another - 'wrong' - relationship. In *Enichem* and *Dumon*[60] it was clear that the Member States had to notify certain measures or information to the Commission, but this obligation existed only between the Member States and the Commission, without having (side-)effects for third parties.

The other way round, sometimes a provision seems relevant from the point of view of whether, *in abstracto*, the relationship between two legal subjects may be affected, but there is another issue: we also have to know *what* a private individual or public authority *etc.* is bound to do. Put differently, even when one is able to conclude that the parties to a certain relationship are within the ambit of the relevant rules, it is also important to ascertain what is the substance of the obligation at issue. This has to be considered in the light of the concrete dispute. For example, State A agrees with State B to regulate, within a period of 5 years, the flow of a river,[61] in particular to reduce considerably the danger of flooding. This is undoubtedly in the interest of - at least - the people living along the river. The relationship between these individuals and the public authorities responsible for the regulation of the river is affected by this agreement. Yet, whether the provisions of the Agreement are relevant for a concrete dispute will depend on what the dispute is about and, in the light of that, whether the obligation is sufficiently defined *for the purpose* it is relied upon. If, for instance, after 5 years, it appears that nothing has been done and the riverbank-dwellers seek a declaration that the authorities failed in their obligation to undertake action, a court should be able to give this. However, if the riverbank-dwellers want to claim that certain particular and well-defined works must be carried out, a court will probably turn down such a request, since at this point, it is up to the authorities to decide and plan what to do and the court is not in a position to do that instead. Yet, the court could act again if the measures taken looked so arbitrary and so obviously insufficient, that they could never be considered as measures that could ever contribute to reducing considerably the danger of flooding.

The case of *Annalisa Carbonari*[62] provides an example of a situation where the content of the obligation was not defined with sufficient precision in the Directive at issue, neither were the institutions named which bore the obligation to pay the relevant remuneration. Under Directive 75/363,[63] as amended by Directive 82/76,[64] trainees in specialized medicine were supposed to get appro-

---

[60] Case 380/87 *Enichem* [1989] ECR 2491; Case-C-235/95 *Dumon* [1998] ECR I-4531.

[61] Or, alternatively, there is a directive which provides for similar measures. The same example may also hold true for, for instance, an arrangement between two autonomous regions within one single state.

[62] C-131/97 *Carbonari* [1999] ECR I-1103.

[63] OJ 1975, L 167/14.

[64] OJ 1982, L 43/21.

priate remuneration. So far, there was, according to the ECJ, an unconditional and sufficiently precise obligation imposed upon the Member States. However, the Directive did not define what level of remuneration had to be regarded as 'appropriate', neither did it indicate the methods by which that remuneration was to be fixed. Furthermore, the Directive did not enable the national court to determine what body should be liable to pay the remuneration.

In another situation, the substance of the obligation may be very well-defined, but for some other reason the application of the provision must be postponed. For instance, in *Wijsenbeek*[65] it was suggested by the ECJ that the full exercise of the right to move and reside freely in the Member States of the Union depended on the adoption, by the Council, of common rules on controls at external frontiers and immigration, visa and asylum policy.[66] In other words, there was perhaps a clear provision, but its full application was conditional upon measures to be taken, in this case by the Council.

Indeed, in the ECJ's case law there are many variations on this theme and they are well known in relation to the conditions for direct effect, namely unconditionality and sufficient precision. This is, however, not confined to EC law. In national law there are also rules which are either vague or incomplete (or both) and which need further implementation by, for instance, statutory instruments in order to be fully operational. As such, they do not admit judicial application in all respects.[67] Similarly, in national legal contexts, considerations of justiciability (i.e. courts must remain within the limits of their judicial function) have implications for the question whether a concrete claim will be sustained or dismissed. Whether a claim can be based on a legal rule, is a matter of interpretation of that rule and judicial interpretation has its limits. In relation to the specific Community law context problems are, to some extent, caused by the fact that Community law provisions are sometimes used as a panacea for legal claims which can not be substantiated: in some disputes parties read in Community law provisions certain obligations which, when using a little (legal) common sense, they cannot possibly contain.[68] On the other hand it must be admitted that, in particular when considered from a purely national law perspective, the interpretation of Community law provisions may be sometimes rather unexpected and surprising.

---

[65] C-378/97 *Wijsenbeek* [1999] ECR I-6207.

[66] The Court was not entirely clear on this point. Cf. para. 43 of the judgment.

[67] Cf. however above, paragraph 2.2, where it is explained that much depends on the question for what purposes the provisions are relied upon. This also holds true for national law.

[68] For instance, when it is claimed that Article 2(4) of Directive 76/207 (as cited), allowing for positive measures, obliges the Member States to adopt such measures.

4.3   Defining legal consequences

Perhaps somewhat surprisingly, in the EC Treaty there is just one provision providing for legal consequences *in* the Member States in case of incompatibility with the Treaty. It is Article 81(2) EC, which provides for automatic nullity of anti-competitive agreements or decisions. In secondary Community law, some indications as to the legal consequences of a breach are given only now and then.[69] For general guidance on this issue, one has to look at the case law of the ECJ. Yet, even in that case law surprisingly little can be found. Indeed, the general dicta of the Court about the role of national courts to protect the rights individuals derive from EC law are widely known.[70] There are some - until now rather exceptional - cases where the ECJ defines the consequences of procedural defects, like *CIA Security* and *Unilever*.[71] And there are plenty of cases where the Court limits itself to the finding that Community law 'precludes the application of [national law that is contrary to EC law provisions]' or that the 'Member States are precluded from adopting [national provisions that are incompatible with EC law]' or that 'national courts must refrain from applying [the contrary provisions]' or something similar.[72] However, the ECJ does not usually say what the consequences should be, beyond the finding of incompatibility and the subsequent disapplication or setting aside of the contrary national provisions.[73]

---

[69] And, moreover, often in less precise terms. Cf. Article 6 of Council Directive 93/13/EEC (unfair terms in consumer contracts), OJ 1993, L 95/29, which declares the prohibited clauses 'non-binding on the consumer', Article 3 of Directive 2000/35/EC of the European Parliament and the Council (late payment in commercial transactions), OJ 2000, L 200/35 , stipulates 'unenforceability' of the contractual provisions at issue, or Article 4 of Directive 76/207 (as cited), which stipulates that discriminatory provisions in collective agreements etc. shall be, or may be declared, null and void.

[70] Initially and often still coupled with direct effect, but in some cases also disconnected from direct effect. Cf. *Francovich* (as cited), para. 32.

[71] See, however, also the case law on Article 88(3) EC Treaty.

[72] These findings relate, indeed, not only to procedural defects, like non-notification, but also to more substantive defects. Cf. for instance Case C-262/97 *Engelbrecht* [2000] ECR I-7321 and Case C-481/99 *Heininger* [2001] ECR I-9945. Furthermore, note that the inapplicability may concern national law in general, thus national legislation (cf. Case C-109/99 *Association Basco-Béarnaise des Opticiens Indépendants* [2000] ECR I-7247) or an individual decision (cf. Case C-224/97 *Ciola* [1999] ECR I-2517) or, arguably, national case law (cf. Case C-215/97 *Bellone* [1998] ECR I-2191 and C-456/98 *Centrosteel* [2000] ECR I-6007). Interesting in this respect are also the consequences of a judgment rendered in an Article 226 proceedings: such a judgment entails 'a prohibition having the full force of law on the competent national authorities against applying a national rule recognized as incompatible with the Treaty ...'. Cf. Case C-101/91 *Ten Oever* [1993] I-4879. For courts this must also imply a setting aside obligation.

[73] Cf. Case 106/77 *Simmenthal* [1978] ECR 629. Cf. about this yet in relation to another problem Betlem in chapter IV.

From cases like *Lück* and, more recently, *IN.CO.GE*[74] we learn that, apart from the obligation to disapply the national rule which is contrary to Community law, the national court should apply, from among the various procedures available under national law those which are appropriate for protecting the individual rights conferred by Community law. In other words, the issue of further legal consequences shifts to the national legal order. Or, as one eminent scholar put it, in relation to what he calls the general *remedy of setting aside*, 'the form which the remedy may take and the procedures in accordance with which it has to be put into operation are to be determined by the national legal systems'.[75] Several separate questions can be distinguished in this respect.[76]

In the first place, there is the question how the setting aside of national rules is to be effected. Should it be done by disapplication as such, or should it lead to non-existence, invalidity, inopposability, absolute or relative nullity, illegitimacy, voidness, loss of force, or whatever classifications there may exist in national law? The ECJ has up until now refrained from indicating into which legal category the 'obligation to set aside' falls. The choice of any of these concepts, as well as their meaning and scope, is left to the national legal system. To this one may add that even the meaning and scope of the nullity sanction of Article 81(2) EC Treaty and the consequences it may have for other sanctions is not an entirely clear matter.[77]

In the second place, procedures in which the setting aside will be deployed, are, somewhat naturally, determined by national law. It is in the context of the national court procedures - administrative, civil, criminal - that a party may raise the setting aside issue. The type of the court procedure also influences the way in which inapplicability will 'operate'.

In the third place, setting aside will usually translate into more specific remedies, such as restitution, compensation, rescission of a contract, interim relief, declaratory relief, order of specific performance, which could possibly include the certainly not undisputed order to legislate,[78] acquittal in criminal proceedings; it may also result in an administrative decision being annulled, entirely or partially, environmental permit being withdrawn or changed etc., all depending on what is possible under national law.

---

[74] Case 34/67 *Lück* [1868] ECR 346; Joined Cases C-10-22/97 *IN.CO.GE* [1998] ECR I-6307.

[75] Van Gerven (2000), at p. 509.

[76] Apart from the frequently debated procedural issues like time limits, standing etc., which I will not address here.

[77] For a brief overview see Van Gerven (2001).

[78] I.e. legislation in order to meet EC law obligations. For instance, in the *Waterpakt*-case, discussed elsewhere in this volume by Jans & Prinssen (chapter V), the Court of Appeal in The Hague held that in the light of the doctrine of separation of powers, it was not up to a court to give such an order; published in [2001] *M&R* no. 95, with case note by Jans and de Jong.

Considered in this perspective, where Community law stops, i.e. at the point of setting aside, national law takes over. Although as of this point everything seems to be left to the national legal system, there is, as is well known, an increasing EC law intrusion at this stage too. The most obvious examples are the requirements imposed by the ECJ governing compensation in case of non-contractual liability[79] and interim relief,[80] while other remedies, like restitution[81] and judicial review,[82] do not escape the Court's interference either. So far, this is nothing new. However, upon closer consideration, the setting aside remedy raises a number of intriguing problems.

In the search for parameters that should help to find out whether a provision is relevant in a concrete case, we already came across the phenomenon that a provision may affect a legal relationship not only directly but also by way of side-effects. These effects occur, in particular, where the provision at issue does not itself regulate the relationship, but where it influences the application of a rule which *does* directly regulate the relationship.[83] The incompatibility of the provision with Community law has consequences for the rule at issue and therefore also, though indirectly, for the relationship. Considered against this background, the setting aside may also lead to somewhat perplexing results. Where incompatibility of national law and Community law provisions leads to the setting aside of the former, in combination with an abstract and objective review of national law, the setting aside remedy makes almost every provision 'a provision which is relevant for the dispute', provided that an indirect challenge of the validity of national law is possible.

In this respect again[84] much depends on what the national legal system allows for. Usually, in certain areas of law a mechanism such as an incidental plea of illegality is by and large allowed, with as a consequence that (almost) everybody may raise it. A good example is provided by criminal law proceedings where Community law is relied upon in defence against a criminal charge.[85] Also in proceedings which may perhaps be characterized as 'private law enforcement' something comparable will often happen. The two *Piageme* cases[86] and

---

[79] *Francovich* (as cited) and subsequent cases.

[80] *Facortame* and *Zuckerfabrik* case law; Case C-213/89 [1990] ECR I-2433 and Joined Cases C-143/88 and C-92/89, [1991] ECR I-415

[81] Joined Cases C-192-218/95 *Comateb* [1997] ECR I-165.

[82] Cf. Case C-120/97 *Upjohn* [1999] ECR I-223. See also Case C-380/01 *Schneider*, pending, OJ 2001, C 348/14.

[83] Cf. above, paragraph 4.1.

[84] Like in relation to remedies and procedures.

[85] Most extreme - and unsuccessful - example of such a defence provides Case C-226/97 *Lemmens* [1998] ECR I-3711.

[86] Case C-369/89, [1991] ECR I-2971 and Case C-85/94, [1995] ECR I-2955, also known as *Peeters I* and *Peeters II*.

the *CIA* case were all brought under the Belgian Law on Commercial Practices. Under this law, injunctive relief may be sought against a 'seller' if he acts in breach of good commercial practice[87] and the conduct is likely to cause harm to other businessmen or consumers. In these cases, the 'sellers' relied in their defence on the fact that the allegedly infringed provisions of national law ran counter to Community law directives and therefore could not be applied as basis for the claim brought by the plaintiffs. Apparently, from the point of view of Belgian law there was no problem in raising the plea of illegality. However, it is conceivable that in other legal systems or in other types of proceedings, the person who wants to raise such a plea successfully, must at least fall within the protective scope of the (Community) norm he relies on. To put it differently, a nexus between factual interest and legally protected interest may be required. Or is the setting aside requirement so absolute that the national legal context does not matter?

Interestingly, looking at it the other way round, the intertwined concepts of legal review and setting aside may put well-established case law of the ECJ under pressure, or at least some aspects of it. Since setting aside operates independently of the public or private characteristics of the parties, it thwarts the non-horizontal direct effect of directives doctrine. Moreover, the abstract and objective means of review in the context of a plea of illegality, in combination with a presumption that the national court knows why it asks preliminary questions, seems to interfere with the ECJ's case law on 'internal situations'. In *Guimont* and *Angonese*[88] the Court circumvented the issue of internal situation and left it to the national Court to decide what to do,[89] although, strictly speaking, neither the concrete situation of Guimont nor that of Angonese fell within the protective scope of the relevant EC law provisions. In *Guimont*, the question whether national provisions on the characteristics of Emmenthal cheese were contrary to Article 28 of the EC Treaty was relevant for the criminal proceedings instituted against Mr. Guimont. The national court indicated in its reference that persons may not be prosecuted for a rule which itself is contrary to a higher ranking legal provision. *Angonese* was concerned with the Casa di Risparmio policy imposing an indirectly discriminatory language requirement, which was, *in abstracto*, incompatible with Article 39 of the EC Treaty. Again, in its reference for preliminary ruling, the national court indicated that under Article 1418 and 1421 of the Italian Civil Code, Angonese could take advantage of a nullity with an *erga omnes* effect.[90]

---

[87] I.e. *inter alia*, if he infringes, in the exercise of an economic activity, any duty imposed by law and regulation which may relate to any area of law, be it tax law, criminal law, social law, competition law etc., EC law included.

[88] C-448/98 *Guimont* [2000] ECR I-10663 and *Angonese* (as cited).

[89] In both cases the ECJ just stated that Article 28 and Article 39, respectively, 'precludes' the measures at issue.

[90] Cf. para. 7 of the Opinion of AG Fennelly.

The actual consequences of legal review and the subsequent setting aside will depend on many more aspects of national law. Setting aside is, in my view, not so much a general remedy, but rather an incomplete remedy. In some cases it may indeed suffice that a national court disapplies national provisions that are contrary to the relevant Community law provisions, or that it simply finds that there is a breach of EC law.[91] However, in other cases such a disapplication may result in a lacuna. Although it is conceivable that a court declares inapplicable national rules contrary to Community law provisions without going so far as to secure for the individual concerned the legal position which he would have had if the State had complied with Community law obligations, usually the lacuna should be filled. In order to resolve the dispute, the national court should either apply the relevant Community law provisions or it must fill the lacuna in some other way, in particular by interpretation.[92]

The combination of, on the one hand, rather absolute dicta of the Court and, on the other hand, the incomplete character of the setting aside remedy, which is, moreover, for its application very closely interwoven with national law, results in very different outcomes in the different Member States.[93] Sometimes the 'precludes-finding' of the Court, i.e. the finding by the Court that Community law precludes the application of the national rule at issue, will tend more to give a clear signal to the national legislator, without, however, giving satisfaction to the individual in a concrete case. The main question is indeed when, and how far, the ECJ should interfere in defining the legal consequences of the setting aside remedy. The problem is that the guidance the Court has given until now is certainly not unambiguous.[94]

It is submitted that with the explicit introduction of the legality review as took place in *Kraaijeveld*,[95] defining the legal consequences of both substantive

---

[91] For instance in a criminal case, or where declaratory relief is sought or where a simple disapplication of an exception to the main rule results in a situation in conformity with Community law.

[92] For the from Community point of view unsatisfactory aftermath of the *Piageme* saga see Verhoeven (2000), at p. 333-334. In some cases the ECJ seems to be a bit too optimistic about the possibilities the technique of interpretation offers in this respect. Cf. Joined Cases C-240-244/98 *Océano* [2000] ECR I-4941, and the comment by Stuyck in *CMLRev.* 2001, p. 719-737, in particular at p. 734.

[93] Comparable divergences also occur in relation to other procedural defects. See on this Jans & Prinssen in chapter V.

[94] *CIA Security* and *Piageme* (as cited), on the one hand, and *Faccini Dori* (as cited) and *El Corte Inglés* (Case C-192/94, [1996] ECR I-1281), on the other, are just two examples. Cf. also Gillieux (1998), at p. 120, who states that the ECJ '... n'apparait pas avoir clairement pris en compte toutes les implications spécifiques au contrôle objectif de légalité dans lequel le respect de la hiérarchie des normes est avant tout privilégié'. However, he also points out that '... ce reproche découle de la conception juridique française, alors que le contrôle de la légalité des actes normatifs a reçu en Europe des solutions variables ...'. The Court has to take that into account.

[95] And independently what is claimed in this contribution, namely that direct effect should be rejected.

and procedural incompatibility between national law and Community law is one of the issues which will become important in the next few years and which merits more attention.

5 Uniformity v. divergence

Doing away with direct effect will certainly not drastically change the issues facing legal doctrine and practice in relation to the question how to give effect to Community law within the Member States. There will, however, be a shift in focus, away from direct effect as a central concept to a number of questions which, as a matter of fact, are topical already.

The review of compatibility of national law with Community law and the exclusionary effect of the setting aside remedy re-emphasize the crucial role of the doctrine of supremacy as a driving force beyond the legal effects of Community law. Supremacy will indeed remain an important conflict-resolving mechanism in cases of incompatibility between national and Community law provisions.[96] To this one may add that we are not dealing with a kind of ruthless primacy. There is room for mitigation of effects of supremacy which are too harsh, on grounds of other considerations, both EC and national, such as general principles of law or other common sense requirements. For instance, legal certainty may entail the need to annul a decision *ex nunc* instead of *ex tunc*, or to uphold at least certain legal consequences. Reasons of 'procedural economy' may dictate that a decision should not be annulled if the outcome would not be any different after redress of a formal defect. A contract may be declared null and void, but harsh consequences may be mitigated by applying the principles of reasonableness and equity. The prohibition of abuse of rights may be relevant for answering the question what remedy is appropriate and proportionate in a concrete case, once incompatibility is established.[97] In brief, legal certainty, effective settlement of disputes, hardship etc. must be balanced against the need to secure the full effectiveness of Community law and, in fact, also the legality of State action.

The application of Community law in the Member States is already now intimately linked with national law. It is merely stating the obvious to say that if Community law is treated in the same way as national law, the relationship will be reinforced. Where national law takes over, procedural rules and other much less visibly operating mechanisms determine what is going to happen to the relevant Community law provisions. National laws differ and so do the

---

[96] To make things clear: doing away with direct effect does not mean doing away with supremacy.

[97] Cf. Case C-373/97 *Diamantis* [2000] ECR I-1705 and the comment on this case by Anagnostopoulou in *CMLRev.* 2001, p. 767-780.

outcomes in terms of application of Community law.[98] The problem goes deeper than imposing constraints upon remedial and procedural autonomy. The methods or rules which govern the deployment of legal norms are also relevant. In addition to divergence in remedies and procedures, there is also divergence at the stage of translating Community law into national legal categories.[99]

In this respect, the Court of Justice will continue to play a crucial role. Not only in explaining the meaning and scope of Community law provisions, but not least in relation to the question whether a Community law provision should be considered as relevant for a certain legal relationship. It will also be called upon to define legal effects and consequences in cases of non-compliance with Community law provisions.[100] Certain aspects may possibly also be regulated by the Community legislature. There is no doubt that Community law - the Community Court or legislature - will interfere in this respect. The proper question is how far should the interference go. In principle, I endorse the point of view that 'what is good for national law is also good for EC law'.[101] However, this does not always hold true. For a start this is because, in my view, Community law may set higher standards for its enforcement.[102] Moreover, it is also a matter of seeing the relationship between Community law and national law in its proper perspective. Where an order to legislate would normally amount to a constitutional enormity, from a Community law perspective the national legislature is in a different position: complying with the Community law obligations can be compared to a kind of delegated activity or a matter of execution rather than an act of a sovereign legislature. Similarly, where, for instance, only a constitutional court is allowed to review the legality of a national Act of Parliament, for the same reason it is not readily understandable why the same should hold true if the Act is reviewed in the light of the EC law provisions.

In my opinion, if one accepts a world without direct effect or uses the term to describe a wide range of effects,[103] the leading questions are not so much 'if it is necessary, and if so, on whose authority, on what grounds and in what form to delimit such wide applicability',[104] but rather how to safeguard, a certain level of, first, uniformity and, second, effectiveness of EC law provisions. The preliminary question is then indeed, as Jans and Prinssen put it elsewhere in

---

[98] Cf. Jans & Prinssen in this volume's chapter V.

[99] Cf. above, paragraph 4.3.

[100] In my opinion, cases discussed hereabove, like *CIA Security, Unilever Italia, Angonese, Guimont, Piageme* are not about direct effect, but rather about consequences of incompatibility.

[101] Cf. Jans & Prinssen, chapter V, paragraph 3.

[102] Cf. also Prechal (2001), at p. 47-50.

[103] Cf. above, paragraph 3.

[104] Preface to the present volume.

this volume, what kind of differences are acceptable and what not?[105] Although the authors still focus on direct effect, in fact they have already written the next instalment of the legal serial.

---

[105] See on these questions also Van Gerven (2000).

CHAPTER III

More than an 'Infant Disease'

Individual Rights, EC Directives, and the Case for Uniform Remedies

dr. Angela Ward

1 Introduction

It has been eighteen years since Judge Pescatore famously illu-
minated the fundamental principle of 'primacy' in EC constitutional law, by
unpacking its underlying premises, and foreshadowing a future characterized by
simplification of the rules on direct application of Community law in national
legal systems. He argued that the 'purpose of any legal rule...[was] to achieve
some practical aim' and that 'direct effect', including its operation in the EC
legal system, was 'nothing but the ordinary state of the law'.[1] Implicit then, in
Pescatore's reasoning, seemed the suggestion that once the 'democratic ideal'[2]
of Europe had firmly taken root, reference to 'direct effect' would become redun-
dant. Effective application of EC rules would become sustainable independent of
more detailed doctrine and logic.

Unfortunately the reverse has occurred. The rules on enforcement of unimplemented EC directives have become particularly convoluted, taking on a
complexity that was, in all likelihood, unforeseen in Pescatore's time. In terms
of contentious issues, scholars and other commentators were largely occupied,
in the early 1980s, by the ramifications flowing from the 'direct applicability' of
regulations under Article 249 EC as opposed to the 'direct effect' of directives[3]
the latter having been developed via Court of Justice case law.[4] Yet, Member
State constitutional problems notwithstanding, this represented the limits of the
'technical' difficulties marring domestic judicial enforcement of EC directives.[5]
The key rules governing national application of badly transposed, or wholly
untransposed, directives remained fairly simple. It involved a two-stage process.
First, an investigation was necessary into whether the relevant provisions of the
directive in question were worded imperatively, and with sufficient clarity, to
be enforceable irrespective of national legislation. Second, courts were obliged
to determine whether the body against whom enforcement of the directive was
sought was a governmental authority, or in the words of the Court of Justice,
an 'emanation of the state'.[6]

---

* Angela Ward is grateful to Jolande Prinssen for comments, and to all of the participants at the Conference "Direct Effect; Rethinking a classic of EC legal doctrine", held on 1 June 2001 at the University
   of Amsterdam.

[1] Pescatore (1983), at p. 177.

[2] Ibid. at p. 158. For contemporary arguments in support of abandonment of direct effect see Prechal
     (2000).

[3] Winter (1972).

[4] Case 41/74 *van Duyn* [1974] ECR 1337.

[5] Timmermans (1979).

[6] Case 152/84 *Marshall I* [1986] ECR 723; Case 8/81 *Becker* [1982] ECR 53; Case C-188/89 *Foster* [1990]
     ECR I-3313. Kvjatkovski (1997).

However, a great deal of jurisprudential water has flowed under the bridge of EC constitutional law since Judge Pescatore presided at the Court of Justice. The result has been obfuscation of some of the principles that were central in the establishment of the EC's quasi-federal legal system.

First, in 1991, and somewhat surprisingly, the Court of Justice in *Francovich*[7] decoupled the notion of 'individual rights' from that of 'direct effect', even though the latter had hitherto been a *sine qua non* for the conferral of the former. In other words, the Court of Justice opened up a significant new constitutional frontier by ruling that, even if a directive was not clear, unconditional and precise, individual applicants were entitled, in some circumstances, to payment of compensation from Member States which have failed to transpose the directive's substantive terms.[8] The alienation of the notion of 'individual rights' from that of 'direct effect' was taken further in 1996. In the *Kraaijeveld* case,[9] in the context of a dispute concerning interpretation of the environmental impact assessment Directive (EIA Directive),[10] the Court of Justice cited the familiar principle that 'where the Community authorities have, by a directive, imposed on Member States the obligation to pursue a particular course of conduct, the useful effect of such an act would be weakened if individuals were prevented from relying on it before their national courts'.[11] However the Court stopped short of ruling that the parts of the EIA Directive in issue were directly effective.

Second, not long after the publication of Pescatore's 'Infant Disease' article, the doctrine of sympathetic interpretation crept into Court of Justice case law. Like the principle of State liability founded in the *Francovich* case, the duty of sympathetic interpretation did not depend on a finding that the Directive

---

[7] Joined Cases C-6/90 and C-9/90 *Francovich* [1991] ECR I-5357.

[8] Court of Justice cases that have developed the *Francovich* notion of State liability in damages include Joined Cases C-46/93 and C-48/93 *Brasserie du Pêcheur* [1996] ECR I-1029; Joined Cases C-178/94, C-179/94 and C-188-190/94 *Dillenkofer* [1996] ECR I-4845; Case C-392/93 *British Telecommunications* [1996] ECR I-1631; Joined Cases C-283/94, C-291/94 and C-292/94 *Denkavit* [1996] ECR I-5063; Case C-5/94 *Hedley Lomas* [1996] ECR I-2553; Case C-127/95 *Norbrook Laboratories* [1998] ECR I-1531; Case C-319/96 *Brinkmann I* [1998] ECR I-5255; Case C-302/97 *Konle* [1999] ECR I-3099; Case C-321/97 *Andersson* [1999] ECR I-3551; Case C-140/97 *Rechberger* [1999] ECR I-3499; Case C-424/97 *Haim II* [2000] ECR I-5125; Case C-150/99 *Stockholm Lindöpark* [2001] ECR I-493. For a recent commentary see Tridimas (2001). On damages claims against private sector for breach of Competition law see Case C-453/99 *Courage* [2001] ECR I-6279, Opinion of AG Mischo of 22 March 2001.

[9] Case C-72/95 *Kraaijveld* [1996] ECR I-5403.

[10] Council Directive 85/337/EEC, OJ 1985, L 175/40, amended by Council Directive 97/11/EC, OJ 1997, L 73/5.

[11] At para. 56. The same approach was taken in Case C-435/97 *WWF* [1999] ECR I-5613, para. 69; Case C-287/98 *Linster* [2000] ECR I-6917, para. 32.

concerned was clear, unconditional and precise. Rather, it bound national judges to interpret national laws passed for the purpose of implementing directives in conformity with the latter, in so far as it is was possible to do so.[12] Later the doctrine was expanded to include all Member State laws falling within the scope of a directive, whether or not the national measures were passed before or after the directive's entry into force.[13] However, the rule on sympathetic interpretation was also contracted, in that it was established that Member State judges were not bound to make *contra legem* interpretation of national law[14] (even though sometimes it appeared they were being directed to do so),[15] and nor could national courts apply the rule on sympathetic interpretation to aggravate criminal liability.[16] For a time it was thought that the duty to interpret national law in conformity with directives operated even prior to the date of the entry into force of the directive in issue,[17] but this approach has not been followed in recent Court of Justice case law.[18]

Thirdly, even though the Court of Justice ruled in the 1994 *Faccini Dori* case[19] that directives were not to have 'horizontal' effect in disputes involving private sector actors, and that no obligations could be cast on such 'individuals' by the grace of unimplemented directives, the Court has consistently answered questions referred by national judges on the meaning of directives. It has done so even in litigation of a purely private nature.[20] Only exceptionally has the Court explained why, in constitutional terms, such questions require an answer.[21] Given the explosion, in the 1990s, of regulatory directives that address their requirements to private sector actors, as opposed to Member State governments, the impact of this development, for improving enforcement, should not be underestimated.

---

[12] Case 14/83 *Von Colson and Kamann* [1984] ECR 1891. For recent examples of the doctrine of sympathetic interpretation see Case C-365/98 *Brinkmann II* [2000] ECR I-4619; Joined Cases C-240-244/98 *Océano* [2000] ECR I-4941; Case C-456/98 *Centrosteel*, [2000] ECR I-6007. For a discussion see the contribution of Betlem in this volume's chapter IV. The rule on sympathetic interpretation has also been applied with respect to international treaties entered into by the EC, and interpretive obligations that follow for national law. See Case C-89/99 *Schieving-Nijstad* [2001] ECR I-5851.

[13] Case C-106/89 *Marleasing* [1990] ECR I-4135.

[14] Case 80/86 *Kolpinghuis* [1987] ECR 3969.

[15] E.g. Case C-421/92 *Habermann-Beltermann* [1994] ECR I-1657.

[16] *Kolpinghuis* (as cited); Case C-168/95 *Arcaro* [1996] ECR I-4705.

[17] Case C-156/91 *Mundt* [1992] ECR I-5567, para. 23 of the Advocate General's Opinion.

[18] See in particular *Centrosteel* (as cited) and the comments by Betlem in chapter IV.

[19] Case C-91/92 *Faccini Dori* [1994] ECR I-3325.

[20] For a recent example see Case C-381/98 *Ingmar* [2000] ECR I-9305.

[21] Case C-185/97 *Coote* [1998] ECR I-5199.

Fourthly, from the mid-1990s, it emerged in a series of judgments, that directives could have 'incidental effect' on the interests of private sector actors.[22] Under this doctrine, national judges are obliged to disapply national technical regulations if, in breach of an EC directive, they have not been notified to the European Commission by a Member State government. It is now well established that this rule operates in litigation in which one individual is pitted against another, and despite the fact that adverse effects can result for one of them.[23]

Fifthly, while the practice of the Court of Justice has vacillated over time, there has been a steady tendency toward intensifying review of national sanctions and procedural rules accompanying national enforcement of Community rules, including directives.[24] In Judge Pescatore's time, review of sanctions and procedural rules to secure application of directly effective measures was largely left to Member State courts, subject to compliance with the guidelines fixed in *Rewe/Comet*.[25] In this sense then, the Court of Justice has, in comparison with the position in the early 1980s, substantially deepened its foray into judicial territory traditionally occupied by Member State courts. It has done so, at least partly, under the imperative of providing 'individuals' with effective judicial protection.[26] This has included, on the back of the *Francovich* litigation, elaboration of comprehensive rules on Member State liability to compensate breach of some types of EC rule. These override national laws supplying lower standards of government liability for damages.[27]

Finally, in a related development, the Court of Justice and the Court of First Instance have, in the last 18 years, exponentially developed rules on judicial review of EC measures alleged by private parties to be unlawful. Of most significance, for present purposes, is the fact that some modest steps have been taken toward refining the rules operative in Article 288 EC damages claims, and to the advantage of 'individual' applicants. As will be shown, this improvement in the law on remedies is intimately bound up in the principles on Member State liability in damages that have evolved post-*Francovich*.

This article will explore the last two of the above six developments. Some of the main contours of Court of Justice reliance on 'individual rights' will

---

[22] For a detailed discussion see e.g. Dougan (2000).

[23] Case C-194/94 *CIA Security* [1996] ECR I-2201; Case C-443/98 *Unilever Italia* [2000] ECR I-7535. This doctrine was attenuated in Case C-226/97 *Lemmens* [1998] ECR I-3711.

[24] The literature on this topic is voluminous, but see for example Bridge (1984); Curtin (1990); Tash (1993); Van Gerven (1995); Hoskins (1996); Biondi (1999); Dougan (2002); Van Gerven (2000).

[25] Case 33/76 *Rewe* [1976] ECR 1989 and Case 45/76 *Comet* [1976] ECR 2043. The limited parameters of Court of Justice review in this field were mentioned by Pescatore (1983), at p. 176.

[26] For a classic example see Case 222/84 *Johnston* [1986] ECR 1651.

[27] See the cases cited above, note 8.

first be mapped out, and its weaknesses highlighted. It will be illustrated that, despite some recent improvements, significant problems remain for those who challenge the legality of EC measures before the Court of First Instance and the Court of Justice.

Remedies and procedural rules operative at national level are affected by this, and in a way that relates to the theme of uniformity. Given the continuing prevalence of the notion of 'individual rights' in Court of Justice case law, it will be here argued that the imperative of constitutional coherence militates in favour of restricted Court of Justice review of Member State sanctions and procedural rules. To this end, it would be preferable if principles formulated to improve national enforcement of (lawful) EC directives were maintained at the same level as rights which individuals enjoy when they question the conduct of *EC institutions*, and challenge the legality of EC legal instruments. That said, however, any rules that *are* developed by the Court of Justice pertaining to national remedies and procedural rules would be best applied across the full spectrum of the 'national implementation' board. That is, in the interests of legal certainty, they should be attached to all cases involving inadequate implementation of directives, and rather than being confined to the 'classic', though increasingly obsolete,[28] conundrum of how to enforce directly effective directives against governmental authorities.

2 Individual what? The parameters of Court of Justice discourse on 'rights'

Two eminent scholars have recently observed that there is 'considerable conceptual confusion'[29] around the use by the Court of Justice of the language of rights, alleging that the Court uses the term right 'indiscriminately'.[30] Further, they have neatly summarized the ethos underpinning the original rationale for the deployment of the notion of individual rights in EC Constitutional law:

'It may well be that by invoking the language of individual rights, the ECJ tries to benefit from the mystique of the term in order to ensure that the requirements which it formulates are more readily accepted in the national legal orders. After all, in the supranational context the protection of individual citizens' rights seems a much more laudable project than merely stipulating that the Member States must be controlled'.[31]

---

[28] Prechal (2000).

[29] Prechal & Hancher (2002).

[30] By Prechal (2000), at p. 1057.

[31] Prechal & Hancher (2002), at p. 104-105.

This suggestion, it is submitted, accumulates further cogency upon close examination of the *Van Gend en Loos* case itself. As was pointed out by Pescatore, the
'new legal order' referred to by the Court had, as its distinguishing characteristic, the participation of 'individual' Member State nationals as 'subjects' of the
system, enjoying both 'rights' and carrying 'obligations'.[32] It was, as Pescatore
observed, 'a highly political idea, drawn from a perception of the constitutional
system of the Community, which is at the basis of *Van Gend en Loos* and which
continues to inspire the whole doctrine flowing from it'.[33]

There was a perceived need, therefore, to elaborate legal principles to support
enforcement of EEC law, as it then was, within national law. To this end the
Court drew on established rules on 'self-executing treaties', under which 'clear
unconditional and precise international agreements could potentially create
rights and obligations for individuals'.[34] From this it followed in Court of Justice
case law, and fairly soon after (in *Rewe/Comet* and *San Giorgio*), that such
'directly effective' rules must not be rendered, under the weight of Member State
rules on remedies and procedures, virtually impossible or excessively difficult to
enforce; and nor were sanctions and procedures applicable to directly effective
EC measures to be less favourable than that attached to analogous claims of a
purely domestic nature.[35]

The Court then, it is submitted, made recourse to the concept of 'individual
rights' under the weight of two imperatives. The first was the need to isolate
a *political* justification for legal 'supranationalism',[36] particularly in the absence
of a supremacy clause or other provisions in the original Rome Treaty unequivocally supporting it.[37] Second, it was called in aid to help persuade national
judges to adopt and develop their roles as 'Community' judges, and supply the
necessary sanctions[38] to enforce rules emanating from the 'new legal order'.[39]

Confusion later ensued on the parameters and purposes of these principles.
At the outset, it is important to underscore the role of political processes,
or at least gaps therein, in the evolution of the 'rights' discourse. Given that
political actors did not, at successive Inter-Governmental Conferences, codify, or
even modify, fundamental constitutional principles formulated by the Court of
Justice, the latter was bound to continue its reliance on the notion of 'individual
rights' in establishing, over the years, constitutional supranationalism.[40] In

---

[32] Case 26/62 *Van Gend en Loos* [1963] ECR 1.

[33] Pescatore (1983), at p. 158.

[34] *Danzig* PCIJ, Ser. B, No 15 (1928). Discussed by Winter (1972), at p. 429.

[35] *Rewe* and *Comet* (as cited); Case 199/82 *San Giorgio* [1983] ECR I-3595.

[36] Weiler (1981).

[37] See further *Van Gend en Loos* (as cited); Ward (2000a), Chapter 1.

[38] *Von Colson and Kamann* (as cited).

[39] *Van Gend en Loos* (as cited).

[40] Weiler (1981).

other words, Treaty amendment would have eased the task confronting the Court.[41] Reliance on 'individual rights' may, it is submitted, have been at least diminished, if reference could have been made by the Court to clauses or declarations in the EC Treaty codifying the supremacy of precisely defined EC rules over conflicting national measures.[42] In this respect a comparison with United States constitutional law is instructive. The United States rule on self-executing treaties makes no reference at all to individual rights and obligations. It rather requires an investigation of whether the treaty concerned 'operates of itself without the aid of any legislative provisions'.[43]

The prevailing distinction in Article 249 EC between directly 'applicable' regulations, and directives which were to be binding 'as to the result to be achieved' left the evolution of rules on the impact of directives (post the found-ing of the *Van Duyn* rule on direct effect of directives)[44] in the hands of the Court of Justice. As is well-known, it was the wording of Article 249, and the difference contained therein between directives and regulations, which prompted the Court of Justice in the *Faccini Dori* case to decline the introduc-tion of horizontal direct effect of directives, and reiterate that unimplemented directives could not cast 'obligations' on private sector actors.

However this was destined to generate conceptual difficulties.[45] They largely, although not exclusively, arose from parallel developments in rules on Member State enforcement of directives. As noted above,[46] the Court continued to elabo-rate the rule on sympathetic interpretation of national laws falling within the scope of directives, introduced 'incidental' effect of directives on private sector actors (which was bound up with Member States obligations to notify technical standards to the EC Commission), and pursued the practice of answering, largely without explanation, questions on the interpretation of directives in disputes involving private sector actors. If these developments did not result in the conferral of 'obligations' on individuals via the judicial application of unimplemented directives, they at the very least resulted in detrimental effects on their interests.

More important was the activation of the concept of 'individual rights' in the wholly novel *Francovich* context. In an action for damages against the Italian State, the Court of Justice ruled that, while the key substantive provisions of a

---

[41]   For suggestions of this kind see CELS (1997).

[42]   Ibid. at p. 404-405.

[43]   Chief Justice Marshall *Foster and Elam* v. *Neilson* 27 US (Pet.) 253, 314 (1829). Discussed by Winter (1972), at p. 428-429.

[44]   *Van Duyn* (as cited).

[45]   Which numerous scholars have valiantly sought to clarify. Coppel (1994); Hilson & Downes (1999); Dougan (2000).

[46]   In paragraph 1.

Directive guaranteeing an employee's wages in the event of the insolvency of an employer[47] were 'unconditional and sufficiently precise' to be directly effective, the 'donor' of the right was not.[48] It was held that the Directive did 'not identify the person liable to provide the guarantee, and the State cannot be considered liable on the sole ground that it has failed to take transposition measures within the prescribed period'.[49] However the Court added, and herein lies the innovation, that if the 'result prescribed by the directive...entail[ed] the grant of rights to individuals', which were identifiable 'on the basis of the provisions of the directive',[50] then an injured party need only prove causation, in order to found an action for damages against the defaulting Member State.[51] Even though the notion of 'individual rights' has been given a measure of further definition in subsequent case law, it being accepted, for example, that EC rules that *do* satisfy the requirements of direct effect attract the *Francovich* State liability test,[52] the concept continues to create difficulties.[53] Most importantly, the qualities that a directive needs to have, if it falls short of direct effect, in order to be considered one vesting 'individuals' with 'rights', are not entirely clear.

Dillenkofer[54] concerned liability in the event of total failure to implement a directive. It was observed that Article 7 of Directive 90/314 on package travel, package holidays, and package tours[55] prescribed the result to be achieved by implementation, which was 'an obligation for the [travel] organizer to have sufficient security for the refund of money paid over and for the repatriation of the consumer in the event of insolvency'.[56] The Court further held that the 'persons having rights under Article 7 are sufficiently identified as consumers, as defined by Article 2 of the Directive' and that this was 'not affected by the fact that...the Directive leaves the Member States considerable latitude as regards the choice of means for achieving the result it seeks'.[57] It was noted that the 'fact that States may choose between a wide variety of means for achieving the result prescribed by a directive is of no importance if the purpose of the directive is to grant to individuals rights whose content is discernable with

---

[47] Council Directive 80/987/EEC, OJ 1980, L 283/23.

[48] *Francovich* (as cited), at para. 22.

[49] Ibid. at para. 26.

[50] Ibid. at para. 40.

[51] Subject to the residual role for national law described in paras. 42 to 45 of the judgment.

[52] *Brasserie du Pêcheur* (as cited).

[53] See for example *Three Rivers District Council and Others v. Governor and Company of the Bank of England* [2000] 2 WLR 1220.

[54] As cited.

[55] OJ 1990, L 158/59.

[56] At para. 34.

[57] At para. 44.

sufficient precision'.[58] The Court of Justice therefore viewed the Directive as one vesting 'individuals' with 'rights' for the purposes of imposing damages liability. Yet, the inquiry pursued in *Dillenkofer* was not markedly different from that employed by the Court when considering whether relevant provisions of a directive are directly effective.

The same difficulty is perhaps better illustrated by the *British Telecommunications* case.[59] There it was held, in the context of damages liability for incorrect transposition of a directive by the United Kingdom Government, that the relevant provision was 'imprecisely worded',[60] and that this was one of the factors which militated against an entitlement to compensation.[61]

Finally, there are at least two other areas in which the Court of Justice has made recourse to the concept of individual rights, but which stood independently of the direct effect doctrine. With respect to the non-contractual liability of *Community institutions* under Article 288(2), the Court of Justice has long held, under the *Schöppenstedt* formula, that, when the Community acts in areas of wide policy discretion, compensation will not be payable unless the institution concerned has committed a sufficiently serious breach of a superior rule of law for the protection of the 'individual'.[62] In addition to this, the ruling of the Court of Justice in *FMC* confirms that, even when the heart of a private parties' complaint is not failure of a Member State government to properly implement directly effective EC law, but is rather concerned with redress for loss arising from *invalid* EC measures, the 'individuals' concerned remain entitled to 'effective judicial protection'.[63] National judges are bound to ensure that Member State remedies and procedural rules that attach to such actions do not 'adversely affect the actual right of individuals to *rely on Community law*'.[64] This contrasts with the position when an applicant seeks improvement of a national remedy attached to Member State breach of a directly effective EC rule. There 'individual rights' referred to an entitlement to enforce *substantive EC measure that are clear, unconditional, and precise.*

Reference to direct effect in either Article 288(2) actions, or validity claims, would of course, make little sense. The Court of Justice is invited in such cases

---

[58] At para. 45.

[59] As cited.

[60] Article 8(1) of Council Directive 90/531/EEC on the procurement procedures of entities operating the water, energy, transport and telecommunications sectors, OJ 1990, L 297/1.

[61] For the approach taken by the House of Lords to State liability, see the *Three Rivers* case (as cited) and the comments by Jans & Prinssen in their contribution to this volume's chapter V.

[62] Case 5/71 *Schöppenstedt* [1971] ECR 975; Joined Cases 83/76, 94/76, 4/77, 15/77 and 40/77 *HNL* [1978] ECR 1209.

[63] Case C-212/94 *FMC* [1996] ECR I-389, para. 58.

[64] Ibid. at para. 65.

to rule on the legality of EC measures, and not whether a *lawful* EC measure is enforceable in its own right. Interestingly, however, the effective remedies principles relied on by the Court of Justice in the *FMC* case had its genesis in, attempts to enforce national compliance with *valid* EC law. Yet in this latter context, it has been intimately bound up with the doctrine of direct effect.[65] For example the Court of Justice recently reiterated that:

> '*in the absence of Community rules.......it is for the domestic legal system of each Member State to lay down the detailed procedural rules governing actions for safeguarding rights which individuals derive from the direct effect of Community law. However, such rules must not be less favourable than those governing similar domestic action; nor may they make it impossible or excessively difficult in practice to exercise rights conferred by Community law'.*[66]

3 Ramifications of reliance on 'individual rights' for the development of effective sanctions against EC institutions

3.1 Liability of Community institutions under Article 288(2)

Advocate General Léger in *Hedley Lomas* counseled against fleshing out the content of *Francovich* liability in damages by reference to the non-contractual liability of Community institutions under Article 288(2). He observed as follows:

> '*..the two types of liability do not have the same foundation. Member States are subject to a hierarchy of legal norms which does not exist in the Community.....Article 215 [now Article 288] of the Treaty can influence the rules applicable in domestic law in the case of State liability for breach of Community law only if it has the effect of* improving *the protection of individuals relying on Community law.... it is somewhat paradoxical to want to align State liability for breach of Community law with Article 215 rules* which are judged to be unsatisfactory *unduly stringent and affording insufficient protection for the right to effective judicial relief'.*[67]

---

[65] *Rewe* and *Comet* (as cited).

[66] Case C-228/98 *Kharalambos Dounias* [2000] ECR I-577, para. 58 (my emphasis). See similarly Joined Cases C-52/99 and C-53/99 *Camarotto and Vignone* [2001] ECR I-1395, para. 21; Case C-78/98 *Preston* [2000] ECR I-3201, para. 31.

[67] *Hedley Lomas* (as cited), paras. 143-145 (emphasis in original).

This advice was not followed, with the Court adopting the competing counsel of Advocates General Mischo in *Francovich* and Tesauro in *Brasserie du Pêcheur*. The Court of Justice, in *Brasserie du Pêcheur*, effectively married the notion of the 'individual rights', in the context in which it was understood within the *Schöppenstedt* test of Article 288(2), with that of 'individual rights' as elaborated in *Francovich*. By merging the two, the Court committed itself to 'parallelism' in the development of rules on compensation for damage. It held that 'the conditions under which the State may incur liability for damage caused to individuals by breach of Community law cannot, in the absence of particular justification, differ from those governing the liability of the Community in like circumstances'.[68]

Doubt has been cast on whether importing the Article 288(2) test into the realm of Member State liability in damages has resulted in the formulation of rules offering a sufficiently rigorous deterrent against Member State breach of Community law.[69] However, recent developments in the case law have shown that linkage of Article 288(2) with the rules on State liability has had an 'upward' influence, by eroding an important barrier to the payment of damages by Community institutions.[70]

One significant shortcoming in Article 288(2) case law has been the approach taken by the Court of Justice in determining whether the institution whose conduct has been questioned acted in an area in which a wide discretion was enjoyed, or in which little or no discretion was enjoyed.[71] The distinction is important, because a much more rigorous test for liability is imposed in the former situation, as opposed to the latter. If the measure in issue was promulgated in the context of wide discretionary powers, then under the test laid down in *Schöppenstedt*, the applicant was bound to prove, in addition to the existence of a causal link, that there has been a sufficiently serious breach of a superior rule of law for the protection of the individual, and that the institu-

---

[68] *Brasserie du Pêcheur* (as cited), at para. 42. See also Case C-352/98P *Bergaderm* [2000] ECR I-5291, para. 41. Doubt has been cast on the extent to which the Court of Justice has taken active interest in developments in Article 288 case law, in elaborating rules on State liability. See Tridimas (2001), at p. 321; Van Gerven (1998).

[69] See e.g. Jans & Prinssen in chapter V, and their discussion of *Three Rivers*. Note that the German Federal Court in *Brasserie du Pêcheur* [1997] 1 CMLR 971 held that, despite the ruling of the Court of Justice in *Brasserie du Pêcheur*, damages were not payable by the German Government. This was so because the loss suffered by the applicant was not viewed by the Federal Court as having been caused by breach of EC law vesting individuals with rights. However, the House of Lords in *R v. Secretary of State for Transport ex parte Factortame Ltd and Others* [2000] *EuLR* 40 awarded compensation.

[70] Tridimas (2001).

[71] AG Leger in *Hedley Lomas* observed at para. 129 that Article 288(2) case law in this field was characterized by 'diversity', and was subject to 'extremely disparate conditions'.

tion has manifestly and gravely disregarded the limits on the exercise of its powers.[72] However, if the institution or institutions concerned had only limited or no discretion, which will generally be the case with respect to particularized administrative measures, the applicant need only prove that the relevant act was unlawful, and that it caused the loss sustained.[73]

The difficulty of this distinction, from the perspective of access for 'individuals' to an effective judicial remedy, lay in the fact that there was a marked propensity toward categorizing challenged instruments as 'wide discretion' measures. This even occurred when the applicant was seeking compensation for tightly prescribed administrative rules.[74] This was one of the reasons for the traditionally low statistical success of Article 288(2) compensation claims.[75]

This trend, however, may be in the process of reversal, due to the combined effects of the rulings of the Court of Justice in *Bergaderm*[76] and *Freshmarine*.[77] In the former case, the Court of Justice, collapsed the *Schöppenstedt* formula, into the *Brasserie du Pêcheur* test for State liability.[78] *Bergaderm* concerned an attempt to obtain compensation with respect to a Directive restricting the use of an allegedly carcinogenic molecule in cosmetic products.[79] The Court of Justice observed that where a Member State or a Community institution has only considerably reduced discretion 'the mere infringement of Community law may be sufficient to prove a sufficiently serious breach'.[80] However, in *Bergaderm* itself, the Court of Justice declined to adopt the applicant's argument that the Directive in reality

---

[72] *Schöppenstedt* (as cited); *HNL* (as cited).

[73] E.g. Case 145/83 *Adams* [1985] ECR 3539; Case T-390/94 *Schröder* [1997] ECR II-501, para. 51. However, as Tridimas has observed, the case law is not consistent. For example, generally, whether a breach is 'serious' requires an examination of whether the institution enjoying a wide discretion has manifestly and gravely disregarded the limits of its powers (eg. Case C-152/88 *Sofrimport* [1990] ECR I-2477). However, this test has not been applied to administrative measures, when they entail the exercise of wide discretionary powers. For a discussion see Tridimas (2001). For a detailed study of Article 288 see Heukels & McDonnell (1997).

[74] See further Ward (2000a), p. 313-318.

[75] As AG Tesauro pointed out in his Opinion in *Brasserie du Pêcheur*, at the time of that case only 8 successful actions had been brought under Article 288(2), at footnote 5 of his Opinion.

[76] As cited.

[77] Case T-178/98 *Freshmarine* [2000] ECR II-3331.

[78] See in particular at paras. 41 to 44. For a discussion see Tridimas (2001). The *Bergaderm* approach has been employed subsequently. See for example Case T-18/99 *Cordis* [2001] ECR II-913, para. 45; Case T-30/99 *Bocchi* [2001] ECR II-943, para. 50; Case T-52/99 *T Port* [2001] ECR II-981, para. 45; Joined Cases T-198/95, T-171/96, T-230/97, T-174/98 and T-225/99 *Comafrica* [2001] ECR II-1975, para. 134.

[79] Council Directive 76/768/EEC, OJ 1976, L 262/169.

[80] At para. 44.

amounted to an individual decision (and therefore warranted examination under Article 288(2) by reference to the simple formula reserved to non-discretionary administrative measures). The Court held that 'the general or individual nature of a measure taken by an institution is not a decisive criterion for identifying the limits of the discretion enjoyed by the institution in question',[81] and that the Court of First Instance had made no error of law in obliging the applicant to prove that the Community institution concerned manifestly and gravely disregarded the limits on its discretion.

Yet, *Bergaderm* paved the way for the Court of First Instance to take this very step in the *Fresh Marine* case. The applicant, a Norwegian company, sought compensation for a Commission Regulation imposing provisional anti-dumping duties, and which had prevented the applicant from selling salmon in the European Community.[82] Traditionally such measures have been viewed by the Community judicature as 'legislative' in nature, with compensation being payable only on satisfaction of the strict *Schöppenstedt* formula.[83] However, the Court of First Instance ruled that the case before it had 'special features'.[84] These were grounded in the fact that the damage arose from the allegedly unlawful conduct of the Commission in examining a report to check whether the applicant had complied with undertakings given in the course of an anti-dumping investigation. The Commission's (erroneous) assessment that such undertakings had been breached led to the promulgation of the anti-dumping Regulation which the applicant challenged. The Court of First Instance thus took the view that the Commission's allegedly unlawful conduct took place in the course of an administrative operation which specifically and exclusively concerned the applicant. That operation did not involve any choices of economic policy and conferred on the Commission only very little or no discretion.[85] The Court of First Instance cited the *Bergaderm* case in concluding as follows:

> '*mere infringement of Community law will be sufficient, in the present case, to lead to the non-contractual liability of the Community...In particular, a finding of an error which, in analogous circumstances, an administrative authority, exercising ordinary care and diligence would not have committed will support the conclusion that the conduct of the Community institution was unlawful in such a way as to render the Community liable under Article 215 [now Article 288] of the Treaty'.*[86]

---

[81] At para. 86.

[82] EC Regulation 2529/97, OJ 1997, L 346/63.

[83] Case 121/86 *Epicheiriseon Metalleftikon* [1989] ECR 3919; Case T-167/94 *Nölle* [1995] ECR II-2589.

[84] *Freshmarine*, para. 57.

[85] Ibid. at para. 57.

[86] Ibid. at para. 61.

A further relaxation of Article 288(2) rules also merits mention, even though it appears to have occurred independent of elaboration of rules on Member State liability for damages. There was a time when an applicant seeking Article 288(2) compensation was also bound to prove, in addition to the substantive test, that they belonged to a 'limited group'.[87] This was altered in 1992, so that it need only be shown that the applicant belonged to a 'clearly-defined group'.[88] This features the obvious advantage of preventing preclusion of compensation, merely because a large number of legal entities were affected by unlawful conduct. It is safe to assume that the old 'limited group' rule will have no operation in State liability cases, given that the test to be applied in both types of liability are now the same.

3.2 Article 230(4) nullity review

In comparison, however, there has been no improvement in the rights of 'individuals' to effective judicial protection in Article 230 EC nullity actions. If anything, there has been a tightening of direct access to the Court of First Instance, particularly in the context of judicial review of EC directives.[89] Despite indications that emerged in *Codorníu*,[90] that legislative measures may, in some circumstances, be of 'individual concern' to those affected by them, there has been no relaxation of standing rules in order to accommodate judicial review of directives via the Article 230 procedure.[91] Not only does the requirement of 'individual concern' continue to block claims at the threshold of *locus standi*, 'direct concern' has additionally emerged as a barrier.[92] Further, Article 230 applicants are required to prove that their 'interests' have been affected by the impugned measure, in the proceedings in that it brought about 'a distinct change' in their legal position.[93]

---

[87] *HNL* (as cited), at para. 7; Case 238/78 *Ireks-Arkady* [1979] ECR 2955.

[88] Joined Cases C-104/89 and C-37/90 *Mulder II* [1992] ECR I-3061, para. 16.

[89] For a detailed exposition see Arnull (2001).

[90] Case C-309/89 *Codorníu* [1994] ECR I-1853.

[91] E.g. Case C-298/89 *Gibraltar* [1993] ECR I-3605; Case C-10/95P *Asocarne* [1995] ECR I-4149.

[92] Joined Cases T-172/98 and T-175-177/98 *Salamander* [2000] ECR II-2487. On direct concern generally see also Case C-386/96P *Dreyfus* [1998] ECR I-2309; Case C-391/96P *Compagnie Continentale* [1998] ECR I-2377; Case C-403/96P *Glencore Grain* [1998] ECR I-2405; Case C-404/96P *Glencore Grain* [1998] ECR I-2435. Note that the applicant in Case T-135/96 *UEAPME* [1998] ECR II-2335 was considered to be directly and individually concerned by a Directive, but this was due solely to the peculiar features of the procedure leading to the adoption of the Directive. For a discussion see Ward (2000a), at p. 233-235.

[93] Eg. Joined cases T-125/97 and T-127/97 *Coca-Cola* [2000] ECR II-1733, [2000] 5 CMLR 467, para. 77; Joined Cases T-83/99 *Carlo Ripa di Meana* [2000] ECR II-3493, para. 30. For further examples and a detailed discussion see Arnull (2001), at p. 45-48.

Moreover, even if an individual can satisfy both *locus standi* requirements, and prove that a directive is (substantively) illegal, the remedy attached to Article 230 review remains relatively muted. All the Court of First Instance is able to do is declare the offending measure void under Article 231, leaving the institution concerned, pursuant to Article 233, to take the measures necessary to comply with the judgment. Unlike national courts which are seized of disputes grounded in Community law, the Court of First Instance is not bound to provide an effective, proportionate, and dissuasive sanction[94] to correct the wrongdoing found to exist. This is significant, given the scale of Court of Justice concern for national courts to supply remedies and procedural rules to secure the effective enforcement of EC law.

So, for example, when the European Commission has unlawfully withheld information in breach of Commission Decision 94/90 on public access to documents,[95] the Court of First Instance will only annul the decision refusing access, and views itself as having no authority to order that the documents concerned are made available.[96] Similarly, the Court of First Instance lacks the power to require the release of funds that have been unlawfully withheld by an EC institution.[97] Given these difficulties, it is unfortunate that the package of reforms to the EC judicial architecture approved at the Nice IGC did not include an amendment expanding on the range of remedies available under Article 230.[98]

The relative impotence of the Court of First Instance with respect to sanctions is magnified when it is compared with its arbitration jurisdiction under Article 181 of the EC Treaty. In a recent case there was some doubt as to whether the Court of First Instance had been seized under its Article 230(4) powers, or pursuant to Article 181. Once it was decided that the matter at hand was really one calling for arbitration, rather than nullity of an EC measure under Article 230(4), the Court of First Instance was able to order the Commission to pay out a precise sum of money to correct its unlawful conduct. This would not have been possible, had the dispute been classed as one arising under Article 230(4).[99]

---

[94] *Von Colson and Kamann* (as cited).

[95] OJ 1994, L 46/58.

[96] E.g. Case T-123/99 *JT's Corporation* [2000] ECR II-3269; Case T-14/98 *Hautala* [1999] ECR II-2489.

[97] For an example where such an order was requested see Case T-468/93 *Frinil-Frio Naval* [1994] ECR II-33. For a detailed discussion of the shortcomings of sanctions under Article 230 see Ward (2000a), at p. 249-256.

[98] The changes introduced under Nice are canvassed by Johnston (2001).

[99] Case T-26/00 *Lecureur* [2001] ECR II-2623.

3.3   Article 234 validity review

This vista represents, however, only half the picture. If the Court of First Instance is unable to take jurisdiction, under Article 230(4), to judicially review allegedly unlawful EC directives, Member State courts may be required to review national measures falling within its scope. This may be so even in the face of obstructive Member State rules. In *Borelli*[100] the applicant pointed out, in Article 230(4) proceedings, that a preliminary decision of Italian authorities, which effectively blocked the award of aid from the Commission under the European Agricultural Guidance Fund, was not judicially reviewable under Italian law. This, it was contended, meant that the applicant had to be given *locus standi* under Article 230(4) to challenge the Commission's ultimate (negative) decision on grant of aid. In denying the applicant standing, the Court of Justice ruled as follows:

> 'It is.....for the national courts to rule, if necessary after a preliminary reference to the Court, on the lawfulness of the national measure at issue, on the same terms as they would review any final measure which, taken by the same national authority, might adversely affect third parties and, therefore, those courts must hold an action brought for this purpose to be admissible, even if the domestic rules of procedure do not so provide in such a case'.[101]

More recently the Court has reached a similar conclusion. It has affirmed that 'the existence of a judicial remedy against any decision of a national authority refusing the benefit of a fundamental right conferred by the Treaty is essential in order to secure for the individual effective protection for his rights'.[102]

A duty on national courts to guarantee access to a (judicial) avenue of redress was hinted at in *Salamander.*[103] The Court of First Instance was asked to declare admissible nullity proceedings brought by a series of private undertakings with respect to Directive 98/43/EC[104] banning tobacco advertising. In rejecting the argument that the fundamental rights to effective judicial review, as reflected in Articles 6 and 13 of the European Convention of Human Rights, obliged the Court to grant *locus standi*, reference was made to the duty of *national legal systems* to protect these rights. The Court indicated that the 'correct' avenue of

---

[100] Case C-97/91 *Borelli* [1992] ECR I-6313.

[101] Ibid. at para. 13. For a discussion of *Borelli* see Garcia de Enterria (1993).

[102] *Kharalambos Dounias* (as cited), para. 64. See, however, the Opinion of AG Jacobs in Case C-50/00P *UPA*, judgment of 25 July 2002, nyr, in which the AG argues, at paras. 54 to 58, that imposition of an obligation on national courts to craft a remedy to accommodate validity claims would be an undesirable development.

[103] As cited.

[104] OJ 1998, L 213/9.

redress was the action for validity, entailing as it does recourse to Article 234 reference. It was held that due to Article 10 of the EC Treaty, Member States were obliged 'to ensure that the system of legal remedies and procedures established by the EC Treaty and designed to permit the Community judicature to review the lawfulness of acts of the Community institutions is comprehensive'.[105] The Court added that even if a reference for a preliminary ruling were less effective than an Article 230(4) annulment action that would not entitle 'the Court to usurp the function of the founding authority of the Community in order to change the system of legal remedies and procedures established by Articles 173 and 177 of the Treaty and by Article 178 of the EC Treaty'.[106]

It remains open to doubt whether the Article 234 EC validity mechanism provides an adequate and appropriate means of contesting the legality of EC rules, including directives.[107] On the one hand, some significant barriers have been overcome. It was once thought that challenge to directives in national courts could only be launched *after* the expiry of the date for implementation,[108] and that this represented a significant lacuna in access to justice in the EC system. However, it has recently emerged that 'pre-emptive strikes' may be made in national courts, so that individuals can prevent the entry into force of a directive, by challenging its validity prior to the final date set for transposition.[109] Further, as mentioned above, it now seems established that any obligations on national judges to disapply, or even improve, Member State rules on sanctions and procedures which are elaborated in the context of failure of Member States to comply with *lawful* EC measures, must equally be extended to actions for validity. So much can be inferred from rulings of the Court of Justice which have established that, as a general rule, charges levied either by invalid EC measures, or by Member State laws that breach prohibitive EC measures, must be repaid.[110] As the Court observed in the *FMC* case, such claims 'must be made in accordance with the detailed procedural rules laid down by national law, always provided.....that such rules are not less favourable than those governing similar domestic claims and are not so framed as to render virtually impossible or excessively difficult the exercise of rights conferred by the Community legal system'.[111]

---

[105] Para. 74. See also Case C-321/95P *Greenpeace* [1998] ECR I-1651. For a recent discussion see Arnull (2001), at p. 49-51.

[106] Para. 75.

[107] For a detailed discussion see AG Jacobs in *UPA* (as cited), at paras. 38 to 44.

[108] AG Tesauro in Case C-63/89 *Assurances du crédit* [1991] ECR I-1799.

[109] R v. *Secretary of State for Transport ex parte Imperial Tobacco Ltd* [2000] *EuLR* 70.

[110] Charges unlawfully levied must in general be repaid under Community law, whether the illegality is sourced in an unlawful EC measure, or a Member State charge imposed in breach of EC rules. See most recently Joined Cases C-441/98 and C-442/98 *Kapniki Mikhailidis* [2000] ECR I-7145. For a detailed discussion see Dougan (1999).

[111] *FMC* (as cited), at para. 63.

On the other hand, cogent arguments can be made that the interests of justice would be better served by broadening access to the Article 230(4) nullity procedure, rather than destroying claims via the Article 234 procedure. It is contended that legal certainty would be improved through challenge to directives within the time limit provided by under Article 230(4), rather than relying of the vagaries of potentially multiple references from national courts (in which different grounds for invalidity might be raised). It is also contended that the principle of equality is in jeopardy, because petition to the Community judicature depends on disparate Member State rules on remedies.[112]

To this might be added the fact that there is no automatic entitlement to an Article 234 validity reference, the applicant being obliged to convince the national judge that there is a 'serious' doubt as to the validity of the directive.[113] Any reference that is sent may not be returned for over two years. In addition, confusion arises if parallel attempts are made before the Court of First Instance and the national courts to challenge the legality of an EC rule, if an applicant has managed to satisfy Article 230 standing rules before both a national court and the Court of First Instance.[114] As for the back-up supplied by the Article 288(2) damages mechanism, which stands independently of Article 230(4) review, this has been described as a 'sticking plaster'; it being preferable to scrutinize the impugned act before it causes damage.[115]

For some of these reasons, and on several additional grounds, Advocate General Jacobs counseled recently for a change in the law, in his Opinion *UPA*. The Advocate General is in favour of abandoning the requirement that the applicants seeking to challenge a measure are differentiated from all others affected by it, in the same way as the measure's addressee.[116] This, he observed, is not required by the text of Article 230; a provision which has been, on the contrary, subject to creative interpretation in the context of the range of measures which can be challenged within its rubric,[117] the institutional actors that may bring suit,[118] and the grounds of review.[119] He noticed that strict rules on standing for Article 230 (4) were 'increasingly untenable' in the light of the

---

[112] Arnull (2001). This was one of several points made by AG Jacobs in *UPA* (as cited), at paras. 38 to 44, casting doubt on whether the validity mechanism supplies effective judicial review.

[113] Case 314/85 *Foto-Frost* [1987] ECR 4199. For an example of a case in which the applicant failed to so persuade the national judge see *R* v. *Secretary of State for the Environment, Transport and the Regions ex parte International Air Transport Association* [1999] 1 CMLR 1287.

[114] The position was, however, recently clarified in C-344/98 *Masterfoods* [2000] ECR I-11369.

[115] Arnull (2001).

[116] *UPA* (as cited), para. 59.

[117] Ibid. para. 68.

[118] Ibid. para. 69.

[119] Ibid. para. 70.

Court's case law, largely directed to Member State judicial tribunals, on effective judicial protection,[120] and advised that the time was ripe for the development of a new test. Rather than considering whether the applicant is 'differentiated' in the sense described above, the Advocate General took the view that 'a person is to be regarded as individually concerned by a Community measure where, by reason of his particular circumstances, the measure has, or is liable to have, a substantial adverse effect on his interests'.[121]

A step in the same direction was recently taken by the Court of First Instance in *Jégo-Quéré*.[122] There the Court of First Instance declared admissible a challenge by French commercial fishermen to a Regulation banning the use of fishing nets having mesh of a certain size. The Court prescribed a change in the law to the effect that a person should be regarded as individually concerned by a Community measure of general application that affects him directly, if the measure in question affects his legal position in a manner which is both definite and immediate, by restricting his rights or imposing obligations on him.[123] The number and position of others affected was also considered by the Court of First Instance to be irrelevant, with the Court affirming that access to a court is one of the constituent elements of a Community based on the rule of law,[124] account taken of the legal traditions of the Member States, Articles 6 and 13 of the European Convention on Human Rights, and Article 47 of the EU Charter of Fundamental Rights.[125]

However, the ECJ did not follow AG Jacobs, nor did it accept the CFI's approach in *Jégo-Quéré*. In *UPA* the Court ruled that:

> '[A]lthough this last condition (individually concerned; editors) must be interpreted in the light of the principle of effective judicial protection [...]such an interpretation cannot have the effect of setting aside the condition in question, expressly laid down in the Treaty, without going beyond the jurisdiction conferred by the Treaty on the Community Courts.*

> While it is, admittedly, possible to envisage a system of judicial review of the legality of Community measures of general application different from that established by the founding Treaty and never amended as to its principles, it is for the Member States, if necessary, in accordance with Article 48 EU, to reform the system currently in force.'[126]

---

[120] Ibid. para. 98

[121] Ibid. para. 60.

[122] Judgment of the Court of First Instance of 3 May 2002, nyr.

[123] Ibid. at para. 51.

[124] Ibid. at para. 41.

[125] Ibid. at paras. 41 and 42.

[126] *UPA* (as cited), paras. 44 en 45.

4 Setting the boundaries: Court of Justice regulation of Member State remedies and procedural rules?

Given the reluctance, then, of the Court of Justice and the Court of First Instance to improve the position of 'individuals' when they challenge the legality of EC rules, under Article 230(4), caution is warranted with regard to the obligations cast on Member State judges to upgrade national remedies and procedural rules. The mandate of the Court to craft law in this field is very weak. The principle of effectiveness can only be linked, in terms of express Treaty provisions, to the Article 10 duties on Member States to secure faithful enforcement of EC law,[127] while the rule on non-discrimination was even more flimsily carved out as a general principle of law.[128] Substantially judicial creativity was therefore required in developing these rules. The 'rights' of 'individuals' were recruited to fill this vacuum.

The same creativity has, however, not been evident in case law developing Article 230(4) and, at least traditionally, under Article 288(2). Acute disjuncture between the rights of individuals before Community courts, as opposed to national courts, might precipitate legitimacy problems in the EC constitutional system, particularly in the eyes of Member State judges.[129] For example, the English courts sent a strong signal, prior to the elaboration of State liability rules, that they would not tolerate the imposition of a less onerous test for damages liability with respect to wrong-doing by United Kingdom government authorities than that which applies to Community institutions under Article 288(2).[130] As one commentator has observed, courts 'which consistently adopt a creative approach to the interpretation of written provisions lack credibility when they seek refuge in the letter of the law to justify a given outcome'.[131]

The Court of Justice refused in the *Faccini Dori* case[132] to abandon the notion of 'individual rights' as a principal rationale for the enforcement of Directives in national law. Further, the notion 'individual rights' was elevated to the status of the foundation on which to ground Member State liability in damages. Given then the increasing, rather than decreasing, importance of the role of the 'individual' in enforcing Community law, irresistible comparisons will be drawn of their position when Member State, as opposed to Community, misconduct is in issue.

---

[127] E.g. *Francovich* (as cited), at para. 36.

[128] For a discussion see Tridimas (1999), p. 279-281.

[129] Johnston (2001), at p. 506.

[130] *Bourgoin SA and Others v. Ministry for Agriculture, Fisheries and Food* [1986] QB 716

[131] Arnull (2001), at p. 50.

[132] As cited.

The cause of 'uniform treatment' is important beyond the field of State liability. Given that the 'rights' of the 'individual' to effective judicial protection continues to drive large swathes of Court of Justice case law, constitutional coherence demands that more is not asked of Member State courts, within the rubric or remedies and procedures, than that which would be available before the Court of Justice and the Court of First Instance. Indeed, this was reflected in a Court of Justice ruling, in which the Court was asked whether the *Johnston*[133] right to an effective judicial remedy bound national courts to undertake merits review of the decisions of administrative authorities. This question was answered in the negative in *Upjohn*,[134] with respect to refusal to of a United Kingdom authority to grant a marketing authorization of a medicinal drug, in alleged breach of Directive 65/65 on approximation of laws relating to proprietary medicinal products.[135] It was observed that:

> '...where a Community authority is called upon, in the performance of its duties, to make complex assessments, it enjoys a wide measure of discretion, the exercise of which is subject to a limited judicial review in the course of which the Community judicature may not substitute its assessment of the facts for the assessment made by the authority concerned. Thus, in such cases, the Community judicature must restrict itself to examining the accuracy of the findings of fact and law made by the authority concerned and to verifying, in particular, that the action taken by that authority is not vitiated by a manifest error or misuse of powers and that it did not clearly exceed the bounds of its discretion... Consequently, Community law does not require the Member States to establish a procedure for judicial review of national decisions revoking marketing authorizations, taken pursuant to Directive 65/65 and in the exercise of complex assessments, which involves a more extensive review than that carried out by the Court in similar cases'.[136]

There is, however, a more practical reason for restraint. The Court of Justice and the Court of First Instance have long been laboring under an ever increasing case load, which has led to substantial delays in the issue of judgments. Delay in the context of references for preliminary ruling were addressed at the Nice IGC, and more specifically by the introduction of the Article 225(3) amendment. It allows for Article 234 references to be sent to the Court of First Instance, rather than the Court of Justice, in specific areas provided by Statute.[137] Further, 'The Report by the Working Party on the Future of the European Communities'[138]

---

[133] As cited.

[134] Case C-120/97 *Upjohn* [1999] ECR I-223.

[135] OJ 1965, p. 369, OJ English Special Edition 1965-66/20.

[136] Paras. 34-35.

[137] Johnston (2001), at p. 507-510.

[138] Reproduced in Dashwood & Johnston (2001).

encouraged national courts to be bolder in their application of Community law. Concerns over 'docket control' has been one of the justification for restricting Article 234 review of EC Title IV measures on visa, asylum, and immigration policy,[139] even though these rules apply with respect to some of the most vulnerable 'individuals' in Europe. All this tends to suggest that enhancement of the efficiency of the judicial system would ensue if Member State courts retained primary responsibility for review of sanctions and procedural rules for compliance with the principles of effectiveness and non-discrimination, and also avoid Court of Justice involvement in the *minutiae* of national law.[140]

What follows, then, is a survey of some relatively recent developments, in which the minimalist approach here advocated may not have been followed. They concern:

(i) possible failure to secure 'uniform' treatment in the event of Member State as opposed to Community misconduct;

(ii) deployment of difficult distinctions with respect to the rules on payment of interest;

(iii) vacillation of the jurisdictional boundary between the Court of Justice and Member State courts when reviewing sanctions and procedural rules.[141]

4.1 Uniform treatment?

4.1.1 Interim relief

The field of interim relief is one area where problems that gestated in Article 230(4) review have been exported to the national level. The Court of Justice has held that national judges are not only obliged to apply Article 242 and 243 rules on interim relief, rather than Member State rules on this subject, when considering the validity of EC measures. They will equally be bound to do so in cases in which the compatibility of national laws with Community measures is in issue, given that 'the dispute in both cases is based on Community law itself'.[142] Due, however, to the substantive test operative pursuant to Articles 242 and 243, the inevitable result may be that it will be

---

[139] Albors-Llorens (1998); Ward (2000b).

[140] See Biondi (1999), at p. 128, 'By subjecting the national rule to a close and detailed scrutiny, the Court gets too involved in the facts of the case. In doing so, not only does the Court almost usurp the function of the national judge, but it does not even contribute to the coherent application of EC law'.

[141] For arguments, however, in favour of Court of Justice review of both rights and the content of remedies see Van Gerven (2000), at p. 526 et seq.

[142] Joined Cases C-143/88 and C-92/89 *Zuckerfabrik* [1991] ECR I-415, para. 20; Case C-465/93 *Atlanta* [1995] ECR I-3761, para. 24.

easier to obtain an interim order in 'validity' actions, than in 'compatibility' disputes. The reasons for this are as follows.

Advocate General Léger in *Hedley Lomas* observed that the imposition on national legal systems EC rules on interim relief, elaborated in the context of EC Treaty Articles 242 and 243 (the interim relief provisions governing Article 230 nullity review) had been mistaken. It has, he contended, made it more difficult to obtain temporary suspension orders before Member State courts.[143] The same is evidenced by the ruling of the Court of Justice in *Emesa Sugar*.[144] There it was held that the fact that domestic rules on interim relief would have ordered temporary suspension of a national measures, in circumstances when EC rules would not, in no way affected 'the conditions under which the temporary protection of individuals must be ensured in proceedings before the national courts'.[145]

The source of the problem lies in the substantive test formulated by the Court of Justice, and more particularly the element pertaining to 'Community interest'. The Article 242 and 243 criteria require Member State courts to first determine whether there is a serious doubt as to the validity of the measures. If it is so satisfied, the Court must make a reference to the Court of Justice under Article 234. Under the Article 242 and 243 criteria, interim relief must be granted by the national judge if there is a situation of urgency, in that serious and irreparable harm will result if the order is not made.[146] *But*, all the while, the court is bound to take account of the 'interest of the Community'.[147] This means that the national court must, *inter alia* 'first examine whether the Community act in question would be deprived of all effectiveness if not immediately implemented'.[148]

In validity proceedings, in which an applicant seeks to obstruct the enforcement of EC legislation, the 'interest of the Community' may militate against the award of an interim order temporarily suspending a measure that has been elaborated through EC legislative processes. Yet, when the compatibility of Member State law with EC rules is questioned, the 'Community interest' might be expected to weigh in favour of temporary disapplication of national measures blocking the enforcement of a (lawful) EC measure, and which threaten its uniform application. The inclusion, then, of the 'Community's interests' among the criteria Member State courts are bound to apply when considering whether to grant interim relief, imperils the Court's objective of ensuring that the condi-

---

[143] *Hedley Lomas* (as cited), at para. 144. The AG cited W. Dänzer-Vanotti, "Der Gerichtshof der Europäischen Gemeinschaften beschränkt vorläufigen Rechtsschutz", BB 15, 30 May 1991, p. 1015.

[144] Case C-17/98 *Emesa Sugar* [2000] ECR I-675.

[145] Ibid. at para. 70.

[146] *Zuckerfabrik*, paras. 23 and 24; *Atlanta*, paras. 32 and 36-38; *Emesa Sugar*, para. 69.

[147] *Zuckerfabrik*, para. 30; *Atlanta*, para. 42. See similarly *Emesa Sugar*.

[148] *Zuckerfabrik*, para. 31; *Atlanta*, para. 43.

tions for the issue of such orders are 'the same', whether an action concerns the validity of EC law or the compatibility of national rules with (lawful) Community measures. It may therefore be desirable to adjust the interim relief criteria employed by the Court of First Instance, and imposed on national courts, in order to achieve the parity of treatment that the Court seeks.

4.1.2 Excusable error

In *Fantask*[149] the Court of Justice ruled that the Danish Government could not rely on the domestic legal notion of excusable error in order to evade payment of a tax levied in breach of Directive 69/335 concerning indirect taxes on the raising of capital.[150] This was so even though it had been argued that the tax had been levied over a period of ten years, without the authorities or those against whom the charge was being levied being aware that they were unlawful. The Court of Justice held that the Danish rule on 'excusable error' rendered recovery of the tax excessively difficult, and had 'the effect of encouraging infringements of Community law which have been committed over a long period'.[151]

Yet the Court of Justice has itself limited the temporal effects of its rulings, precisely because of the hardship that would result from correcting protracted breach of EC rules, and when the wrongdoer might have assumed their conduct to be lawful. In *Defrenne II* the Court of Justice restricted the results flowing from its finding of direct effect of Article 141 (ex 119) EC rules on equal pay for equal work between men and women.[152] The Court observed that the failure of the Commission to bring an Article 141 action against Member States who had breached Article 141 'was likely to consolidate the incorrect impression as to the effects of Article 119'.[153] Could not the same be said for the Commission's failure with respect to the Danish Government's implementation of Directive 69/335? The Court concluded in *Defrenne II* that 'all the interests involved, both public and private, make it impossible in principle to reopen the question as regards the past'.[154] Yet it is not clear why the Danish rule on excusable error failed to withstand the same test; especially given that there was no evidence that it was inapplicable to analogous claims of a purely domestic nature.

---

[149] Case C-188/95 *Fantask* [1997] ECR I-6783

[150] OJ 1969, L 249/25; OJ English Special Edition (II)/12, as amended.

[151] At para. 40.

[152] Case 43/75 *Defrenne II* [1976] ECR 455

[153] Ibid. at para. 73.

[154] Ibid.

4.1.3   The raising of new arguments on appeal

It is submitted that national laws prohibiting applicants from raising new arguments on appeal, from administrative to judicial authorities, should also be considered compatible with Community law, provided that they respect the principle of non-discrimination. As Advocate General Jacobs pointed out in his Opinion in *Peterbroeck*[155] in Article 230(4) annulment proceedings, the applicant is bound by rule Article 42 of the rules of procedure of the Court of Justice. It provides 'no new plea in law may be introduced in the course of proceedings unless it is based on matters of law or of fact which come to light in the course of the procedure',[156] although the Community courts may take account of the existence of *res judicata*, and of its own motion, at any stage of proceedings.[157]

It was surprising, therefore, that the Court of Justice declined to follow the Opinion of the Advocate General in *Peterbroeck*, holding instead incompatible with Community law a Belgian rule which prohibited the raising of new arguments if 60 days had elapsed since it was lodged with an appeal court from the tax authorities.[158] The Court has subsequently, however, held justified national rules prohibiting judges, in civil suits, from raising arguments of their own motion, including those pertaining to Community law,[159] at least in the context of appeal from superior courts. It held in *Van Schijndel* that:

'[that] limitation is justified by the principle that, in a civil suit, it is for the parties to take the initiative, the court being able to act of its own motion only in exceptional cases where the public interest requires intervention. That principle reflects the conceptions prevailing in most of the Member States as to the relations between the State and the individual; it safeguards the rights of the defence; and it ensures proper conduct of proceedings by, in particular, protecting them from the delays inherent in examination of new pleas'.[160]

Further, post-*Peterbroeck* the Court of Justice has also sanctioned a national provision laying down a three month time limit for lodging an application for annulment of an arbitral award. The Court observed in *Eco Swiss* that this period

---

[155] Case C-312/93 *Peterbroeck* [1995] ECR I-4599.

[156] Ibid. at para. 31 of his Opinion. See similarly his Opinion in Joined Cases C-430/93 and C-431/93 *Van Schijndel* [1995] ECR I-4705, paras. 32 and 42.

[157] Ibid. at para. 24, citing Joined Cases 29/63, 31/63, 36/63, 39-47/63, 50/63 and 51/63 *Usines de la Providence v. High Authority* [1965] ECR 911, per AG Roemer.

[158] *Peterbroeck*, para. 21.

[159] *Van Schijndel* (as cited).

[160] Ibid. at para. 21. For a critique see Biondi (1999), at p. 1277-1278.

was not 'excessively short compared with those prescribed in the legal systems of other Member States', and did not 'render excessively difficult or virtually impossible the exercise of rights conferred by Community law'.[161] This tends to suggest that *Peterbroeck* may indeed be confined to its 'special features',[162] involving as it did a restrictive time limit on the raising of new arguments on appeal from an administrative to a judicial authority, as opposed to limits on the arguments that can be raised at different stages of the judicial process.

4.2   Payment of interest

Doubt may also be cast on whether 'minimum harmonization' of Member State remedies and procedural rules is reflected in Court of Justice involvement in the question of payment of interest. The Court of Justice held in *Marshall II*, and with respect to the Equal Treatment Directive, that the requirement of full compensation, in the context of damages claims, meant that the award of interest could not be ruled out by national law; it was viewed by the Court as an essential component of compensation for the purposes of restoring real equality of treatment.[163] It was also held in *Brasserie du Pêcheur* that exclusion of pure economic loss, especially in the context of commercial litigation, 'would be such as to make reparation of damage practically impossible'.[164]

Prior to this, the necessity or otherwise of payment of interest (to secure compliance with the principle of effectiveness) was considered by the Court of Justice to be a question for the national courts. With respect to charges improperly levied, it was for Member State courts 'to settle all ancillary questions relating to the reimbursement of charges improperly levied, such as payment of interest, including the rate of interest and the date from which it must be calculated'.[165]

Court of Justice review of payment of interest at national level has led to some peculiar results. In *Sutton*,[166] in a dispute concerning invalid carer's allowance (withheld in breach of Directive 79/7 on the principle of equal treatment in matters of social security)[167] the Court declined to apply the *Marshall II* principle on interest. In *Sutton* the payment of interest for in arrears benefits was not

---

[161] Case C-126/97 *Eco Swiss* [1999] ECR I-3055, para. 45.

[162] *Peterbroeck*, para. 16.

[163] Case C-271/91 *Marshall II* [1993] ECR I-4367, at paras. 24-32. See also Joined Cases C-397/98 and C-410/98, *Metallgesellschaft* [2001] ECR I-1727, para. 94.

[164] *Brasserie du Pêcheur* (as cited), at para. 87. See also *Metallgesellschaft*, at para. 91.

[165] *Metallgesellschaft*, at para. 86; Case 26/74 *Roquette Frères* [1976] ECR 677, paras. 11 and 12; Case 130/79 *Express Dairy Foods* [1980] ECR 1887, paras. 16 and 17.

[166] Case C-66/95 *Sutton* [1997] ECR I-2163.

[167] OJ 1979, L 6/24.

considered to be an essential component of the right to obtain social security benefits under the equal treatment conditions as reflected in Directive 79/7. *Marshall II* was distinguished on the basis that it concerned a claim for compensation, in which interest had to be payable.

Sutton is difficult to reconcile with a recent Court of Justice ruling. In *Metallgesellschaft* the Court took the view that interest lost as a result of (unlawful) payment of advance of taxation by an undertaking, in breach of the rules on freedom of establishment, was 'not ancillary'.[168] Rather it was viewed as 'essential' if the loss sustained was to be rectified.[169] This was so even though the dispute between the applicant and the United Kingdom tax authorities might not necessarily be viewed as a 'compensation' dispute, in which case it would have automatically attracted the *Marshall II* principle on interest.

It is submitted, therefore, that the availability of interest, in claims based on Community law, is a matter best left for the decision of national courts, who can test the relevant Member State laws for compliance with the principles of effectiveness and non-discrimination. Any Court of Justice regulation of this issue should be limited to the demand for a minimum standard that reflects rules on interest operative in the context of Article 288(2) liability.[170] Extension of any principle that is in place to *Sutton* style cases of unlawfully withheld payments would help coherence in the law.

4.3 Vacillating boundaries and the principle of non-discrimination

The principle of non-discrimination poses special problems. Which court, Community or national, should isolate the appropriate comparator to determine whether rights grounded in Community law are protected by the same remedies and procedural rules as are extended to analogous claims of a purely domestic nature? Once selected, which Court should decide whether the principle of non-discrimination has been breached?

The Court of Justice has wavered over this issue. In a battery of cases concerning recovery of unlawfully levied charges, and the compatibility of national time limits for their recovery with the principle of non-discrimination, the Court of Justice decided all aspects of the non-discrimination test, declaring, in all the circumstances, national time limits in issue compatible with Commu-

---

[168] *Metallgesellschaft*, para. 87.

[169] Ibid. at para. 95.

[170] *Ireks Arkady* (as cited), para. 20; Lenaerts e.a. (1999), paras. 11-060 to 11-061. For arguments, in favour of comprehensive, 'Community wide' rules on payment of interest see AG Van Gerven in *Marshall II* (as cited).

nity law.[171] Yet, with respect to claims that repayment of unlawfully levied charges would lead to the unjust enrichment of a trader, the Court has left all aspects of the principles of effectiveness and non-discrimination for resolution by national courts, although it has provided guidelines.[172]

Further, in a case addressing whether pension payments were made in compliance with a Community regulation,[173] the Court held that it was solely for the national court to consider whether 'individuals in a domestic situation similar' to the applicants 'may have recourse to the procedure' on which they relied.[174] The Court observed that 'the national court must ensure that the principle of equivalence is observed by permitting recourse to that procedure under the same conditions for applicants based on Community law as for similar applications based on domestic law'.[175]

Inconsistency of this kind has also occurred with respect to EC rules on equal treatment of men and women. In *Draehmpaehl*[176] the Court of Justice isolated the appropriate comparator for assessing whether a 'non-discriminatory' payment of compensation had been made with respect to breach of the Equal Treatment Directive.[177] This was deemed to be the normal remedy available under German civil and labour law.[178] The sum offered under German law (capped as it was to three months lost wages) was considered by the Court of Justice as falling beneath these standards, at least with respect to an applicant who would have been appointed, but for the discrimination. Yet in *Preston*,[179] in an equal pay dispute, the Court of Justice declined to make such an intimate assessment of national law, and left it to the House of Lords to decide if a six month time limit, to run from date of dismissal, breached the principle of non-discrimination.[180] In conformity with the approach employed in the earlier *Levez* case,[181] the Court of Justice supplied guidelines to *assist* the national court in

---

[171] Case C-231/96 *Edis* [1998] ECR I-4951; Case C-260/96 *Spac* [1998] ECR I-4997; Joined Cases C-279-281/96 *Ansaldo Energia* [1998] ECR I-5025; Case C-228/96 *Aprile* [1998] ECR I-7141; Case C-343/96 *Dilexport* [1999] ECR I-5025. For a discussion see Biondi (1999), at p. 1272-1276.

[172] Joined Cases C-192-218/95 *Comateb* [1997] ECR I-165; *Kapniki Mikhailidis* (as cited).

[173] Council Regulation 1408/71 on the application of social security rules employed persons, self-employed persons, and members of their families moving within the Community, OJ 1971, L 149/2; OJ English Special Edition, 1971 (II) 416, as amended.

[174] *Camarotto and Vignone* (as cited), para. 40

[175] Ibid.

[176] Case C-180/95 *Draehmpaehl* [1997] ECR I-2195.

[177] Council Directive 76/207/EEC, OJ 1976, L 39/40.

[178] *Draehmpaehl*, paras. 28 and 41.

[179] As cited.

[180] [2001] 3 All ER 947.

[181] Case C-326/96 *Levez* [1998] ECR I-7835.

deciding this issue. While it ruled out recourse to the United Kingdom *Equal Pay Act* as the appropriate comparator for assessing remedies supplied by national law to protect Article 141 EC equal pay rules, it held as follows:

'*the national court - which alone has direct knowledge of the procedural rules governing actions in the field of employment law - must consider both the purpose and the essential characteristics of the allegedly similar domestic actions.... the national court must consider whether the actions concerned are similar as regards their purpose, cause of action and essential characteristics...the principle of equivalence would be infringed if a person relying on a right conferred by Community law were forced to incur additional costs and delay by comparison with a claimant whose action was based solely on domestic law...the national court must take into account the role played by that provision in the procedure as a whole, as well as the operation and any special features of that procedure before the different national courts... various aspects of the procedural rules cannot be examined in isolation but must be placed in their general context. Moreover, such an examination may not be carried out subjectively by reference to circumstances of fact but must involve an objective comparison, in the abstract, of the procedural rules at issue.*'[182]

It is submitted that the approach taken in *Preston* represents the better of the two here described. Given both the 'distance' of the Court of Justice from procedural rules operative at national level, and the problem of inordinate burdening, already mentioned, of the case load of the Court of Justice, it is difficult to find cogent reason for comprehensive Court of Justice review of Member State law for compliance with the principle of non-discrimination. This is a matter best policed by Member State courts, subject to guidelines from Luxembourg of the kind offered in *Preston*.

5 Procedural rules and remedies and non-directly effective directives

As has already been illustrated, much of Court of Justice case law on Member State remedies and procedural rules has been underpinned by the discourse on 'rights'. Community rules vesting 'individuals' with 'rights' are the only measures attracting State liability in damages;[183] 'individuals' have been held by the Court to be entitled, with respect to directly effective EC rules, to access to effective, non-discriminatory remedies and procedural rules.[184] The

---

[182] *Preston*, paras. 56-62.

[183] See above, at paragraph 2.

[184] *Rewe* and *Comet* (as cited), as affirmed by the Court of Justice in numerous cases. See recently *Kharalambos Dounias* (as cited).

same has been extended to challenge to the validity of Community measures, due to the entitlement of 'individuals' to rely on Community law.[185]

Where does this leave us, then, with respect to remedies and procedural rules that attach to claims in which reference to a directive is required to solve a dispute between two private parties? In this context reference to 'individual rights' is illogical, given that one of the two litigants loses out as a result of reliance on the directive by the other. Does this therefore mean that principles formulated by the Court of Justice regulating Member State sanctions and procedural rules should have no application in disputes entailing recourse to the doctrine of sympathetic interpretation, or when a national court simply asks a question on the meaning of a directive (and the litigation is horizontal), or when incidental effect is in issue, and one party has called for the disapplication of national regulatory standards which, in breach of a directive, have not been notified to the Commission?[186]

It is submitted that this question should be answered in the negative. The overriding imperative should be legal certainty, and the disastrous complexity that would ensue if the Court's already difficult case law on sanctions and procedures were to take on a further dimension. Confining the principles of effectiveness and non-discrimination to directives having direct effect, or which vest individuals with rights, would lead to such a result.

Thus far this is the path that the Court of Justice has chosen to tread, albeit in the absence of an express declaration that is was doing so. The duty on national judges to supply an effective remedy has been invoked by the Court in three cases in which horizontal enforcement of the Equal Treatment Directive[187] has been sought by one private party against another; namely *Dekker*,[188] *Coote*,[189] and *Draehmphael*.[190] Legal certainty would be improved if the Court of Justice were to formulate a specific rule extending rules on Member State remedies and procedural rules to all disputes turning on the effects of an unimplemented directive in national law. This could perhaps be based, as is the case in the context of validity review, on an entitlement to 'rely on Community law'.[191]

---

[185] *FMC* (as cited).

[186] See above, paragraph 1.

[187] As cited.

[188] Case C-177/88 *Dekker* [1990] ECR I-3941.

[189] As cited.

[190] As cited.

[191] *FMC* (as cited).

6 Conclusion

Rather than withering away into the constitutional history of the European Community, the 'individual' has remained the fulcrum on which rests direct application of EC directives in national legal systems, albeit at the cost of some coherence in the law. Further, the concept of 'individual rights' has had a potent impact on the elaboration of rules on remedies to correct unlawful conduct, whether the perpetrator is a Member government authority or a Community institution. It has spearheaded liberalization of Article 288(2) damages liability, opened out the Article 234 avenue for validity challenge, and bound national judges to alter and enhance national sanctions and procedural rules in disputes concerning Community law. The cause of 'individual rights' is yet, however, to permeate Court of Justice case law concerning Article 230(4) nullity actions, although powerful arguments have been laid before it in its favour.

Given the absence of express delineation, in constitutional documents, of the hierarchy of rules in the EC legal system, the challenge confronting the Community judicature remains in maintaining 'uniformity' in elaborating rules on judicial remedies. This involves ensuring that the 'individual' is treated with an even hand, irrespective of the context in which illegal measures are passed; that is whether a Community institution or a Member State government is at fault. This is by no means any easy task, but it is one that seems destined to be shouldered primarily at the judicial level, given scant political will to tackle the challenges here canvassed through legislative initiative or constitutional reform.

CHAPTER IV

The Doctrine of Consistent Interpretation

Managing Legal Uncertainty

dr. Gerrit Betlem

1 Introduction

This contribution seeks to find a middle way between a practitioner orientated paper, focussing on giving an overview of recent developments in the case law of the European Court of Justice (ECJ), and a more scholarly contribution exploring possible reforms in legal doctrine. The overview examines cases by the ECJ dealing with aspects of the principle of consistent interpretation which were hitherto unsettled or which highlight its sometimes hidden nature.[1] In certain situations - so-called horizontal relations between private parties - there is debate in the legal literature whether either consistent interpretation or direct effect has been used. The reforms seek to develop a parallelism between these two doctrines - direct effect and consistent interpretation - as well as suggest ways and means for coping with legal uncertainty. Finally, the examination of one of the fundamental means of giving effect to European Community law before national courts - consistent interpretation - is placed in the broader context of the two other mechanisms developed by the ECJ to ensure the effect of EC law at the national level: direct effect and State liability. More particularly, the complex interaction between the latter two is noted following the 2001 ECJ ruling in *Metallgesellschaft*.[2]

What is meant by 'consistent interpretation'? In broad conceptual terms, a norm of EC law is used as an aid to the interpretation of another rule; the latter is the one actually being applied by a court (or other authority) but is construed in the light of the former. That is to say, it is being interpreted consistently with the hierarchically higher norm of EC law. As will become apparent below, this method thus differs fundamentally in theory from the doctrine of direct effect where a court simply applies the relevant norm of Community law as such (directly), if necessary, displacing any conflicting rules of its national law. The method involving consistent interpretation seeks to solve a clash between conflicting norms regulating the same issue or between a higher ranking norm constraining the effect of a lower rule by way of choosing between different possible interpretations. The impact of the rule of EC law on national law is therefore an indirect one.

There is a close analogy with interpretive techniques employed by courts in jurisdictions with a written constitution in order to solve conflicts between their legislation and the constitution, in German: *verfassungskonforme Auslegung* (interpretation in conformity with the Constitution).[3] A conflict between the Constitution and another lower ranking norm is solved by construing the latter consistently with the former. By the same token, national courts employ this

---

[1]   The paper builds on Betlem (1993), p. 204 et seq. and Betlem (1995).

[2]   Joined Cases C-397/98 and C-410/98 *Metallgesellschaft* [2001] ECR I-1727.

[3]   Wissink (2001), No. 168.

technique in the context of the impact of public international law on domestic legislation. Generally speaking, it is a canon of interpretation that statutes should not be so construed that they would violate international law, whenever another possible interpretation remains.[4]

A good example is the UK House of Lords 1999 *Pinochet* judgment, where the (English) State Immunity Act of 1978 was interpreted in conformity with the law of nations. The Act entitles a former head of state to immunity from prosecution in the performance of official duties. According to the House of Lords, 'those functions can[not], as a matter of statutory interpretation, extend to actions that are prohibited as criminal under international law. In this way one can reconcile, as one must seek to do, the provisions of the Act of 1978 with the requirements of public international law'.[5]

Also in the Community legal order does this canon apply. In fact, the doctrine of consistent interpretation works within several contexts, as a matter of EC law. Three levels can be distinguished. First, the national law level for giving effect to EC law within the domestic legal sphere. Secondly, the level of secondary Community law which must be construed in conformity with primary EC law.[6] And thirdly, the level of the Community legal order (primary and secondary law) vis-à-vis public international law.[7] Here one is dealing with interpreting Community law in conformity with the international legal obligations incumbent on the EU. In turn, this may require an interpretation of - again - national law giving effect to, say, a Community law regulation. The whole track of national-EU level must be construed in accordance with the overarching instrument of public international law.[8] In all three spheres a form of indirect effect is given to the higher norm by using it to inform the construction of the lower one. Hereafter, the discussion is limited to the impact of EC law, in particular directives, on domestic law, i.e. the interpretation of national law in conformity with a directive.

---

[4] See generally Prechal (1995), p. 201 and, in WTO context, Cottier & Schefer (1998) at p. 88; on English law, see Hunt (1998), p. 14-25 and Chapter 8.

[5] *Regina v. Bartle and the Commissionar of Police for the Metropolis and Others Ex Parte Pinochet*, [2000] 1 A.C. 147, per Lord Philip of Worth Matravers.

[6] See e.g. Case C-352/95 *Phytheron* [1997] ECR I-1729; Case C-135/93 *Spain v. Commission* [1995] ECR I-1651, para. 37; Case C-90/92 *Dr Tretter* [1993] ECR I-3569.

[7] See in particular Case C-284/95 *Safety Hi-Tech* [1998] ECR I-4301, para. 22; Case C-61/94 *Commision v. Germany* [1996] ECR I-3989 (Re International Dairy Agreement); Case C-70/94 *Werner* [1995] ECR I-3189, para. 23 and Case C-83/94 *Leifer* [1995] ECR 3231, para. 24: GATT and the Dual Use Goods Regulation.

[8] See most recently Case C-89/99 *Schieving-Nijstad* [2001] ECR I-5851, para. 55.

2 The doctrine of consistent interpretation: the Von Colson principle

Until around the 1990s, the legal literature on EC law focussed on one mode of giving effect to Community law before national courts: the doctrine of direct effect (in combination, of course, with supremacy).[9] The significance of the doctrine of consistent interpretation as a an equally important method of giving effect to EC law was not appreciated in full. Presently, textbooks still tend to devote many more pages to direct effect than to consistent interpretation, but the doctrine's autonomous value is generally appreciated.[10] Indeed, it can be said that it is currently the main form of ensuring effect of directives whether correctly, incorrectly or not transposed at all.[11] In the light of its theoretical origins in the relationship between public international and domestic law this is unsurprising; a potential conflict of norms in that sphere would first of all be addressed by a 'defusing' interpretation.

Under EC law, the doctrine of indirect effect has priority over direct effect. In the event of a potential conflict between a European Community and a domestic norm, a court will first seek to neutralize such a clash by way of 'reconciling interpretation'. It is only where this proves to be unfruitful that the doctrine of direct effect is employed, setting aside the national law provision and directly applying the European one.[12] The interpretive obligation is relevant to two distinct situations: both where the directive in question has and has not been properly transposed.[13] Indeed, because Community law requires that the result envisaged by the directive must be attained in law and in fact, judicial interpretation and application will often be decisive for the correct transposition of it.[14] Numerous references for preliminary rulings have been made in this context. A notable example is the Transfer of Undertakings Directive which, in fact, gave rise to so much case law - all after correct and timely transposition - that the Council adopted a codified version to enhance manageability of the rules.[15] Where the legislature has timely and correctly transposed the directive

---

[9] See e.g. Louis (1990), p.107.

[10] Representative texts are Craig & De Búrca (1998) and Hartley (1998).

[11] Wissink (2001), p. 49.

[12] Opinion of AG Darmon in Case C-177/88 *Dekker* [1990] ECR I-3941, at I-3958; Prechal (1995), p. 205; Lauwaars & Timmermans (1997), p. 100.

[13] Prechal (1995), p. 210 et seq.; see for an example of the decisiveness of a directive even after correct transposition, *British Horseracing Board* v. *William Hill*, [2001] 2 CMLR 12 (p. 215).

[14] Case C-300/95 *Commission* v. *UK* [1997] ECR I-2649 (Re: Product Liability Directive).

[15] Council Directive 2001/23/EC of 12 March 2001 on the approximation of the laws of the Member States relating to the safeguarding of employees' rights in the event of transfers of undertakings, businesses or parts of undertakings or businesses, OJ 2001, L 82/16.

- the normal situation - a court is unlikely to encounter the boundaries of acceptable interpretation. However, in the absence of such a transposition - the pathological situation - and where there is some discrepancy between the wording of the directive and the implementing legislation, Community law does require a certain judicial creativity.[16]

The requirement of consistent interpretation in situations of transposition deficiencies follows from the *Von Colson* case. There the ECJ held that 'all the authorities of the Member States' must interpret their national law in the light of the wording and the purpose of the directive in order to achieve the result referred to in the third paragraph of Article 189 (now Article 249) EC.[17] The courts must, insofar as they are given discretion to do so under national law, construe and apply that law, and in particular the implementing legislation in conformity with the requirements of Community law (para. 28).

This interpretive obligation was extended in *Marleasing*[18] where the ECJ elaborates as follows:

'[I]n applying national law, whether the provisions in question were adopted before or after the directive, the national court called upon to interpret it is required to do so, as far as possible, in the light of the wording and purpose of the directive...' (para. 8).

The cited passage has become the standard terminology.[19] The ECJ subsequently even prescribed to the national court the outcome of this exercise and held that the requirement to construe national law in conformity with the Directive 'precludes' the interpretation of the former in such a manner that other grounds of nullity of companies than the ones listed in the Directive apply (para. 9; the *Marleasing* case involved company law). It follows that the Community law doctrine of consistent interpretation goes further than a general spur to 'reconciling interpretation'. In fact, in outcome - and even in formulation: 'Community law precludes application of national law' - the result is the same as for direct effect, despite, as is well-known, the absence of direct effect of directives in horizontal relations (dispute between two private parties). The way effect was given to the Directive in the present case boiled down to a 'prohibition' for the Spanish court to apply a provision of the Civil Code insofar as it would produce a result not envisaged by the Directive.[20]

---

[16] Prechal (1995), p. 214; Jans (1994), p. 237.

[17] Case 14/83 *Von Colson and Kamann* [1984] ECR 1891, para. 26; see also Case 79/83 *Harz* [1984] ECR 1921.

[18] Case C-106/89 *Marleasing* [1990] ECR I-4135.

[19] See most recently Case C-456/98 *Centrosteel* [2000] ECR I-6007 and Case C-365/98 *Brinkmann II* [2000] ECR I-4619.

[20] See also Case C-421/92 *Habermann-Beltermann* [1994] ECR I-1657 and more recently, *Centrosteel* (as cited).

It seems to me that this obligation not to apply a rule of national law if it is contrary to a directive, as a matter of interpretation of domestic law where there is a choice between different relevant rules, is one of the most important aspects of the doctrine. The crucial point is that as long as no legal vacuum is created by the impact of the directive, courts will stay within the bounds of interpretation.[21] They simply apply another rule of domestic law or, like in *Marleasing* itself, decline to apply a general provision of contract law to the specific situation in hand, which can be regarded as interpreting the scope of that rule in the light of the facts of the dispute and a directive. Consider a situation comparable to *Marleasing*, where reliance on a ground of nullity of a company under Spanish law was blocked. National contract law lays down a requirement to register a contract subject to the sanction of nullity for non-compliance with this requirement.[22] If and when a directive rules out such a registration, all the national court has to do is to simply uphold the contract as a matter of construing the three types of rules in issue: the registration requirement, the nullity of contracts rules and the directive. Admittedly, the impact of a directive in such a context may be regarded as stretching the notion of interpretation, but it is doctrinally quite acceptable in my view.[23]

To date the most far-reaching application of consistent interpretation has been confined to sanctioning infringements of the prohibition of sex discrimination as laid down in Directive 76/207/EEC on Equal Treatment of Men and Women,[24] where an employer - despite the absence of direct effect - was held liable in a situation where there would not have been liability under the applicable national rules. The ECJ ruled that the mere breach of this prohibition suffices for civil liability 'without there being any possibility of invoking the grounds of exemption provided for by national law' (*Dekker* case).[25] In other words, the national court was obliged not to apply any grounds of justification and the requirement of fault, as applicable to the dispute under the Dutch tort law system. In the *Draehmpaehl* case from 1997,[26] the ECJ affirmed its decision in *Dekker*. The pattern is becoming familiar: because the limits to liability under,

---

[21] Cf. Lenz e.a. (2000), p. 519-520, analysing what they call *l'invocabilité d'exclusion*: a blocking effect by a directive on national law.

[22] See Case C-215/97 *Bellone* [1998] ECR-I 2191.

[23] See also Opinion of AG Jacobs in *Centrosteel* (as cited), para. 36. But see Arnull (2000), p. 94: cannot be called interpretation at all.

[24] Council Directive 76/207/EEC of 9 February 1976 on the implementation of the principle of equal treatment for men and women as regards access to employment, vocational training and promotion, and working conditions, OJ 1976, L 39/40; see for a Proposal to amend the Directive, OJ 2000, CE 337/204.

[25] *Dekker* (as cited).

[26] Case C-180/95 *Draehmpaehl* [1997] ECR I-2195.

in this case, German law may not be applied, the employer - in the context of the doctrine of consistent interpretation - incurs more liability than under German law applied in isolation (that is without the Directive). However, it should be noted that German law had introduced a *lex specialis* into its law of damages, restricting recovery in sex discrimination cases. Not surprisingly, these restrictions were contrary to EC law. Now that the Directive precludes its application, the *lex generalis* of the Civil Code will have to be applied. In itself that cannot be objectionable of course. Neither could one say that the ECJ forced an interpretation of German law *contra legem* (i.e. effectively redrafting express wording) by introducing a sanction which was not in place at all.[27]

What these cases do illustrate is the level of uncertainty parties are confronted with in coping with conflicts between directives and national provisions and the scope for reconciling them as a matter of interpretation.[28] According to Advocate General Jacobs, this type of uncertainty is in fact less acceptable than to grant fully fledged horizontal direct effect to directives: that is, he argued in favour of the latter partly because of a worse state of legal uncertainty under the doctrine of consistent interpretation.[29] However, others argue that the level of legal uncertainty in the interpretation context is acceptable and not fundamentally different from the purely national context.[30] To an extent, this uncertainty is inevitable, in my view, and inherent in the notion that there must be some ambiguity in the national rule for it to be construed consistently with Community law ('... as far as possible...').

Less satisfactory is that the ECJ has not always been consistent in determining the duties EC law imposes on the national courts. As noted above, prescribing that a directive precludes the application of a rule of national law, as in *Marleasing*, is a far reaching obligation which leaves little scope for any interpretive role by those courts. It is not so that in subsequent cases the ECJ has retreated from this somewhat radical approach because it followed exactly this pattern in the *Centrosteel* case of 2000 (see further below). What looked like a retreat from *Marleasing* in some cases in this interim is apparently not a general rule.[31] In the next paragraphs, further factors contributing to the uncertainty surrounding consistent interpretation will be examined.

---

[27] Cf. Opinion of AG Van Gerven in *Marleasing* (as cited).

[28] See also Craig (1998), p. 53.

[29] Opinion of AG Jacobs in Case C-316/93 *Vaneetveld* [1994] ECR I-763, para. 31.

[30] A. O'Neill, Presentation at Conference 'Enforcing Community law before national courts: ten years of Francovich', Trier, Academy of European Law, 14 May 2001; cf., in WTO context, Cottier & Schefer (1998).

[31] See in particular Case C-334/92 *Wagner Miret* [1993] ECR I-6911, where the ECJ leaves it up to the national court to decide whether it can give a consistent interpretation (probably not, para. 22) without 'dictating' the outcome.

2.1 The time factor: is expiry of transposition period for directives relevant?

One aspect of the doctrine of consistent interpretation which contributes to legal uncertainty and is controversial in legal doctrine concerns the relevance or otherwise of the expiry of the transposition period.[32] In one interpretation of *Kolpinghuis* the interpretive obligation applies even before expiry of the transposition period (although legal doctrine frequently criticizes this result).[33] A more balanced approach to this issue, according to Advocate General Jacobs,[34] is to distinguish between a broad and a narrow duty to construe national law in conformity with EC law. The narrow duty relates to the specific implementing provisions. If these are in force before the deadline for transposition has expired, those provisions must be construed in the light of the directive. Consequently, the narrow duty concerns situations of timely implementation and can be assimilated to what has been termed above 'normal' consistent interpretation. The broad duty, on the other hand, concerns all the relevant national law and operates especially in cases of non-implementation. The Advocate General contends that this duty can only apply after expiry of the period for implementation to prevent that the national court would be obliged to pre-empt any action by the national legislature.

Taking up the thread of parallelism in the application of the doctrines of direct effect and consistent interpretation, it would be advantageous if the basic attributes of the two doctrines do not differ too much; the less unnecessary complexity, the easier it is for practitioners to manage the doctrines and thereby give effect to Community law. As said, there is authority for the view that it follows from the *Kolpinghuis* judgment that national courts have to start applying consistent interpretation before expiry of the period for transposition of the directive. As is well-known, a directly effective provision of a directive can only be relied upon after that period has expired. In fact, the ECJ went as far as saying that it cannot produce any effect capable of being taken into account by national courts before that date.[35]

In the light of such apparent and unjustified inconsistency between direct effect and consistent interpretation it is no surprise that national courts have queried the ECJ on various occasions whether they indeed must ignore the transposition deadline. For example in *Mendes Ferreira* it was asked, in the context of the Directives on compulsory car accidents insurance, whether such

---

[32] See e.g. Ehricke (1999), p. 553-559.

[33] Case 80/86 *Kolpinghuis* [1987] ECR 3969. See e.g. the Opinion of AG Darmon in Joined Cases C-87-89/90 *Verholen* [1991] ECR I-3757, para. 15. See also Craig (1998), p. 45 and Prechal (1995), p. 23-24.

[34] Opinion of AG Jacobs in Case C-156/91 *Mundt* [1992] ECR I-5567.

[35] Case 148/78 *Ratti* [1979] ECR 1629, para. 47.

interpretation had to be employed even where the accident took place before the end of the transposition period.[36] Unfortunately, the ECJ did not give an answer as that particular point was not relevant in the light of the answers to other questions.

However, guidance on this matter can be gleaned from *Centrosteel*.[37] It deals with the Directive on commercial agents and basically follows up an earlier judgment of the ECJ, the case of *Bellone*.[38] Indeed, *Centrosteel* concerns exactly the same situation as the earlier *Bellone* judgment, namely the possible invalidity of a contract under Italian law where it was not entered in a register for commercial agents, whereas, under the Directive no such requirement of registration is allowed. The national court knew that this had already been decided in *Bellone*, but expressed its doubt as to how to apply the ruling in the absence of direct effect between individuals which would seem to entail that it could not disapply the Italian Act with the registration requirement. Accordingly, the single issue before the ECJ is how to give effect to the Directive between private parties.

The ECJ acknowledged that the situation here is identical to *Bellone* and recalled that it had ruled that the Directive precludes imposing this registration requirement. Does that mean that the Directive thus imposes an obligation on a private person? It does not. Citing the *Marshall I* and *Faccini Dori*[39] cases to confirm that a directive cannot of itself impose obligations on individuals, the Court likewise reiterates its standard phrase on consistent interpretation (... as far as possible interpret relevant national law, whether adopted before or after the Directive in the light of Directive's wording and purpose, para. 16 ...).[40] It follows that in keeping with settled case law, consistent interpretation is employed to block the application of a provision of national law at odds with a directive in a dispute between private parties.

The next paragraph does more than merely confirm previous judgments. For the ECJ says: 'Where a court is seised of a dispute falling within the scope of the Directive and arising from facts postdating the expiry of the period for transposing the Directive, the national court, in applying provisions of domestic law or settled domestic case-law ...', must interpret that law so as to conform with the aims of the Directive (para. 17). The new elements here are: (i) facts postdating expiry transposition period and (ii) reference to case law. In no other ruling on consistent interpretation has the Court included a reference to the

---

[36] Case C-348/98 *Mendes Ferreira* [2000] ECR I-671; Council Directives 72/166/EEC, OJ 1972, L 103/1, 84/5/EEC, OJ 1984, L 8/17 and 90/232/EEC, OJ 1990, L 129/33.

[37] As cited.

[38] *Bellone* (as cited); Council Directive 86/653/EEC, OJ 1986, L 382/17.

[39] Case 152/84 *Marshall I* [1986] ECR 723; Case C-91/92 *Faccini Dori* [1994] ECR I-3325.

[40] Citing *Marleasing, Wagner Miret, Faccini Dori* (all as cited) and Joined Cases C-240-244/98 *Océano* [2000] ECR I-4941.

temporal aspect regarding the facts of the dispute having taken place after the period for transposition has expired.

It now also refers to settled domestic case law, which is important but less relevant to the issue of parallelism between direct effect and consistent interpretation. Of course, where the national law consists of case law any required reinterpretation cannot be limited to legislation alone. This significance of national courts' case law regarding the interpretation of domestic law in the light of directives has been emphasized previously by the ECJ, albeit in a different context. In an infringement action judgment regarding the Product Liability Directive, it held that an infringement action by the Commission for incorrect implementation may be premature in the absence of domestic case law (except where any discrepancy between the Directive and the national law is *a priori* irreconcilable and only one interpretation, contrary to the Directive, is conceivable).[41] In other words, without such case law, it cannot be determined whether the Directive had indeed been incorrectly transposed. As for *Centrosteel*, the incompatibility between the Directive and Italian law was in fact produced by case law of the Italian *Corte di Cassazione* and not by any legislative provision.[42] It is probably for that reason that the ECJ now included a reference to settled domestic case law in the '*Marleasing* formula'. It is in this light, that the ECJ rules in para. 18 of *Centrosteel* that it does not have to deal in detail with the substantive questions in hand as the Italian court 'may' resolve them 'on the basis of the Directive' and its case law on consistent interpretation.

Unfortunately, regarding the more important new element of *Centrosteel*, the inclusion of the term 'postdating', the Court is not unequivocal as to whether it is indeed included as a conditional requirement of the doctrine of consistent interpretation. Ambiguity remains as the facts of the dispute here apparently did relate to an event postdating the expiry of the Directive's transposition period so that the inclusion of this factor does not impose an additional constraint on the national court in this particular dispute. Also, the operative part of the judgment does not include it. The 'postdating' issue is an *obiter dictum* here which could not affect the outcome of the Court's ruling, unlike in the cited *Mendes Ferreira* case where the facts of the dispute before the national court occurred before that crucial date. In other words, if the ECJ had answered the preliminary questions on consistent interpretation in the latter case it would also have had to confirm its introduction of the postdating-restriction in *Centrosteel* and thus rule that the Directive could not be given any effect. Subsequent references for preliminary rulings in situations pre-dating expiry of the transposition period are needed to determine the precedent value of *Centrosteel* on this point.

---

[41]   *Commission* v. *United Kingdom* (as cited); Council Directive 85/374/EEC, OJ 1985, L 210/29.

[42]   Opinion AG Jacobs, para. 36. But as is apparent from para. 17 of the ECJ's judgment, that the Italian Supreme Court had subsequently changed it case law in line with the Directive.

Tentatively, in recollection of the fact that the absence of horizontal direct effect was also first introduced in an *obiter dictum* in *Marshall I*, it is concluded that the ECJ in *Centrosteel* has silently overruled its earlier (also somewhat cryptic) holdings in *Kolpinghuis* about the role of the transposition period in the doctrine of consistent interpretation.[43] Albeit terse and without any reasoning, it has now brought this doctrine into line with direct effect by limiting the interpretive obligation on national courts to facts occurring after expiry of the relevant directive's transposition period.

2.2 Limits to consistent interpretation: the ECJ's inconsistent *Arcaro* judgment

Since the cited *Kolpinghuis* case, it is well-established that the general principles of law place limits on the interpretive obligation. It will be remembered that the ECJ had first decided in this case that also in the context of criminal liability where the State sought to invoke EC law to the detriment of an individual the courts are obliged to give indirect effect to a directive (the preliminary question asked whether a court *was allowed* to do so). By contrast, it ruled out any possibility for the State to rely on direct effect as against an individual (so-called inverse vertical direct effect). It then considered that the interpretive obligation 'is limited by the general principles of law which form part of Community law and in particular the principles of legal certainty and non-retroactivity' (para. 13). Because the Court refers to non-retro-activity in particular, it would seem that this reasoning focuses on the criminal liability context, without indicating what the law is in other contexts (civil and adminis-trative law).

It is true that in *Arcaro*[44] the ECJ in general terms addresses the issue of consistent interpretation in the State v. citizen situation, but the relevant passage (the 'obligation of the national court to refer to the content of the directive when interpreting the relevant rules of its own national law reaches a limit where such an interpretation leads to the imposition on an individual of an obligation laid down by a directive which has not been transposed...', para. 42) is not reiterated in subsequent case law. The mere imposition of an obligation on individuals is here put forward as a limit to the interpretive obligation without any reference to the general principles of law, which is difficult to tally with the cited judgments in *Dekker* and *Draehmpaehl* where additional obligations certainly were imposed

---

[43] Support for this view may also be gleaned from the denial of any need to interpret a directive before expiry of the transposition date and without transposition; implicitly this covered consistent interpreta-tion, see Case C-165/98 *Mazzoleni* [2001] ECR I-2189, para. 17.

[44] Case C-168/95 *Arcaro* [1996] ECR I-4705.

as a result of indirect effect in the civil law context. *A fortiori*, the ECJ continues in the quoted passage by referring to criminal liability.[45]

Moreover, it follows from the subsequent *Display Workers* case[46] that the approach to limit consistent interpretation through the application of general principles of law (rather than a blanket reference to the imposition of obligations) still constitutes current law. Consequently, still no explicit decision by the ECJ has been made about the limits to the interpretive obligation in civil and administrative cases. For the Court in this case, again, says that the courts' duty to construe their national law in conformity with a directive 'is not unlimited, particularly where such interpretation would have the effect to' determine or aggravate an individual's criminal liability (para. 24). Interestingly, and for the first time, the ECJ specifies the nature of the limit in this type of case (criminal law: State v. citizen) by referring to the 'principle that a provision of the criminal law may not be applied extensively to the detriment of the defendant, which is the corollary of the principle of legality in relation to crime and punishment' (para. 25). In addition, the Court explains its approach by pointing to the *nulla poena* principle as formulated in Article 7 ECHR.[47]

This case law is not determinative for the application of the principle of legal certainty outside the criminal law context. But it is clear now that one must distinguish criminal cases from others because the crucial principle in *Re Display Workers* - the legality principle or *nulla poena sine lege* - only applies to criminal liability. Or, in the words of Advocate General Jacobs, affirming the well-established principles of the doctrine of indirect effect, that 'it may well lead to the imposition upon an individual of civil liability or a civil obligation which would not otherwise have existed'.[48]

It is a matter of appreciation when the principle of legal certainty will preclude an attempt by the State to invoke a non-transposed directive against a private person in the context of administrative law. The mere fact that the individual is worse off cannot be enough as this is just what happened in the *Dekker* and *Draehmpaehl* cases (cited above). Decisive is not whether consistent interpretation boils down to a kind of direct effect by the back door nor whether additional obligations are imposed on individuals, but whether the outcome of a directive-conform interpretation of the applicable national law in the case in hand (civil or administrative) is acceptable in the light of the general principles of law.[49]

---

[45] See also Editorial, "The incidental effect of directives", *ELRev.* 1999, p. 1-2, *inter alia* pointing to Case C-2/97 *IP* [1998] ECR I-8597, para. 26.

[46] Joined Cases C-74/95 and C-129/95 *Procura della Republica* v. *X* [1996] ECR I-6609.

[47] See also the Opinion of AG Ruiz-Jarabo Colomer, paras. 43-63.

[48] Opinion in *Centrosteel* (as cited) para. 35.

[49] Prechal (1995), p. 242.

In the civil law context, a distinction must be made between cases where the State acts against a citizen and horizontal cases (citizen v. citizen). In the latter situation the question arises *whose* legal certainty should prevail: the one of the private party seeking to rely on a directive which should have been transposed into national law at that time, or the legal certainty of the person who invokes the national law which, contrary to EC law, had not been adapted to the directive? If and when, in horizontal civil law situations, the possibility of any imposition of obligations on private parties is denied at all by way of consistent interpretation, this is detrimental to the rights of another private person - the one invoking the directive; it also prevents the full effect of the directive (*effet utile*). In addition there would be unequal treatment of citizens in States which have and which have not (yet) transposed the directive.[50] In civil law, it would seem that the requirements of legal certainty are satisfied because every private person is able to ascertain on what date the directive must be transposed.[51]

2.3 Disguised indirect effect and the communitarization of private international law

Both the acceptance of ECJ rulings and the manageability of the modes of giving effect to Community law would benefit from a more explicit reference to and better reasoned ruling on how exactly a directive can impact on a dispute between private parties in the continuing lack of horizontal direct effect. On several occasions the Court simply interprets the directive in issue, prescribes the result in unequivocal terms (... Community law precludes ...) and leaves it to the parties and commentators to work out that this probably was a ruling on consistent interpretation rather than direct effect because the dispute does not involve a public authority. Such 'disguised indirect effect' is all the more unsatisfactory where fundamental doctrinal issues on the relationship between EC and domestic law are at stake. This critique may be levied against the Court's judgment in the *Ingmar* case where it decided on the territorial scope of the Commercial Agents Directive, implicitly settling an important theoretical question on the interrelationship between Community law and national systems of private international law (conflict of laws), without citing any cases on how to give effect to the ruling in this horizontal dispute.[52] Briefly, as this is not the place to deal with private (international) law issues, this case established a rule in that the Directive entitling a commercial agent to compensation upon termination of the contract by the principal is applicable even where the whole

---

[50] Dommering-van Rongen (1991), p. 42; Wissink (2001), No. 264.

[51] Opinion AG Jacobs in Joined Cases C-206 and 207/88 *Zanetti I* [1990] ECR I-1461 and in Case C-359/88 *Zanetti II* [1990] ECR I-1509, at I-1471.

[52] Case C-381/98 *Ingmar* [2000] ECR I-9305.

contract is governed by the law of a third State. The salient feature of this case is that the agent was based and operating in the UK but the principal was based in California, USA. Under relevant rules of private international law, the parties had exercised a choice of law for Californian law. English law was thus excluded, including, of course, these protective rules on agent compensation based on the Directive. In issue was therefore the territorial scope of a protective rule from a directive: is that scope determined by the directive itself or by the private international law of the Member State? The English Court of Appeal in its reference to the ECJ seems to assume that the latter will be the case because it seeks guidance on interpreting the Directive in the light of the English law principles on mandatory rules, i.e. rules of English law which apply to a contract even where the whole contract is governed by another legal system.[53]

The ECJ does not consider the dimension of the national private international law but focuses on the scope of the Directive as such, thus bypassing those rules of English law on mandatory rules, and prescribes the application of the protective regime of the Directive whenever the situation is closely connected with the Community such as in this case where the agent is operating in England. Effectively, the judgment constitutes a Communitarization of the Member States' rules on private international law through directives in addition to specific harmonization of these systems as such on the basis of Article 65 EC Treaty.[54]

In terms of legal uncertainty, is this a surprising judgment? Most likely not. This ruling is not wholly unexpected for the national court involved as itself had already pointed out that the same outcome would be quite possible and even likely where it would apply the doctrine of mandatory rules of English law (which are of course based on the 1980 Rome Convention on the law applicable to contractual obligations).[55] However, the ECJ does not refer to how to give effect to its ruling; one must assume that consistent interpretation will be possible. For the referring court had already established that a 1993 Statutory Instrument gave effect to the Directive and therefore considered it necessary to refer the case to the ECJ. Still, the absence of guidance by the ECJ may cast doubt on the consistency of its case law, in particular in cases which seems to belie the denial of horizontal direct effect and cause confusion on whether one deals with direct effect or with consistent interpretation.

---

[53] *Ingmar GB* v. *Eaton Leonard Technologies* [1999] *European Commercial Cases* 49 (C.A.).

[54] Van Hoek (2001). See generally Basedow (2000).

[55] OJ 1998, C 27/34 (consolidated version).

2.4 The 'incidental' effect of directives

This uncertainty about the delineation between the two techniques is most notable where it coincides with the uncertainty about the limits to the ECJ's rejection of horizontal direct effect. The decisive impact of a directive in disputes involving two private parties proved controversial in the literature. Commentators debate whether the ECJ's case law is inconsistent or not or propose new terminology to explain the apparent contradictory cases, such as 'incidental effect'.[56] Three cases in particular have fuelled this debate: *Pafitis*, *Ruiz Bernáldez* and *CIA Security*.[57] This is not the place for a detailed analysis of these judgments. Suffice it to say that in my opinion, they can all be 'pigeon holed' under direct effect and consistent interpretation, the two received methods of giving effect to EC law, and should not be seen as moving away from doctrinal orthodoxy.

In *Pafitis*, according to Advocate General Tesauro, the dispute before the national court concerned an act adopted by public authorities, i.e. the Greek Central Bank and a temporary administrator acting on its behalf, who were responsible for the management of the formal defendant, a bank in the form of a public limited company, under Greek law regarding banking supervision.[58] In effect, the directive in issue was relied upon to preclude the application of these decisions by public authorities, even though the case in formal terms concerned two private parties.

As for *Ruiz Bernáldez*, the national court regarded the dispute as involving consistent interpretation of Spanish civil law, including the regulated contractual relations between the insurance company and the insured as well as the third party victims, in the light of the Directives on compulsory motor insurance for traffic accidents.[59] In fact, this case is virtually identical to *Marleasing* and

---

[56] Editorial, "The incidental effect of directives", *ELRev.* 1999, p. 1-2.

[57] Case C-441/93 *Pafites* [1996] ECR I-1347; Case C-129/94 *Ruiz Bernáldez* [1996] ECR I-1829; Case C-194/94 *CIA Security* [1996] ECR I-2201.

[58] Opinion AG at para. 25. Given the role of the public authorities with respect to the bank's legal position, one can compare this to the role of public law licences in civil disputes, see English Court of Appeal, *R. v. Durham County Council ex parte Huddleston*, [2000] WLR 1484, [2000] 2 CMLR 313, No. 18. See generally on this issue, Lackhoff & Nyssens (1998), p. 397-413.

[59] Opinion AG Lenz in *Ruiz Bernáldez* (as cited), at para. 4. See also *Mendes Ferreira* (discussed above): the national court explicitly refers to consistent interpretation of the Portuguese Civil Code in light of directives on compulsory motor insurance; and see House of Lords, *White and the Motor Insurer's Bureau*, [2001] 2 CMLR 1 where these same Community law rules were taken into account to interpret an Agreement between the Motor Insurer's Bureau and the Secretary of State which implemented a directive. Even though the House of Lords held that the interpretive obligation did not apply because the Agreement was not legislation it reached exactly the same result. A term of the Agreement excluding liability of the insurer was construed narrowly in conformity with the directive.

Centrosteel in that they all involve an exhaustive list of conditions laid down in a directive - in *Ruiz Bernáldez* a list of permitted exclusions of liability - which preclude the application of additional conditions or exemptions in the national law. The crucial point is that Community law opposes any reliance on such 'forbidden fruits' of the national law by way of consistent interpretation. This seems to me to be fundamentally different from imposing any fresh - additional - obligations on the private party concerned; only the latter would indeed constitute the banned horizontal direct effect of a directive.[60]

The third noted case, *CIA Security,* has attracted the most attention and is perhaps the most confusing given the apparent contradictory views on the chosen *modus operandi* between the ECJ and its Advocate General: the former approaches the case entirely as a matter of (traditional) direct effect whereas the latter refers to the consistent interpretation of the relevant Belgian legislation on commercial practices.[61] In my view, this case deals with direct effect alone - not with any possible impact of the directive in terms of an aid to the interpretation of substantive national law dealing with the same issues as the directive. More generally speaking, the case involves the interaction between public and private law in the sense that the status and validity of public law regulatory standards determine the private law obligations between private parties (as is common in environmental and consumer protection law). Undoubtedly, the Directive in issue does not intend to regulate relations between private persons (as a directive on, say, unfair contract terms in consumer contracts obviously does). Directive 83/189/EEC in fact exclusively concerns the relationship between the European Commission and the Member States and imposes on the latter the duty to notify legislation on technical standards before they are adopted so that the Commission can verify their compatibility with the free movement of goods (ex ante supervision).[62] How can a failure to notify by a Member State be determinative for a dispute between two competitors before a civil court?

The answer is that non-contractual (private law) obligations between these parties under Belgian law were dependent on the lawfulness of technical standards adopted under Belgian public law. One producer of alarm systems, Signalson, contends that its competitor, CIA Security, markets defective systems as they do not comply with the Belgian standards, whereupon CIA Security sues Signalson and seeks an injunction restraining further statements about CIA

---

[60] See also the English Court of Appeal in *R. v. Durham County Council ex parte Huddleston* (as cited), at Nos. 25-26 per Sedley LJ, who thinks that the ECJ's body of case law about this distinction is coherent.

[61] Opinion of AG Elmer in *CIA Security* (as cited), para. 72.

[62] Weatherill (1996), p. 129-204. Council Directive 83/189/EEC of 28 March 1983 laying down a procedure for the provision of information in the field of technical standards and regulations, OJ 1983, L 109/8, as amended by Directive 94/10/EC of the European Parliament and the Council, OJ 1994, L 100/30. Consolidated in Directive 98/34/EC of the European Parliament and the Council, OJ 1998, L 204/37.

Security's allegedly unlawful/defective product. In broad terms, the legal basis for this action in most Member States would be the law of tort (negligence or breach of statutory duty; libel).[63] In a counterclaim, Signalson sues CIA Security, also seeking an injunction, in this case to restrain further sales of the allegedly unlawful product, being contrary to national law (Belgian) standards. It is readily appreciable that ascertaining the non-contractual rights and obligations between the competitors depends on the validity/lawfulness of the Belgian product standards. The direct effect of the Directive therefore arose as an incident in a tort action. It is well-known that the ECJ did consider the Directive to produce direct effect and held that the 'breach of the obligation to notify renders the technical regulations concerned inapplicable, so that they are unenforceable against individuals' (para. 54).[64] The public law issue of the lack of notification had to be decisive in the private law context as the very unlawfulness of one competitor's conduct or the other was linked to these standards; if they are unenforceable in that they must be disapplied for being contrary to a higher ranking norm, this unenforceablity cannot be dependent on the public or private nature of the enforcer. The salient feature of this case is that effectively a competitor seeks compliance with national law product standards, just like an enforcement agency or other public authority would. The former cannot 'revive' rules which would have been 'pronounced dead' with respect to the latter.[65]

Admittedly, the decisive role in a horizontal dispute of a failure by a Member State to notify rules of domestic law to the European Commission increases legal uncertainty for private parties (albeit, of course as a matter of direct effect and not as the allegedly even more uncertain doctrine of consistent interpretation). Even more problematic is that failures by States during the notification procedure (i.e. failure to suspend adoption of rules, which had been notified, during a required stand-still period) can determine the outcome of a contractual dispute between two private companies. The ECJ nevertheless did extend the *CIA Security* ruling from the tort to the contract context in *Unilever Italia,*[66] contrary to the proposal of Advocate General Jacobs. Leaving aside the fact that the procedural defect here is not a non-notification as such but a far less obvious procedural requirement, assessing the acceptability of *Unilever Italia* depends on whether or not one focuses on the similarity in enforcement rules (as noted

---

[63] The legal basis under Belgian law was the Law of 14 July 1991 on Commercial Practices, Art.s 93 and 95, which prohibit unfair trading practices.

[64] Cf. the similar legal and factual setting in Case C-77/97 Österreichische Unilever [1999] ECR I-431.

[65] Opinion of AG Elmer in Case C-194/94, [1996] ECR I-2201, para. 71. See also Lord Hoffman in *Seymour Smith*, [1997] 2 CMLR 904, as cited by Jans & Prinssen in this volume's chapter V, paragraph 2.4 and the Opinion of AG Jacobs in Case C-443/98 *Unilever Italia* [2000] ECR I-7535, paras. 64-71.

[66] *Unilever Italia* (as cited).

above) by public authorities and competitors in unfair competition litigation. Advocate General Jacobs thought that the result of *CIA Security* was acceptable in its own context but should be applied with caution and certainly should not be extended to the contractual sphere.[67]

In favour of the ECJ's ruling that the national court must also here refuse to apply the procedurally defective regulatory standards one could point to an analogy with the impact of other public law incompatibilities on disputes between private parties. First of all, *Unilever Italia* is unproblematic in terms of explaining the result as a matter of direct effect. In fact, the ECJ clarifies, albeit somewhat in the abstract, the limited scope of the non-horizontal direct effect of directives as confirmed in the *Faccini Dori* case (paras. 50-51). Only where the relevant substantive norm of the directive in issue itself is being invoked by one citizen against another and as such imposes new or additional obligations, compared to the existing position under national law, on that private party, does this limit to direct effect apply. In both *CIA Security* and *Unilever Italia*[68] the private party affected by the ECJ's non-enforceability of the technical measures relied on these measures in a dispute with another private party. No party invoked a Community law directive either to make the other liable or by contrast to relieve that party of liability because of a substantive liability provision under that directive.

On the contrary, the contractual or tortious liability in issue in these cases was determined by national law alone. Decisive for that liability was (non-)compliance with a technical standard of - again - national law, in this case public law. However, if that standard is incompatible with a superior rule of law, it cannot be enforced. In the tort context, neither a public authority nor a private actor, who is effectively engaged in private enforcement of these standards, can do so. In the contractual sphere, a non-enforceable labelling requirement cannot be invoked to be relieved of a contractual obligation to pay for delivery of goods not labelled in accordance with such rules; in other words, breach of these (unenforceable) national rules does not constitute the alleged breach of contract. The superior rule of law here is of course one of an EC law directive so that EC law also determines the consequences of this public law conflict for the private law dispute. A similar scenario is entirely conceivable in many legal systems where such standards would be conflicting with a superior rule of national law (or a directly effective Treaty). This public law incompatibility (whether EC or domestic, e.g. in States with a written Constitution) is a preliminary issue in the private law dispute. In other words, the private law liability is dependent on the resolution of this public law incompatibility. Therefore, if an EC law directive

---

[67] Opinion AG, paras. 71, 98, 111. The Advocate General noted the limits introduced by Case C-226/97 *Lemmens* [1998] ECR I-3711. See also Dougan (2000), p. 598.

[68] And, as said, in *Österreichische Unilever* (as cited).

is determinative, the decision of the liability question has nothing to do with a horizontal direct effect of directives. Admittedly, the public-private law nexus is closer in the tort than in the contract sphere. However, it is still there; examples are the possible impact of human rights issues such as privacy in the contractual labour law context or contracts which contents are determined to a considerable extent by law.[69]

The legal certainty issue is a different matter; assessments will differ on when a situation becomes too uncertain, as they did between the ECJ and Advocate General Jacobs. Perhaps unfortunately, the ECJ did not consider the lack of transparency during the Commission's evaluation of the technical norms; to an extent, the existence of other procedural defects than full scale non-notification is unknowable by private parties.[70] In addition, the connection between any incentives on Member States to stimulate notification and determining a breach of contract in the light of notification defects is remote. The detrimental effect of the ruling on contractual certainty may thus be seen as unjustified.[71] On the other hand, is the result of *Unilever Italia* so different from the impact of other forms of incompatibility of administrative law rules with superior norms of law (as pointed out above), notably a written constitution? If such an incompatibility is raised in a dispute between two private persons the party who seeks to rely on the rule in issue could probably not have known in advance that the court would disapply it because of this incompatibility. This type of uncertainty is inevitable and likely to become more prevalent even in the UK under the Human Rights Act (see further below, at 2.6).[72]

2.5 Inverse vertical indirect effect of Community law: a bridge too far?

The Court has consistently ruled in well established case law that a State can never invoke a non-implemented directive as against an individual.[73] To be more precise, all these cases where a possible direct effect result-

---

[69] See in particular *Ruiz Bernáldez* (as cited), para. 20 and operative part: Directive precludes reliance on incompatible contractual clauses. In addition, a hindrance to marketing a product in the form of these national technical standards is relevant in both the tort law and the contractual context, see ECJ in paras. 46-47 of *Unilever Italia* (as cited).

[70] Weatherill (2001), p. 181.

[71] Weatherill (2001), p. 182.

[72] Through the technique of consistent interpretation which applies to predating legislation. As a result, according to Leigh & Lustgarten (1999) 'all settled interpretations of earlier legislation should be open to reconsideration', p. 511.

[73] From Case 14/86 *Pretore di Salò* v. *X* [1987] ECR 2545, *Kolpinghuis, Arcaro, Procura della Republica v. X* (all as cited), to, most recently, Joined Cases C-304/94, C-330/94, C-342/94 and C-224/95 *Tombesi* [1997] ECR I-3561.

ing in the imposition of an obligation on an individual by a directive as such (so-called inverse vertical direct effect) was considered, concerned the criminal liability of these individuals under the relevant domestic criminal law. However, in my view the ECJ has denied this possibility for the wrong reason. It ruled that as directives cannot impose an obligation as such on individuals than *a fortiori* this cannot be possible for the benefit of the State.[74] It thus linked this situation of potential inverse direct effect (State v. individual) to the denial of possible horizontal direct effect of directives (individual v. individual). In this same case law, the ECJ did accept the applicability of the interpretive obligation, albeit, of course, subject to the limits imposed by the general principles of law (e.g. legal certainty, legality principle or *nulla poena*). Unlike Advocate General Mischo, who only considered it acceptable that national courts *may* take account of untransposed directives as an aid to the interpretation of domestic criminal law to confirm an interpretation based on other considerations, the ECJ held that the national court *must*, as a matter of Community law, achieve a consistent interpretation within the general principles limits.[75] The Court's approach to the effects - or lack of it - in the State v. individual context is problematic as it is quite possible to argue in favour of horizontal direct effect of directives[76] but still deny *any* reliance on a non-transposed or wrongly transposed directive by the State against an individual under either direct effect or consistent interpretation.

The issue of the legal effect of a directive as between private parties (horizontal effect) does not coincide with the issue of the legal effect of a directive in the situation of inverse vertical effect, such as in *Kolpinghuis*. It is a broader question to ask whether directives may ever impose obligations on private parties than to ask whether they can produce horizontal direct effect.[77] If the first question is answered negatively, *nobody* will be able to rely upon a directly effective provision of a directive against a private person (neither State nor individual). The second question is narrower in scope in that a possible acceptance of horizontal direct effect between private parties *inter se* does not necessarily decide the question whether direct effect may be invoked by the State vis-à-vis a private party. Put differently, a lack of horizontal effect is not a necessary precondition for the ruling that a directive cannot produce inverse vertical effect as these are separate questions.[78] As for consistent interpretation, the present situation is that provided the courts stay within the bounds of the general principles of

---

[74] *Pretore di Salò* v. *X* (as cited), at I-2570.

[75] Opinion of AG Mischo in *Kolpinghuis* (as cited), para. 27; ECJ in paras. 12-14.

[76] As three Advocates General have: see Opinion of AG Van Gerven in Case C-271/91 *Marshall II* [1993] ECR I-4367, Opinion of AG Jacobs in *Vaneetveld* (as cited) and Opinion of AG Lenz in *Faccini Dori* (as cited).

[77] Arnull (1988), p. 44.

[78] Arnull (1988).

law, obligations may be imposed on individuals through the mediation of the applicable domestic law even where it is the State that is acting against it. It is recalled that the cases so far have been concerned with criminal liability alone suggesting that an imposition of obligations in a civil law context beyond what applies on the basis of national law alone is possible.[79]

Given the fact that in practice, courts can be required to reach exactly the same result through either direct effect or consistent interpretation, it is anomalous to allow States to benefit from the latter but not the former. It is therefore submitted that Member States should not be allowed to plead directives which they have not (correctly) implemented as an aid to the interpretation of national law. One could paraphrase a well worn legal adage here and argue: *quod licet bovi non licet Jovi.* Private persons who derive protection from a directive are entitled to rely on them even against private parties but never should the State be able to rely on them because the State should not benefit from its own wrong doing. This so-called *estoppel* argument or *nemo auditur,* invoked by the ECJ to justify direct effect against the State in favour of individuals, should be adopted here as a basis for denying any possibility for Member States to invoke directives before national courts under both direct effect and the doctrine of consistent interpretation (except, of course, to construe national law after correct transposition).[80] The notion of *estoppel* is here used in a more narrow sense than under the current ECJ's case law. It is here restricted from forming part of the justification for ('normal' vertical) direct effect to bar reliance on directives by Member States without their proper transposition.[81] So unlike the present situation, it is my proposal to streamline the two doctrines in this respect. Both doctrines could thus be applied in parallel in this type of situation. Such a proposed parallelism would reduce complexity in the application of the two doctrines and thus enhance legal certainty.

2.6 Comparative note: 'the English *Marleasing*' (Human Rights Act 1998, S. 3)

It may be helpful to put the doctrine of consistent interpretation in a wider, comparative, perspective and to note its prominent role in terms

---

[79] Opinion of AG Jacobs in *Centrosteel* (as cited), para. 35. In the horizontal context, this is of course exactly what happened in the *Dekker* and *Draehmpaehl* cases (as cited).

[80] Cf. Morris (1991): inverse direct effect in civil law perhaps possible but difficult to reconcile with *estoppel.* But see Wissink (2001), No. 284, arguing that reliance on *estoppel* here would lead to unequal treatment of cases between public and private actors and would compromise the effectiveness of Community law.

[81] For an early critical assessment of the use of *estoppel* in the current state of the law, see Wyatt (1983), p. 241 and also Prechal (1995), p. 255-260.

of giving effect to higher ranking law as a matter of interpretation as opposed to direct effect. In 1998, the UK legislature adopted the Human Rights Act (HRA)[82] in order to incorporate most, but not all, of the fundamental rights laid down in the 1950 European Convention for the Protection of Human Rights and Fundamental Freedoms. The HRA came into force in October 2000. In constitutional terms, the status of so-called Convention rights under the HRA within the UK legal order is comparable to European Community law: both systems require that English law, both statutory and common law, be compatible with the 'European' norms. There is, however, an important difference between the powers of the courts in the event of a perceived incompatibility. The HRA does not empower the courts - unlike under the doctrine of direct effect of EC law - to set aside an English Act of Parliament where it conflicts with the HRA.[83] At most, they can issue a declaration of incompatibility which does not affect the validity, continuing operation or enforcement of the provision in respect of which it is given nor is it binding on the parties to the proceedings in which it is made (S. 4(6)). By contrast, Section 3 of the HRA obliges the courts to interpret legislation, both primary and secondary, whenever enacted, 'so far as it is possible to do so ...' and to give effect to it 'in a way which is compatible with the Convention rights'. The wording of this English duty of consistent interpretation is, of course, almost identical to the ECJ's formulation in *Marleasing*. In fact, it has been modelled on it. It has therefore been suggested that the limits to the HRA duty should be drawn along similar lines as the limits to the *Marleasing* formula.[84]

A similar far reaching impact is to be expected under this parallel interpretive obligation.[85] It has been argued that this provision requires a different approach to statutory interpretation than so far prevalent in England. Not only is there a stronger pointer to the courts under the HRA to reach compatibility, i.e. stronger than the rule which allowed consistent interpretation when there is ambiguity. Consistent interpretation is considered possible and must be achieved as long as the statute is not distorted. Most importantly, a purposive approach to statutory interpretation is required in this context, just like in the context of giving effect to EC law. In positive terms courts must proceed from a presumption of compatibility and achieve congruity unless the wording of the statute makes that clearly impossible.[86] As the HRA is still recent, it is too early

---

[82] Available on the Website of HMSO, URL: www.legislation.hmso.gov.uk/acts.htm (Acts of the UK Parliament).

[83] See generally e.g. Beloff (1999), p. 11; Lindell (2000), p. 399 and Leigh & Lustgarten (1999).

[84] Bamforth (1999), p. 169

[85] Cf. Edwards (2000); Leigh & Lustgarten (1999), p. 511; House of Lords, *R. v. DPP, ex parte Kebilene*, [1999] 3 WLR 972, [1999] 4 All ER 801: 'Section 3(1) enacts a strong interpretive obligation', per Lord Steyn.

[86] Beloff (1999), p. 29; Leigh & Lustgarten (1999), p. 538-539; Starmer (2001), p. 28.

to assess the full impact of it on legal practice.[87] However, given the numerous cases in which it has been invoked already, there can be no doubt about its significance.

These cases include a ruling of the Court of Appeal, acknowledging that the HRA is an instrument of constitutional significance. In addition, it considered the HRA's interpretive obligation (Section 3) and held that '[t]he consequence of Section 3 is that legislation which affects human rights is required to be construed in a manner which conforms with the Convention wherever this is possible'.[88] Finally, in that same case, the Court of Appeal proved itself willing to indeed ensure conformity by reading words into a criminal law statute which had introduced a mandatory life sentence for a second serious offence (popularly referred to as the 'two strikes and you're out' law). The Court of Appeal found that a compatible reading of this statute, thus preventing a contravention of the Convention rights, required it to construe the notion of 'exceptional circumstances' to mean 'no significant risk to the public'. Without the insertion of the latter, the imposition of such a mandatory life sentence on a person who does not pose a risk to the public would be disproportionate and in breach of the ECHR. Significantly, consistent interpretation here produced a result in line with judicial practice before the adoption of the statute, the 1997 Crime (Sentences) Act, which removed the Court's power to take this factor into account; before the HRA, the courts were unable to reach this result by way of interpretation.[89]

Accordingly, this early experience with the interpretive obligation under the Human Rights Act reflects the predicted convergence with the purposive and result oriented approach to statutory interpretation under the *Marleasing* formula. One can expect the courts to adopt this 'European style' canon of interpretation whenever a potential conflict between Convention rights and English law arises. To support this view, it is significant to note that the House of Lords in *Webb* has accepted wholeheartedly the ECJ's ruling requiring a drastic reinterpretation of the relevant English statutes.[90] This national court no longer emphasizes the limits to consistent interpretation in terms of distorting the meaning of a statute but instead focuses on reaching the directive's result if at all possible.[91]

---

[87] See for an overview Starmer (2001).

[88] R. v. *Offen and Others* [2001] 1 WLR 253, No. 104.

[89] Cf. "Ruling neutralises 'two strikes' law", *The Guardian*, 10 November 2000.

[90] *Webb* v. *EMO Air Cargo (UK) Ltd (No 2)*, [1996] 2 CMLR 990, [1995] 4 All ER 577, [1995] 1 WLR 1454.

[91] Hunt (1998), p. 121-122; Craig (1998), p. 49-50: albeit subject to a distinction between cases involving express implementing legislation or not. Note in particular the contrast with the House of Lords' first judgment in *Webb* (the reference to the ECJ), [1992] 4 All ER 929, [1993] 1 WLR 49: emphasis on further consideration of possibility to reach a consistent interpretation; reference to limits of the duty: no distortion of statute.

To conclude the comparison, what does this development teach us about the issue of legal uncertainty inherent in the doctrine of consistent interpretation? It must follow from the fact that now that the English legislature has voluntarily adopted the ECJ's approach to consistent interpretation in the context of the Human Rights Act that it finds the inevitable uncertainty created by this doctrine acceptable - certainly more acceptable than a setting aside of primary legislation as a matter of direct effect, as this is not possible under the HRA.[92] Surely, this can be seen as an indication for the acceptability of the ECJ's insistence on consistent interpretation: if this is good enough for English law than why would it not be good enough for EC law as well?

3 Direct effect and Francovich liability: independent but not unconnected

Finally, a brief comparison may be made not with a comparable doctrine of consistent interpretation under domestic law, but between on the one hand the theme pursued above - parallelism between direct effect and consistent interpretation - and the interrelationship between direct effect and the *ultimum remedium* of ensuring the effectiveness of Community law before national courts: the liability of the State for breaches of EC law or *Francovich* liability.[93] It has been noted above that in legal practice, the issue of direct effect will only arise after the courts have first attempted to solve a conflict between Community and national law by way of interpretation and thus giving priority to the technique of consistent interpretation over the technique of direct effect. After the recognition of such State liability as a matter of Community law in 1991,[94] the question arose as to the interrelationship between the now three ways EC law may be invoked at national level. The ECJ itself indicated quite clearly that only where a solution could not be reached by direct effect and consistent interpretation, does State liability come into play.[95] Should this approach to methodological priority also mean that where an individual failed to rely on direct effect, there is no longer a right of reparation either?

It is recalled, that such a radical approach to the subsidiary nature of *Francovich* liability had been rejected by the ECJ in *Brasserie du Pêcheur* in that it did not accept the arguments of several governments that State liability should not be available at all where the provisions infringed have direct effect. However, in

---

[92] See also Hunt (1998), p. 298, suggesting a full interpretive obligation on English courts to ensure compliance with the UK's obligations under international human rights law.

[93] See for an account of recent developments Tridimas (2001).

[94] Joined Cases C-6/90 and C-9/90 *Francovich* [1991] ECR I-5357.

[95] *Faccini Dori* (as cited), paras. 27-29.

that same case, the ECJ did recognize some impact of a potentially unacceptable failure to invoke direct effect by an individual in the context of the principle that a victim is obliged to mitigate the loss, i.e. the injured party must show reasonable diligence in either avoiding altogether or limiting the extent of the loss or damage, or risk having to bear the damage himself.[96] What does this mean in practice? Can an individual be 'punished' for failing to raise a plea of direct effect? What exactly is required of an individual in terms of awareness of possible conflicts between EC and national law?

The ECJ provides some further guidance on this matter in *Metallgesell-schaft*.[97] The dispute concerns a complex factual and legal situation regarding English tax law and the alleged discriminatory treatments of companies with subsidiaries based in other Member States compared to those with daughters within the UK in terms of their entitlements to tax relief. What is of interest here is a line of argument adopted by the UK tax authorities regarding the noted duty to mitigation of loss. They contended, as a defence against the *Francovich* claim, that the company should have applied for tax relief even though this was not available under English law, in order to challenge any ensuing refusal to do so by the tax authorities and invoke the primacy and direct effect of Community law. The UK cited *Brasserie*'s rulings - reasonable diligence on the part of the victim to limit the loss - and argued that this meant using all the legal remedies available. The national court asked the ECJ whether it was allowed under Community law to refuse or reduce a damages claim on the sole ground that this route had not been followed by the claimants.

According to the ECJ, the UK's argument amounts to 'criticising the plaintiffs for complying with national legislation' and for not launching an apparently pointless appeal. The ECJ considers it contrary to the principle of effectiveness to demand of private persons to be aware of and challenge the incompatibility of domestic law with directly effective Community law.[98] It ruled that it would be contrary to Community law (read: the principle of effectiveness) if national courts refused or reduced a claim on the sole ground that the plaintiffs had failed to make use of all legal remedies, including setting aside unambiguous national tax law.

---

[96] Joined Cases C-46/93 and 48/93 *Brasserie du Pêcheur* [1996] ECR I-1029, paras. 18-23 and 84-85.

[97] *Metallgesellschaft* (as cited).

[98] See para. 106, which reads: 'The exercise of rights conferred on private persons by directly applicable provisions of Community law would, however, be rendered impossible or excessively difficult if their claims for restitution or compensation based on Community law were rejected or reduced solely because the persons concerned had not applied for a tax advantage which national law denied them, with a view to challenging the refusal of the tax authorities by means of the legal remedies provided for that purpose, invoking the primacy and direct effect of Community law'.

What is one to make of these passages? To the very least they constitute a mitigation of the mitigation of loss defence, one might say. In *Brasserie*, the ECJ had ruled that a victim's duty to mitigate the loss included to avail himself in time of *all* legal remedies (para. 84). One could thus quite reasonably infer that these remedies include a reliance on direct effect and supremacy. On the other hand, it is also reasonable to assume that one is asking too much of private persons if they have to ascertain any possible conflict between national law and Community law and then fail to comply with the applicable national rules (thereby even exposing themselves, in certain circumstances, to the imposition of sanctions). It is one thing for citizens to be able to do so if they take such an initiative but quite another to 'punish' them for failing to have taken this route. The one Community principle of effectiveness in this case curtailed not so much the application of domestic remedies but restricted the application of another principle of Community law: the duty to mitigate one's loss. In terms of positioning the remedy of damages in the wider context of other Community mechanisms of legal protection, the ECJ has strengthened the autonomous character of the *Francovich* liability with this ruling. It would seem to follow that the ECJ would take the same line where the interrelationship between consistent interpretation and *Francovich* liability is at stake.

4   Conclusion

This paper has reviewed a number of ECJ cases particularly relevant to the conceptualisation and legal circumscription of the doctrine of consistent interpretation. They reveal the fundamental importance of this technique; indeed, as a mode of giving effect to Community law before national authorities it takes priority over direct effect. The scope of this interpretive obligation remains uncertain to a degree. In part this is inevitable as the technique functions to resolve conflicts between incompatible norms. However, legal uncertainty could be reduced if the ECJ would be prepared to provide more extensive reasoning in its judgments. In particular, a highly critical discussion of the *Arcaro* judgment concludes that its precedent value is next to nothing. An enhancement of legal certainty would be to bring the conditions for applicability as far as possible in line with direct effect. It has been argued that such a parallelism has already been achieved insofar as the issue of expiry of the transposition period is concerned. In addition, the paper suggests a reconsideration of the case law on consistent interpretation in actions by the State versus individuals. Relying on the estoppel principle, no effect whatsoever (direct and indirect) should be allowed in favour of the State in the context of defective transposition of directives. The paper also considers the delineation between consistent interpretation and direct effect, notably in the light of controversial cases establishing so-called incidental effects and offers possible explanations for their seemingly inconsistent nature.

In considering whether the doctrine gives rise to unacceptable legal uncertainty, a comparison with the interpretive obligation incumbent on British court under the Human Rights Act is made. Not only are there notable similarities in the application of both doctrines, the English law rule confirms the importance of this method as an alternative to direct effect and justifies its level of uncertainty. Finally, the interrelationship between consistent interpretation and *Francovich* liability is considered in the light of recent case law exploring the role of the doctrine of direct effect in the context of a compensation claim.

CHAPTER V

Direct Effect: Convergence or Divergence?

A Comparative Perspective

prof. dr. Jan H. Jans & Jolande M. Prinssen, LL.M

1 Introduction

It is somewhat surprising that after 40 years' development of EC law, of the case law of the European Court of Justice (ECJ) and academic debate, there are still major differences in the way national courts apply one of the key doctrines of European law: the doctrine of direct effect. As a result of direct effect, national courts are bound to apply Community law in order to achieve effective legal protection of individuals and uniform application[1] of Community law. Yet, because the manner in which directly effective provisions are deployed in the national legal systems is fundamentally governed by national (procedural) law, the application and enforcement of directly effective provisions may produce very different outcomes in the various Member States.

One might ask why bother at all with the question of differences and similarities in the application of the doctrine of direct effect by the various national courts. The answer of course must be that these differences may affect the very rationale of the doctrine, providing effective legal protection and ensuring the uniform application of Community law. Differences significantly affecting these objectives cannot be accepted. Furthermore, if there are 'unacceptable' differences in the light of these principles, the question of harmonization, whether through the agency of the ECJ or by the Council's enacting the necessary directives, has to be discussed.

The objective of this contribution is therefore to present you with some ideas concerning what kind of differences in application have to be accepted and what kind of differences are not acceptable. Without any attempt to be comprehensive we shall illustrate our views using examples of judgments coming from various jurisdictions.

2 National case law and the direct effect doctrine 'as such'

The right of private parties to invoke directly effective provisions of Community law needs no further elaboration. Whenever a provision of Community law is 'unconditional and sufficiently precise', individuals may rely on this provision before a national court.[2] Furthermore, as far as the consequences of conflicting national law are concerned the ECJ ruled in *Simmenthal*:

'that every national court must... apply Community law in its entirety and protect the rights which the latter confers on individuals and must accordingly set aside any

---

[1] Cf. on the requirement of 'uniform application' Van Gerven (2000), p. 501-536, in particular at p. 504-505, who makes it perfectly clear that this requirement does not preclude all national differences.

[2] Cf. Case 8/81 *Becker* [1982] ECR 53. Cf. about these conditions more extensively Prechal in this volume's chapter II.

provision of national law which may conflict with it, whether prior or subsequent to the Community rule'.[3]

Thus a national court is bound to give precedence to directly effective Community law over conflicting provisions of national law.

2.1 Questioning the doctrine and its consequences; Dutch, French and Spanish case law

It goes without saying that it is not acceptable in a given case for a national court to refuse outright to apply the doctrine of direct effect. Nor for the national court to refuse to accept its consequences fully. We agree with Van Gerven, who stated that in relation to rights which Community law confers on individuals, the answer must necessarily be that their content should be the same throughout the Community.[4] When national courts do question the direct effect doctrine, the result will generally be that Community-based rights will be applied differently in the various Member States. Of course these kinds of clear-cut examples of European disobedience are rare. But then again examples can be found in various national legal orders where national courts have applied the doctrine in a more restricted manner than required by the ECJ.

A judgment of a Dutch Court of Appeal in the so-called *Waterpakt* case comes close to such outright disobedience.[5] In that case the Court of Appeal refused to apply a directly effective provision of the Nitrate Directive[6] by referring to a pending infringement procedure before the ECJ. In order to avoid divergent rulings the Court of Appeal decided to stay the procedure and wait for the judgment of the ECJ. In our view this is incompatible with the independent nature of the doctrine. As early as in *Van Gend en Loos* the ECJ ruled that the existence of infringement procedures does not mean that individuals cannot plead the infringement of Treaty obligations by public authorities before a national court.[7]

---

[3] Case 106/77 *Simmenthal* [1978] ECR 629 (para. 21).

[4] Van Gerven (2000) at p. 526. See also the conclusion of AG Jacobs in Case C-150/99 *Stockholm Lindöpark* [2001] ECR I-493, where he states that although it is in principle for the national courts to determine whether the conditions for liability are met, the question of the grant of rights to individuals is more properly a matter for the ECJ (para. 52).

[5] Hof (Court of Appeal) The Hague (2.8.2001), *Waterpakt*, published in *M&R* 2001, no. 95, with case note by J. Jans and M. de Jong.

[6] Council Directive 91/676/EEC, OJ 1991, L 375/1.

[7] Case 26/62 *Van Gend en Loos* [1963] ECR 1. See also Case 28/67 *Mölkerei-Zentrale* [1968] ECR 585, where the ECJ ruled that proceedings brought by an individual are intended to protect individual rights in a given case. Infringement proceedings are intended to ensure uniform application of Community law. They 'have different objects, aims and effects, and a parallel may not be drawn between them'.

We would also like to suggest that the French reluctance[8] to accept the doctrine in judicial review of *individual* decisions of public authorities seems to be at odds with the requirements laid down in the case law of the ECJ. Here we are referring to the French, so-called *Cohn-Bendit*[9] case law, according to which directives may not be invoked by individuals before French courts in support of an action against an *individual* administrative act:

'les directives ne sauraient être invoquées par les ressortissants de ces Etats à l'appui d'un recours dirigé contre un acte administratif individuel'.

With the observation of the *Conseil d'Etat* in the same case that 'à défaut de toute contestation sur la légalité des mesures réglementaires prises par le gouvernement français pour se conformer aux directives arrêtées par le Conseil des communautés européennes', it has acknowledged that it is permitted to challenge the validity of the underlying implementing legislation. This second element of the *Cohn-Bendit* judgment, 'an escape route',[10] can be regarded as an application of the ECJ's *Kraaijeveld* judgment before it even existed.[11] This escape route has been used and developed by the *Conseil d'Etat* for a more Community law friendly approach in subsequent cases.[12] However one major problem is still that in cases where no implementing national legislation exists, the escape route is more or less non-existent.

In our view, the French reluctance is only acceptable if, in all individual cases where there is objectively speaking a conflict between an individual decision and directly effective provisions of a directive, the French administrative law courts come to the conclusion that the individual decision is either in violation of the implementing national legislation (and will therefore be annulled) or the implementing legislation is in conflict with the directive and should be set aside (and as a result, the individual decision will also be annulled). It is however unacceptable if, where there is a conflict between an individual decision and a directly effective provision of a directive, the French approach results in the individual decision being upheld.[13]

While there seems to be a reluctance in France to accept direct effect as a means to review *individual* decisions, but rather a preference to review the legal-

---

[8]   To be more precise: the reluctance of the French *Conseil d'Etat*. The French *Cour de Cassation* has never had any problems with the doctrine of direct effect; see Plötner (1998), p. 45.

[9]   Conseil D'Etat (22.12.1978), *Cohn-Bendit*, Rec. p. 524. English translation in [1980] 1 CMLR 543.

[10]   Words of Plötner (1998), p. 49.

[11]   Case C-72/95 *Kraaijeveld* [1996] ECR I-5403, see also our remarks in the following paragraph.

[12]   See on these developments Plötner (1998), p. 49-50.

[13]   In the terminology of Van Gerven (2000): this would either affect the content of a Community right or one could even say that French public law does not provide an *adequate* remedy.

ity of the national legislation, the reverse appears to be true in Spain. In Spain, a set of cases are reported where lower courts rejected reliance on unimplemented directives on the ground that they can *only* apply directly effective provisions in the *absence* of national implementing measures, and that they lack competence to review the legality of national implementing law.[14] In the authors' opinion this case law is in outright conflict with the Court's judgment in *Kraaijeveld*. In that case the Court ruled that:

> '[I]n particular, where the Community authorities have, by directive, imposed on Member States the obligation to pursue a particular course of conduct, the useful effect of such an act would be weakened if individuals were prevented from relying on it before their national courts, and if the latter were prevented from taking it into consideration as an element of Community law in order to rule whether the national legislature, in exercising the choice open to it as to the form and methods for implementation, has kept within the limits of its discretion set out in the directive'.[15]

This statement of the ECJ makes it perfectly clear that there is a duty for national courts to review the legality of national implementing legislation. It should however be noted that in later judgments the Spanish Constitutional Court has accepted that national courts have to set aside national legislation which is in contravention of Community law directives.[16]

To some extent elements of both the French and Spanish approaches can be found in the way administrative law courts apply the doctrine in the Netherlands. Sometimes judicial review focuses on the legality of individual decisions in the light of directly effective provisions of EC law; in other instances the Dutch courts have a strong preference for reviewing the legality of the underlying legislation.[17] However neither method is excluded in principle and there seem to be no fundamental reasons for choosing one approach rather than the other.

Neither the French reluctance to review *individual* decisions of administrative authorities in contravention of directly effective provisions of EC law, nor

---

[14] By Nogueres & Barbero (1993), p. 1148 and 1149, in referral to Tribunal Supremo (30.11.1991) Rep. 5371, reproduced in 83 *Noticias C.E.E.* 1991, p. 121-124.

[15] *Kraaijeveld*, para. 56.

[16] Díetz-Hochleitner (1998), p. 197, referring to Tribunal Constitucional 28/1991 (14.2.1991) and 64/1991 (22.1.1991), *BOE* of 15.3.1991 and 24.4.1991, where the Constitutional Court declined its constitutional function with regard to conflicts between national law and Community law. See also Nogueres & Barbero (1993), who at p. 1149 make reference to the fact that in spite of the pronouncement of the Constitutional Court, the Supreme Court (5.6.1991) reiterated its traditional doctrine as to its lack of competence to oversee the compatibility of national law with Community directives.

[17] See on this more extensively Jans & de Jong (2002).

the Spanish reluctance to review the legality of national implementing *legislation*, are justified by the case law of the ECJ. This is unacceptable if it means that rights of individuals are denied as a result. It should be stressed that application of the doctrine of direct effect and the corresponding obligation for national courts to ignore conflicting legislative and administrative acts must be considered essential to the enforcement of Community law. This implies that national courts are bound to apply directly effective provisions of a directive, both in the absence of implementing national legislation, if necessary by annulling a conflicting administrative decision, and where there is national implementing legislation, by reviewing its legality. In addition, a national court may not on its own authority make the application of the direct effect doctrine depend upon the completion and result of an infringement procedure, as a Dutch Court of Appeal did in *Waterpakt*.

2.2 Formulating the conditions; the House of Lords in the *Three Rivers* case

On the face of it, the case law of the ECJ on the conditions for provisions of directives to be directly effective seems simple and straightforward. Provisions must be 'unconditional and sufficiently precise' before they can be relied upon in a national court.[18]

However, it is clear from the *Three Rivers* judgment of the House of Lords that things are not always that straightforward.[19] The case concerned a legal action started by more than 6000 depositors of the BCCI against the Governor and the Bank of England. The BCCI was a Luxembourg bank which also carried out its business in the UK. The Bank collapsed in the early 1990s. The principal cause was fraud on a vast scale perpetrated at a senior level. One cause of action was alleged breaches of Community law, in particular the First Banking Directive.[20]

According to the House of Lords, Community law is capable of conferring upon individuals the right to claim damages from a national authority by two distinct routes. The first one was described as the right to claim damages against the State or an emanation of the State (like the Bank of England) for the non-implementation or misimplementation of Community law, which can be based

---

[18] Cf. *Becker* (as cited).

[19] House of Lords (18.5.2000), *Three Rivers District Council and Others* v. *Governor and Company of the Bank of England*, [2000] 2 WLR 1220.

[20] Council Directive 77/780/EEC, OJ 1977, L 322/30 (by now replaced by Directive 2000/12/EC of the European Parliament and the Council, OJ 2000, L 126/1). We will not discuss the other cause of action 'tort of misfeasance in public office'. See on this Andenas (2000) in his case note on the *Three Rivers* case.

upon the principle of direct effect ('*Becker*'-type liability).[21] The second route is based upon the principle of State liability ('*Francovich*'-type liability).[22] However, according to the House of Lords, the conditions which must be satisfied in order to establish a right of damages 'are so closely analogous that they can be taken to be [...] the same.' Subsequently the House of Lords formulated the critical questions in this *BCCI* case as follows: whether 'the Directive of 1977 entails the grant of rights to individual depositors and potential depositors and whether the content of those rights is identifiable on the basis of the provisions of the Directive'.

Its conclusion was that it was not possible to discover provisions which entail the granting of rights to individuals, as the granting of rights to individuals was not necessary to achieve the results which were intended to be achieved by the Directive (harmonization). In short, according to the House of Lords, the relevant provision did not create rights for individuals and, as a consequence, the depositors of BCCI could neither rely on the doctrine of direct effect nor on the principle of State liability.

With all respect, we have some problems with the House of Lords' approach.[23]

First of all, we are not aware of any case law of the ECJ stating that there are indeed two routes (State liability and direct effect) by which damages can be claimed. It was our belief that the route of State liability was 'invented' by the ECJ to fill the gaps left by the doctrine of direct effect in this respect. In the case of non-implementation and misimplementation and other conflicts with national law, reliance on directly effective provisions of EC law normally results in application of the necessary Community law provisions. The purpose of direct effect is to ensure that provisions of Community law prevail over national provisions. On the other hand, the right to reparation is a necessary corollary of the direct effect of the Community provision whose breach caused the damage sustained.

Nor are we aware of any case law of the ECJ which states that the conditions for 'direct effect' ('unconditional and sufficiently precise') are more or less the same as those for State liability (individual rights, sufficiently serious breach,

---

[21] In reference to *Becker* (as cited). The House of Lords noted that in order for there to be liability under this principle the rights said to have been conferred by the Directive must be 'unconditional and sufficiently precise'.

[22] In reference to Joined Cases C-6/90 and 9/90 *Francovich* [1991] ECR I-5357. For this the House of Lords quoted the well known *Dillenkofer* judgment: 'the Directive entails the grant of rights to individuals, the content of those rights is identifiable on the basis of the provisions of the Directive and a causal link exists between the breach of the state's obligation and the loss and damage suffered by the injured parties'; Joined Cases C-178/94, 179/94 and 188-190/94 *Dillenkofer* [1996] ECR I-4845, para. 22.

[23] And we are not alone in our criticism. Cf. Wissink (2002) and Andenas (2000).

causal link, damages). Of course the Court made it clear in *Brasserie* that direct effect implies that these provisions confer rights on individuals upon which they are entitled to rely directly before the national courts and that breach of such provisions may give rise to reparation.[24]

Arguably, what the House of Lords should have done was first to assess whether or not the relevant provisions of the First Banking Directive were directly effective (by considering whether they were unconditional and sufficiently precise in either the *'Becker'* or *'Kraaijeveld'* way) and, if this was the case, come to the conclusion that individual rights were at stake which might give rise to *Francovich*-style liability. The Lords' approach should however be reserved for provisions of directives which do not have direct effect. In that case a detailed analysis of the substantive content becomes relevant. After all, a provision of Community law may lack direct effect and still give rise to rights of individuals.[25] On this, we would also like to refer to the dissenting opinion of Lord Justice Auld in the Court of Appeal. He came to the conclusion, in our opinion rightly so, that the First Banking Directive:

'imposed clearly defined obligations on Member States and on their regulatory bodies and, in doing so, gave rise to corresponding Community law rights on individuals in the position of the plaintiffs to enforce those obligations, if necessary by an action for damages'.[26]

What the House of Lords did however was something completely different: it did not discuss the direct effect of the Banking Directive, but analysed the provisions of the Banking Directive from a very - in our opinion, too - narrow viewpoint concerning 'individual rights'. The real question was not whether the Directive's primary objective is to provide guarantees and safeguards to individual or groups of savers and other creditors of the BCCI and other banking institutions, but whether public authorities failed to meet their directly effective obligations under the Directive and whether individuals suffered damage as a result.

In this respect the French case law after *Parodi*[27] has been referred to,[28] where the French *Cour de Cassation*, among other French courts, did provide for protection of the depositors under the First Banking Directive. By contrast, the

---

[24] Joined Cases C-46/93 and C-48/93 *Brasserie du Pêcheur* [1996] ECR I-1029, para. 23 (with regard to the Treaty provisions on free movement of goods).

[25] See for example Joined Cases C-6/90 and 9/90 *Francovich* [1991] ECR I-5357.

[26] Court of Appeal (4.12.1998) *Three Rivers District Council and Others v. Governor and Company of the Bank of England*, [2000] 3 CMLR 1, 152.

[27] Case C-222/95 *Parodi* [1997] ECR I-3899.

[28] By Andenas (2000), p. 401.

tendency in Germany is to undertake banking supervision in the public interest only, and not to protect individual interests of bank creditors.[29] In view of these different approaches, the House of Lords should at least have referred the matter to the ECJ as to whether the provisions in question have direct effect, and/or whether a violation gives rise to State liability. Considering the same differences, it is hard to see how the Lords could have regarded the issue as an *'acte clair'*.[30] After all according to the *Cilfit* doctrine, it is not sufficient that the matter is clear to the Lords, but they must be convinced that the correct application of Community law is equally obvious to the courts of other Member States and the ECJ.[31]

Against this background, we would like to emphasize that national courts do not normally have any discretion about whether or not to accept the direct effect of a provision of Community law; it either does have direct effect or it does not.[32] Furthermore we would like to suggest that national courts should *especially* exercise extreme caution when they *deny* the direct effect of provisions of Community law. National courts need to be fully aware of this. If there is an 'arguable'[33] case for accepting the direct effect of a given provision of Community law, national courts should not deny the direct effect without referring the case to the ECJ.[34]

2.3 Horizontal direct effect or not; Spanish and Italian approaches

In well established case-law, the ECJ has rejected horizontal direct effect of directives, that is to say, the possibility of directly invoking a directive against an individual and imposing an obligation upon an individual.[35] According to the Court, a directive may not in itself impose obligations on an individual and a provision of a directive may not be relied upon as such against an individual. In this respect, national courts generally reject reliance on directly effective provisions of directives in litigation between private parties.[36]

---

[29] Andenas (2000), p. 400-403, where he criticizes the fact that the House of Lords did not make any reference to developments in French and German case law.

[30] In the same vein Wissink (2002).

[31] Case 283/81 *Cilfit* [1982] ECR 3415 (para. 16).

[32] See however paragraph 4 below, where we discuss to what extent it is possible that provisions of Community law have direct effect according to national (constitutional) law where they do not meet the standard EC law conditions for direct effect.

[33] For instance, where national courts in other jurisdictions have accepted that a given provision of Community law is directly effective.

[34] By way of an extended analogy of the ECJ's ruling in Case 314/85 *Foto-Frost* [1987] ECR 4199.

[35] Cf. Case C-91/92 *Faccini Dori* [1994] ECR I-3325 and Case C-192/94 *El Corte Inglès* [1996] ECR I-1281.

[36] See quotations made in several of the national reports in: *Les Directives Communautaires: effets, efficacité, justiciabilité*, Stockholm XVIII FIDE-congress 1998 (I).

For example the House of Lords has rejected horizontal direct effect because a directive has no effect upon the private rights of parties.[37]

There are but few exceptions in national case law, where the direct application of directives in private litigation was accepted. For instance in Spain, the *Tribunal Supremo* has held on a few occasions that the Directive relating to unfair terms in consumer contracts[38] may produce horizontal direct effect.[39] And Italian courts have also sometimes acknowledged the direct effect of directives in relationships between individuals.[40] In this respect a judgment of the Italian *Corte di Cassazione* is mentioned, where it upheld a decision which recognized horizontal direct effect by stating that although the ECJ denies the horizontal direct effect of Directives, 'this does not rule out that the national court may and shall judge as if the conflicting national law did not exist'.[41]

Although it could be said that the effective application of Community law and the protection of at least one party is increased by the 'national' acknowledgement of horizontal direct effect, it is debatable whether this divergent application of Community law is acceptable. Because imposing an obligation upon an individual by way of direct effect may be unacceptable from a European law point of view, it is not inconceivable that national courts would be obliged, on the basis of Article 10 EC, to exclude the application of the directly effective provision of a directive between individuals, even where such an application is in accordance with national constitutional law. We will come back to this issue later in paragraph 4 of this contribution. Yet in private litigation national courts, following the case law of the ECJ, generally consider the appropriate enforcement mechanism to be the duty to interpret national legislation in light of the Directive and reserve the application of directly effective provisions for emanations of the State.[42]

---

[37] E.g. House of Lords *Duke* v. *Gec Reliance* (11.2.1988) [1988] 1 CMLR 719 and House of Lords *Regina* v. *Secretary of State for Employment ex parte Seymour Smith* [1997] 2 CMLR 904.

[38] Council Directive 93/13/EEC, OJ 1993, L 95/29.

[39] Díetz-Hochleitner (1998), p. 199, in reference to Tribunal Supremo (8.11.1996), RJA 1996/7954, Tribunal Supremo (30.11.1996), RJA 1996/8457 and Tribunal Supremo (5.7.1997), RJA 1997/6152.

[40] See the examples mentioned by Adinolfi (1998), p. 1331.

[41] By Adinolfi (1998), p. 1331 and 1332, in reference to Corte di Cassazione (3.2.1995), No. 1271, *Dir. Lav.* 1995, II, 8. In this respect, Adinolfi also mentions Italian Court of Cassation (27.2.1995) No. 2275, *Riv. dir. internaz* 1995, 448, where the Court corrected its approach.

[42] See for example on 'indirect effect' in UK Courts and the scope of the interpretative obligation in horizontal disputes Craig (1997), in particular at p. 528-535. See also Betlem in this volume's chapter IV.

2.4 Horizontal side-effects of vertical direct effect; examples of national (mainly English, German and Dutch) case law

In spite of the consistent rejection of horizontal direct effect, the ECJ has on several occasions accepted the possibility of reliance on directives between individuals. Where, in a case like *CIA Security*, the Court holds that the relevant obligation may be relied on between individuals and national courts are bound to set aside the national measure because of its incompatibility with the Directive, the directly applied provision will certainly affect the legal position of the individuals concerned.[43] Moreover, the Court has confirmed the direct effect of provisions of a directive in proceedings against the State in situations where the application of these provisions could easily have legal consequences for third parties.[44] Without entering the discussion on this complicated issue, it seems that the Court is willing to accept the direct effect of directives, where the application of the directive, although clearly affecting the legal relationship of individuals, does not *in itself* amount to imposing an obligation on an individual.[45] That is to say, Community law provisions which impose obligations on the Member States can be directly invoked both in proceedings against the State and in proceedings between individuals to prevent the application of national legislation which is inconsistent with the directive in question. The Court seems to have accepted the possible horizontal side-effects of the application of this type of (disguised vertical)[46] direct effect.

---

[43] Cf. Case C-194/94 *CIA Security* [1996] ECR I-2201, Case C-85/94 *Piageme II* [1995] ECR I-2955, and more recently, Case C-443/98 *Unilever Italia* [2000] ECR I- 7535. See also the observation of Lord Hoffman in *Regina* v. *Secretary of State for Employment ex parte Seymour-Smith*, [1997] 2 CMLR 904, p. 909, where he rejected the submission that *CIA Security* could be regarded as a departure from the rejection of horizontal direct effect because this case should be regarded as plainly distinguishable: 'there is not hint in the judgment of the Court that it intended to depart from its jurisprudence [...] the case was one in which, unusually, the issue in litigation between private parties was whether, as a matter of public law, the manufacturer was doing something unlawful. If the regulation alleged to have been infringed could not be enforced against him by the State, it could not be right for the defendant to say that his alarm system did not comply with the law'.

[44] Cf. Case 103/88 *Fratelli Costanzo* [1989] ECR 1839, *Kraaijeveld* (as cited) and Case C-435/97 *World Wildlife Fund (WWF)* [1999] ECR I-5613. However, in Case C-221/88 *Busseni* [1990] ECR I-495 the Court rejected the possibility of invoking a provision of a directive against the State because this would amount to imposing an obligation on the private parties involved. On the issue how this approach can be reconciled with *Fratelli Costanzo*, see Jans e.a. (1999), p. 76 and 77.

[45] Cf. Case C-443/98 *Unilever Italia* [2000] ECR I- 7535. See also Gilliams (2000), Dougan (2000) and Betlem in this volume's chapter IV (paragraph 2.4) as to the interpretation of this case law.

[46] Term used by Dougan (2000).

Application of this kind of enforcement can be found in relation to the public procurement directives. For example in Sweden, a judgment of the Supreme Administrative Court has been reported where the Court, referring to Directive 92/13,[47] allowed a private litigant to contest the rights of another individual, who had already been granted a public procurement contract under Swedish law.[48]

Other interesting observations can be made in this respect by examining national case law on the environmental impact assessment directive (EIA Directive) and its application in so-called trilateral legal relations.[49] National case law involving the EIA obligation shows that there are differences in judging the acceptability of horizontal side-effects of the (vertical) direct effect of directives.

The *Huddleston* case provides a clear example where horizontal side-effects were accepted.[50] In this English case judicial review was sought by Huddleston. The Court of Appeal had to ascertain what to do about a statutory planning regime which, in breach of a directive, enabled a company, in this case Sherburn, to revive a mining permission without providing an EIA. In answer to the question whether the application of the direct effect of the Directive would be entering the forbidden territory of horizontal direct effect, Lord Justice Sedley concluded that although Sherburn would be subjected to more onerous conditions for the grant of the permission, to give the directive direct effect would not 'impose an obligation in the objectionable sense - that is to say, to interpose a new obligation in the relations between individuals or retrospectively to criminalise the activity of one of them. It is to prevent the State, when asked by a citizen to give effect to the unambiguous requirements of a directive, from taking refuge in its own neglect to transpose them into national law'.

The Dutch Council of State adopted the same approach where it allowed an interested party to invoke the EIA Directive, which resulted in annulment of an authorization granted to a company (Aramide) because no EIA had been carried out.[51] However a Belgian case has been reported where the Council of State rejected direct effect in a similar situation to *Huddleston* in view of the horizontal effect. There, the Belgian Council of State refused to apply the same

---

[47] Council Directive 92/13/EEC (public procurement), OJ 1992, L 76/14.

[48] By Eliasson, Abrahamsson & Mattsson (1998), p. 397 (Swedish Supreme Administrative Court, 26.6.1996, Case RÅ 1996, Ref. 50). This case seems to be a straightforward application of the *Fratelli Costanzo* doctrine. Cf. also Irish High Court (17.6.1997) *SIAC Construction* v. *Mayo Country Council*, referred to by Travers (1998), p. 188.

[49] Council Directive 85/337/EEC, OJ 1985, L 175/40, amended by Council Directive 97/11/EC, OJ 1997, L 73/5.

[50] Court of Appeal (8.3.2000) *Regina* v. *Durham Country Council and others ex parte Rodney Huddleston*, [2000] 2 CMLR 313.

[51] Dutch Council of State (19.12.1991), *Aramide*, AB 1992/122.

directive in a case where the claimants contested a building permit granted without an environmental assessment because:

> 'la jurisprudence citée par les requérants vise le cas où un citoyen pourrait se prévaloir d'une obligation mise à charge de l'Etat par une directive, que l'exception à la règle générale qui a ainsi été admise par la Cour de justice ne saurait être étendue au cas où, comme en l'espèce une obligation est mise à charge d'un citoyen'.[52]

A decision of the German *Bundesverwaltungsgericht* seems to take a similar view as the Belgian Court. In this case the *Bundesverwaltungsgericht* recognized that the EIA Directive could be invoked in order to contest a planning decision for a government-built highway.[53] The *Bundesverwaltungsgericht* observed:

> 'Ob der einzelne aus diesen Bestimmungen subjektive Rechte für sich herleiten kann, spielt in diesen Zusammenhang keine Rolle. Die Möglichkeit des gemein-schaftsbürgers, sich auf hinreichend genaue und unbedingte Richtlinienvorschriften zu berufen, ist nicht eine Voraussetzung, sondern lediglich eine Folge der unmittel-bare Wirkung. Sie ist nicht geeignet, Aufschluß darüber zu geben, ob der Richtlinien-inhalt im säumigen Mitgliedstaat objektivrechtlich gilt. Ebenfalls keine Rolle spielt hier, daß eine unmittelbare Anwendung einer nicht umgesetzten Richtlinie zu Lasten Privater nicht in Betracht kommt; denn hier handelt es sich um ein Vorgaben, dessen Träger der Staat ist.'

This case concerned an application for planning permission by a public author-ity. The final sentence of the paragraph quoted, seems to imply that if it were a private person who had applied for planning permission, the *Bundesverwaltungs-gericht* would not have accepted the horizontal consequences. In this respect it should also be noted that there is a lively debate concerning the pros and cons of these kinds of horizontal effects in German doctrine.[54]

In the authors' opinion this Belgian and German case law fails to acknowl-edge the Court's case law. After all, in *Kraaijeveld* and *WWF* the Court seems to have accepted these kinds of horizontal effects.[55] In our view, having accepted these horizontal side-effects the ECJ has created a duty for the national courts to apply the vertically directly effective provision in question. However, as it may be difficult for national courts to distinguish acceptable horizontal side-effects from the unacceptable horizontal direct effect of directives, national courts should refer questionable cases to the ECJ. Because the acceptability of these side-effects

---

[52] Conseil D'Etat (21.9.1993), *Reintjes*, Recueil des arrêts No. 44.142.

[53] Bundesverwaltungsgericht 100, 238 (25.1.1996), *DVBl.* 1996, p. 677, *NJW* 1997, p. 144

[54] Cf. Ruffert (1996), p. 76-77 in particular.

[55] *Kraaijeveld* and *WWF* (as cited). See also *Unilever Italia* (as cited).

goes to the heart of the doctrine of direct effect, it is for the Court to rule on the issue and it should not be left to the national courts. To avoid divergence the general approach for national courts should therefore (again) be: if there is a prima facie case for direct effect, direct effect should only be rejected after a reference to the ECJ.

2.5 Conclusions

Are differences with respect to the doctrine of direct effect acceptable? We would like to stress again the rationale of the doctrine, on the one hand to provide effective legal protection and, on the other, to ensure 'uniform' application of Community law. The case law of the ECJ shows that national law which affects the doctrine of direct effect 'as such' is incompatible with Community law and cannot be accepted.

In view of that, it is our opinion that there should be no national discretion in what we would like to call the 'standard setting' of the direct effect doctrine as a doctrine of EC law. By this we mean that all issues concerning questions like: what are the conditions to be applied for assessing direct effect, what are the consequences in terms of supremacy of directly effective provisions, and what is the relationship between direct effect and concepts like indirect effect and State liability and the enforcement procedure under Article 226 EC etc., should be decided by the ECJ. In other words, the ECJ should have the monopoly in terms of *shaping the contours* of the doctrine as such; it is the ECJ that rules exclusively on the question whether and, if so, under what circumstances, a Community law provision does or does not have direct effect.

In this respect, it should be noted that the Dutch refusal to apply the direct effect doctrine in anticipation of the decision of the ECJ in the enforcement procedure, where no support for this approach can be found in the case law of the ECJ, can not be accepted. And by persevering in its rejection of the possibility of relying on directives against individual administrative acts in the absence of implementing measures, the *Conseil d'Etat* also goes against the EC standard for the application of directly effective provisions of Community law. Furthermore, the judgment of the House of Lords in the *Three Rivers* case, where it decided - perhaps implicitly - that the condition of 'individual rights' must be applied in liability and direct effect cases alike, and no reference was made to the ECJ, seems to fail to acknowledge national differences (by courts and in literature).

In view of the maxim *in dubio, pro direct effect* national courts should be very cautious about denying the direct effect of a given provision of Community law and, in cases of real doubt, should refer the case to the ECJ. Diverging national judgments, resulting from different national approaches in respect of the key elements of the doctrine, are not acceptable and should be avoided as far as possible.

3 National case law and the 'modalities' of applying the doctrine of direct effect; the Berkeley case

The rulings of the Court in cases like *Rewe/Comet* make clear that some national differences are to be considered inherent in Community law.[56] In the absence of specific Community rules it is for the Member States to determine the competent courts and applicable procedural rules for legal proceedings relevant to the enforcement of Community law. The two well known basic conditions of the so-called *Rewe*-test are that these rules may not be less favourable than those relating to similar 'domestic' remedies (principle of non-discrimination) and that these rules may not make the exercise of Community rights virtually impossible or excessively difficult (principle of effectiveness).[57] It must be acknowledged that the case law of the ECJ in *Rewe/Comet* implies the legitimacy of national differences concerning the modalities of applying the direct effect doctrine.

The judgment of the ECJ in *Upjohn* suggests that national differences in the *intensity* of, and the *methods* used in, judicial review must also be accepted, and are only subject to a *Rewe*-test.[58] So it might (or might not, for that matter) be correct to state that the 'Wednesbury unreasonableness' test applied in English judicial review leaves more latitude to public authorities than the legitimacy tests normally applied by German *Verwaltungsgerichte* and that, even though the various approaches of Dutch administrative law courts differ from those employed by both the English and the German courts, these differences are acceptable.

We would like to illustrate these national differences with a judgment of the House of Lords in the *Berkeley* case.[59] This case involved the granting of a planning decision by the Secretary of State for the Environment for a development of the Fulham Football Club. Lady Berkeley, who lives near the site, and who, according to the written judgment 'has taken a course on Ecology and was concerned about the effect of the development on the diversity of species in the Thames' took legal action. She argued, among other things, that the grant of planning permission should be quashed on the ground that it was *ultra vires* because no Environmental Impact Assessment (EIA) had been undertaken as required by the relevant directive.

---

[56] Case 33/76 *Rewe* [1976] ECR 1989; Case 45/76 *Comet* [1976] ECR 2043 and Case 265/78 *Ferwerda* [1980] ECR 716.

[57] Cf. Prechal (2001).

[58] Case C-120/97 *Upjohn* [1999] ECR I-223.

[59] House of Lords (6.7.2000) *Berkeley v. Secretary of State for the Environment and Others, Journal of Environmental Law* 2001, p. 89-105, case law analysis by Upton.

In the Court of Appeal the judge had stated that even if an EIA was required, he would as a matter of *discretion* refuse to quash the permission. The reason was that in his opinion the absence of the EIA 'had no effect on the outcome of the inquiry and could not possibly have done so'. UK planning law allowed the judge to exercise his discretion in this way. However, the House of Lords disagreed with the approach taken by the Court of Appeal. Although UK planning law, in providing that the Court 'may' quash an *ultra vires* planning decision, clearly confers a discretion upon the Court, the House of Lords doubted:

'*whether, consistently with its obligations under European law, the Court may exercise that discretion to uphold a planning permission which has been granted contrary to the provisions of the Directive. To do so would seem to conflict with the duty of the Court under Article 10 (ex Art. 5) of the EC Treaty to ensure fulfilment of the United Kingdom's obligations under the Treaty*'.

In other jurisdictions, in Germany and the Netherlands for instance, we find that judges have the same kind of discretion.[60] In Germany the courts generally will exercise their discretion; Dutch courts will not. So once again: national, even intra-national, divergences. Acceptable or not?

It is clear that the problems in this case are of a different order compared to those in the *Three Rivers* case. They are not about direct effect 'as such', but rather concern the question what role national *procedural* rules play in the case of conflicts between national law and EC measures with directly effective provisions: i.e. the modalities of applying the doctrine of direct effect.[61]

The House of Lords' approach in the *Berkeley* case, where 'discretion' was discussed in the context of Article 10 EC, is in the authors opinion a correct one. We would like to advocate the same approach in respect of matters such as national rules on court fees, consequences of procedural errors, statutory limitations, compulsory representation, *locus standi*, etc. Even though national case law shows that these rules have a considerable effect on the outcome of national procedures, national discretion should be respected as long as these rules do not affect the effectiveness of legal protection.

Of course the Community legislator can intervene by enacting relevant directives. However, we would not be in favour of too general an approach by the Council. A directive on, for instance, *locus standi* for non-governmental organizations might make perfect sense in the areas of consumer and environmental law; but in other areas (e.g. tax and social security law) it might not. Only the 'rough edges' of national procedural law should be removed by Community harmonization and a case-by-case approach is to be preferred.

---

[60] See on this more extensively Jans & De Jong (2002).

[61] Or, in the terminology of Van Gerven (2000): this is not a matter of 'rights' or 'remedies' but of 'procedures'.

Thus, with regard to the modalities of applying the doctrine of direct effect, as a general rule we would suggest to respect national discretion. If in a given situation the results are unsatisfactorily, it is up to the Council to harmonize that area. In exceptional circumstances the Court can intervene on the basis of the second *Rewe* condition of effectiveness, as it has done in cases like *Emmott*[62] and (though not explicitly) *Océano*.[63] In recent literature some scholars have tried to explain the tension between the need for uniformity on the one hand and national discretion on the other by using the concept of 'proportionality'.[64] Maybe the concept of 'subsidiarity' is more precise in this context: what is good for domestic law should be, in principle, good enough for Community law.[65]

4 Direct effect from the perspective of minimum harmonization

Direct effect as a doctrine of EC law does not allow national standard setting. But how does this relate to the various doctrines of direct effect and/or self-executing provisions of European and international law as a doctrine of *national constitutional* law? We have seen that national courts have on occasion applied directly effective provisions even before the Court had recognized such an effect. It is legitimate to wonder whether national courts are entitled to confer direct effect on a provision of Community law or an EU-framework decision, irrespective of the fact that the relevant provision does not have direct effect from a Community law point of view.

In our opinion these questions are primarily, if not exclusively, governed by national (constitutional) law. In this respect, the case law of the ECJ on the conditions for direct effect can be regarded as a form of minimum harmonization.

Support for this idea can be found in the *Brasserie* case, where the Court considered direct effect to be only a 'minimum guarantee' (and State liability its 'necessary corollary').[66] Furthermore, as regards the conditions governing State liability, it stated that a Member State may incur liability under less strict conditions on the basis of national law.[67] Even stronger support can be found in the *Dior* case, where the Court ruled that Community law does not prohibit

---

[62] Case C-208/90 *Emmott* [1991] ECR I-4269.

[63] Joined Cases C-240-244/98 *Océano* [2000] ECR I-4941.

[64] Van Gerven (2000), p. 533; Prechal (2001), p. 39-58 and Biondi (1999).

[65] See also the conclusion of A.G. Jacobs in Joined Cases C-430/93 and 431/93 *Van Schijndel* [1995] ECR I-4705.

[66] *Brasserie du Pêcheur*, para. 20.

[67] *Brasserie du Pêcheur*, para. 66.

the legal order of a Member State according to individuals the right to rely directly on Article 50(6) of TRIPs or oblige the courts to apply that rule of their own motion even if this provision is not, by virtue of Community law, directly effective.[68]

In this respect, we would also like to refer to the Court's judgment in the *Sievers* and *Schrage* cases.[69] In these cases a German court was seeking to ascertain whether the limitation in time of the possibility of relying on the direct effect of Article 141 EC[70] precludes national provisions of less restrictive character. The ECJ ruled that the limitation of the possibility of relying on the direct effect of Article 141 EC was not intended in any way to deprive the workers concerned of the opportunity of relying on national provisions laying down a principle of equal treatment. The Court went on to add that national provisions having the effect of ensuring application of the principle of equal pay for male and female workers contribute to the implementation of Article 141 EC, in compliance with the obligation which is incumbent on the Member States. As a result it concluded:

'In such circumstances, the principle of legal certainty inherent in the Community legal order, which may move the Court, exceptionally, to limit the possibility of relying on a provision which it has interpreted, does not fall to be applied and does not preclude the application of national provisions which ensure a result which conforms with Community law'.

All the cases cited above seem to suggest, although without explicitly dealing with the issue, that more 'liberal' national approaches with respect to direct effect are allowed. More 'liberal' must be interpreted in the sense of the capability of producing 'more legal protection' and a 'more effective application of Community law'. So Community law does not preclude, as a matter of principle, judgments at the national level accepting the direct effect of directives by virtue of national law.

The necessary consequence of this is also that national courts first have to assess whether there is a Community law based right for the individual to rely on Community law or to claim damages. If the European conditions for a successful claim are not met, national courts should subsequently consider whether the claim can be based on national law. For instance: in cases of State liability there is no reason for Dutch courts not to discuss State liability on the basis of Dutch

---

[68] Joined Cases C-300/98 and C-392/98 *Dior* [2000] ECR I-11307.

[69] Joined Cases C-270/97 and C-271/97 *Sievers* and *Schrage* [2000] ECR I-929.

[70] As a result of the *Defrenne II* and *Barber* case law where the Court ruled that overriding considerations of legal certainty required it to limit, to a certain extent, the retroactive effect of the relevant Treaty provision; Case 43/75 *Defrenne II* [1976] ECR 455 and Case C-262/88 *Barber* [1990] ECR I-1889.

public law if the more stringent *Francovich/Dillenkofer* test has failed. In other words, national courts must be aware of the fact that national law can play a role above the minimum level of ECJ case law standards.

A possible area of application of the notion of minimum harmonization outside the First Pillar of Community law might well be in the context of the Third Pillar's Framework Decisions (Art. 34 EU Treaty). The fact that Article 34 states that they shall not entail direct effect does not imply that Member States could not allow 'their' individuals to rely on Framework Decisions before national courts, if this is allowed under their national (constitutional) law. The 'they shall not entail direct effect' of Article 34 EU cannot be taken to have harmonized national constitutional law.

The only real problem concerns cases where national courts would accept 'horizontal direct effect' (individual *v.* individual) or 'inverse vertical direct effect' (State *v.* individual) of directives or would apply the doctrine of indirect effect in a manner which would affect legal certainty of private individuals. With respect to 'inverse vertical direct effect' it is necessary to appreciate that the ECJ's case-law seeks to prevent a Member State from taking advantage of its own failure to comply with Community law. Accepting 'inverse vertical direct effect' by virtue of national law would circumvent this and, in the authors' view, is unacceptable.[71]

As far as 'horizontal direct effect' and 'indirect effect' are concerned, the issue becomes more complex. It is true that a directive may not by itself create obligations for individuals and a provision of a directive may therefore not be relied upon as such against an individual. By accepting 'horizontal effect' on the basis of national law, the directive 'does not however create the obligations 'by itself'. The source of the obligations is not the directive, but national law.

On the other hand, legal certainty remains a problem. The judgment in *Kolpinghuis* illustrates how the options of national courts can be influenced by general principles of Community law.[72] In this, criminal, case the ECJ found, in answer to the question how far the national court *may* or must take account of a Directive as an aid to the interpretation of national law, that in light of general principles of law a directive cannot on itself have the effect of determining or aggravating the liability in criminal law of persons who act in contravention of the provisions of that directive. In this respect, it considered the question whether or not the period prescribed for implementation has expired to be of no relevance to '*the limits which Community law might impose* on the obligation or power of the national court to interpret the rules of its national law in light

---

[71] See on inverse vertical (in)direct effect more extensively Betlem in this volume's chapter IV, paragraph 2.5.

[72] Case 80/86 *Kolpinghuis* [1987] ECR 3969.

of the Directive'.[73] In brief, general principles of law may limit the powers of national courts to give effect to Community law. Yet, future case law of the ECJ will have to show more clearly to what extent these principles, in particular the principle of legal certainty, affect more 'liberal' national approaches with respect to (in)direct effect (in criminal as well as civil and administrative context).

5 Conclusions

Our survey of the case law has shown considerable differences in the way national courts apply the doctrine of direct effect. What are the main reasons for this? First we would submit that the ECJ has thus far been unable to settle some major unanswered doctrinal questions (e.g. individual rights as a precondition for direct effect; what are the exact boundaries between unacceptable horizontal and permitted vertical direct effect). In the absence of guidance from the ECJ and in the light of the reluctance of many national courts to apply the *Cilfit* criteria for preliminary rulings, it is not surprising to find national divergences here.

The second reason however is that differences in the way national courts apply the doctrine are inherent in the Community legal system as such. There never has been, nor will there ever be a uniform system of legal protection within the Member States of the EU. The question should not therefore be: are national differences acceptable, but rather: what kind of differences are acceptable and what are not?

Unacceptable differences are those which concern the shaping of the doctrine as such (conditions, scope, content). The doctrine of direct effect sets a standard with respect to the interpretation of Community law, and thus falls within the competence of the ECJ. However, except for those cases where this would affect legal certainty as a general principle of Community law, more 'direct effect' is allowed on the basis of national (constitutional) law and could therefore remain a source of national differences.

What should be done about national differences? With respect to differences concerning the modalities: nothing at all. We have to learn to live with it. In exceptional cases national courts and the ECJ may intervene on the basis of Article 10 EC. The second *Rewe* condition of 'effectiveness' limits national peculiarities in this respect. At the end of the day it is the ECJ that rules on the ultimate interpretation of the second *Rewe* condition; unacceptable differences will be 'harmonized' if the Court finds these differences incompatible with the requirement of 'effectiveness'.

---

[73] Para. 15 (italics by the authors). See also joined Cases C-74/95 and C-129/95 *Procura della Republica* v. *X* [1996] ECR I-6609 (para. 31).

Furthermore, the Council might want to regulate national procedural rules in a directive. However, we would not favour too general an approach and we would suggest that there is no *general* competence to harmonize this issue.[74] The extent to which national procedural rules affect the effectiveness of the direct effect doctrine will depend very much on the substantive rules at issue. Restrictive national rules on *locus standi* (in particular with regard to third party access) will, for example, have a greater negative impact in areas of consumer and environmental law than in tax or social security law.

To avoid unacceptable differences we submit that national courts should make more use of the preliminary rulings procedure. The statement of the House of Lords in the *Three Rivers* case that it did not find it appropriate to make a reference for a preliminary ruling, because it regarded the issue as clear cut, is not convincing at all. Of course we understand the reluctance many national courts feel about using the preliminary rulings procedure and we appreciate why the *Cilfit* criteria are not always applied in the strict sense of that judgment. But judgments at national level which go to the heart of the direct effect doctrine without guidance by the ECJ should, as far as possible, be avoided. In this respect we would like to stress that national courts do have to take developments in other jurisdictions more seriously (as required by *Cilfit!*). Nowadays judgments can only rarely be found where there is an explicit reference to foreign case law. In our view, if a national court wanted to interpret Community law differently from the interpretation already given in another Member State, it could not be maintained that this provision of Community law could be regarded as an *acte clair*.

Finally, the ECJ should also make up its mind about some key doctrinal issues and give clearer guidance. If it wants to be accepted as a constitutional court it should act like one.

---

[74] Perhaps with the exception of Art. 308 EC; see Jans & de Jong (1999).

CHAPTER VI

Direct Effect in Germany and France

A Constitutional Comparison

prof. dr. Jörg Gerkrath

DIRECT EFFECT

1 Introductory remarks

As can easily be guessed from the title, the purpose of this paper is to scrutinise the doctrine of direct effect from the point of view of German and French constitutional law. The merit for framing the subject goes to Eijsbouts. His suggestion allowed me to work on a topic which turned out to be a very challenging but still insufficiently explored one. Though the general issue of the relationship between national constitutions and European integration, as well as the principle of supremacy, has been studied from the domestic constitutional law perspective, up to now, the principle of direct effect has apparently been neglected to some extent by constitutional lawyers. The three following paragraphs intend to show why the point of view of constitutional law is particularly relevant (1.1), why the comparative analysis seems to be appropriate (1.2) and why the choice of Germany and France is convenient (1.3).

1.1 The relevance of the constitutional law position

The relevance of constitutional law with regard to the principle of direct effect has been abundantly discussed in the *Van Gend en Loos* case itself, especially by the three intervening Governments (Germany, Belgium and the Netherlands[1]) who denied jurisdiction to the ECJ on the ground that the issue of the effect of an international treaty in (Dutch) internal law must be determined, according to well-established international law practice, exclusively by (Dutch) constitutional law. In response, Advocate General Roemer pointed out in his Opinion that:

'it is impossible to clarify the real legal effects of an international agreement on the nationals of a Member State without having regard to the constitutional law of that Member State. But, on the other hand, it is clear that the question does not refer exclusively to problems of constitutional law'.[2]

The reception of the 'direct effect doctrine', as it has been developed by the ECJ since 1963, within the national legal orders is without any doubt one of the most interesting aspects of what may be called today 'European constitutional law'. As this concept, however, may be given at least three different meanings, which all relate to the principle of direct effect, it calls for some clarification. Taken in the first sense, the controversial expression 'European constitutional law' suggests

---

[1]   Three out of six governments at the time intervened with strong submissions which indicates that the concept of direct effect probably did not accord with the intention of those States when they became parties to the EC Treaty.

[2]   Case 26/62 *Van Gend en Loos* [1963] ECR 1.

the emergence of a Constitution for Europe.[3] In this context, the shaping of the doctrine of direct effect appears indeed to be a capital step within the process of 'constitutionalization' of the Treaties themselves and could be considered as one of the pillars of the EC's 'constitutional charter'.[4] In a second sense, the penetrating of EC Law (and international law) in the national legal orders and the acceptance of the direct effect doctrine is a matter of national constitutional law and will fall, in an increasing number of Member States, under special constitutional provisions. Some of these special clauses which make European integration a topic of national constitutional law may also be called 'European constitutional law'.[5]

Finally, in a third sense, 'European constitutional law' also has a 'horizontal' dimension. The European States, members of the Council of Europe, and *a fortiori*, the Member States of the European Union, share a common constitutional heritage which only the comparative approach can make visible.[6] This is well known in the field of protection of fundamental rights where the ECJ has deduced general principles of law from common constitutional standards within the Member States. Nevertheless, the comparative method can also be helpful when national judges are confronted with similar problems.

For the purpose of this limited contribution, the principle of direct effect will therefore be examined solely from the point of view of national constitutional law. Considerations on the administrative law practice or the positions of ordinary courts will only be made if they concern closely enough the constitutional law issue. This will make it possible, in return, to embody the question of direct effect of EC Law within the broader subject of direct effect of international law. The focus will be put on the question how constitutions respond to the claim of international (and Community) law to generate rules enjoying direct applicability within the national legal orders which is one manner to approach the old issue of the relationship between legal orders.[7]

1.2 The appropriateness of the comparative approach

Many reasons plead for a comparative analysis in the present field of study. As Prechal puts it elsewhere in this volume, the concept of direct effect causes confusion because of various national perceptions - or even

---

[3] See Gerkrath (1997).

[4] See Stein (1981), at p. 3, who considers the *Van Gend en Loos* judgment 'the cornerstone for the constitutional evolution' within the Community.

[5] German authors sometimes refer to what they call *nationales Europaverfassungsrecht*, cf. Häberle (1995), p. 308. See also Gerkrath (1997), at p. 21 et seq. and p. 129 et seq.

[6] Cf. Grewe & Ruiz Fabri (1995).

[7] See Vandamme & Reestman (2001). See also the very substantial contribution of De Visscher (1952), notably at p. 559 et seq.

'national sub-doctrines'- of the classic EC doctrine.[8] A comparison of these perceptions, which derive naturally from different legal traditions formed in the course of centuries, but also from different constitutional options taken by the Member States more recently, might contribute to facilitating mutual understanding. Within the field of 'European constitutional law' the comparative approach appears furthermore to be particularly fertile as a means of understanding the phenomena of European integration and the emergence of a 'multilevel constitutionalism'.[9] Finally, comparative law is a discipline which allows sometimes to reconsider unsatisfactory national solutions to legal problems shared with other Member States.[10]

But choosing the comparative approach also involves special constraints: one has to be very cautious with the legal terms and expressions used by courts and scholars in different national contexts. They need to be clarified and should be used uniformly. A rapid glance at the case law and the legal writings in the two countries studied here reveals, however, that the contrary is true. In France the vocabulary varies from one author to another and, moreover, the terms such as *immediateté, effet direct, applicabilité directe* and *invocabilité* are employed with sometimes divergent meanings.[11] In Germany we will encounter equivalent expressions such as *Durchgriff, unmittelbare Geltung, unmittelbare Wirkung, Direktwirkung* and *unmittelbare Anwendbarkeit* or *unmittelbare Anwendung* as well as similar problems of differentiation.[12]

The main difficulty caused by this profusion of terms is to retain a singular (English) terminology which makes it possible to confront the two national viewpoints properly. In order to avoid further confusion, the comparison will be based on the following distinction between 'direct applicability' and 'direct effect':[13]

I. The concept of 'direct applicability' concerns the relation between a treaty (or any other act of international or Community law) and the national legal order. Saying that such an act is 'directly applicable' means that it will become part of the domestic legal order without any formal measure of reception or transformation. Hence, direct applicability proceeds from domestic constitutional law, at least with regard to traditional international law.[14] In theory, a treaty which enjoys direct applicability, will be

---

[8] In chapter II, paragraph 2.1.

[9] Pernice (1999).

[10] Vitzthum (1998).

[11] Cf. Sauron (2000), p. 38, who presents a chart representing the three main examples of terminology and signification.

[12] See Jarass (1994) p. 68 et seq. Cf. also Klein (1988).

[13] This distinction appears indeed essential for the understanding of the doctrine of direct effect and will be followed strictly hereafter.

[14] Whereas EC regulations are 'directly applicable in all Member States' according to Art. 249 EC.

in force as a part of domestic law upon its ratification by the contracting parties. This is of course legal fiction because even States whose constitutions reflect a 'monist' attitude toward international law, do in general maintain some formal requirements which must be fulfilled prior to any application.[15]

2. The notion of 'direct effect' goes further than 'direct applicability'. It concerns the relation between a rule of external origin and the individuals within the national legal order. Since the advisory opinion of the Permanent Court of International Justice of 3 March 1928, there can be no doubt that, 'the very object of an international agreement, according to the intention of the contracting Parties, may be the adoption by the Parties of some definite rules creating individual rights and obligations and enforceable by the national courts'.[16] In international law, 'self-executing' treaties are still rather rare and the principle of direct effect of such law is at the mercy of state courts which often give restrictive interpretations.[17] Within the European Community, on the contrary, the Court of Justice, invoking the 'spirit' of the treaties, considers direct effect as an element of the very nature of EC Law. Furthermore, the existence of the preliminary ruling procedure and the persuasive method followed by the Luxembourg Court have made the national judges become the common judges of Community law.[18] The effectiveness of the principle of direct effect depends indeed very much on the behaviour of the national courts. As the ECJ stated in *Van Gend en Loos*: it's up to the national courts to protect the rights which are conferred upon individuals by Community law and which become part of their legal heritage. In order to answer the question whether a rule has direct effect or not, it is either necessary to look at the 'intention of the contracting Parties'[19] or to consider 'the spirit, the general scheme and the wording of those provisions'[20], which is merely a (constructive) method for interpreting this intention. Nevertheless, this is a matter of international law and not

---

[15] E.g. publication of the Treaty in an Official Journal. Cf. Art. 55 of the French Constitution.

[16] *Danzig* PCIJ, Ser. B, No. 15 (1928), at points 17-18.

[17] E.g. the case law of French courts with regard to the UN Convention on the rights of children, see 3.1.1 below.

[18] See Mancini (1989), p. 606: 'It was by following this courteously didactic method that the Luxembourg judges won the confidence of their colleagues from Palermo to Edinburgh and from Bordeaux to Berlin; and it was by winning their confidence that they were able to transform the procedure of Art. 177 into a tool whereby private individuals may challenge their national legislation for incompatibility with Community law'.

[19] According to the PCIJ's advisory opinion of 3 March 1928.

[20] According to the ECJ, *Van Gend en Loos* (as cited).

of domestic constitutional law. Direct effect is closely linked to direct applicability because no rule can be enforced by national judges without having complied with the constitutional requirements for its formal reception. Still, direct effects are inherent to a treaty. They pre-exist its formal reception, but they remain latent as long as the constitutional hurdles have not been jumped over.[21] The conditions for direct effect of Treaty provisions or other forms of Community law have been set out by the ECJ since *Van Gend en Loos*. Accordingly, a rule has direct effect whenever it is clear, unconditional and does not require any national implementation measure, or, in the words of Pescatore, 'whenever its characteristics are such that it is capable of judicial adjudication'.[22] Although these far-reaching effects of a rule do not proceed from the Constitution but from the Treaty itself, they cannot be attained in presence of conflicting constitutional law.

Therefore, this contribution will focus on direct applicability and direct effect as defined above. Any other consequences of the doctrine of direct effect in the widest sense, e.g. *invocability*, the duty of consistent interpretation or State liability, will be left aside. These are either questions of judicial process or of administrative law and will be dealt with by more authorized contributors.[23]

1.3   The convenience of the choice of Germany and France

The selection of these two Member States appears appropriate for several reasons. The German-French co-operation is indeed often referred to as a 'motor' for European integration and, as such, the couple is naturally predestined to be a choice object of comparative analysis.[24] The recent case law of the German and French constitutional courts constitutes moreover an interesting field for comparative studies.

Since the well-known *Maastricht* decision of the German Federal Constitutional Court (FCC) of 12 October 1993,[25] the question of domestic effect of EC law has again become a potential source of conflict between the German Court and the ECJ. The two main issues are, firstly, where to draw the border-

---

[21]   Cp. F. Rigaux, quoted by Joliet (1983), p. 292.

[22]   Pescatore (1983), p. 176.

[23]   Cf. especially the contributions of Prechal, Betlem and Jans & Prinssen in this volume's chapters II, IV and V.

[24]   See for instance N.N. (1998). On the question whether there is already a German-French legal science, cf. Beaud (1999).

[25]   Often quoted as the *'Brunner'* decision, BVerfGE (collection of decisions of the FCC) vol. 89, p. 155 et seq. English translations have been published in [1994] 1 CMLR 57 and [1994] ILM 388.

line between the effect of Community law and the authority of national constitutional law and, secondly, who will fix this border-line. Compared to the situation under French law, the topic becomes particularly stimulating because
the French *Conseil constitutionnel* has developed quite a different doctrine with
regard to the relation between Community law and domestic constitutional law.

This could of course be considered as a direct consequence of the contrasting
general attitude of the two Constitutions with respect to international law. The
French Constitution of 1958 is indeed considered as being 'monist' while the
German Basic Law (BL) of 1949 is known as 'moderately dualist'.[26] But, as
a matter of fact, these differences, which are important in legal theory, have
to be tempered in practice especially with regard to Community law.[27] The
divergent positions of the two Courts may also be explained by the very different
standing they enjoy within their national political system and by their different
competences. But these undeniable differences should not be exaggerated. The
main reason is to be found in their attitude towards Community law and their
self-image as 'guardians of the Constitution'.

Concerning Community law but also international law in general, it appears,
indeed, that 'what the Constitution says' seems to be pretty similar in France
and Germany, both countries having 'constitutionalized' their membership
within the European Communities and the European Union by specific clauses
which were introduced in 1992.[28] The comparison of 'what the judges say that
the Constitution says'[29] intends to underline to what extent the dogmatic position of the *Bundesverfassungsgericht* contrasts with the more pragmatic attitude
of the *Conseil constitutionnel*. The German Basic Law, which is often referred to
for its 'openness' to European integration, is interpreted in a very defensive way
while the French Constitution, which is deeply marked by the classic concept of
national sovereignty, is construed in a rather harmonious manner.

As a matter of fact, 'what the Constitution says' (2) does only deal with the
question of direct applicability, whereas 'what the judges say' (3) refers to both:
direct applicability and direct effect.

---

[26] See for example Autexier (1997), p. 152.

[27] On the question whether the debate between monism and dualism is still useful, see Daillier (1998),
p. 9.

[28] Other Member States like Portugal (Art. 7 §§ 5 and 6) and Austria (Art. 23 a-f) have also introduced such
special clauses. Cf. Grewe & Oberdorff (1999).

[29] Referring to a statement made by Charles Evans Hughes, judge and later president of the US Supreme
Court, in a speech in 1908: 'the Constitution is what the judges say it is'. See C.E. Hughes, Speech
before the Elmira Chamber of Commerce, Addresses and Papers, quoted by Van Alstyne (1969), p. 2.

2 What the Constitution says

With regard to the substance of constitutional law, there are stronger similarities than one might expect, considering the fact that the French Constitution is generally presented as belonging to those inspired by 'monism', whereas the German Basic Law passes for a convenient example of the theory of 'dualism'. As we will see in the following, these distinctions have lost much of their force of conviction and must be handled with caution with regard to Community law. As both Constitutions contain general provisions with respect to international law and international organisations but also special clauses on European integration, these two aspects will be presented separately.

2.1 General clauses on the domestic effect of international law

The embodiment in the Constitution of articles dealing *inter alia* with the effect and the force of international law within the national legal order is a phenomenon which has been analysed under the name of 'international constitutional law'.[30] De Witte characterizes it as 'that part of constitutional law which deals with the external relations of the State and the domestic effect of international law'.[31] For the purpose of this contribution, only the rules concerning the domestic effect of international law will be examined.

2.1.1 The German Basic Law

The *Grundgesetz* of 23 May 1949 includes four articles regarding international law and institutions (Arts. 24, 25, 26 and 59(2)) and one additional provision about the jurisdiction of the FCC in this field (Art. 100(2)). Article 24 BL relates to the participation of the Federation within the International Community of States. It explicitly entitles 'the Federation' to transfer (by legislation) 'sovereign powers to intergovernmental institutions' (Art. 24(1)).[32] Furthermore, it rules that 'for the maintenance of peace, the Federation may join a system of mutual collective security', and that 'in doing so it will consent to such limitations upon its rights of sovereignty as will bring about and secure a peaceful and lasting order in Europe and among the nations of the world' (Art.

---

[30] See the pioneer work of Mirkine-Guetzévitch (1933) and more recently Favoreu (1993).

[31] De Witte (1995), p. 149.

[32] The 38th amendment of the BL of 12 December 1992 introduced a new section 1a) to Art. 24: 'Insofar as the States [*Länder*] are responsible for the exercise of state rights and the discharge of state duties, they can, with consent of the Government, delegate sovereign powers to institutions for neighborhood at state borders'.

24(2)). Finally, it declares that 'for the settlement of disputes between states, the Federation will accede to agreements concerning international arbitration of a general, comprehensive, and obligatory nature' (Art. 24(3)).

Coupled with the wording of the preamble and Article 26, which indicate that the German People adopted the Basic Law 'animated by the purpose to serve world peace' and that 'acts tending to and undertaken with intent to disturb the peaceful relations between nations ... are unconstitutional', Article 24 manifests one of the fundamental choices of the constituent power. Its decision, in favour of a strong integration of Germany within the international Community, is often summarized by using the image of 'openness' or 'friendliness' of the German legal order towards international law (*offene Staatlichkeit, Völkerrechtsfreundlichkeit*).

Two provisions, Article 25 and Article 59(2), deal with the position of the rules of international law within the German legal order. At first glance, they seem to attribute different effects to the 'general rules of international law' on the one hand and to 'treaties' on the other hand. Under the title 'Public international law and federal law', Article 25 BL proclaims indeed that:

'The general rules of public international law constitute an integral part of federal law. They take precedence over statutes and directly create rights and duties for the inhabitants of the federal territory'.

Thus, Article 25 could lead to the impression that the Basic Law takes a 'monist' attitude at least towards 'the general rules of public international law'.[33] In fact, the distinction between monism and dualism has been progressively abandoned in Germany in favour of a more practical approach based on the technical operation of reception or transformation. Accordingly, the Basic Law distinguishes between 'the general rules of international law' which have been introduced on the whole into German law by virtue of Article 25 and 'international agreements' which need to be transformed one by one.[34] This view is confirmed by Article 100(2) BL which attributes jurisdiction to the FCC on the question 'whether a rule of public international law is an integral part of federal law'.[35] The wording of Article 100(2) presupposes indeed implicitly the existence of two spheres of law.

---

[33] See Dupuy (2000), p. 391 who underlines the ambiguity of certain constitutions but quotes Art. 25 BL as revealing clearly the 'monist option' of the German Constitution.

[34] See Autexier (1997) p. 152 et seq.

[35] Art. 100(2) indicates indeed that : 'Where, in the course of litigation, doubt exists whether a rule of public international law is an integral part of federal law and whether such rule directly creates rights and duties for the individual (Art. 25), the Court obtains a decision of the Federal Constitutional Court'.

The situation of treaties is governed by Article 59 BL. The President, who represents the Federation in its international relations, 'concludes treaties with foreign states on behalf of the Federation'. According to Article 59(2):

'Treaties which regulate the political relations of the Federation or relate to matters of federal legislation require the consent or participation, in the form of a federal statute, of the bodies competent in any specific case for such federal legislation. As regards administrative agreements, the provisions concerning the federal administration apply mutatis mutandis'.[36]

Nothing is said about the validity and the applicability of treaties within the domestic legal system nor about their ranking. Each treaty or administrative agreement needs to be transformed either by a federal statute or a legal act of the executive power.

2.1.2   The French Constitution

The rules which constitute French 'international constitutional law' are not embodied in one single document as in Germany.[37] According to the preamble of the Constitution of 4 October 1958: 'The French people solemnly proclaims its attachment to the Rights of Man and the principles of national sovereignty as defined by the Declaration of 1789, confirmed and complemented by the Preamble to the Constitution of 1946'. These three documents form, together with a number of 'fundamental principles acknowledged by the statutes of the Republic', what is known in France as *bloc de constitutionnalité*.[38] Thus, one has to refer to the preamble of 1946 and the Constitution of 1958 in order to assemble the relevant rules.

Section 14 of the preamble of the Constitution of 1946 delivers a first, though imperfect and ambiguous, indication specifying that 'the French Republic complies with the rules of public international law'. This is completed by section 15 which allows, 'subject to reciprocity', that 'France consents to limitations of sovereignty necessary for the organisation and the defence of peace'.

Since the founding of the Fifth Republic, the monist tradition, initiated by Articles 26 and 28 of the Constitution of 1946, continues throughout part VI of the Constitution entitled precisely: 'on treaties and international agreements'. According to Article 53:

---

[36] The last sentence signifies that the conclusion of such administrative agreements may require prior approbation by the *Bundesrat* according to Art. 80(2).

[37] A comprehensive and well documented introduction to the French situation is to be found in: Conseil d'Etat (2000).

[38] In a famous decision of 16 July 1971 on the freedom of association, the *Conseil constitutionnel* referred for the first time to the preamble of the Constitution of 1958. As a result, he conferred full constitutional value not only to the preamble of 1958 but also to the preamble of 1946 and the declaration of 1789.

'Peace treaties, commercial treaties, treaties or agreements relating to interna-
tional organisation, those that commit the finances of the State, those that modify
provisions which are matters for statute, those relating to the status of persons, and
those that involve the cession, exchange or addition of territory, may be ratified or
approved only by virtue of an Act of Parliament. They shall not take effect until they
have been ratified or approved'.

The most significant provision is, however, to be found in Article 55 which rules
that:

'Treaties or agreements duly ratified or approved shall, upon publication, prevail
over Acts of Parliament, subject, in regard to each agreement or treaty, to its applica-
tion by the other party'.

This clause is generally presented as a rule governing the authority of international treaties in the national legal order. In fact, the requirements laid down
by Article 55 do not only concern the question of supremacy of a treaty vis-à-vis
Acts of Parliament but constitute first of all conditions for its applicability in
the broadest sense.[39] A treaty, duly ratified and applied by the other contracting
party, will indeed become applicable upon publication in the *Journal officiel de la*
République française which is considered as being typical for a monist system.[40]
    The three conditions of applicability laid down by Article 55, 'due ratification',
'publication' and 'reciprocal application' of the treaty, are nevertheless very strict
and difficult to apply in court. Additionally, the formulation of Article 55 appears
to be particularly unsatisfactory because its wording only fits bilateral agreements and does not include international customary law. Thus, Article 55 opens
the door to more or less 'dualist' interpretations as we will see in the following.
    As a first result, the short presentation of German and French international
constitutional law clearly reveals that the antagonism between a claimed 'dualist' German *Grundgesetz* and an assumed 'monist' French Constitution fails to
provide an adequate theoretical scheme of comparative analysis. Both Constitutions share an approach vis-à-vis international law which might be qualified as
being open to far-reaching but still 'home-steered' integration. Further parallels
have appeared with the introduction of special articles on European integration.

2.2 Special provisions on European integration

Until 1992, both Germany and France participated actively in
the process of European integration without encountering major obstacles due to

---

[39] Cf. Alland (2000), p. 379.
[40] Cp. Grewe & Ruiz Fabri (1995), p. 105.

their domestic constitutional law. Both ratified the founding treaties, the various amendment treaties or acts and accession treaties without being forced to adjust their Constitutions. Neither the German nor the French Constitution as adopted in 1949 and 1958 contained special provisions with regard to the process of European integration. The only reference to a 'united Europe' was to be found in the preamble of the *Grundgesetz*, which still indicates that the German People adopted it 'animated by the purpose to serve world peace as an equal part in a unified Europe'.[41]

This state of apparently peaceful co-existence between somewhat static constitutional provisions and the dynamic evolution of the founding treaties of the Communities ceased with the signature of the Treaty on European Union on 7 February 1992. Both Member States were indeed confronted with important constitutional challenges during the ratification procedure of the Treaty and both decided to amend their Constitution. In France, this was the direct and inevitable result of a decision of the *Conseil constitutionnel* declaring the Treaty contrary to the Constitution.[42] In Germany, it was the other way round. The political decision to amend the Basic Law, did not prevent several German members of the European Parliament and a former high ranking official of the European Commission from lodging constitutional complaints with the *Bundes-verfassungsgericht*. That court's decision finally opened the way for Germany's ratification of the Treaty but also formulated severe limits for the future development of the European Union.

As a result, the Basic Law has been enriched by a new Article 23, and a new title XV (Arts. 88-1 to 88-4) has been added to the French Constitution. Though there are undeniable differences in spirit and wording, which will be examined hereafter, these new 'European Articles' are similarly structured and follow common objectives. Both start indeed with a section about the conditions of the State's participation within the Union, followed by a section on the transfer of powers and both terminate with indications on the role of the national Parliament. It seems appropriate to follow this analogy in structure and found the comparison upon the three elements.

---

41 Not to forget Art. 24(2) which authorizes the Federation to join a system of mutual collective security and to 'consent to such limitations upon its rights of sovereignty as will bring about and secure a peaceful and lasting order in Europe'.

42 A 'première' in France. The *Conseil constitutionnel* had to decide three times on the Treaty of Maastricht: twice on the question of the constitutionality of the Treaty itself and once on the constitutionality of the statute authorizing its ratification. There are thus three 'Maastricht decisions': *Maastricht 1*, decision No. 92-308 (9.4.1992), Rec. p. 55, *Maastricht 2*, decision No. 92-312 (2.9.1992), Rec. p. 76 and *Maastricht 3*, decision No. 92-313 (23.9.1992), Rec. p. 94.

2.2.1 Participation in the European Union

Article 23(1) of the Basic Law, as well as Article 88-1 of the French Constitution, authorize explicitly the participation of the respective Member State in the European Union. There are, however, striking differences. Article 23 BL states indeed that:

'To realise a unified Europe, Germany concurs to the development of the European Union which is bound to democratic, rule of law, social, and federal principles as well as the principle of subsidiarity and provides a protection of fundamental rights essentially equivalent to that of this Constitution'.

Whereas Article 88-1 of the French Constitution declares that:

'The Republic shall participate in the European Communities and in the European Union constituted by States that have freely chosen, by virtue of the treaties that established them, to exercise some of their powers in common'.

There are obviously three main differences. The first one is a difference in attitude towards the process of integration. The Basic Law takes an attitude which might be qualified as 'offensive'. The Federal Republic is indeed called upon to 'concur to the development of the Union' (wirkt bei der Entwicklung der EU mit) which means logically that all federal institutions have a duty to do so. Furthermore, several constitutional principles are 'projected' in the direction of the Union which is required to respect them. As these principles are clearly of national origin one might find that this is a kind of 'constitutional imperialism' especially in the field of fundamental rights. In comparison, the position of the French Constitution appears to be rather 'defensive' stating that the Republic merely 'participates' in the Communities and the Union. Underlining that the Member States have freely chosen to do nothing more than 'exercise some of their powers in common', Article 88-1 seems to be inspired by an attitude of fear to lose sovereignty.

The second difference is one in perception of the nature of the Union. The French Constitution insists indeed on the existing elements of traditional international nature (constituted by states and established by treaties) whereas the Basic Law exposes a 'federal' or 'constitutional' vision of the Union (united Europe, federal principles). Beside these differences, both States have, however, 'constitutionalized' their participation in the Union. Therefore they cannot anymore withdraw from the Union without prior modification of their Constitution.

The third difference concerns the process of European integration. The Basic Law seems indeed to take into account the dynamic 'development of the

European Union' whereas the French Constitution reflects a static vision of the
Union.

2.2.2   Transfer of powers

The transfer of state powers is the second common element in
the structure of the two 'European clauses'. In this field, the German Basic Law
took the option of a general clause allowing such transfers 'for the foundation
of the European Union as well as for changes in its contractual bases' while the
French Constitution agrees to the transfers necessary for the purpose of each
treaty individually. But before continuing the comparison, let us bear in mind
the wording of Article 23(1) which asserts that:

> 'The Federation can, for this purpose and with the consent of the Bundesrat,
> transfer sovereign powers. Article 79(2) & (3) is applicable for the foundation of
> the European Union as well as for changes in its contractual bases and comparable
> regulations by which the content of this Constitution is changed or amended or by
> which such changes or amendments are authorised'.

The corresponding French formula is to be found in Article 88-2 which is
composed of two sub-sections introduced respectively in June 1992 and January
1999 after the decisions of the *Conseil constitutionnel* declaring the Maastricht
and Amsterdam Treaty contrary to the Constitution. Thus, Article 88-2 is now
composed as follows:

> 'Subject to reciprocity and in accordance with the terms of the Treaty on European
> Union signed on 7 February 1992, France agrees to the transfer of powers necessary
> for the establishment of European economic and monetary union.
>
> Subject to the same reservation and in accordance with the terms of the Treaty
> establishing the European Community, as amended by the Treaty signed on 2 October
> 1997, the transfer of powers necessary for the determination of rules concerning
> freedom of movement for persons and related areas may be agreed'.

This time, the comparison seems to reveal a difference with regard to the extent
to which transfers of powers are authorized. Similar to Article 24, Article 23
permits to transfer sovereign powers by legislation with the consent of the
Bundesrat. This is valid for the present and the future of the Union. Article
88-2 of the French Constitution, on the contrary, only authorizes the transfer
of powers which is strictly necessary to realize the objectives of the two treaties
it mentions. Future amendment treaties will therefore probably require further

additions to Article 88-2.[43] This apparent difference is, however, not as important as it seems. Article 23 indicates that Article 79(2) & (3) BL applies if a future transfer of powers implies amendments to the Constitution. This means that a majority of two thirds is required in both houses of Parliament and the material limits of amendment must be respected.[44]

2.2.3 Association of national parliaments

The role of the national parliaments is also governed by the two Europe-articles. The rather detailed rules on this point are to be found in Article 23(2)-(7) of the Basic Law and in Article 88-4 of the French Constitution. These provisions are similarly motivated by the wish to strengthen the place of the Parliaments and to associate them more closely to the decision-making procedure within the Union. Though they do not concern immediately the subject of direct effect, they also belong to European constitutional law and deserve to be quoted here. Article 23(2)-(7) has the following content:

'*(2) The* Bundestag *and the* Länder, *by their representation in the* Bundesrat, *participate in matters of the European Union. The Government has to thoroughly inform* Bundestag *and* Bundesrat *at the earliest possible time.*

(3) The Government allows for statements of the Bundestag *before it takes part in drafting European Union laws. The Government considers statements of the* Bundestag *during deliberations. Details are regulated by federal statute.*

(4) The Bundesrat *has to be included in the deliberations of the* Bundestag *insofar as it would have to participate in a domestic measure or insofar as the* Länder *would be accountable domestically.*

(5) Insofar as, in the area of exclusive legislative competence of the Federation, the interests of the Länder *are affected or insofar as, in all other cases, the Federation has legislative competence, the Government considers the statement of the* Bundesrat. *If legislative competences of the* Länder, *the installation of their agencies, or their*

---

[43] Art. 88-3 introduces also a specific derogation allowing citizens of the Union to vote and stand as a candidate in municipal elections.

[44] Art. 79 is about amendment of the Constitution. Its first paragraph provides that the Constitution 'can be amended only by statutes which expressly amend or supplement the text thereof ... (2) Any such statute requires the consent of two thirds of the members of the *Bundestag* and two thirds of the votes of the *Bundesrat*. (3) Amendments of this Constitution affecting the division of the Federation into *Länder*, the participation on principle of the *Länder* in legislation, or the basic principles laid down in Arts. 1 and 20 are inadmissible'.

procedures are centrally affected, the opinion of the Bundesrat *has to be considered
as decisive for the Federation's deliberation; the responsibility of the Federation for
the whole state has to be maintained in the process. The consent of the Government
is necessary in matters possibly resulting in higher expenses or lower revenues for
the Federation.*

*(6) The Federation shall delegate the exercise of rights of the Federal Republic
of Germany as a member of the European Union to a representative of the* Länder
nominated by the Bundesrat *if exclusive legislative competences of the* Länder *are
centrally affected. These rights are exercised with participation of and in coordination
with the Government; the responsibility of the Federation for the whole state has to
be maintained in the process.*

*(7) Details of Paragraphs (4) to (6) are regulated by a statute requiring the
consent of the* Bundesrat'.

Thus, both houses of the German Parliament are associated to the European
decision-making procedure on the national level. The most challenging element
is to be found, however, in paragraph 6. This disposition makes it possible for
a representative of the *Länder* to exercise rights of the Federation on the level
of the European Union if exclusive legislative competences of the *Länder* are
centrally affected.[45] This could also be considered as a consequence of direct
effect.

Article 88-4 of the French Constitution indicates much more laconically that:

*'The Government shall lay before the National Assembly and the Senate any
drafts of or proposals for instruments of the European Communities or the European
Union containing provisions which are matters for statute as soon as they have
been transmitted to the Council of the European Union. It may also lay before
them other drafts of or proposals for instruments or any document issuing from a
European Union institution. In the manner laid down by the rules of procedure of
each assembly, resolutions may be passed, even if Parliament is not in session, on the
drafts, proposals or documents referred to in the preceding paragraph'.*

As a matter of fact, these special clauses on European integration which have
been introduced in both Constitutions do not refer explicitly to the question of
domestic effect of Community law. This question must therefore be answered

---

[45] Since the coming into force of the Maastricht Treaty, Art. 203 (ex 146) EC provides indeed that 'The
Council shall consist of a representative of each Member State at ministerial level, authorized to commit
the government of that Member State'. Cf. also Gerkrath (1995).

according to the general provisions about international law as presented above. In the end it is generally up to the judges to say what the Constitution signifies.

3 What the judges say that the Constitution says

National judges often have a rather reserved position vis-à-vis international law. The main reason for such an attitude is precisely to be found in their quality of 'national' judges rather than in their claimed 'unfamiliarity' with international law. Their jurisdiction is indeed founded on the Constitution and they will only consider international law as part of the domestic legal order if the Constitution says so in clear and unequivocal terms.[46] The constitutional provisions concerning international law give, however, substance for divergent interpretations. The role of the national judges, and in particular the conception which constitutional judges have of their own jurisdiction, appears thus to be at least as important in practice as the Constitution's wording.[47] Having compared the wording in the first part of this contribution, it is thus indispensable to examine the case law of the two constitutional courts which will reveal important differences with regard to the domestic effect of international and Community law.

A comparison of the case law of the French *Conseil constitutionnel* and the German *Bundesverfassungsgericht* must take into account the fact that there are important differences between the two institutions. These differences do not only concern their composition, but also their standing in the legal system and their competences. The German Court benefits certainly from an exceptionally powerful status.[48] In comparison, the *Conseil constitutionnel* appears humble and its attributions modest. One should not forget, however, that the *Conseil* is at the origin of a 'veritable political revolution' transforming itself into the guardian of individual rights.[49]

Both Courts have the power to construe the Constitution with final authority vis-à-vis all the other institutions. Or, in other words, they deliver the authentic interpretation of the Constitution *erga omnes*. One must not forget, however, that besides the constitutional judges, the ordinary judges will also be called to intervene. Their role is necessarily stronger in France than in Germany where an ordinary court, faced with a question of constitutionality, will normally have

---

[46] Such 'judicial self-restraint' may also be explained by a reference to the separation of powers principle, which prevents the judge to act as a legislator. Cp. on this point Daillier (1998), p. 16.

[47] See Dupuy (2000), p. 394.

[48] Cp. Grewe & Ruiz Fabri (1995), p. 85.

[49] Cf. Rousseau (1993), p. 60 et seq.

to obtain a preliminary decision from the *Bundesverfassungsgericht*.[50] No similar procedure exists in France.

As a matter of fact, we will find in both countries judicial interpretations of the constitutional provisions on international and EC law (3.1). These are of course of special interest for the comprehension of the national visions of the principles of direct applicability and direct effect. But, in the case law of the *Bundesverfassungsgericht*, we will also find a couple of decisions containing interpretations of certain clauses of the Basic Law which do not have any apparent link with Community law but which are, nevertheless, construed in a sense which relates to the doctrine of direct effect (3.2).

3.1   ... interpreting the specific clauses on international and EC law

On the one hand, the *Bundesverfassungsgericht* and the *Conseil constitutionnel* have both acknowledged direct effect of EC law as a principle notwithstanding the domestic Constitution. But, on the other hand, they have also both established more or less precise limits which need to be analysed.

3.1.1   The principle of direct effect is generally accepted under the domestic Constitution

The *Bundesverfassungsgericht* already mentioned the principle of direct applicability of EC regulations in an early decision from 18 October 1967 quoting the wording of Article 249 (ex 189) EC.[51] Four years later, on 9 June 1971, in the *Lütticke* case, the FCC acknowledged the direct effect of Article 90 (ex 95) EC as it had previously been declared by the ECJ.[52] In its decision, the Federal Court argued that Article 24 BL does not only allow to transfer powers to intergovernmental institutions but also requires that the domestic authorities must recognize the law adopted by them. The FCC even agreed with the ECJ in considering that the doctrine of direct effect is necessary to realize the subjective rights of the citizens within the Common Market.[53] Three years later, the FCC, in the case known as *Solange 1*, declared that 'Article 24 BL does not in fact entitle to transfer sovereign rights but opens up the national legal order, ... thus giving room to the direct effect and direct applicability of law coming from another source within the national territory'.[54] Hence, there can be no doubt:

---

[50] According to Art. 100 BL.

[51] BVerfGE vol. 22, p. 293. The decision concerns also the question of the Court's jurisdiction, it will be discussed below at 3.2.

[52] Case 57/65 *Lütticke* [1966] ECR 205.

[53] BVerfGE vol. 31, p. 174.

[54] BVerfGE vol. 37, p. 280, 'der unmittelbaren Geltung und Anwendbarkeit eines Rechts aus anderer Quelle innerhalb des staatlichen Herrschaftsbereichs Raum gelassen wird'.

direct effect and applicability is compatible with the Basic Law. However, this is not without limits, as the Court underlines in the same decision.

In another well known decision, dating from 22 October 1986 (*Solange 2*), the German Court pronounced itself on the question of direct effect of Community regulations according to Article 249 EC. It did so, however, considering direct effect of regulations as a result of the command to apply EC law given by the national ratification act which embraces Article 249 EC. Furthermore, the Court added, that this command, based on Article 24 BL is not without constitutional restraints.[55]

Finally, on 8 April 1987, in the *Kloppenburg* case, the *Bundesverfassungsgericht*, acting on an individual constitutional complaint against a judgment of the *Bundesfinanzhof*, clearly took a position on the question of direct effect of EC directives. Arguing against the case law of the ECJ on direct effect of directives and unwilling to refer this question to the ECJ throughout the preliminary ruling procedure, the *Bundesfinanzhof* had refused indeed to apply Directive 77/388/EEC.[56] As a result, the FCC, presenting a detailed analysis of the case law of the ECJ on the question of direct effect of directives, decided that this case law did not exceed the limits of judicial interpretation and consequently annulled the judgment of the *Bundesfinanzhof*.[57]

In France, the *Conseil constitutionnel* did not have so many occasions to pronounce on the question of direct applicability or direct effect. There are, however, several decisions which show that the French constitutional court is not hostile to it. The first reference to the principle is to be found in two decisions of 30 December 1977.[58] The *Conseil* was asked to control the constitutionality of two budgetary statutes which had been contested because they did not contain any provisions about certain agricultural levies established by EC regulations. Referring to the wording of Article 249 EC, the *Conseil* indicated clearly that the validity (*'force obligatoire'*) of the dispositions of the regulation 'does not depend on an intervention of Member States' authorities'.

In a second decision, of 25 July 1991, on the French statute authorizing the ratification of the implementing convention of the 'Schengen' agreement, there is a rather mysterious passage about the link between direct effect of decisions of the 'Schengen executive committee' and judicial review.[59] The *Conseil* admits indeed that the convention of 19 June 1990 does not submit this executive committee to any judicial control. But it also considers that neither the institu-

---

[55] BVerfGE vol. 73, p. 375.

[56] OJ 1977, L 6/13.

[57] BVerfGE vol. 75, p. 223, in particular at p. 235 et seq.

[58] Decisions No. 77-89 DC and No. 77-90 DC, *Prélèvement isoglucose*, (30.12.1977), Rec. p. 46 et seq., RJC I-54.

[59] Decision No. 91-294 DC, *Accord de Schengen*, (25.7.1991), Rec. p. 91, RJC I-455.

tion itself, nor its attributions, are contrary to the Constitution 'as no stipulation of the convention confers the decisions of this committee any direct effect in the territory of the contracting parties'. Thus, the implementing measures adopted by French authorities are submitted to judicial control by French courts.

A last reference to direct effect is to be found in a recent decision on the constitutionality of the statute on the social security budget for 1998.[60] Considering the principle of equal treatment between pharmaceutical laboratories and wholesalers, the *Conseil* takes into account a Council Directive of 31 March 1992, 'not yet implemented'.[61] Consequently, the *Conseil constitutionnel* seems to admit the possibility of directives deploying direct effects.

Since a well-known decision of 15 January 1975, it is clear that the *Conseil constitutionnel*, acting as constitutional court, refuses to review the conformity of a statute vis-à-vis a treaty. Implicitly, it thus invited the ordinary courts to exercise this type of control.[62] It is also well known that the *Cour de cassation* (since 1975) and the *Conseil d'Etat* (since 1989) agree to ensure that treaties 'duly ratified or approved' prevail 'upon publication' over Acts of Parliament, 'subject to its application by the other party'.

Therefore, it appears to be more interesting to have a look at the most recent case law of the two highest ordinary courts in order to present briefly their position with regard to direct applicability or direct effect of international and EC Law and to discover their interpretation of the pertinent constitutional provisions.

With regard to international agreements, the three conditions of applicability mentioned by Article 55 of the Constitution furnish a structure to present the rich case law. First of all, both *Conseil d'Etat* and *Cour de cassation* refuse to apply a treaty which has not yet been published in the Official Journal.[63] This is of course rather prejudicial considering that the publication sometimes takes a couple of months or is simply neglected by the administration.[64] In a recent judgment, the *Conseil d'Etat* accepted furthermore to verify the regularity of the procedure of conclusion of an agreement according to the requirement laid down in Article 55.[65] As to the condition of reciprocity, the *Conseil d'Etat* refers this

---

[60] Decision No. 97-393 DC, *Loi de financement de la sécurité sociale pour 1998*, (18.12.1997), Rec. p. 320, RJC II-721.

[61] At point 16 of the decision; Council Directive 92/25/EEC, OJ 1992, L 113/1.

[62] Decision 74-54 DC, *Intérruption volontaire de grossesse*, (15.1.1975), Rec. p. 19, RJC I-30. The situation is different when the *Conseil* acts as judge on the regularity of elections

[63] See Conseil d'Etat (13.7.1965), *Société Navigator*, Rec. p. 423 and Cass. Civ. 1 (16.5. 1961), [1961] *Dalloz* p. 489.

[64] The link between the requirement of publication and direct effect has recently been stressed by a 'circulaire' of the Prime minister, cf. *RGDIP* 1997, p. 591.

[65] See Conseil d'Etat (18.12.1998), *Sarl du parc d'activité de Blotzheim*, Rec. p. 483, *RFDA* 1999, p. 315.

question systematically to the Minister of foreign affairs[66], while the *Cour de cassation* considers it to be satisfied as long as the treaty has not been officially repealed by the executive power.[67]

The way these three conditions of applicability are handled by the *Conseil d'Etat* reveals clearly a 'dualist' attitude which has been confirmed by the judgment in the *Sarran* case of 30 October 1998. The *Conseil d'Etat* states indeed that the prevalence granted to international agreements by virtue of Article 55 of the Constitution 'does not apply, within the internal order, to dispositions of constitutional value'.[68] Difficult to find a more explicit formula to explain the theory of dualism.

Concerning the question of direct effect of treaty provisions, the case law on the UN Convention on rights of children from 26 January 1990 furnishes an example of divergent interpretation by the highest French courts. The *Cour de cassation* decided indeed that the provisions of this convention 'cannot be invoked in court, because they are not directly applicable' without considering these provisions one by one.[69] The *Conseil d'Etat*, on the contrary, recognized, first implicitly and later explicitly, the possibility of 'immediate applicability' of certain provisions of the same convention.[70]

With regard to customary international law, it has been mentioned above that the French Constitution is not as explicit as the German Basic Law. Section 14 of the preamble of 1946 refers indeed to 'the rules of public international law' without further specification and Article 55 does only deal with agreements. It is therefore not surprising that the *Conseil d'Etat* refuses to give prevalence to customary international law over statutes. Thus, customary international law exists in the domestic order but does not prevail over statutory law.[71]

With respect to EC Law, the position of the ordinary French courts does not differ fundamentally from the position of the *Conseil constitutionnel*. The *Conseil d'Etat* is, however, somewhat 'reluctant' to recognize direct effect of directives. It does not accept indeed, since the famous *Cohn-Bendit* case in 1978, that an individual may invoke a directive against an individual act of the administration.[72] Thus, the case law restrains the 'effectiveness' of the direct

---

[66] Cf. Conseil d'Etat Ass. (9.4.1999), *Madame Chevrol-Benkeddach*, Rec. p. 115, *RFDA* 1999, p. 937.

[67] The Conseil constitutionnel considered that the condition of reciprocity (contained in section 15 of the preamble of 1946) was satisfied in the case of the Maastricht Treaty as Art. 52 (ex Art. R) states that 'this treaty shall enter into force ..., provided that all the instruments of ratification have been deposited ...'.

[68] Cf. Dupuy (2000), p. 406.

[69] Cass. Civ. 1 (10.3.1993), *Lejeune*, *RGDIP* 1993, p. 1051. In two following judgments this formula has been 'softened'. See Braunschweig & de Gouttes (1995), p. 878 and Alland (1998), p. 213 et seq.

[70] Conseil d'Etat (29.7.1994), *Préfet de la Seine-Maritime c. Abdelmoula*, *RGDIP* 1995, p. 502 and Conseil d'Etat (10.3.1995), *Demirpence*, Rec. p. 610. See Alland (1998), p. 210 et seq. for further references.

[71] Conseil d'Etat (6.6.1997), *Aquarone*, Rec. p. 206, *RFDA* 1997, p. 1068. See Alland (1997), p. 1054.

[72] Conseil d'Etat (22.12.1978) *Cohn-Bendit*, Rec. p. 524. English translation in [1980] 1 CMLR 543.

effect doctrine. The most important limits have been fixed by the constitutional courts themselves.

3.1.2   Both constitutional courts maintain limits to direct effect deriving from domestic constitutional law

The study of the case law concerning European integration reveals a common tendency of the *Bundesverfassungsgericht* and the *Conseil constitutionnel* to use some circumscribing constitutional restraints in the field of European integration. These restraints are, however, quite different in substance. On the one side, the *Conseil constitutionnel* has developed a doctrine based on the 'essential conditions of the exercise of national sovereignty', on the other side, the *Bundesverfassungsgericht*, developed specific restraints founded on the protection of fundamental rights and the principle of democracy.

In an early decision, the *Conseil constitutionnel* made a distinction between 'limitations of sovereignty' which it considered to be allowed and 'transfer of sovereignty' which it held contrary to the Constitution.[73] Strongly criticized, this distinction has been definitely abandoned since a decision from April 1992, known as *Maastricht 1*.[74] In this decision, the *Conseil constitutionnel* inaugurated a new approach based on 'transfer of competences' similar to the wording of Article 88-2. Since then it considers that:

'*the respect of national sovereignty does not prevent France from concluding, on the basis of the dispositions of the preamble from 1946 and subject to reciprocity, international agreements in order to participate in the creation or in the development of a permanent international organisation having legal personality and being invested with decisional powers by virtue of transfer of competences consented by the Member States*'.

Called to verify, according to Article 54 of the Constitution, whether 'an international commitment contains a clause contrary to the Constitution' the *Conseil* applies a three step test. The Treaty will indeed be held contrary to the Constitution not only if it contains a clause which is incompatible with the Constitution but also if it affects the constitutionally guaranteed rights or freedoms, or if it infringes the 'essential conditions of the exercise of national sovereignty'.[75] The sense of this apparently undetermined notion has been explained by the *Conseil*. It refers to the duty of the State to 'ensure the respect of the institutions

---

[73]   Decision No. 76-71 DC, *Assemblée européenne*, (30.12.1976), Rec. p. 15, RJC I-41.

[74]   Decision No. 92-308 DC, *Traité sur l'Union européenne*, (9.4.1992), Rec. p. 55, RJC I-497.

[75]   Cf. the most recent Decision No. 99-408 DC, *Traité portant statut de la Cour pénale internationale*, (22.1.1999), Rec. p. 29. See also Flauss (2001), p. 48.

of the Republic, the continuity of the nation's existence, the guarantee of the citizens' rights and freedoms'.[76] The *Conseil* also indicated that the transfers of competences may affect the 'essential conditions of the exercise of national sovereignty' either by their 'nature' or because of the 'modalities' which are chosen to accomplish them.[77]

In Germany, the Federal Constitutional Court has developed quite a different conception concerning the relationship between EC Law and the Constitution. Already in the decision *Solange 1*, in 1974, the Court states that Article 24 BL does not make it possible to 'invalidate the identity of the effective German Constitution by an intrusion in its constitutive structures'. In this context, the function of the Court is sometimes compared to 'bridge guard' controlling the extent to which Community law is allowed to step over and to enter the German legal order.[78]

Two main restraints have been pointed out by the Court: the protection of fundamental rights on a level which is equivalent to the protection given by the Basic Law and the respect of the democratic principle. Concerning the first aspect, there is a long succession of decisions starting in 1967 and ending in 7 June 2000.[79] According to the latest decision, the Court makes clear that it will only control the constitutionality of EC Law if an applicant shows in detail that the protection of fundamental rights within the Community is no longer equivalent to the protection assured by the Basic Law.[80]

The second aspect concerns the principle of democracy. In the *Maastricht* decision of 12 October 1993, the *Bundesverfassungsgericht* referred indeed to this principle in order to declare that it requires limits to be set to the transfer of powers to the institutions of the European Union.[81] The Court considered especially that the dynamic interpretation of the Community Treaties must not result in a treaty amendment because in this case 'such interpretations of competencies would not have any binding effect in Germany'.[82]

These extracts clearly show that the acknowledgement of the principle of direct effect is limited. Community law may have direct effect, provided that it does not conflict with basic principles and values enshrined in the Basic Law. Interestingly, several provisions of the Basic Law have been construed in a manner which connects them to the doctrine of direct effect even though they do not have any apparent link with international or Community law.

---

[76] See decision No. 91-294 DC, *Accord de Schengen*, (25.7.1991), Rec. p. 91, RJC I-455.

[77] Decision No. 97-394 DC, *Traité d'Amsterdam*, (31.12.1997), Rec. p. 344, RJC II-727.

[78] This image has been used by one of the judges. Cf. Kirchhof (1994), p. 11. See also Puissochet (2000), p. 86 et seq.

[79] For an overview cf. Kokott (1996).

[80] Decision of 7 June 2000, BverfGE vol. 102, p. 147. See Zimmer (2001), p. 3.

[81] BVerfGE vol. 89, p. 155.

[82] Ibid., p. 210.

3.2 ... interpreting other constitutional clauses related to the principle of direct effect

The case law of the German *Bundesverfassungsgericht* comprises several such decisions concerning articles of the Basic Law which do not show *a priori* any apparent link with EC law. Nevertheless they will be construed by the Court in a manner conferring on them a close connection with the question of direct effect. Where there are no comparable decisions to be found in the case law of the *Conseil constitutionnel*, three examples can be detected in German case law.

In the first place, there is Article 101(1) BL which declares extraordinary courts inadmissible and states that 'no one may be removed from the jurisdiction of his lawful judge'. In the *Solange 2* case, the *Bundesverfassungsgericht* indicates that the Court of Justice has to be considered as 'the lawful judge' when it decides on preliminary questions following Article 234 EC. Therefore, an individual can challenge the refusal of an ordinary court to ask for a preliminary ruling of the ECJ as being contrary to Article 101(1) BL. If such a refusal is found to be arbitrary, the *Bundesverfassungsgericht* will overrule the incriminated judgment.[83] This interpretation of Article 101(1) BL confers direct effect on Article 234 EC.

In the second place, Article 38(1) BL is construed as an individual right to participate in the democratic process of legitimization of the sovereign power. In the *Maastricht* decision of 12 October 1993, the *Bundesverfassungsgericht* had first of all to solve a problem of jurisdiction. Indeed, according to Article 93(1)(4a) BL, constitutional complaints introduced by individuals must be based on the allegation of a violation of their fundamental rights. According to the FCC, such a complaint could be based on Article 38 BL which guarantees 'general, direct, free, equal and secret elections' of the deputies in the German *Bundestag*.

For the first time it construed this right as a subjective right of each citizen 'to concur to the legitimization of the state power by the people on the federal level'. Consequently, the FCC reasoned, the right of a complainant from Article 38 BL can be violated if competences of the German Parliament are transferred to an intergovernmental organ of the European Union or the European Community to such an extent 'that the minimum requirements of democratic legitimation of the sovereign power the citizen is faced with are no longer fulfilled'.[84]

According to the FCC there are therefore limits to the transfer of powers to the Community institutions and there is a breach of Article 38 BL 'if an Act that opens up the German legal system to the direct validity and application of

---

[83] For an example see, BVerfGE vol. 75, p. 223, decision of 8 April 1987, *Kloppenburg*.

[84] Cf. BverfGE vol. 89, p. 172. Translation by the author ('unverzichtbare Mindestanforderungen demokratischer Legitimation der dem Bürger gegenübertretenden Hoheitsgewalt').

the law of the - supranational - European Communities does not establish with sufficient certainty the intended programme of integration'.[85] The reasoning of the FCC is clearly influenced by the principle of direct effect. In order to resume its argumentation in a single phrase: the democratic principle laid down in Articles 20 and 38 of the German Basic Law imposes limits to the transfer of powers to Community institutions because the citizens are (directly) faced with their sovereign power and because the law adopted by them will apply directly in the Member States.

In the third place, the FCC decided that constitutional complaints under Article 93(1)(4a) BL may now be introduced directly against measures of Community law. This question had been answered negatively in the first place (decision from 18 October 1967) because Community regulations are not 'acts of the German public authority'. But in the *Maastricht* decision, the Court altered its jurisprudence explicitly indicating that acts emanating from the 'public authority of a supranational Organisation' do also affect the beneficiaries of the protection of fundamental rights in Germany.[86] Hence, it is again the doctrine of direct effect of Community acts which justifies a solution apparently contrary to the intent of the Basic Law.[87]

Such an assimilation of acts of the Community institutions to acts of the German public authority appears indeed as a logical consequence of the direct effect doctrine. The procedural repercussions decided by the *Bundesverfassungsgericht* are, however, contrary to EC law. One might proclaim that Community acts have to be submitted to the same standards of judicial review as any act of German law, precisely because they affect individuals in Germany in the same way.[88] But the jurisdiction on the validity of Community law must remain with the Court of Justice.

These three examples illustrate that the doctrine of direct effect as developed by the Court of Justice and acknowledged by the national (constitutional) judges may sometimes generate a kind of 'boomerang effect'. Suddenly, national constitutional provisions which have not been written for this purpose will produce effects with regard to the European Union: the ECJ will become a 'lawful judge' in Germany, the principle of democracy (of the Basic Law) will limit the development of the European Union and the decision-making power of the Community institutions will be considered as 'public authority' on the German territory. As

---

[85] Ibid., p. 187. Translation drawn from [1994] 1 CMLR 57.

[86] Ibid., p. 175.

[87] According to Art. 93(1)(4a) 'The Federal Constitutional Court decides: (...) on complaints of unconstitutionality, being filed by any person claiming that one of his basic rights (...) has been violated by public authority'.

[88] The parallel to the above quoted passage in the decision of the *Conseil constitutionnel* in the *Schengen* decision (25.7.1991) is obvious.

with the principle of direct effect itself, these are all consequences which occur only within integrated or 'mutually overlapping' legal systems.[89]

4   Conclusion

The comparison between French and German constitutional law and jurisprudence with regard to the question of domestic effect of international law in general and of EC law in particular leads to three final remarks.

Firstly, this comparison clearly shows, that the divergent constitutional options in favour of 'monism' or 'dualism' tend to become more and more secondary in practice. A clause like Article 55 of the French Constitution actually operates - in anticipation and under several conditions - a sort of general reception of international treaties. Thus, it appears that in the bottom dualism subsists and that the option in favour of monism, whether it is taken by the constitution or by the case-law, constitutes merely 'a modality of dualism'.[90]

Secondly, the comparison of the case-law of the *Bundesverfassungsgericht* and the *Conseil constitutionnel* also revealed some interesting similarities corroborating the existence of common principles and values, which the 'guardians of the Constitution' defend legitimately. As it has been shown above, both courts accept - within certain limits - the principle of direct effect, especially in the field of EC law. In spite of undeniable and important differences in drawing these limits, the two courts notably agree on the necessity to maintain the constitutionally guaranteed rights or freedoms of the citizens. Furthermore, they also seem to agree on the point that Community measures with direct effect must be submitted to the same standards of judicial control as measures taken by national authorities.[91]

Finally, it is striking to see that the case law of the different French courts concerning the question of direct effect is not necessarily convergent. Compared to Germany, the French system appears to be dominated by the briefness of the dispositions of the preamble of 1946 and of Article 55, which altogether are rather elliptical, and by the coexistence of several orders of jurisdiction. As a result, this leads to the consequence that the direct effect of a treaty may be accepted or refused depending on the court to which the matter will be referred to (*Conseil d'Etat* or *Cour de cassation*). In Germany, such a situation is rendered impossible. According to Article 100 BL, ordinary courts must obtain a decision

---

[89] The expression is from Bieber (1988), p. 147.

[90] See Combacau & Sur (2001), at p. 180.

[91] This results from the above quoted passage in the *Schengen* decision of the *Conseil constitutionnel* (Decision No. 91-294 DC, *Accord de Schengen*, (25.7.1991), Rec. p. 91, RJC I-455) and the *Maastricht* decision of the Bundesverfassungsgericht, BVerfGE vol. 89, p. 175.

from the Federal Constitutional Court 'where ... doubt exists whether a rule of public international law is an integral part of federal law and whether such rule directly creates rights and duties for the individual'. Therefore, the issue of direct effect is under the central control of the Constitutional Court through a mechanism of preliminary ruling (art. 100 (3)BL).

CHAPTER VII

The Direct Effect of Public International Law

prof. dr. André Nollkaemper

1 Introduction

In the *LaGrand* case,[1] the International Court of Justice (ICJ) was confronted with the question whether a German national should have been able to rely, in a criminal procedure in courts of the United States, on Article 36 of the Convention on Consular Relations.[2] This provision determines the obligations of a State in which a foreign national is detained towards the detained person and towards the State of which that person is a national. It provides that, at the request of the detained person, the detaining State must inform the consular post of the State of which that person is a national of the individual' s detention 'without delay' and 'shall inform the person concerned without delay of his rights'. Article 36 had not been transposed into a rule of national law of the United States and, because of conflicting provisions of national law, the United States courts had not given it effect.[3] The International Court of Justice had to consider whether the failure to give effect to Article 36 was in violation of public international law.

The ICJ answered this question in the affirmative. It held that Article 36, paragraph 1 of the Convention on Consular Relations creates individual rights[4] and that individuals must be able to exercise these rights in the national courts of the states party.[5] The United States courts' application of a rule of national law that precluded them from attaching legal consequences to the Article, violated the Convention. Though the Court did not express it in these terms, in effect the ICJ' s judgment implies that in the circumstances of the case, the United States courts should have applied international law.[6]

In doctrinal terms, borrowed from the law of the European Community, one could say that the judgment implied that the United States courts should, in

---

*   André Nollkaemper would like to thank Ward Ferdinandusse for helpful comments on an earlier version of this chapter.

1   *LaGrand* case (*Germany* v. *United States*), judgment of 27 June 2001, [2001] 40 ILM 1069.

2   Vienna Convention on Consular Relations, 1963, UNTS Nos. 8638-8640, vol. 596, p. 262-512.

3   The application of Art. 36 had been considered but rejected in the following decisions: United States Court of Appeals (Ninth Circuit), *Karl LaGrand* v. *Stewart*, 170 F.3d 1158 (24.2.1999); United States Court of Appeals (Ninth Circuit), *Karl LaGrand* v. *Stewart*, 133 F.3d 1253 (16.1.1998).

4   *LaGrand* case, para. 77.

5   Ibid., paras. 89-90.

6   Technically, the ICJ is only concerned with the implementation of international law by states as legal entities and not with the specific position of the courts. However, as will be further explained in paragraph 5 below, given the decisions of many states to allow for the application of international law, its judgments may have direct consequences for the application of international law by national courts.

the circumstances of the case, have granted 'direct effect' to Article 36(1). The principle of 'direct effect' as used here, means that a national court (or any other national organ) applies a provision of international law not transformed into national law as a rule of decision in the national legal order.[7]

The judgment is a rare statement of an international court and is relevant to the direct effect of public international law. The scarcity of practice of international courts is reflected in the marginal role of the concept in international legal doctrine. While the concept plays a key role in the doctrinal understanding of the application of EC law by national courts and takes center stage in the textbooks on EU law,[8] the leading textbooks on public international law do not consider direct effect to be a matter of much interest and relegate the topic effect to national law.[9]

The *LaGrand* judgment is reason to reconsider in this contribution the silence in international legal scholarship on the direct effect of public international law and, more in particular, to consider in which respect the direct effect of a rule of international law is determined by public international law. The main thesis of the author is that the position that direct effect of public international law is not a matter governed by international law, is based on an oversimplifying dichotomy between public international law and national law. While public international law does not control direct effect in the way that is done by EC law, many courts across the world do not make the effect they give to international law exclusively dependent on their national legal systems. The concept of direct effect straddles the boundaries of international and national law and indeed illustrates the problems of the traditional dichotomy between international and national law.

The contribution is structured as follows. Before exploring the influence of international law over direct effect, paragraph 2 defines in more detail the concept of direct effect. Paragraph 3 explains that the fact that direct effect is

---

[7] The term 'rule of decision' is used to distinguish 'direct effect' from 'indirect effect', which refers to the application of international law as a means of interpretation of national law. The distinction is well established in EC law, see Betlem in this volume's chapter IV. While the distinction between direct and indirect for many purposes is unhelpful, see Knop (2000), for the purposes of this chapter the problems relating to the distinction can be left aside.

[8] See e.g. Hartley (1994), chapter 7 & 8; Craig & de Búrca (1998), p. 163-212; Kapteyn & VerLoren van Themaat (1998), p. 82-89.

[9] See e.g. Brownlie (1998), who treats the issue briefly on p. 50-51 and notes that 'The whole subject resists generalization, and the practice of states reflects the characteristics of the individual constitution'. Also Shaw (1997) confines himself in chapter 4 to a discussion of how various states proceed. A similar approach is taken in Sorensen (1968), p. 166. More appreciative of the significance of international law for the question of direct effect is the treatment in Cassese (2001), in particular p. 173-174, and more generally p. 166-181.

conditional on validity and supremacy, limits the degree in which direct effect can be controlled by international law. Paragraph 4 argues that the degree and depth of voluntary acceptance of direct effect nonetheless have made the concept a reality in the interface between international law and national law. Paragraph 5 explores, for those states that have accepted direct effect, the international and national legal determinants of direct effect.

2 The concept of direct effect

In order to determine to what extent international law governs direct effect, it first is necessary to define more precisely what is meant by 'direct effect'. It is understood in this contribution that a national court gives 'direct effect' to a rule of international law if it applies that rule as such, without that rule being transformed into a rule of national law. This does not mean that the rule of international law is applied *irrespective* of national law. For there always needs to be a rule of national law authorizing the courts to apply international law. It means, however, that the specific contents of the rule that is applied has not been transformed into a rule of national law.

When considering to what extent direct effect is governed by international law, we need to distinguish direct effect from two closely related concepts: validity and supremacy. Validity (also referred to as 'domestic validity') means that a rule of international law has legal force in the national legal order, without there being a requirement that the rule is transformed in a separate rule of national law. In some cases validity is barely distinguishable from direct effect, because the mere fact that a rule is valid may allow organs to apply it and, thus, to give it effect. However, as will be further discussed below, in other cases criteria additional to validity apply before a rule of international law can be given effect, and for that reason the concepts of direct effect and validity cannot be equated. A decisive reason for keeping the concepts of validity and direct effect separate is conceptual consistency with EC law.[10] The close relationship and interactions between public international law and EC law[11] makes it recommendable to use similar concepts for similar legal phenomena. Validity, then, is a necessary but not always sufficient condition for direct effect.[12]

'Supremacy' explains that when a rule of international law is valid in the national legal order but conflicts with a rule of national law, international law prevails over national law. The concept is distinct from direct effect, since in

---

[10] Case 6/64 *Costa/ENEL* [1964] ECR 585; see below paragraph 3.

[11] Leben (1998), at p. 295, noting that the distinctive features of the operation of Community law 'almost all exist but in a far less developed and efficient state in the international legal order'.

[12] Similarly Iwasawa (1986), at p. 645.

many cases rules of international law can have direct effect without a conflict arising and without need to resort to a conflict rule. Nonetheless, supremacy is critical to direct effect. A rule of international law that by virtue of its nature or contents could have direct effect can be rendered powerless when, according to applicable conflict rules, national law prevails in case conflict. It would be meaningless to say that a rule of international law has direct effect if that rule because of a lack of supremacy cannot be applied (cannot be given effect). In all cases where international law conflicts with national law, direct effect thus presumes supremacy. This definition follows the distinction between supremacy and direct effect in EC law.[13]

The distinction between validity and supremacy on the one hand and direct effect on the other, means that the principle of direct effect is a *conditional* principle. It exists only in those cases where international law has acquired validity and when, in case of conflict, it is supreme over national law. It is under these conditions that the concept of direct effect can determine the *specific* consequences under which international law can be applied.

What these specific conditions are depends on the circumstances of the case. Direct effect is best understood as a compound concept that may refer to a wide variety of different conditions or factors that explain, assuming the conditions of validity and supremacy are satisfied, whether or not a court can apply international law.[14]

As noted above, in some cases validity is a sufficient condition for direct effect. In national legal orders in which international law as such is valid, courts in some cases routinely apply (give effect to) international law, without considering any other 'specific' conditions. Examples are decisions on immunities in states that do not have an immunity statute. If a foreign state is sued, the national courts in such states do not examine whether that principle has 'direct effect' but simply apply the international law rule on immunities. The same is true for decisions of national courts (or the ECJ)[15] on the validity, suspension or termination of treaties. For instance, the ECJ in the *Racke* case considered the validity of a EC regulation that suspended a treaty with the Socialist Republic of Yugoslavia, without considering whether the rules on suspension of treaties in question had direct effect.[16] Direct effect here is simply the result of the

---

[13] E.g. Hartley (1994), at p. 234. Note, however, that because in EU law supremacy by definition follows direct effect, the concepts are not always clearly separated.

[14] A similar approach to direct effect as a compound concept is taken by Iwasawa (1986).

[15] The concepts relevant to the relationship between international law and national law are equally applicable to the relationship between international law and EC law.

[16] Case C-162/96 *Racke* [1998] ECR I-3655, para. 47. See Kuijper (1998), in particular at p. 21-22. Also in domestic law direct effect (in the narrow sense discussed below) does not appear to be relevant in determining validity of treaties, see Conforti & Labella (1990).

normal operation of the law and is not a concept with independent explanatory or normative force.

In different factual constellations, however, courts consider that the mere validity of a rule is not sufficient for its judicial application. This holds in particular in cases which do not concern a typical interstate case where the courts, as organs of the state, apply international law to protect the rights of other states (such as a case involving state immunity) but concern disputes between a private party and a state. An example is a case involving a claim based on international human rights law. In most states, courts considering the application of international human rights law will not be satisfied with a determination that this law is valid in the national legal order, but will examine whether certain additional conditions are fulfilled. These additional conditions are essentially twofold, generally indicated as subjective and objective direct effect.[17]

First, in many states courts inquire whether the private party bringing a claim based on international law has a 'right' or 'legal interest' that is protected by international law or, in reverse cases in which international law is applied vis-à-vis individuals, whether the rules in question are binding on individuals. This is the so-called requirement of subjective direct effect.[18] This requirement, which may be translated in issues of standing or invocability,[19] can be a formidable threshold, since most courts perceive international obligations as determining legal relationships between states and as being of no legal interest to private parties. It causes, for instance, the virtual absence of a role of the national judiciary in the application of international environmental law.[20]

Second, courts will generally only apply rules at the request of, or vis-à-vis, private persons when such rules by virtue of their contents lend themselves for judicial application.[21] This is the requirement of objective direct effect. This

---

[17] The distinction is made, e.g., in Simma (1997), at p. 85. See also Vázquez (1992), who distinguishes between the question whether a treaty is self-executing and whether individuals have standing to invoke it. He rightly notes that the two issues may overlap: 'standing doctrine addresses the same issue that the courts sometimes address as a 'self-execution' issue: whether the duty imposed by the treaty gives rise to a correlative primary right of the litigant such that the litigant may enforce the rule in court' (p. 1141).

[18] This also is the conceptual underpinning of the notion of direct effect in EC law, see chapter III by Ward in this volume, paragraph 2 and paragraph 4. But see Case C-72/95 *Kraaijeveld* [1996] ECR I-5403, para. 56.

[19] Vázquez (1992), at p. 1133 et. seq.

[20] Bodanksy & Brunnée (1998).

[21] See also Vázquez (1992), at p. 1123, noting that a treaty is enforceable in the courts only if *it establishes judicially enforceable obligations*. If it is instead hortatory, a litigant claiming that the defendant has violated the treaty will lose on the merits because the treaty does not require the defendant to behave

requirement corresponds to the prevailing conceptualization of direct effect in EC law, where direct effect is made contingent on unconditionality and precision of the norm in question.[22] For instance, the *Hoge Raad* of the Netherlands holds that the direct effect of a rule of public international law is determined by the question whether it is of 'such a kind that the provision can simply function as an objective rule in the national legal order'.[23] In some states this requirement is considered in terms of the question whether the concerned rules are self-executing.[24]

It is not easy to understand why in cases involving, for instance, the application of rules on immunity, validity or termination of treaties courts mostly do not expressly employ a test of justiciability but do so in cases involving the determination of rights or duties of private parties. This can best be explained by the fact that because states accept as the default position that international law is *not* applied in disputes involving private parties, additional criteria are applied to ascertain that it is a case that lends itself for judicial rather than legislative or executive decision-making. The relative clarity of the norm then helps determining which branch is to give effect to the rule of international law at issue in the case. Direct effect than becomes a means to separate powers between the branches of government.

It follows that the term 'direct effect' can be used in two forms: a generic form referring to all cases where a court can use international law as a rule of decision (in which form validity can be a sufficient condition) and a more narrow form in which it refers to certain additional criteria that apply when claims based on international law are made by or against private parties.[25] In literature, and also in regard of EC law, the term mostly is used in the latter sense.[26]

---

otherwise than he has been behaving. Even if the ultimate objective may be to establish obligations affecting the individual, the individual's suit may be dismissed as premature because the treaty does not purport to establish those obligations itself.

[22] Case 8/81 *Becker* [1982] ECR 53. See Prechal in her contribution to this volume's chapter II.

[23] Hoge Raad (Supreme Court), 30.5.1986, NJ 1986/688, para. 3.2, reproduced in *Netherlands Yearbook of International* Law 1987, p. 392.

[24] In the United States this test was formulated in the US Supreme Court decision in *Foster* v. *Neilson*, 27 US (2 Pet.) 253, 314 (1829). See for analysis the articles by Iwasawa (1986) Vázquez (1992) and Koh (1991). As observed by Vázquez (1992), p. 1141, the distinction is not sharp and the term 'self-executing' in some cases is used to refer to subjective rather than objective direct effect.

[25] The fact that these criteria are 'additional' has led some observers to qualify direct effect as a 'shield' that may preclude actual application of international law. However, this qualification is not helpful. When the default position is accepted that international law applies primarily between states, the criteria that allow courts to apply international law at request of a private party could just as well be considered as a sword. See for the debate in the context of EU law Prechal (2000), at p. 1047-1048.

[26] That also holds for use of the concept in EC law, see e.g. chapter VI by Gerkrath in this volume (paragraph 2).

However, the distinction between these two meanings is conceptually troublesome. The question whether a court can apply a rule of international law depends on a wide variety of issues, of which the question whether a private plaintiff or defendant is involved is only one example. Another relevant question is whether the application of international law concerns the merits of the case or preliminary issues (such as immunities). Yet another question is, which remedies the plaintiff seeks. In case where a plaintiff seeks a mere declaration of compatibility of a national act with international law, the court may not require more than validity. In such a case, a rule of international law can very well have direct effect, even though it is raised by a private party, but does not expressly create rights (subjective direct effect) for private parties.[27] On the other hand, if a private party seeks compensation, as a remedy for a violation of a rule of international law, or the setting aside of national law that conflicts with international law, validity may not be enough and the court may want to seek to establish whether the rule of international law intends to provide a right to the plaintiff.[28] It all depends on the context in which the rule is invoked: one and the same rule may have direct effect in some cases but not in others.

The larger point is that 'direct effect' is best considered as a compound concept consisting of various criteria that, depending on the circumstances of the case, in combination determine the effect of a norm. The concept of direct effect can group such diverse factors. But it is not helpful to give the notion independent explanatory power or normative power that would help to integrate and understand such diverse issues. It is not a separate test that needs to be fulfilled before courts can apply international law.[29] For particular purposes, such as the general question considered in this chapter, it is helpful to group these factors under direct effect. But otherwise there is a strong case to be made against using the concept as an independent explanatory tool for understanding which rules can and cannot be applied by national courts.[30]

---

[27] Similarly Iwasawa (1986), at p. 646-640. Cf. Case C-377/98 *Biotechnological inventions* [2001] ECR I-7079, para. 54, in which the ECJ noted: 'Even if .. the [Convention on Biological Diversity] contains provisions which do not have direct effect, in the sense that they do not create rights which individuals can rely on directly before the courts, that fact does not preclude review by the courts of compliance with the obligations incumbent on the Community as a party to that agreement'. The use of language here is confusing, because also in reviewing compliance the ECJ would give effect, be it for a different purpose, to the treaty in question.

[28] Iwasawa (1986), p. 690 who, however, employs a narrow concept of 'direct applicability' and notes that even when a treaty is not directly applicable, it still may have legal effect because, for instance, a court may strike down a law that conflicts with that treaty. In the terminology used here, there is no reason not to say that also in the latter case the treaty has direct effect.

[29] Similarly Vázquez (1992), at p. 1115.

[30] Vázquez (1992), at p. 1120 rightly finds applicable the observation that Louis Henkin made with regard to the political questions doctrine: the concept of direct effect can be seen as 'an unnecessary, deceptive

It needs to be acknowledged that this use of terminology differs from that used in the practice of many states which use 'direct effect' as a separate test to restrict the application of international law by the courts. However, such uses cloud the relevant legal and policy uses and are best avoided.

The consequence for the purposes of this chapter is that it is not helpful to examine in the abstract the international legal status of the principle of direct effect, but rather to examine to what extent the determinants of direct effect are influenced by international law.

3 The conditional nature of direct effect

The fact that direct effect is contingent on validity and supremacy has consequences for the degree in which direct effect is governed by international law.

It generally is thought that both validity and supremacy are not governed by public international law. As to validity, many states, in particular those in which parliamentary approval is not a precondition for the entry into force of treaty obligations, consider themselves at liberty to separate their international rights and obligations from the national legal order and to disallow their organs to apply rules of international law that are not made part of national law. No international court has said that these practices as such are 'illegal' and that international law is, out of its own force, valid in the national legal order. Even the European Court of Human Rights, that supervises a part of international law that is particularly integrated with national law, has held that while incorporation of the European Convention in national law would be a faithful method of applying the Convention,[31] the European Convention formally is neutral as to

---

package of several established doctrines that has misled lawyers and courts to find in it things that were never put there and make it far more than the sum of its parts'. Similarly Koh (1991), at p. 2361 and p. 2383 (stating that the sole relevant question is whether the plaintiff has stated a claim upon which relief can be granted) and McDougal (1977), p. 77. The point is comparable to that made in respect of EC law by Prechal (2000), p. 1047-1069.

[31] Case of *Ireland* v. *the United Kingdom* (18.1.1978), Appl. 5310/71, EHRR, Ser. A, No. 25, para. 239. A similar position was taken by the UN Committee on Economic, Social and Cultural Rights, noting that 'while the Covenant does not formally oblige States to incorporate its provisions in domestic law, such an approach is desirable. Direct incorporation avoids problems that might arise in the translation of treaty obligations into national law, and provides a basis for the direct invocation of the Covenant rights by individuals in national courts. For these reasons, the Committee strongly encourages formal adoption or incorporation of the Covenant in national law'. UN Doc E/C.12/1998/24, CESCR General comment 9 of 3 December 1998, para. 8.

the mode of implementation and does not require incorporation.[32] What matters
is that the substance of the guaranteed rights should in fact be enjoyed by
individuals.[33]

The same holds for supremacy of international law. It is true that the ICJ
has stated that 'international law prevails over domestic law'.[34] However, state
practice shows no general acceptance of supremacy of international law in
the national legal order,[35] and in the absence of international decisions to the
contrary, it is a safe conclusion that the effects of this rule are confined to the
international sphere and do not extend to the national sphere.[36]

---

[32] Case of *Swedish Engine Drivers' Union* v. *Sweden* (6.2.1976), Appl. 5614/72, EHRR, Ser. A, No. 20,
     para. 50 (stating that the Convention does not lay down 'for the Contracting States any given manner
     for ensuring within their internal law the effective implementation of any of the provisions of the
     Convention'). See also Frowein (1993), noting that while Articles 1 and 13 may suggest an obligation
     to apply the Convention directly, the fact that six of the original contracting parties did not allow
     for incorporation makes an interpretation to that effect implausible. But see African Commission on
     Human and Peoples Rights, Communication No. 129/94, *Civil Liberties Organization* v. *Nigeria* (holding
     that the Act of the Nigerian Government to nullify the domestic effect of the Charter constitutes an
     affront to the African Charter on Human and Peoples Rights).

[33] Janis, Kay & Bradley (2000), p. 472. See on general international law: Lauterpacht (1978), p. 566
     (writing that the proposition that international law is applicable by municipal courts ipso facto, by virtue
     of a rule of international law superior and independent of the will of the State 'is a theory and not a
     rule of existing law').

[34] Advisory Opinion on *the Applicability of the obligation to Arbitrate under Section 21 of the United Nations
     Headquarters Agreement of 26 June 1947*, ICJ Rep. (1988) p. 12-35, at p. 34.

[35] Many states consider themselves at liberty to adopt or keep in place laws that violate or do not
     give full effect to international law. In states that do not grant rules of international law automatic
     effect in national law (like the United Kingdom) *a fortiori* there is no supremacy. In countries that
     employ the so-called 'later-in-time rule', international law prevails only over earlier legislation. If the
     legislature adopts domestic laws contrary to the treaty-obligations, it thereby disallows the courts to
     apply international law. See e.g. U.S Supreme Court, *Chae Chan Ping* v. *US*, 130 U.S. 581 (1889) (holding
     that a treaty is the equivalent of an act of Congress, 'to be repealed or modified at the pleasure of
     Congress. In either case the last expression of the sovereign will must control').

[36] See for a typical cautious judgment: Permanent Court of International Justice, *Interpretation of the
     Memel Statute*, PCIJ Ser. A/B, No. 49, p. 336. Cf. ECHR, judgment of 9 December 1994, *The Holy
     Monasteries* v. *Greece*, A. 301-A, stating that Article 13 of the Convention 'does not go so far as to require a
     remedy whereby the laws of a Contracting State may be impugned before a national authority as being in
     themselves contrary to the Convention'. Tammes (1962), at p. 163 (stating that the fact that the majority
     of states do impose restrictions on the extent to which national law or the constitution may be put to
     the test of conventional international law 'rules out the possibility that any wrong general international
     law is at present constituted by enacted or self-imposed restrictions on the courts in the application of
     international law over national law'); Fitzmaurice (1986), p. 587-66. Scholarly opinions that argue that
     the supremacy of international law means that also in the national legal order national law yields in case
     of conflict are few and far between; Erades (1980), at p. 415 (arguing that municipal law that is contrary

Both as to validity and supremacy, the silence of international law contrasts with EC law. In the *Costa/ENEL* case, the ECJ said:

'*By contrast with ordinary international treaties, the EEC Treaty has created its own legal system which, on the entry into force of the Treaty*, became an integral part of the legal systems of the Member States and which their courts are bound to apply' (emphasis added).[37]

And as to supremacy, the Court said that:

'*The integration into the laws of each Member State of provisions which derive from the Community, and more generally the terms and the spirit of the Treaty*, make it impossible for the States, as a corollary, to accord precedence to a unilateral and subsequent measure over a legal system accepted by them on the basis of reciprocity' (emphasis added).[38]

It follows that Community law becomes automatically part of the legal systems of the Member States regardless of their constitutional law with respect to the relationship between international and domestic law and that it prevails over national law in case of conflict. It is this combination of validity and supremacy that creates the precondition for direct effect as a powerful principle of EC law.

Public international law lacks those preconditions. Without the unqualified acceptance of the principles of validity and (whenever a conflict arises) supremacy, direct effect lacks the essential force to penetrate the national legal orders and to empower national courts to apply international law where national law fails.[39] The absence of compulsory or even automatic validity and supremacy

---

to international law shall yield to the latter, and that international law of necessity would be supreme in the domestic legal order); Amador (1974), p. 19-20, stating that international law prevails over municipal law with all the consequences which necessarily derive from the admission that the later is the inferior order in the hierarchy of legal norms. If international law would oblige a state to undertake something or to refrain from undertaking something, 'it cannot be suggested that a provision of its internal legislation which is contrary to, or incompatible with, that obligation, can possibly be valid. Such a provision would in fact be null and void; and hence it could not even be relied on *internally* as a defence to an international obligation'.

[37] *Costa/ENEL* (as cited), at p. 593.

[38] Ibid. at p. 593-594.

[39] See Buergenthal (1992), at p. 320-321, noting that 'a treaty that, as a matter of international law, is deemed to be directly applicable is not self-executing ipso facto under the domestic law of the states parties to it. All that can be said about such a treaty is that the States party thereto have an international obligation to take whatever measures are necessary under their domestic law to ensure that the specific provisions of the treaty ..., not only of its substantive obligations, are accorded the status of domestic law'.

means *a fortiori* that states are at liberty to determine, according to their own national legal systems, the conditions[40] and consequences[41] of direct effect. For it is *prima facie* implausible that if international law would be agnostic on validity and supremacy, it would impose limitations on a principle that is contingent on these concepts. All this excludes what Iwasawa called the 'given-theory': the idea that international law would determine whether or not a particular rule of international law has direct effect.[42]

4   The voluntary acceptance of direct effect

The fact that public international law does not *oblige* states to allow for direct effect in the same manner as is done by EC law, does not negate the influence of international law over direct effect.

A large and increasing number of states that have made public international law part of the national legal order, grant it precedence in case of conflicts, and allow courts to apply directly rules of international law. These developments have been detailed elsewhere[43] and need not be considered here. There also are many examples of states where international law is not formally part of national law, yet where national organs consider themselves empowered, possibly even obliged, to give effect to international law by applying it in conjunction with national law and by construing national law in conformity with international law.[44]

One could say that all these states allow the inroads of international law by voluntary choice, unguided by sense of legal obligation. However, there appears sufficient acceptance of the notion of international law as 'higher law' that must be given effect in the national legal order, to accept that the better position is that states generally do allow for internal effect by voluntary acceptance of a perceived, even if unarticulated and certainly unenforceable, obligation under

---

[40] This of course also holds for the procedural conditions governing the actions of interested parties that seek to protect their legal interests under a treaty; also here the liberty left by EC law (see Case C-228/98 *Kharalambos Dounias* [2000] ECR I-577, para. 58) is magnified.

[41] For instance, this holds for question whether international law can be applied directly in horizontal sphere; in public international law there is not the beginning of the relative uniformity that exists on this point in EC law. This applies also to the European Convention of Human Rights, see Van Dijk & van Hoof (1998), at p. 22-26.

[42] Iwasawa (1986), at p. 650.

[43] E.g. Cassese (1985); Vereshchetin, (1996); Stein (1994).

[44] These uses fall outside the definition of 'direct effect' given above, but are indicative of the opening of national systems towards international law. See for the open attitude of courts in the United Kingdom Higgins (2000).

international law.[45] In this situation, the position that public international law is neutral on the matter of validity and supremacy seems too narrow.[46]

It must also be considered that the distinction with EC law on this point is only a relative one, since some degree of voluntary acceptance is also present in EC law. Also in EC law supremacy eventually exists by virtue of constitutional acceptance, as can be seen from the decision of the German Constitutional Court as well as other constitutional courts that have placed limits on the supremacy of Community law.[47]

The doctrinal question whether the openness of international law is construed in terms of an implementation of an obligation or as a voluntary choice, for many states is a question of academic interest only. In actual practice, in a large number of states the reality is that validity and, to a lesser extent, supremacy are given, and that in those cases direct effect is as much a reality as it were in the case that validity and supremacy were to be determined by public international law itself. As Lauterpacht notes, while the independence of international law as a rule of decision 'is conceded by the State and is revocable at its instance... so long as it lasts ... it has the effect of elevating to the authority of a legal rule the unity of international and municipal law'.[48] The position advocated here thus holds that for those states that allow judicial application of international law, the determination of whether there is an abstract international law principle proclaiming direct effect is of little help in understanding and explaining their practice. Beyond the recognition that international law cannot force direct effect, a wide range of cases opens in which direct effect functions and can explain interactions between international and national law.

It might be thought that if the direct effect of a rule of international law is contingent on a prior decision by a state to consider international law as part of the national legal order, it is no longer possible to speak of direct effect of *international* law, for the rules would need to be considered as rules of national law. However, that inference would be incorrect. Rules of international law that

---

[45] Morgenstern (1950), at p. 92, noting that the significance of the constitutional trend lies in the fact that states have felt impelled to provide, in their most fundamental law, for the supremacy of international law within the state.

[46] There is truth in the observation of Morgenstern (1950), stating that true supremacy of public international law would be 'obscured by the fact that, owing to the absence of compulsory judicial dispute settlement in the international sphere, responsibility is not always the automatic consequence of violation of rules of law' (p. 91).

[47] German Federal Constitutional Court, 12 October 1993, *Brunner* [1994] 1 CMLR 57 and [1994] ILM 388. See also the decision of the Danish Supreme Court, 6 April 1998, *SEW* 1998, p. 398; *Ars Aequi* 1999, p. 121, with case note by Kortmann, who points out that Italy and Sweden have adopted a similar position (p. 124).

[48] Lauterpacht (1978), at p. 548.

are accepted as part of the national legal order remain fully subject to the secondary rules of international law, including interpretation, modification and termination, and in that respect remain, while incorporated in national law, fully part of the international legal order. One then could say that one and the same rule then is part of two legal systems, or, more precisely, that in respect of that rule at least the distinction between the legal systems is not sharp. This opens the door to a conceptualization of direct effect as a concept straddling the distinction between international and national law.

5 The determinants of direct effect

The mechanisms of public international law that influence direct effect, in those countries that allow for it, are diffuse and not well organized. Divergences between the practices of the courts of states are significant. The differences that exist between the practice of the courts of member states of the EU,[49] notwithstanding the fact that in the EU responsibility for determination of direct effect in the final instance rests with the ECJ,[50] is magnified in public international law. These differences are in keeping with the normal process of auto-appreciation in the application of international law.[51]

Yet, in state practice some common patterns can be identified. Most states accept that public international law contains some rules that by virtue of their nature or contents are intended to be applied by national courts and are suitable for application by these courts. While for international law it is irrelevant whether such rules are applied as part of national law (after transformation) or applied directly, in those states that do allow for international law to be applied directly, the nature or contents of these rules generally will lead to courts granting them direct effect.

Rules on immunity can be mentioned as an example. By their very nature, these rules generally are applied by national courts. This was recognized in the advisory opinion on *Difference relating to immunity from legal process of a special rapporteur of the Commission on Human Rights*, in which the ICJ stated:

'When national courts are seized of a case in which the immunity of a United Nations agent is in issue, they should immediately be notified of any finding by the Secretary-General concerning that immunity. That finding, and its documentary expression, creates a presumption which can only be set aside for the most compelling reasons and is thus to be given the greatest weight by national courts'.[52]

---

[49] See Jans & Prinssen in this volume's chapter V.

[50] Art. 234 EC Treaty.

[51] Weil (1992), at p. 220.

[52] ICJ Reports 1999, p. 62, para. 61.

The Court found that the Government of Malaysia had the obligation to inform the Malaysian courts of the finding of the Secretary-General that Dato' Param Cumaraswamy was entitled to immunity from legal process.[53] In this particular case, Malaysia had implemented the obligations to grant immunity in their national law,[54] but had they not done so, the obligations would have been the same and the courts normally would have to proceed in the same manner. International law requires that states model their national laws in such manner that rules on immunity can be applied by the courts, whether through national laws or direct. In the many states that have not adopted immunity legislation, that requirement generally is given effect by granting direct effect.

Except for rare cases in which immunity is controlled by the 1946 Convention on the Privileges and Immunities of the United Nations which gives controlling authority to the UN Secretary-General and ultimately to the ICJ, the interpretation of the international rule on immunities and the effect given to that rule will primarily depend on the interpretation by the national court. However, as noted above, that is characteristic of the normal process of international law[55] and does not negate the controlling role of international law.

There is no fundamental distinction between rules on immunity of states or UN personnel and international rules that aim to regulate the rights and duties of private parties. The *Danzig* opinion is of continuing relevance here. The PCIJ said that, while in principle a treaty does not create direct rights and obligations for individuals that should be enforceable in national courts,

> 'the very object of an international agreement, according to the intention of the contracting Parties, may be the adoption by the Parties of some definite rules creating individual rights and obligations and enforceable by the national courts'.[56]

International law thus recognizes that states may conclude a treaty that requires the contracting parties to ensure that all or some of its provisions have the status

---

[53] Ibid., dictum para. 2(a).

[54] Provisions relating to the privileges and immunities of persons employed on mission on behalf of the United Nations were incorporated in the subsidiary legislation entitled the Diplomatic Privileges (United Nations and International Court of Justice) Order, 1949. See Statement of the Government of Malaysia in the opinion *Difference relating to immunity from legal process of a special rapporteur of the Commission on Human Rights*, para. 2.7, org/icjwww/idocket/inuma/inumaframe.htm, under 'written pleadings'.

[55] Weil (1992).

[56] *Danzig* PCIJ, Ser. B, No 15 (1928), p. 17-18. See for analysis Van Panhuys (1964), p. 24 et seq. Intent similarly is considered decisive in determining whether international law can be applied in criminal proceedings, see *Presecutor* v. *Tadic, Decision on the Defence motion for interlocutory appeal on jurisdiction*, 2.10.1995, paras. 128-130.

of directly applicable law and be enforced by their domestic courts.[57] Intent will not govern whether these rules are applied as national law or as international law,[58] but for courts in those states that do not require transformation, this will generally mean that they have to apply international law as such, that is: give it direct effect. That decision, then, is a matter of interpretation of international law.[59]

The controlling effect of international law under this criterion is most obvious when states express a negative intent, that is: an intention not to allow for direct effect. An example is the Agreement on international humane trapping standards between the European Community, Canada and the Russian Federation,[60] which provides that:

'This Agreement is not self-executing. Each Party shall implement the commitments and obligations arising from this Agreement in accordance with its internal procedures'.

A national court confronted with a claim by a private person based on the Agreement, generally will determine that it was the intention of the parties not to have courts, without further implementing legislation, apply the agreement and thus will not grant direct effect to the Agreement.[61] For all practical purposes, international law thus will control the effect.

That also can be the case when it follows from a treaty that states agreed to make certain provisions enforceable by individuals before national courts ('positive intent'). That intention primarily will be shown in the subjective element of direct effect. An obvious example are rights contained in the European Convention on Human Rights[62] and other human rights treaties. These treaties require

---

[57] Buergenthal (1992), at p. 319. The EC Treaty, as construed by the ECJ, is precisely such a treaty. See the chapter III by Ward in this volume (paragraph 2).

[58] See Riesefeld (1980), at p. 895-896.

[59] This was already noted by Advocate General Roemer in Case 26/62 *Van Gend en Loos* [1963] ECR 1, at p. 8, who stated that while the question as to the effects of an international agreement on the nationals of a member state does not refer *exclusively* to problems of constitutional law. See for views on the mixed international - national law nature of direct effect also Riesefeld (1980), at p. 896-900; Buergenthal (1992), at p. 319. The interpretation that direct effect *exclusively* is a matter of national law (see e.g. Iwasawa (1986) at p. 650-651) thus is to be rejected.

[60] O.J. 1998, L 42/43.

[61] Bleckmann (1981), at p. 375. Iwasawa (1997), p. 237.

[62] Van Dijk & van Hoof (1998), p. 19, stating that 'The subject-matter regulated by the Convention - the protection of civil and political rights - lends itself eminently to direct effect. In fact, it concerns precisely the protection of rights which can be exercised without further measures being taken by the national authorities; that is: rights which by their very nature are directly applicable'. See also Pisillo-Mazzeschi (1999), in particular (with regard to Art. 5(5) of the European Convention) p. 163.

that their provisions have the status of directly applicable law and be enforced as such by their domestic courts. As noted by the Committee on Economic, Social and Cultural Rights,

'In general, legally binding international human rights standards should operate directly and immediately within the domestic legal system of each State party, thereby enabling individuals to seek enforcement of their rights before national courts and tribunals. The rule requiring the exhaustion of domestic remedies reinforces the primacy of national remedies in this respect. The existence and further development of international procedures for the pursuit of individual claims is important, but such procedures are ultimately only supplementary to effective national remedies'.[63]

Again, while human rights treaties themselves do not express on the question whether the rights should be applied as international law or as national law, in the many states that have made the decision to open their constitutions for directly applicable rules of international law, courts generally will recognize the intention to make the provisions enforceable in domestic courts. That intention is translated in the direct effect of these rights. It is the international law determinants of direct effect of such rules, rather than their exclusive subjection to the diversity of national law, that makes it possible for observers to assess whether particular national judicial decisions on direct effect are 'right' or 'wrong'.[64]

States have not often employed the possibility to conclude treaties that provide that their provisions must be enforceable in the national courts. It commonly is thought that most of the time it does not matter to the states party to a treaty how each of them complies with its provisions, whether they do so by statute, administrative regulation or judicial decrees, as long as they comply with substantive obligations.[65] However, it appears that there is an increasing number of treaties that do envisage or require a role for the national judiciary. Whenever this is done, and states do allow for direct effect, it can be said that the notion of direct effect rests on a characteristic of the treaty or circumstances surrounding the conclusion or termination of the treaty. In that respect direct effect therefore is a matter of international law.[66]

Some states accord direct effect to treaties also in the absence of a manifest intent to make such provisions enforceable by national courts. The practice of the Netherlands is illustrative. As noted, the question whether a norm has direct

[63] UN Doc E/C.12/1998/24, CESCR General comment 9 of 3 December 1998, para. 4.

[64] E.g. Cassese (2001), at p. 174, noting that only in 1991 the French Conseil d'Etat came to the right conclusion that Art. 8 of the European Convention is self-executing.

[65] Buergenthal (1992), p. 320.

[66] Bleckmann (1981), at p. 414 and references above in note 59 .

effect is determined by the question of whether a norm is of 'such a kind that the provision can function as an objective rule in the national legal order'.[67] No express intention of the protection of individual rights usually is required and the emphasis is on objective rather than subjective direct effect. Also this test is a matter of treaty interpretation and in that respect a matter of international law.[68] It is clear, however, that the decision to allow courts to apply such rules as such is not dictated by international law. It can be expected that in the formulation and application of the test of objective direct effect, substantial differences can be shown to exist between states.

Indeed, in several states courts are reluctant to recognize the direct effect of international law, often irrespective of the apparent intention of the parties.[69] In that respect, courts may introduce what may be called 'second order dualism', that is to say, filtering the entry of international law even when the constitution in principle has accepted international law as part of the national legal order.

The influence of international law over direct effect may partly be determined by the practice of international courts and other international institutions. Here a critical difference exists with EC law, however. In infringement cases under Article 226 EC, matters of validity and supremacy and also direct effect in principle are not relevant and the ECJ will only consider compliance with a rule of EC law by the state as a whole. In the preliminary rulings under Article 234, that concern the position of national organs vis-à-vis Community law, the ECJ will, if requested, pronounce on the matter of direct effect. It is not accidental the most directly relevant decision by the PCIJ/ICJ is the *Danzig* opinion, in which the Permanent Court was asked to answer precisely the question of whether the *Beambtabkommen* had direct effect. In cases of alleged breach of international law, courts normally need not reach that issue.

Nonetheless, the determinations of international courts may clarify intent and contents of international rules and may thereby have direct consequence for the direct effect of international law. This is illustrated by the *LaGrand* case. Based on a textual interpretation, the Court found that Article 36(1) of the Convention on Consular Relations created individual rights. It said that:

'Article 36, paragraph 1(b), spells out the obligations the receiving State has towards the detained person and the sending State. It provides that, at the request of the detained person, the receiving State must inform the consular post of the sending State of the individual's detention 'without delay'. It provides further that any communication by the detained person addressed to the consular post of the

---

[67] Hoge Raad (Supreme Court), 30.5.1986 (as cited).

[68] E.g. Hoge Raad (Supreme Court), *Hansa Chemie v. Bechem Chemie* (16.5.1997), *Netherlands Yearbook of International Law* 1999, p. 307.

[69] Conforti (1993), p. 25-34.

*sending State must be forwarded to it by authorities of the receiving State 'without
delay'. Significantly, this subparagraph ends with the following language: 'The said
authorities shall inform the person concerned without delay of his rights under this
subparagraph'* (emphasis added). *Moreover, under Article 36, paragraph 1(c), the
sending State's right to provide consular assistance to the detained person may not be
exercised 'if he expressly opposes such action'. The clarity of these provisions, viewed
in their context, admits of no doubt. It follows, as has been held on a number of
occasions, that the Court must apply these as they stand ... Based on the text of
these provisions, the Court concludes that Article 36, paragraph 1, creates individual
rights...'.*[70]

Once it was established that Article 36(1) created individual rights, Article 36 (2)
of the Convention required national law to enable these rights to be protected
in the national legal order:

*'The rights referred to in paragraph 1 of this Article shall be exercised in conform-
ity with the laws and regulations of the receiving State, subject to the proviso, however,
that the said laws and regulations must enable full effect to be given to the purposes
for which the rights accorded under this Article are intended'.*

In view of Article 36(2), the Court then said that national courts of the United
States should have been allowed to attach legal significance to the violation of
the rights set forth in Article 36(1).[71] One could say that, in terms of the *Danzig*
opinion, the Convention on Consular Relations was considered as a treaty that
requires the contracting parties to ensure that Article 36(1) is given the status of
directly applicable law and be enforced as such by their domestic courts.[72]

From the perspective of the ICJ, the question whether states have made the
provisions part of directly applicable national law or allow for direct effect of
international law (a choice left open by Article 36 paragraph 2) is immaterial.
Not bothered by the question whether implementation of international law in
national law proceeds through incorporation or transformation, the ICJ simply
required that national organs give effect to international law.[73] Presumably, the

---

[70] *LaGrand* case (as cited) para. 77.

[71] Ibid., para. 91.

[72] Buergenthal (1992), at p. 319.

[73] See also para. 125, where the Court stated, on the matter of remedies: 'in cases where the individuals
concerned have been subjected to prolonged detention or convicted and sentenced to severe penalties. In
the case of such a conviction and sentence, it would be incumbent upon the United States to allow the
review and reconsideration of the conviction and sentence by taking account of the violation of the rights
set forth in the Convention. This obligation can be carried out in various ways. *The choice of means must
be left to the United States*' (emphasis added).

Court was aware that the Convention on Consular Relations, under Article IV of the Constitution of the United States, was part of national law and that under certain circumstances it could be given direct effect. But were that not the case, this part of the ruling most probably would have been the same - the fact that the United States did not allow for individuals to exercise treaty-based rights was sufficient to find a breach of international law.

Nonetheless, this part of the judgment, and this point is true of findings of international courts in general, may have a direct relevance for the effect given to international law by national courts in states whose constitution allows for direct effect. The traditional understanding that international courts are not concerned with the modalities of national implementation and only rule on the question whether international law is complied with, neglects the effects of such requirements in the national legal order in those states that do allow for direct effect. When considered from the perspective of the United States, given the fact that it had not transposed the Convention on Consular Relations into a rule of national law and given that its courts in principle are allowed to apply international law directly, the consequence of the ICJ's judgment was that the US Courts should have applied Article 36 rule as such, that is: give it direct effect. In its decision in the *Angel Breard* case, rendered some years earlier, the US Supreme Court had noted that Article 36 'arguably' had direct effect (was 'self-executing').[74] In later cases United States courts took different positions on the matter.[75] While it by no means is certain that the ICJ's judgment in *LaGrand* would be followed directly by the US Supreme Court or other courts, much room for argument has been taken away. International law now would more control the issue than at the time the *Breard* decision was rendered.

The practice of other courts can similarly be relevant. While also the European Court of Human Rights will not pronounce on the question whether the European Convention should be given direct effect, when states do allow for direct effect in their national legal order, the determinations that individuals should have been able to invoke a particular norm, generally will have the result that the courts in question must give the norm direct effect.

---

74 US Supreme Court, *Breard* v. *Greene*, Warden, 000 U.S. 97-8214 (1998). See for earlier judicial decisions in this case: US District Court, E.D. Virginia, *Angel Breard, Petitioner* v. *J.D. Netherland, Warden, Respondent*, 949 F.Supp. 1255 (1996), US District Court, E.D. Virginia, *Republic of Paraguay* v. *George Allen, Governor of Virginia, et al., Defendants*, 949 F. Supp. 1269 (1996), US Court of Appeals, Fourth Circuit, *Breard* v. *Pruett*, 134 F.3d 615 (1998), US Court of Appeals, Fourth Circuit, *Republic of Paraguay* v. *George F. Allen*, 134 F.3d 622 (1998).

75 In *USA* v. *Lombera Carmorlinga*, the U.S. 9th Circuit Courts of Appeals judged that Article 36 did create enforceable rights (*Lombera-Camorlinga*, 170 F.3d at 1244). Rehearing the case, the Court left the question aside (*USA* v. *Lombera Carmorlinga*, U.S. 9th Circuit Courts of Appeals, 6 March 2000, No. 98-50347), but the US Government took the position in this case that Article 36 did not create judicially enforceable individual rights.

Also international institutions with non-legally binding powers can make determinations relevant to the effect that national courts should give to international norms. Indeed, probably precisely because it concerns non-legally binding powers, such institutions may be more outspoken in their views on the direct effect of particular rules of international law. A clear example is General Comment No. 9 of the Domestic application of the Covenant, adopted by the Committee on Economic, Social and Cultural Rights.[76] Against the background of the many states which decline to give direct effect to the Covenant on Economic, Social and Cultural Rights because its provisions would lack objective direct effect (or: be non-self-executing), the Committee stated that:

'It is...important to avoid any a priori assumption that the norms should be considered to be non-self-executing. In fact, many of them are stated in terms which are at least as clear and specific as those in other human rights treaties, the provisions of which are regularly deemed by courts to be self-executing'.[77]

It also referred to a large number of provisions of the Covenant that it considers to be capable of immediate implementation.[78]

Such (quasi-) judicial pronouncements relevant to direct effect should be distinguished from ordinary findings by international courts that national law is in breach of international law. In the *LaGrand* case, the Court noted that the procedural default rule that the United States invoked to justify the non-application of Article 36(2) had the effect of preventing 'full effect [from being] given to the purposes for which the rights accorded under this Article are intended', and thus violated paragraph 2 of Article 36.[79] The Court held that a national rule prohibiting a plaintiff from raising new arguments on appeal was incompatible with international law. In other words, this law was no defense on the international level. Such findings of incompatibility should have consequences for the national level; for future cases that procedural barrier should be removed.[80] However, this type of change normally will not be effectuated by the courts but by legislative act and therefore cannot be construed in terms of direct effect.

---

[76] UN Doc E/C.12/1998/24, CESCR General comment 9 of 3 December 1998.

[77] Para. 11.

[78] It referred to the fact that, in General Comment No. 3 (1990) it cited (para. 10), by way of example, Articles 3; 7(a)(i); 8; 10(3); 13(2)(a); 13(3); 13(4); and 15(3).

[79] Para. 91.

[80] This is far reaching even when compared with EC law. It can be compared to the judgment of the ECJ in Case C-312/93 *Peterbroeck* [1995] ECR I-4599, para. 21, discussed by Ward in chapter III, paragraph 4.1.3.

Pronouncements relevant to direct effect will rarely be considered decisive in national courts.[81] In all cases it depends on the degree in which national systems that have opened for the direct effect of international law allow international law considerations to control determinations in respect of direct effect.

National legal considerations often will qualify and mitigate the influence of international law, as is shown in the wide differences in state practice as regards subjective[82] and objective direct effect.[83] Also the question as to which national rules, especially of a procedural nature, may be invoked to regulate and in particular cases exclude reliance on international law is, also because of the absence of case-law, particularly unsettled and rudimentary. International institutions generally will consider such differences with deference.[84]

Whether a rule of international law, even one that is clearly intended to be granted direct effect, actually is given such effect, depends above all on the national context in which it is applied. This can be illustrated by case law concerning the compatibility of Dutch family law with the ECHR. The Netherlands Supreme Court has determined that, in case of a conflict between

---

[81]   Generally on the effect of international decisions in national courts Schreuer (1974).

[82]   Examples are the practice of the Italian Court of Cassation to deny the European Convention on Human Rights direct effect cited in Harris, O'Boyle & Warbrick (1995), p. 24-25 and the practice of United States courts not to allow direct effect of the ICCPR because the executive branch determined that its provisions would not be self-executing; see e.g. *Beazley* v. *Johnson*, US Court of Appeals for the Fifth Circuit, 9 February 2001, 242 F3d 248. Differences can in particular be seen in such areas of international law as extradition law, where some states do allow private parties to invoke treaties, whereas courts in other states consider that these treaties only grant rights and duties to states.

[83]   This holds prominently for varying decisions on direct effect of the International Covenant on Economic, Social and Cultural Rights; see UN Doc E/C.12/1998/24, CESCR General comment 9 of 3 December 1998, para. 13.

[84]   Illustrative is the position of the Human Rights Committee on the decision of the US not to consider the ICCPR directly effective. The US had said that 'that the decision to declare the Covenant non-self-executing did not limit international obligations under the Covenant' and that it 'only meant that the Covenant could not, in and of itself, provide a cause of action in United States courts... nothing in the Covenant generally, or Article 2 in particular, required States parties to make it self-executing under their domestic law... The real question was not whether the Covenant should be self-executing, but whether the rights accepted by the United States in adhering to the Covenant were, in fact, guaranteed to people within the United States, and whether there was effective recourse and remedies in the event that those rights were violated. If it should be determined that United States law fell short of Covenant standards, then the necessity of corrective legislation would certainly be considered. Human Rights Committee, *Summary Record of the 1405th Meeting*, CCPR/C/SR.1405 24 April 1995, para. 7. The HRC did not consider this to be in violation of the treaty but took 'note of the position expressed by the delegation that, notwithstanding the non-self-executing declaration of the United States, American courts are not prevented from seeking guidance from the Covenant in interpreting American law'; CCPR/C/79/Add.50; A/50/40, 3 October 1995, (paras. 266-304) at para. 276.

the ECHR and provisions of Dutch law, direct effect is not to be granted when it would require setting aside national laws that would lead to gaps in the law that could only be filled by the legislature. A case on point involves a request for adoption made by two women. The plaintiff became pregnant as a result of (anonymous) donor insemination and gave birth to twins. The women, who were living together, applied for adoption. However, Articles 1:227(1) and 228(1g) of the Dutch Civil Code preclude such an adoption as it limits an application for adoption to couples who have been married for at least five years. At this point in time, it was impossible for persons of the same sex to marry, and the applicants argued that the requirement of marriage was contrary to their right to family life within the meaning of Article 8 ECHR. The Netherlands Supreme Court ruled that even if there were an incompatibility between the Civil Code and the Convention, and Articles 8, 12 and/or 14 ECHR would require a more far-reaching recognition in law of the women's relationship than at present:

> 'the necessary measures to obtain such a result would exceed the boundaries of the judiciary's law making capacity. For one thing, it must be determined what requirements of the relationship between the adopting mother and her partner should be satisfied (whether or not similar to a marriage) in order to ensure its stability, in the interests of the child. For another, it must be considered whether it should possibly follow from the special nature of this form of adoption, which abandons the notion of descent, that not all ties with the biological father are severed by the adoption, alternatively - in the situation where the cohabitation involves two males, that the bond with the biological mother as a matter of family law should remain in place. Both the interests of this person and the child need to be taken into account. Furthermore, the wider context of the law of descent in general must be considered'.

These questions could not be resolved by a simple setting aside of the provisions of Articles 1:227(1) BW en 228 (1g) BW and a direct application of the ECHR; therefore, direct effect was denied.[85] In such cases, the outcome is largely governed by national rather than international law.[86] The question has been raised whether such restrictions on the application of international law are compatible with the European Convention, in particular Article 13.[87] However, in the related case *Auerbach*, the European Court on Human Rights held that:

> 'the Supreme Court's finding of a violation of the applicant's rights under Article 14 of the Convention in conjunction with the cost orders issued in the applicant's

---

[85] Hoge Raad (Supreme Court), 5.9.1997, NJ 1998/686.

[86] Also elsewhere the context may strongly influence whether provisions of the European Convention can be given direct effect; Harris, O'Boyle & Warbrick (1995), p. 24.

[87] See Martens (2000).

favour, and its instruction to the legislator to enact new legislation which has in fact occurred, may be regarded as adequate redress'.[88]

Finding that adequate redress had been granted, the Court found the application inadmissible. It thus would appear that the judicial restraint exercised in cases where direct application of international law leads to gaps in the law is generally permissible under the Convention.

6 Conclusion

The conclusions of this contribution can conveniently be drawn by comparing direct effect of public international law with direct effect of EC law, as discussed elsewhere in this volume. The concept of direct effect as it has been considered above, differs from the concept of direct effect of EC law, as the latter concept commonly is confined to the conditions under which private parties can invoke EC law. As explained above, there is no justification for a similarly narrow concept in regard to public international law, and the concept of direct effect involves all cases where national courts, or indeed the ECJ, apply rules of international law that are not transformed in rules of national law or EC law.

Apart from this conceptual difference, the main difference between EC law and public international law with regard to direct effect concerns the degree of autonomy of national legal systems and thereby the relative degree of control exercised by, respectively, EC and international law. While the contours of the concept are largely comparable, public international law leaves more room for the national legal order to determine the conditions and consequences of direct effect.

The result is that the manifestations of direct effect of public international law in state practice vary substantially. The lack of uniformity that even exists in EC law is magnified in regard of public international law to such an extent that one could raise the question whether the concept has any identifiable contents at all and, indeed, is not only a concept of national law.

However, on balance, in view of the large number of states that do employ a principle that allows courts to give effect to international law as a rule of decision, and the weight of international legal determinants of direct effect, one can conclude that direct effect is influenced by international law and that the courts that grant direct effect apply the mandates of international law in a comparable manner as national courts that grant direct effect to EC law. In this respect,

---

[88] *Auerbach v. the Netherlands*, Admissibility Decision of 29 January 2002.

the widespread practice of opening national constitutions to international law had the effect of mitigating the dualism between international law and national law and of piercing through the unity of the state that similarly has character- ized classic international law.[89] National courts then are granted a position in international law that is comparable to their role in EC law.

It is not helpful to say that direct effect, as discussed above, is either a concept of international law (which it does not appear to be given the large differences between states) or of national law (which is too narrow given the similarity in approach across the world). The better view appears to be that it is a *sui generis* concept that characterizes legal effects of norms that straddle the threshold of two legal systems and that indeed qualifies the relevance of that threshold.

---

[89] Fitzmaurice noted in a classical dualist position: 'It is only by treating the State as one indivisible entity, and the discharge of the international obligations concerned as being incumbant on that entity as such, and not merely on particular individuals or organs, that the supremacy of international law can be assured - the atomization of the personality of State is necessarily fatal to this'; Fitzmaurice (1958), p. 88. Cf. the Separate Opinion of Judge Oda in *Difference relating to immunity from legal process of a special rapporteur of the Commisson on Human Rights* (as cited) para. 24 and the Dissenting Opinion of Judge Koroma in the same case, para. 28, both critiquing the fact that the ICJ expressly made reference to the role of the courts of Malaysia, rather than to Malaysia as a unitary state.

CHAPTER VIII

Giving Effect to Customary International Law Through European Community Law

prof. dr. Jan Wouters and Dries Van Eeckhoutte

1 Introduction

Being part of general international law, customary international law[1] is in principle binding on all subjects of international law, including international organisations like the European Union,[2] the European Community and all of the EU's Member States.[3] The breach of rules of customary international law will entail the international responsibility of the subject(s) involved. However, for private individuals, what matters most is the question of whether and to which extent they are able to rely on a rule of customary international law before the courts in order to see their rights protected. In most domestic legal systems, national courts are under certain conditions willing to accept that a private individual invokes a rule of customary international law to interpret a domestic rule in conformity with customary international law; to derive a right out of a rule of customary international law; or - the strongest and most far-reaching use - to contest the legality of a rule of domestic law. However, this last type of reliance on customary international law is especially severely restricted if not rendered impossible in the case law of many States.[4]

Although the case law of the European Court of Justice ('Court of Justice') has for many years taken rules of customary international law into account,[5] it is only very recently, in the *Opel Austria* judgment[6] of the European Court

---

[1] References to customary international law in this contribution mean universal rules of customary international law, and not regional or local customary international law. As to the question of what belongs to 'general international law', see *inter alia* Nöll (1986), p. 60-64.

[2] This contribution will not enter into the ongoing debate concerning the legal personality of the European Union in international law. Suffice it here to note that the question of the EU's proper legal personality has received a fresh impetus from the changes brought about by the Treaty of Nice: see Wouters (2002), at p. 67.

[3] See, specifically with regard to international organisations, ICJ, *Interpretation of the Agreement of 25 March 1951 between the WHO and Egypt*, advisory opinion of 20 December 1980, ICJ Rep. (1980) p. 73, at p. 89-90, para. 37: 'International organizations are subjects of international law and, as such, are bound by any obligations incumbent upon them under general rules of international law (...)'. See *inter alia*, with regard to the relationship between general international law and international organisations, Bleckmann (1977); David (1999), p. 3-22.

[4] The application by national courts of customary international law in various European States has been thoroughly examined by Stirling-Zanda (2000). See also the national overviews in Eisemann (1996).

[5] There is a steadily increasing body literature on this issue. See especially Bleckmann (1975); Elias (2000); Epiney (1999); Ganshof van der Meersch (1975), at p. 181-195; Hoffmeister (1998); Kuijper (2002); Lowe (1998); Meessen (1976); Lenaerts & Van Nuffel (1999), at p. 561-564; Ott (2001); Peters (1997); Puissochet (1998); Schermers (1975); Schwarze (1983); Timmermans (1999); Vanhamme (2001a); Van Panhuys (1965-66).

[6] Case T-115/94 *Opel Austria* [1997] ECR II-39. For annotations, see *inter alia* Fischer (1998); Kahil (1998); Kuijper (1999); Mengozzi (1997).

of First Instance ('Court of First Instance') and in the *Racke* judgment[7] of the Court of Justice, that the Community courts have explicitly relied on customary international law to test the validity of acts of EU institutions.

These two cases raise a variety of issues which will be analysed in this contribution. First, the question arises as to what the precise position of customary international law is in Community law (2).[8] Secondly, *Racke* and *Opel Austria* raise the question under which conditions rules of customary international law can be invoked in Community law in order to challenge the validity of acts of EU institutions or rules of national law. This requires a careful analysis of the reasoning followed in the judgments concerned (3). In the third place, it should be examined how the Community courts' case law on the invocability of customary international law relates to their case law on the invocability of treaties to which the EC is a party (4). It would be interesting to see whether there is any incoherence between the two lines of case law and whether the outcome of a case before the Community courts could differ depending on the formal source of international law involved. Based on the insights acquired in the previous sections, we will end our contribution with some reflections relating to the nature of customary international law (5).

A preliminary remark should be made as to the terminology used in this contribution. The concept of 'invocability' is often used interchangeably with that of 'direct effect'. In the present contribution, however, we prefer the term 'invocability' as it better catches the different manners in which customary international law can be used by private individuals, in particular the review of the legality of domestic (be it national or EC) rules and the interpretation of those rules in conformity with customary international law.[9] The use of the term 'invocability' also helps to distinguish our analysis, which concerns the relationship between the international legal order and domestic (national or EC) legal orders, from the context in which the notion of 'direct effect' is typically used, namely the relationship between rules of Community law and rules of national law.[10] When the term 'direct effect' is used hereinafter, it will be in

---

[7] Case C-162/96 *Racke* [1998] ECR I-3655. See especially the annotations of Barbero (1998); Berramdane (1999); Epiney (1999); Furlan (1999); Gagliardi (1999); Hoffmeister (1998); Klabbers (1999a); Kokott & Hoffmeister (1999); Kuijper (1999); Mehdi (1999); Leray & Potteau (1999); Petit (1999).

[8] This contribution uses the terms 'Community law' and 'EC law' interchangeably. As such, its scope is limited to the 'first pillar' of the EU, which does not exclude the possibility that some of the insights may be relevant for the relationship between customary international law and EU law originating in the second pillar (the EU's common foreign and security policy) and the third pillar (police and judicial cooperation in criminal matters).

[9] See also, with regard to the broader notion of 'invocability', Prechal in this volume's chapter II. See also Ojanen (2000).

[10] Moreover, the European Court of Justice's case law on the relationship between the European Community's legal order and the legal order of the Member States has been responded to in the different

reference to the Court of Justice's well established case law concerning the rights of private individuals derived from Community acts and/or their right to invoke EC law before a national court in order to assess the compatibility of national law with EC law.

2   The position of customary international law in Community law

Much has been written about the initial reticence of the Court of Justice regarding the relationship between general international law and EC law.[11] One can find a specimen of such reticence in the *Dyestuffs* case (1972), a competition law case in which the Court avoided the problem of the limits which customary international law imposes on the EC's jurisdiction in cartel cases.[12] As Timmermans has rightly stressed, the Court's initial reticence can largely be explained from its efforts to safeguard the autonomy of Community law vis-à-vis international law.[13] However, since then the Court of Justice has made numerous references to customary international law, even though the wording used often blurs the precise formal source of the rule (typically, reference is made to 'the general rules of international law',[14] 'the rules of (public) international law',[15]

Member States' legal orders so as 'to conclude that special rules have been developed for the reception of Community law (vis-à-vis international law deriving from other sources) with the result that this is a special regime in each of the Member States'; Fox, Gardner & Wickremasinghe (1996) at p. 37.

[11] See the literature quoted above, note 5.

[12] Case 48/69 *Imperial Chemical Industries* v. *Commission* [1972] ECR 619. As is known, the Court avoided the problem of customary law of jurisdiction by following the Commission's argument that the parent companies outside the EC, by giving pricing instructions to their EC-based subsidiaries, were acting as a single entity so that the Commission's decision could be seen as a simple application of the territoriality principle. One may compare this with the thorough examination of customary international law of jurisdiction by AG Mayras in his Opinion in this case. The Court avoided this question again in Joined Cases 6/73 and 7/73 *Istituto Chemioterapico Italiano and Commercial Solvents* v. *Commission* [1974] ECR 223, paras. 36-41.

[13] Timmermans (1999), at p. 181-183. See already Case 26/62 *Van Gend en Loos* [1963] ECR 1, at p. 12; Case 6/64 *Costa/ENEL* [1964] ECR 585, at p. 593.

[14] See e.g., Case 104/81 *Kupferberg* [1982] ECR 3641, para. 18; Case C-146/89 *Commission* v. *United Kingdom* [1991] ECR I-3533, para. 2; Case C-221/89 *Factortame II* [1991] ECR I-3905, para. 17; Case C-246/89 *Commission* v. *United Kingdom* [1991] ECR I-4585, para. 15.

[15] See e.g. joined Opinion of AG Mischo in Cases C-62/98 and C-84/98 *Commission* v. *Portugal* [2000] ECR I-5171, para. 61; Opinion of AG Darmon in Case C-9/89 *Spain* v. *Council* [1990] ECR I-1401, para. 37.

'principles of international law',[16] or even simply to 'public international law',[17] or 'international law').[18]

This is not to say, though, that through the Community case law, the precise legal status and place of customary international law within the hierarchy of norms has been clear. Before *Opel Austria* and *Racke* the Court of Justice mainly relied on customary international law (2.1) to demarcate the limits of State or EC/EU jurisdiction and powers, (2.2) as providing rules of interpretation and (2.3) as a 'gap-filler' in the absence of specific EC rules. Although this may have been implicit in earlier case law (see below), before the aforementioned judgments the Community courts had not explicitly confirmed the possibility that customary international rules could be relied upon to challenge the validity of Community acts (2.4).

2.1 Customary international law as a limit on State/EC jurisdiction and powers

What has been clear for a long time is that the Court of Justice uses customary international law rules to analyze the boundaries of State or EC jurisdiction and powers. An illustration of this can already be found in the *Van Duyn* case in 1974. The United Kingdom had prevented a national of another Member State from entering and taking up employment within its territory on the ground of the public policy exception to the free movement of workers (Article 39, ex 48, EC). The question was raised whether this amounted to discrimination as no similar restriction was placed upon the United Kingdom's own nationals. In its assessment of the argument of discrimination the Court clearly took notice of customary international law: 'it is a principle of international law, which the EEC treaty cannot be assumed to disregard in the relations between Member States, that a State is precluded from refusing its own nation-

---

[16] See e.g. Case 244/80 *Foglia* v. *Novello* [1981] ECR 3045, para. 24; *Kupferberg*, para. 17; Case 286/86 *Deserbais* [1988] ECR 4907, para. 17; Case C-158/91 *Levy* [1993] ECR I-4287, para. 12; Case C-324/93 *Evans Medical* [1995] ECR I-563, para. 27; Case C-124/95 *Centro-Com* [1997] ECR I-81, para. 56; Joined Cases C-364/95 and C-365/95, *T-Port* [1998] ECR I-1023, para. 60; Joined Cases C-62/98 *Commission* v. *Portugal* (as cited), para. 44 and Case C-84/98, para. 53. See also Case 41/74 *Van Duyn* [1974] ECR 1337, para. 22; Case C-177/96 *Belgian State* v. *Banque Indosuez and others* [1997] ECR I-5659, para. 25; Case C-37/00 *Weber*, judgment of 27 February 2002, nyr.

[17] See e.g. Joined Cases 3/76, 4/76 and 6/76 *Kramer* [1976] ECR 1279, paras. 30-33; *Belgian State* v. *Banque Indosuez and others*, para. 22. See also Joined Cases 89, 104, 114, 116, 117 and 125-129/85 *Woodpulp* [1988] ECR 5193, para. 18.

[18] See e.g. Case C-369/90 *Micheletti* [1992] I-4239, para. 10; Joined Cases C-46/93 and C-48/93 *Brasserie du Pêcheur* [1996] ECR I-1029, para. 34.

als the right of entry or residence'.[19] More recently the Court referred to this principle repeatedly.[20]

A first, albeit implicit acceptance of customary international law as a limitation of the powers of the Community to adopt measures can be found in the *Kramer* case[21] (1976). In this well-known judgment the Court examined *inter alia* whether the Community had the authority to enter into international commitments for the conservation of the resources of the sea. From the relevant Community provisions the Court deduced that the EC does indeed have rule-making authority which *'ratione materiae* also extends - in so far as the Member States have similar authority under public international law - to fishing on the high seas'.[22] The Court has consistently confirmed this case law thereafter.[23]

In *Woodpulp*[24] (1988), the Court of Justice accepted that customary international law acts as a limit on the powers of the European Commission in competition cases. Woodpulp producers from outside the EC contested a decision in which the Commission held that these companies had engaged in price concertation which had the object and effect of restricting competition within the common market within the meaning of Article 81 (ex 85) EC and in which the Commission had imposed fines on them. The applicants submitted that the decision was incompatible with public international law as it exceeded the Community's jurisdiction. The Court considered the argument, but, deeming the place of implementation of infringements of Article 81 to be decisive, it held that the Commission's decision 'was covered by the territoriality principle as

---

[19] *Van Duyn* (as cited), para. 22. See also Joined Cases 115/81 and 116/81 *Adoui and Cornuaille* [1982] ECR 1665, para. 7 (without reference to international law). The reference to international law in *Van Duyn* has been downplayed or downrightly criticized by some authors: see Simmonds (1975), at p. 437; Meessen (1976), at p. 486, who speaks of a 'rather ill-conceived allusion to international law'.

[20] Joined Cases C-65/95 and C-111/95 *Shingara and Radiom* [1997] ECR I-3343, para. 28; Case C-171/96 *Pereira Roque* [1998] ECR I-4607, para. 38; Case C-348/96 *Calfa* [1999] ECR I-11, para. 20; Case C-416/96 *El-Yassini* [1999] ECR I-1209, para. 45; Case C-235/99 *Kondova* [2001] ECR I-6427, para. 84; Case C-63/99 *Gloszczuk* [2001] ECR I-6369, para. 79; Case C-257/99 *Barkoci and Malik* [2001] ECR I-6557, para. 81.

[21] As cited.

[22] *Kramer*, paras. 30-33.

[23] See in particular Case 61/77 *Commission v. Ireland* [1978] ECR 417, para. 63; Case C-258/89 *Commission v. Spain* [1991] ECR I-3977, para. 9; Case C-405/92 *Etablissements Armand Mondiet v. Armement Islais* [1993] ECR I-6133, para. 12; Case C-25/94 *Commission v. Council* [1996] ECR I-1469, para. 42. See also CFI, judgment of 6 December 2001 in Case T-196/99, *Area Cova v. Council and Commission* [2001] ECR II-3597, para. 76.

[24] As cited.

universally recognised in public international law'.[25] As we will note below, the *Woodpulp* judgment was the first case in which the Court accepted to deal at length with arguments of customary international law in order to review the legality of a Community act.

In the *Poulsen* case (1992), the Court for the first time explicitly states that 'the European Community must respect international law in the exercise of its powers' and that therefore provisions of EC legislation have to be interpreted, and their scope limited, in the light of the relevant rules of customary international law at hand.[26] This statement of principle has become well established case law since[27] and will *inter alia* be recalled by the Court in *Racke*.[28] The case raised numerous questions on the relation between a Community Regulation on technical measures for the conservation of fishery resources[29] and the

---

[25] *Woodpulp*, para. 18. See *inter alia* the comments on the Court's reasoning of Van Gerven (1990). In Case T-102/96 *Gencor* [1999] ECR II-753, para. 50, the Court of First Instance held, with reference to *Woodpulp*, that the principle of territoriality is 'a general principle of public international law which the Community must observe in the exercise of its powers'. In the same judgment, the Court of First Instance endorsed the 'effects' doctrine, though, where it held that application of the EC's Merger Control Regulation (EEC Council Regulation 4064/89 of 21 December 1989 on the control of concentrations between undertakings, OJ 1989, L 395/1) 'is justified under public international law when it is foreseeable that a proposed concentration will have an immediate and substantial effect in the Community' (para. 90). The Court then proceeded to examine whether these criteria had been fulfilled in the case at hand, which it found to be the case. See on this case Elias (2000), at p. 24-26.

[26] Case C-286/90 *Poulsen* [1992] ECR I-6019, para. 9. Compare the Opinion of AG Tesauro, para. 4: 'It is clear, in fact, that the provision in question cannot but be interpreted in conformity with the applicable rules of international law'. Compare already the Opinion of AG Darmon in Case C-9/89 *Spain* v. *Council* (as cited), para. 37, who noted that 'the Community, when it exercises jurisdiction which previously devolved on the Member States, is required to comply with the obligations imposed on States by public international law'.

[27] See also, as applied to treaties to which the EC is a party, Case C-284/95 *Safety Hi-Tech* [1998] ECR I-4302, para. 22, and Case C-341/95 *Bettati* [1998] ECR I-4355, para. 20: 'It is settled law that Community legislation must, so far as possible, be interpreted in a manner that is consistent with international law, in particular where its provisions are intended specifically to give effect to an international agreement concluded by the Community'. See also Case C-61/94 *Commission* v. *Germany* [1996] ECR I-3989, para. 52: 'the primacy of international agreements concluded by the Community over provisions of secondary Community legislation means that such provisions must, so far as is possible, be interpreted in a manner that is consistent with those agreements'.

[28] *Racke*, para. 45. See also the Joined Opinion of AG Léger in Cases C-284/95 and C-341/95 *Safety Hi-Tech* [1998] ECR I-4312, para. 33.

[29] EEC Council Regulation 3094/86 of 7 October 1986, laying down certain technical measures for the conservation of fishery resources, OJ 1986, L 288/1.

international law of the sea.[30] A vessel called 'Onkel Sam', registered in Panama and flying the Panamanian flag but otherwise having solely Danish crew, had caught several thousand kilograms of salmon on the high seas in the North Atlantic and was on its way to Poland to sell its cargo there. Engine trouble and bad weather conditions forced its Danish master Poulsen to head for a Danish port. There criminal charges were brought against the master and the owner of the ship (a company governed by Panamanian law wholly owned by a Danish national) for having salmon on board in breach of the Regulation. But could the Regulation apply at all to a non-EU vessel? In answering the preliminary questions posed to it, the Court took account of numerous rules of customary international law of the sea:

- A vessel has in principle only one nationality, that of the State in which it is registered; it follows from this that an EU Member State may not regard that vessel as flying its own flag because of a 'genuine link' between it and the vessel, even if the sole link between the vessel and its State of nationality is the administrative formality of registration.[31]
- The law governing the crew's activities does not depend on the latter's nationality but on the State in which the vessel is registered and, where appropriate, the sea area in which the boat is located.[32] In applying the regulation, this has to be taken into account.
- On the high seas, a vessel is in principle governed only by the law of its flag.[33] In the other sea areas of the Member States, the EC has the power to adopt rules but not in an unconditional manner, since in the exclusive economic zone a vessel enjoys freedom of navigation and in the territorial waters it enjoys the right of innocent passage.[34] Conversely, in the Court's view the regulation may be applied to a non-EU vessel 'when it sails in the inland waters or, more especially, is in a port of a Member State, where it is generally subject to the unlimited jurisdiction of that State'.[35] Only in the latter situation may confiscation of the cargo be ordered, according to the Court.[36] The Court's statement regarding unlimited jurisdiction is somewhat at odds with the case law of a number of States, as shown by

---

[30] See the Opinion of AG Tesauro in *Poulsen*, para. 4: 'Even from a superficial reading it is clear that a number of fundamental principles of international law are at issue'.

[31] *Poulsen*, paras. 12-16. See the considerations of AG Tesauro concerning the treatment in international law of 'flags of convenience' (para. 9). See also the Opinion of the same AG in Case C-62/96 *Commission v. Greece* [1997] I-6730-6733, paras. 9-16.

[32] *Poulsen*, para. 18.

[33] *Poulsen*, para. 22.

[34] *Poulsen*, paras. 24-27.

[35] *Poulsen*, para. 28.

[36] *Poulsen*, paras. 30-34.

Advocate General Tesauro in his Opinion.[37]

- The *pacta tertiis* rule in the customary international law of treaties: the Convention for the Conservation of Salmon in the North Atlantic, signed by the EC in 1982,[38] may not be invoked against non-signatory States (like Panama) and cannot therefore be applied to vessels registered there.[39]

- On one issue of customary international law, namely the immunity of ships in distress, the Court did not provide an answer: holding that this 'does not concern the determination of the sphere of application of Community legislation, but rather the implementation of that legislation by the authorities of the Member States', it left it to 'the national court to determine, in accordance with international law, the legal consequences flowing from such a situation'.[40] It can be deplored that the Court did not give any guidance in this respect: it would have been enlightening to know whether it shares the rather extensive view of its Advocate General on the (in his view, customary law rule of) immunity of a foreign vessel in distress which enters a port of a coastal State.[41]

A year later, the Court used customary international law to determine whether the Community had acted within the confines of its jurisdiction in the *Mondiet* case (1993).[42] A French fisheries company had challenged the validity of a Community regulation which prohibited vessels flying the flag of an EU Member State from keeping on board or using for fishing, including on the high seas, driftnets of more than 2.5 kilometres in length. Referring to its aforementioned *Kramer* case law on the EC's jurisdiction over maritime zones and to the 1958 Geneva Convention on fishing and the conservation of living resources of the high seas and the 1982 Law of the Sea Convention as embodying customary international law, the Court found that the Community had the competence to adopt, for the said vessels, such measures for the conservation of the fishery resources of the high seas.[43]

---

[37] Para. 12. See also the reflections of Slot (1994), at p. 152. Compare, however, Verhoeven (1997), at p. 411, who considers the AG's point of view in this respect 'excessive'.

[38] See OJ 1982, L 378/25.

[39] *Poulsen*, para. 23. The *pacta tertiis* rule is explicitly recalled by AG Tesauro in his Opinion (para. 8).

[40] *Poulsen*, paras. 37-39.

[41] Para. 13. See also the critical remarks of Slot (1994), at p. 153. Compare again Verhoeven (1997), at p. 411: 'La 'situation de détresse' ... permet certes, coutumièrement, à un navire d'entrer dans un port sans l'autorisation à laquelle cette entrée... est en principe subordonnée. Elle n'a pas pour effet de le soustraire de plein droit aux règles en vigueur, qui lui sont applicables comme elles le sont à tout autre navire dûment autorisé à pénétrer dans le port'.

[42] As cited.

[43] Mondiet, paras. 13-15; confirmed in Case C-25/94 *Commission v. Council* (as cited), para. 44.

2.2 Customary international law as providing rules of interpretation

In many cases the Court of Justice has had recourse to the customary international rules of treaty law in order to interpret international agreements to which the EC is a party, or rules of Community law proper.[44] As is known, several topics of the law of treaties are dealt with in two multilateral treaties, namely the 1969 Vienna Convention on the Law of Treaties[45] ('1969 Vienna Convention') and the 1986 Vienna Convention on the Law of Treaties between States and International Organizations or between International Organizations[46] ('1986 Vienna Convention'). However, neither of these two treaties applies to international agreements concluded by the EC or to the EC Treaty itself.[47] The 1969 Vienna Convention does not apply to treaties concluded by the EC as it only applies to treaties concluded between States.[48] As far as the 1986 Vienna Convention is concerned, although it is meant to apply to treaties concluded by international organisations[49] and thus to treaties entered into by the EC, it has not yet entered into force internationally[50] and the Community has not become a party to it. Nevertheless, it is widely accepted that several provisions of these conventions constitute a codification of rules of customary international law on the law of treaties.[51] The 1969 Vienna Convention especially is

---

[44] See also Klabbers (1999b); Kuijper (1998).

[45] Vienna Convention on the Law of Treaties, done at Vienna, 23 May 1969, UN Doc. A/CONF.39/27, UNTS, vol. 1155, p. 331.

[46] Vienna Convention on the Law of Treaties between States and International Organisations or between International Organisations, done at Vienna, 21 March 1986, UN Doc. A/CONF.129/15.

[47] Although the EC Treaty would fall within the ambit of the 1969 Vienna Convention (see Article 5 of the latter), the Convention does not as such apply to it since its entry into force dates only from 27 January 1980 (see Article 4). In addition, several EU Member States are not a party to it: this is the case with Luxembourg, France, Portugal and Ireland (http://untreaty.un.org > Status of Multilateral Treaties Deposited with the Secretary-General).

[48] Article 1 1969 Vienna Convention; see however Article 5 of this Convention, pursuant to which it applies 'to any treaty adopted within an international organization without prejudice to any relevant rules of the organization'.

[49] Article 1 1986 Vienna Convention.

[50] For the 1986 Vienna Convention to enter into force, 35 States have to deposit instruments of ratification or accession (Article 85). Until now, only 26 states have deposited an instrument of ratification or accession (http://untreaty.un.org > Status of Multilateral Treaties Deposited with the Secretary-General (16 October 2001)). See also Manin (1987).

[51] This has been repeatedly stated by the International Court of Justice with regard to the 1969 Vienna Convention: see, *inter alia*, *Legal Consequences for States of the Continued Presence of South Africa in Namibia (South West Africa) Notwithstanding Security Council Resolution 276 (1970)*, advisory opinion of

frequently invoked before the Community courts[52] and is often applied by them in their interpretation and application of international agreements concluded by the Community and of the EC Treaty.[53]

The cardinal rule on the law of treaties, expressed in Article 26 of both conventions, is *pacta sunt servanda*: 'Every treaty is binding upon the parties to it and must be performed by them in good faith'.[54] The Court explicitly refers to this rule in several cases, sometimes to expand on it further.[55] Thus, in *Kupferberg* (1982) and *Portugal* v. *Council* (1999) the rule was its starting point for verifying whether or not to grant direct effect to rules of the 1972 free trade agreement between the EEC and Portugal and the GATT, respectively:

'according to the general rules of international law there must be bona fide performance of every agreement. Although each contracting party is responsible for executing fully the commitments which it has undertaken it is nevertheless free to determine the legal means appropriate for attaining that end in its legal system, unless

---

21 June 1971, ICJ Rep. (1971) p. 16 et seq., at p. 47, para. 94; *Fisheries Jurisdiction* Case (*United Kingdom* v. *Iceland*), judgment of 2 February 1973 (jurisdiction), ICJ Rep. (1973) p. 3 et seq., at p.18, para. 36; *Interpretation of the Agreement of 25 March 1951 between the WHO and Egypt*, advisory opinion of 20 December 1980, ICJ Rep. (1980), p. 73 et seq., at p. 94-96, paras. 47 and 49; *Gabčíkovo-Nagymaros Project* (*Hungary* v. *Slovakia*), judgment of 25 September 1997, ICJ Rep. (1997), p. 7 et seq., at p. 38, para. 46. However, to our knowledge the International Court of Justice has not yet taken a position on the customary international law status of provisions of the 1986 Vienna Convention. It has referred to the International Law Commission's draft articles which led to the said treaty; see ICJ, *Interpretation of the Agreement of 25 March 1951 between the WHO and Egypt*, p. 95-96, paras. 47 and 49.

[52] See for cases in which it was invoked without being addressed by the Court: Case C-268/94 *Portugal* v. *Council* [1996] ECR I-6177, para. 19; Case C-27/96 *Danisco Sugar* [1997] ECR I-6653, paras. 20, 31; Case C-179/97 *Spain* v. *Commission* [1999] ECR I-1251, para. 11; Judgment of 24 January 2002 in Case C-500/99P *Conserve Italia Soc. Coop.* v. *Commission*, nyr, para. 73; Case T-120/99 *Kik* [2001] ECR II-2235, para. 43.

[53] See, apart from the *Racke* and *Opel Austria* cases, Case C-432/92 *Anastasiou* [1994] ECR I-3087, paras. 43, 50; Case C-25/94 *Commission* v. *Council* (as cited), para. 33; Case C-62/98 *Commission* v. *Portugal* (as cited), para. 44; Case C-84/98 *Commission* v. *Portugal* (as cited), para. 53; Case T-2/99 *T-Port* [2001] ECR II-2093, para. 81. See also, with regard to the 1986 Vienna Convention, *Levy* (as cited), para. 19; Case C-327/91 *France* v. *Commission* [1994] ECR I-3641, para. 25; Opinion of AG Lenz in Case 165/87 *Commission* v. *Council* [1988] ECR 5557, para. 35. See on these cases especially Klabbers (1999b); Kuijper (1998).

[54] Article 26 1969 Vienna Convention and Article 26 1986 Vienna Convention.

[55] There are also judgments in which the Court refers to this principle without mentioning the 1969 Vienna Convention: see e.g. Case 142/88 *Hoesch and Germany* [1989] ECR 3413, para. 30.

the agreement, interpreted in the light of its subject-matter and purpose, itself specifies those means'.[56]

The Court has referred to other provisions of the 1969 Vienna Convention too as illustrations of customary international law of treaties. In the Commission's recent infringement cases against Portugal for the latter's cargo-sharing agreements with third countries, the Court held that Article 307 (ex 234) EC follows the principles of international law enshrined in Article 30(4)(b) of the 1969 Vienna Convention, in that its purpose is to make it clear that application of the EC Treaty rules does not affect the duty of the Member State concerned to respect the rights of third countries under a prior agreement and to perform its obligations thereunder.[57] Although the Member States are required to eliminate all incompatibilities between the EC Treaty and the agreements they have concluded with third countries prior to the entry into force of the EC Treaty, in the meantime the relations between the Member State and the third country concerned remain governed by such agreements.

In several cases, the Court has referred to the rules of treaty interpretation as laid down in Article 31 of the 1969 Vienna Convention. It is indeed well established case law by now that 'an international treaty must be interpreted not solely by reference to the terms in which it is worded but also in the light of its objectives. Article 31 of the Vienna Convention of 23 May 1969 on the Law of Treaties stipulates in that respect that a treaty must be interpreted in good faith in accordance with the ordinary meaning to be given to its terms in their context and in the light of its object and purpose'.[58]

Finally, the Community courts have also had recourse to the customary treaty law rules laid down in Article 59(1) of the 1969 Vienna Convention. In *T-Port*, the Court of First Instance did not even take the pain to mention the customary law status of Article 59(1)(a), which was as such not applicable, when

---

[56]   *Kupferberg* (as cited), para. 18; Case C-149/96 *Portugal* v. *Council* [1999] ECR I-8395, para. 35. See also Case C-61/94 *Commission* v. *Germany* [1996] I-3989, para. 30, holding that a provision of the International Dairy Arrangement had to be interpreted taking account of 'the general rule of international law requiring the parties to any agreement to show good faith in its performance'.

[57]   Case C-62/98 *Commission* v. *Portugal* (as cited), para. 44; Case C-84/98 *Commission* v. *Portugal* (as cited), para. 53, each time with reference to Case 812/79 *Attorney General* v. *Burgoa* [1980] ECR 2787, para. 6. See also in this respect the Opinion of AG Tesauro in *Levy* (as cited), point 4. Already in the *Italian Radio Tubes* case the Court referred to this rule of customary international law: Case 10/61 *Commission* v. *Italy* [1962] ECR 1, at p. 10.

[58]   Opinion 1/91 EEA I [1991] ECR I-6079, para. 14; Case C-312/91 *Metalsa* [1993] ECR I-3751, para. 12; *El-Yassini* (as cited), para. 47; Case C-268/99 *Jany* [2001] ECR I-8615, para. 35. See also *Anastasiou* (as cited), para. 43, referring also to 'any subsequent practice in (a treaty's) application' as an interpretative factor within the meaning of Article 31(3)(b) of the 1969 Vienna Convention.

it observed, in order to reject the argument that GATT 1994 should be seen as an international agreement pre-dating the entry into force of the EC Treaty to the extent it replicates the substantive law of GATT 1947, that 'in the relations between Member States of the WTO, and hence parties to GATT 1994, ... it follows from Article 59(1)(a) of the Vienna Convention on the Law of Treaties of 23 May 1969 that GATT 1994 has replaced GATT 1947 with effect from 1 January 1995, when GATT 1994 entered into force'.[59] Likewise, in *Levy* the Court of Justice accepted, referring to Article 59(1)(b) of the 1986 Vienna Convention, that 'the provisions of an international agreement may be deprived of their binding force if it appears that all the parties to the agreement have concluded a subsequent agreement whose provisions are so far incompatible with those of the earlier one that the two agreements are not capable of being applied at the same time'.[60] It did so in answer to an argument of the Commission that ILO Convention No.89 (1948), which France was a party to and which prevented it from giving full effect to the Community law principle of equal treatment of men and women (the convention prohibits night work solely for women), had been by-passed by later human rights treaties and ILO instruments.[61]

2.3 Customary international law as gap-filler

Finally, the Community case law occasionally relies on rules of customary international law as 'gap-fillers' when Community law itself displays lacunae regarding a certain issue. In the area of EC fisheries law, the Court has repeatedly held, starting with *Factortame II*, that, in the absence of specific Community rules on the registration of vessels, 'it is for the Member States to determine, in accordance with the general rules of international law, the conditions which must be fulfilled in order for a vessel to be registered in their registers and granted the right to fly their flag'.[62] A similar reference to customary international law has been made regarding the conditions for granting nationality: in *Micheletti* the Court held that '[u]nder international law, it

---

[59] Case T-2/99 *T-Port* (as cited), para. 81, quoting literally from the Opinion of AG Elmer in Joined Cases C-364/95 and C-365/95 *T-Port* (as cited), para. 16. The AG had not paid attention to the customary law status of the rule laid down in this provision either.

[60] *Levy*, para. 19. One may wonder why the Court chose to refer to the 1986 Vienna Convention rather than to the 1969 Vienna Convention.

[61] The Commission referred in this respect to the Convention on the Elimination of all Forms of Discrimination against Women, concluded in New York on 18 December 1979, ratified by France in 1983, to the 1990 Protocol on ILO Convention No.89, to ILO Convention No.171 of 1990 on night work and to ILO Recommendation No.178 of 1990 on night work.

[62] *Factortame II*, para. 17; Case C-246/89 *Commission v. United Kingdom* (as cited), para. 15; Case C-62/96 *Commission v. Greece* (as cited), para. 22.

is for each Member State ... to lay down the conditions for the acquisition and loss of nationality'.[63] However, the reference to international law in these cases is not unconditional. In the fisheries cases the Court added that, 'in exercising that power, the Member States must comply with the rules of Community law',[64] whereas in *Micheletti* it added that 'due regard' was to be given to Community law.[65]

It is interesting to note that in the fisheries cases from which the aforementioned quotation stems, the Court observed concerning the argument of several Member States that they could define as they saw fit the conditions upon which they grant to a vessel the right to fly their flag under international law, that it 'might have some merit only if the requirements laid down by Community law with regard to the exercise by the Member States of the powers which they retain with regard to the registration of vessels conflicted with the rules of international law'.[66] One could read in this an expression of the Court's preparedness in principle to give primacy to customary international law in case of an outright conflict with norms of Community law.

In the very recent *Weber* case (2002) the Court had to answer a preliminary question from the *Hoge Raad* as to whether work carried out by an employee on the Netherlands section of the continental shelf (Weber worked as a cook on mining installations and ships in that maritime zone) must be regarded as having been carried out in the Netherlands for the purposes of Article 5(1) of the Brussels Convention. The Court gave a positive answer, holding that, 'in the absence of any provision in the Brussels Convention governing that aspect of its scope or any other indication as to the answer to be given to this question, reference must be made to the principles of public international law relating to the legal regime applicable to the continental shelf'.[67]

---

[63] *Micheletti*, para. 10. See also Opinion of AG La Pergola in *Pereira Roque* (as cited), para. 31. The *Micheletti* case law has later been confirmed in Case C-179/98 *Mesbah* [1999] ECR I-7955, para. 29 and in Case C-192/99 *Kaur* [2001] ECR I-1237, para. 19. In para. 20 of the latter judgment, the Court makes clear that it considers this to be a 'principle of customary international law'.

[64] *Factortame II*, para. 17; *Commission* v. *United Kingdom*, para. 17; *Commission* v. *Greece*, para. 22.

[65] *Micheletti*, para. 10.

[66] *Factortame II*, para. 16; *Commission* v. *United Kingdom*, para. 14. Compare, however, Case C-280/89 *Commission* v. *Ireland* [1992] ECR I-6185, para. 24 (with reference to *Poulsen*, paras. 13, 14 and 15): 'under international law a vessel has the nationality of the State in which it is registered and (...) it is for that State to determine in the exercise of its sovereign powers the conditions for the grant of such nationality'. No mention is made here of the need to exercise these 'sovereign powers' in conformity with Community law. This addition was not needed here, though, since in making this statement the Court simply contradicted the argument of Ireland that public international law authorized it to decline to recognize the nationality of vessels which do not have a genuine link with the State whose flag they are flying.

[67] *Weber* (as cited), para. 31. The relevant rules of the international law of the sea are analysed in paras. 32-34.

As the *Micheletti* and fisheries cases already indicated, there are limits to the reliance on customary international law in order to fill certain lacunae of Community law. The Court of Justice will not accept that Member States can invoke competences which they have under customary international law in order to unilaterally modify obligations that are incumbent upon them under Community law. Thus, in a judgment of 9 July 1991, the Court rejected the United Kingdom's argument that the extension of its territorial sea from 3 to 12 miles in 1987 and the adjustment of the baselines which followed therefrom complied with international law so that the resulting new baselines (which were shifted further out to sea than the earlier ones) did not constitute a breach of an EC Regulation on fisheries the scope of which is based on the previous baselines. The Court observed that '[i]nternational law merely authorizes States to extend their territorial sea to 12 nautical miles and, in certain circumstances, to draw the baselines used to measure the breadth of the territorial sea to and from low-tide elevations which are situated within that territorial sea' and that, since 'the decision to make use of the options under the rules of international law' was attributable solely to the United Kingdom, the latter had unilaterally altered the scope of the Regulation concerned.[68] As a result, the effectiveness of the Regulation would be reduced since fishermen from other Member States would be excluded from the zones in which they had hitherto fished and the relative stability of fisheries activities would be disturbed.[69] This judgment shows that reliance by a Member State on customary international law in order to fill a lacuna under EC law - the notion of 'baselines' had not been defined in the Regulation at issue, hence the United Kingdom argued it did not refer to fixed but to ambulatory baselines, i.e. those that are defined from time to time by the Member State concerned - may run against other fundamental values of Community law, such as safeguarding its effectiveness (*effet utile*).

2.4 Reviewing the legality of EU acts based on customary international law?

The question of invocability of customary international law in order to review the legality of Community law is a complex one. As a matter of fact, it requires a positive answer to the following three sub-questions: first of all, is customary international law part of the Community legal order? Secondly, is customary international law invocable before the Community courts in a review of legality? And thirdly, does customary international law have primacy over Community acts?

---

[68] Case C-146/89 *Commission* v. *United Kingdom* (as cited), para. 25.

[69] *Commission* v. *United Kingdom*, paras. 27-29.

As is clear from the analysis until now, the Court of Justice has only given a partial response to these questions in the case law discussed so far. It is true that the Court held in *Poulsen* that 'the European Community must respect international law in the exercise of its powers'[70] and that it has interpreted and applied Community law in conformity with customary international law. In doing so, the Court seems to have made clear that customary international law is part of the Community legal order and that it has the jurisdiction to ensure in this way the compliance of Community law with customary international law.

However, one should not be too excited with this finding. Courts and tribunals in general make a distinction between, on the one hand, the question of whether a treaty or a rule of customary international law is part of their domestic legal order for the purpose of interpreting a domestic rule in conformity with the rule of public international law at hand and, on the other hand, the question of whether a rule of customary international law can be invoked in order to review the legality of a rule of the internal legal order. Usually, the distinction is labelled by using the term 'indirect effect' as opposed to 'direct effect'.[71]

We are thus soon confronted with the second sub-question. Here the case law before *Opel Austria* and *Racke* had likewise not given explicit answers. Reference is often made in this respect to the Court of Justice's judgment in the *International Fruit* case (1972). On the one hand, this judgment could be read as implying that rules of customary international law are part of the Community legal order in a more general way than solely for the purpose of interpreting and applying Community law in conformity with it:

'*According to the first paragraph of Article [234 EC] "The Court of Justice shall have jurisdiction to give preliminary ruling concerning (...) the validity (...) of acts of the institutions of the Community".*

Under that formulation, the jurisdiction of the Court cannot be limited by the grounds on which the validity of those measures may be contested.

Since such jurisdiction extends to all grounds capable of invalidating those measures, the Court is obliged to examine whether their validity may be affected by reason of the fact that they are contrary to a rule of international law'.[72]

However, the Court added two conditions:

---

[70] *Poulsen*, para. 9.

[71] See e.g. Dominicé & Voeffrey (1996), at p. 52-53.

[72] Joined Cases 21 to 24/72 *International Fruit* [1972] ECR 1219, paras. 4-6 (emphasis added).

> *'Before the incompatibility of a Community measure with a provision of interna-*
> *tional law can affect the validity of that measure, the Community must first of all*
> *be* bound *by that provision.*
>
> *Before invalidity can be relied upon before a national court, that provision of*
> *international law must also be capable of* conferring rights on citizens *of the*
> *Community which they can invoke before the courts'.*[73]

From the second quotation it looks as if - presuming the EC as a subject
of international law is bound by a rule of customary international law - the
test to be carried out is whether or not the rule in question is capable of
conferring rights on individuals. However, some caution is required in applying
the judgment to customary international law. In the case at hand, the rule
of international law concerned was a treaty provision, more particularly a provision of GATT 1947. As we will see below, the GATT/WTO case law of the
Community courts displays some particular features (see further 4.3 below).

In any event, the Court of Justice's affirmation that the EC must respect
international law in the exercise of its powers does by no means imply the
invocability of the customary international law for the review of the legality of
Community acts. Subjects of international law, like the EC, are responsible for
executing fully their obligations under international law. Nevertheless, unless
otherwise provided for, they are free to determine the legal means appropriate
for executing these obligations. Consequently, there is no general obligation
under international law to make the rules and principles of international law
invocable in the internal legal order with a view to testing the validity of acts
adopted by organs of that internal legal order.

It is true that a provision of international law can provide for specific rules
concerning the manner in which certain international legal instruments or
provisions have to be implemented in the internal legal order of the subjects
of international law to which they are addressed and/or with regard to their
invocability in that legal order.[74] Nevertheless, the cases in which a particular
international rule or instrument provides for its invocability in the domestic
legal order remain rather exceptional.[75] Moreover, when a subject of international
law decides that rules and principles of international law are invocable in its
internal legal order, there is no rule of international law as to under what
conditions these rules should be invocable. To put it differently, there is no
fixed definition under international law for the concept of invocability or direct

---

[73] *International Fruit*, paras. 7-8 (emphasis added).

[74] An obvious example of such a provision is Article 249 (ex 189), second para., EC, pursuant to which
regulations are directly applicable in all Member States.

[75] Dominicé & Voeffray (1996), at p. 51.

effect.[76] Even between the EU's Member States the definition and the application of the concepts of invocability and direct effect differ widely.[77]

As far as customary international law is concerned, the *Woodpulp* judgment was the first case in which the Court of Justice dealt at length with arguments of customary international law to review the legality of Community acts. Applicants not only argued (i) that the Commission had violated public international law by applying an 'economic repercussions' (in other words, an 'effects') test, but also (ii) that it had infringed Canada's sovereignty[78] and thus the principle of international comity by imposing fines on them and by making reduction of those fines conditional on the producers giving undertakings as to their future conduct, and (iii) that it had infringed the principle of non-interference, by disregarding, in applying its competition rules, the rule that 'where two States have jurisdiction to lay down and enforce rules and the effect of such rules is that a person finds himself subject to contradictory orders as to the conduct he must adopt, each State is obliged to exercise its jurisdiction with moderation'.[79] Although, as we noted above, the Court concluded that Community law was in conformity with customary international law, the *Woodpulp* case can be seen as a first implicit acceptance of the invocability of customary international law for the review of the legality of Community acts.

However, as the Court in its reasoning based itself in the first place on Article 81 EC in order to note that the Commission's decision 'was covered by the territoriality principle as universally recognised in public international law'[80] and only secondarily on a rule of customary international law of jurisdiction, the *Woodpulp* judgment remains somewhat ambiguous. Moreover, the Court did not explicitly address the matter of invocability of customary international law in the Community legal order. To unveil the precise position of customary international law in the Community legal order as to its invocability, one had to await an explicit judgment on the matter.

---

[76] See also Nollkaemper in this volume's chapter VII.

[77] Frowein & Oellers-Frahm (1996), at p. 18 and the various national reports in the same book.

[78] This was a claim of Canadian applicants.

[79] See *Woodpulp*, paras. 6-23. The principle of comity has been invoked a number of times before the Community courts but has never really been applied by the latter. It was invoked but not applied in, *inter alia*, Case 60/81 *IBM* [1981] ECR 2639, para. 4; Opinion of AG Ruiz-Jarabo Colomer in Case C-336/96 *Gilly* [1998] ECR I-2812, para. 41; Opinion of AG Léger in Case C-381/98 *Ingmar* [2000] ECR I-9305, para. 18; CFI, Joined Cases T-24/93, T-25/93, T-26/93 and T-28/93 *Compagnie maritime belge* [1996] ECR II-1201, para. 88. The principle was, however, actively used by AG Fennelly in his Opinion in Case C-219/98 *Anastasiou II* [2000] ECR I-5241, paras. 22, 34 and 41.

[80] *Woodpulp*, para. 18.

3 An analysis of Opel Austria and Racke

In *Opel Austria* and *Racke* a private individual contested the validity of an act of secondary Community law, namely a regulation, on the basis of a rule of customary international law. In both cases, the rule of customary international law concerned the law of treaties: in the first case, the obligation not to defeat the object and purpose of a treaty prior to its entry into force, in the second case the rule of *rebus sic stantibus*. Therefore in both cases the Court was invited to express itself on the position of customary international law in the Community legal order with a view to testing the validity of Community acts.

3.1 The facts of both cases

Opel Austria GmbH, a company incorporated under the laws of Austria which is part of the General Motors Group, is the sole producer of F-15 car gearboxes. It has exported the gearboxes to the EU since 1993 and received Austrian state aid for their production. The European Community was of the opinion that the Austrian state aid had a detrimental effect on trade between Austria and the European Community and that is was thus in violation of the Free Trade Agreement between the EC and Austria.[81] In order to neutralize the detrimental effect that the Austrian state aid had on trade between Austria and the Community, the Council adopted on 20 December 1993 EC Regulation 3697/93.[82] This Regulation introduced, *inter alia*, an import duty of 4,5 % for F-15 car gearboxes produced by Opel Austria. Opel Austria introduced an application for annulment against it.

However, in the meantime, on 13 December 1993, the Council and the Commission had approved, on behalf of the EC and the ECSC, the Agreement on the European Economic Area between the European Community and their Member States on the one hand and, amongst others, Austria on the other ('EEA Agreement').[83] The EEA Agreement, which contained a prohibition on levies equivalent to custom duties, entered into force on 1 January 1994.

Opel Austria argued that the contested Regulation and the EEA Agreement provisions were incompatible. By adopting an incompatible regulation a few weeks before the entry into force of the EEA Agreement, so it argued, the Council had infringed the rule of customary international law, confirmed in both Article 18 of the 1969 Vienna Convention and Article 18 of the 1986

---

[81] OJ 1972, L 300/2.

[82] Council Regulation 3697/93/EC of 20 December 1993 withdrawing tariff concessions in accordance with Article 23(2) and Article 27(3)(a) of the Free Trade Agreement between the Community and Austria (General Motors Austria), OJ 1993, L 343/1.

[83] OJ 1994, L 1/1.

Vienna Convention, according to which a signatory may not defeat the object and purpose of a treaty prior to its entry into force.

The second case, *Racke*, was lodged with the Court of Justice in a reference by the German *Bundesfinanzhof* for a preliminary ruling. The Co-operation Agreement of 2 April 1980 concluded between the European Economic Community and the Member States on the one hand and the Socialist Federal Republic of Yugoslavia on the other ('Co-operation Agreement'), introduced a preferential tariff for the import of wine originating in Yugoslavia. The Council suspended the Co-operation Agreement unilaterally in 1991 by means of a regulation.[84] The reasons given were the fundamental change in circumstances (*rebus sic stantibus*), i.e. the civil war and the disintegration of Yugoslavia. Racke, a German company, imported wine from Yugoslavia (more in particular, from Kosovo) and was thus prejudiced by the suspension of the tariff concessions. It continued to rely on the preferential tariff introduced by the Co-operation Agreement and contested the validity of the regulation suspending the Co-operation Agreement. The litigation with the German Tax Authorities reached the German *Bundesfinanzhof*. The latter asked the Court of Justice whether the Regulation suspending the Co-operation Agreement was valid in the light of the conditions imposed by customary international law for a suspension based on *rebus sic stantibus*.

3.2   An analysis of *Racke*

The point of departure in the Court of Justice's reasoning in *Racke* is quite affirmative and straightforward and builds on the *Poulsen* case (see above 2.1):

'*It should be noted in that respect that (...) the European Community must respect international law in the exercise of its powers. It is therefore required to comply with the rules of customary international law when adopting a regulation suspending the trade concessions granted by, or by virtue of, an agreement which it has concluded with a non-member country.*

It follows that the rules of customary international law concerning the termination and the suspension of treaty relations by reason of a fundamental change of circumstances are binding upon the Community institutions and form part of the Community legal order'.[85]

---

[84] Council Regulation 3300/91/EEC of 11 November 1991 suspending the trade concessions provided for
by the Co-operation Agreement between the European Economic Community and the Socialist Federal
Republic of Yugoslavia, OJ 1991, L 315/1.

[85] *Racke*, paras. 45-46 (emphasis added).

To the extent that any doubts still persisted on this subject, they are hereby clearly resolved. Customary international law is part of the Community legal order.

However, the Court continues on its élan and it also answers the following two questions in the affirmative:

'In those circumstances, an individual relying in legal proceedings on rights which he derives directly from an agreement with a non-member country may not be denied *the possibility of challenging the validity of a regulation which, by suspending the trade concessions granted by that agreement, prevents him from* relying on it, and of invoking, in order to challenge the validity of the suspending regulation, obligations deriving from rules of customary international law *which govern the termination and suspension of treaty relations'.*[86]

Thus, in the case at hand, the Court accepted the invocability of customary international law to review the legality of a Community act and accorded the rule of customary international law primacy over the conflicting rule of secondary Community legislation.

The Court of Justice's position of principle is remarkable and quite progressive. As a matter of fact, only a few domestic courts and tribunals of the Member States reach a similar conclusion. In some Member States, they would not reach such a conclusion because customary international law is not a part of the domestic legal order (e.g. Denmark, where it would require incorporation to be applicable before the Danish judiciary).[87] In other Member States, national courts and tribunals would have refused the invocability of the particular rule of customary international law at hand, i.e. *rebus sic stantibus*, as it concerns the relations between states (and international organizations) and does not intend to confer rights on private individuals. Still in other Member States, even if none of these hurdles applied, the courts and tribunals would, in all probability, have refused to give primacy to rules of customary international law over domestic legislative acts (e.g. the Netherlands, France,[88] United Kingdom, Ireland and Belgium).

Nevertheless, giving the wording of the *Racke* case, one has to be careful not to overstretch the judgment's significance for the question of invocability of customary international law in the Community legal order. Upon closer inspection, the Court restricts its ruling in at least four manners.

First of all, the judgment is restricted to the situation in which an individual invokes a rule of customary international law in order to review the legality of

---

[86] *Racke*, para. 51 (emphasis added).

[87] Harhoff (1996), at p. 173.

[88] See, commenting on *Racke*, Gautron & Grard (2000), at p. 116-117.

a Community act. The Court went out of its way to stress that the case did not concern the question of 'direct effect' of a rule of customary international law:

> '*In this case, however, the plaintiff is incidentally challenging the validity of a Community regulation under those rules [of customary international law] in order to rely upon rights which it derives directly from an agreement of the Community with a non-member country. This case does not therefore concern the direct effect of those rules*'.[89]

It follows from this paragraph and from paragraph 51 of the judgment quoted above that the Court viewed the case rather as one in which a private individual relies on the direct effect of the Co-operation Agreement and, in doing so, *incidentally (de façon incidente/inzident)* challenges the validity of a Community regulation preventing him from relying on the rights granted to him. In such a (limited) situation, the Court in *Racke* makes clear that the individual may invoke obligations that for the EC flow from customary international law.

Secondly, it seems as if the invocability of a rule of customary international law to review the legality of a Community act is furthermore restricted to the situation in which this Community act is, in fact, an implementation of the invoked rule of customary international law. After all, the contested regulation explicitly stated to have been taken on the basis of *rebus sic stantibus*. Therefore, one may wonder whether the *Racke* case does not in a way boil down to an application of the *Nakajima* case law vis-à-vis customary international law. In the latter case, an importer of Japanese typewriters and printers had been imposed an anti-dumping duty. The importer introduced an action for annulment and contended that a provision of the basic anti-dumping Regulation was unlawful and thus void for being contrary to the GATT Anti-Dumping Code. The Court of Justice held that the rules of the GATT agreements are, in principle, not invocable in order to review the legality of a Community act, but added that GATT rules are nevertheless invocable to review the legality when the contested Community act intends to implement an obligation assumed in the context of GATT.[90] In paragraph 48 of *Racke* the Court expressly refers, 'for a comparable situation in relation to basic rules of a contractual nature', to *Nakajima*.

Thirdly, the Court seems to restrict its ruling to rules of customary international law of a *fundamental* nature:

---

[89] *Racke*, para. 47 (text between brackets added).

[90] Case C-69/89 *Nakajima* [1991] ECR I-2069, paras. 28-31; Case C-149/96 *Portugal* v. *Council* (as cited), para. 49. See e.g. Berrod (2000), at p. 443; Vanhamme (2001b), at p. 255.

'Racke is invoking fundamental *rules of customary international law against the disputed regulation, which was taken pursuant to those rules and deprives Racke of the rights to preferential treatment granted to it by the Co-operation Agreement'.*[91]

Although the Court does not define what a *fundamental* rule of customary international law is, it makes clear in the judgment that the principle of *pacta sunt servanda* and the rule of *rebus sic stantibus* belong to this category.[92] In paragraph 51, though, the Court seems to be a bit broader in its formulation by referring more generically to the invocability of 'obligations deriving from rules of customary international law which govern the termination and suspension of treaty relations'.

Finally, the Court does not only restrict the scope of the invocability of rules of customary international law to review the legality of a Community act, but it also rather surprisingly waters down the legality test itself:

'However, because of the complexity of the rules in question and the imprecision of some of the concepts to which they refer, judicial review must necessarily, and in particular in the context of a preliminary reference for an assessment of validity, be limited to the question whether, by adopting the suspending regulation, the Council made manifest errors of assessment *concerning the conditions for applying those rules'.*[93]

With due respect, it must be submitted that the latter restriction, apparently inspired by the Advocate General's Opinion,[94] is not only undesirable, but also legally unacceptable.

Firstly, it is a misconception and oversimplification to hold that rules of customary international law are vague, uncertain and imprecise (see also further 5.1 below). Moreover, the customary rule of *rebus sic stantibus* has been codified in Article 62 of the 1969 Vienna Convention and in Article 62 of the 1986 Vienna Convention.[95] Hence, the rule of customary international law at

---

[91] *Racke*, para. 48 (emphasis added).

[92] *Racke*, paras. 49-50.

[93] *Racke*, para. 52 (emphasis added).

[94] See Opinion of AG Jacobs [1998] ECR I-3677, para. 71. It should be noted, though, that, although he took the view that 'only manifest violations of the law of treaties can give rise to a ruling of invalidity', the AG did not base this on the complexity or imprecision of the rules or concepts in question, but on the fact that in his Opinion the reliance on customary international law by individuals to challenge a Community act 'should be exceptional in the light of the overall purpose and nature of such rules'.

[95] See ILC, *Draft Articles on the Law of Treaties*, UN Doc. A/CONF.39/11/Add.2, Official Records, II, p. 76, para. 2; ILC, *Report of the ILC to the GA* (1963, II) Y.I.L.C. 207, para.2; ICJ, *Fisheries Jurisdiction* Case (*United Kingdom* v. *Iceland*, as cited), at 19, para. 36; ICJ, *Fisheries Jurisdiction* Case (*Federal Republic*

hand has similar characteristics to a treaty provision and the Court of Justice indeed makes an application, further on in its judgment, of the conditions of Article 62(1) of the 1969 Vienna Convention.[96] It is therefore unacceptable to hold that in reviewing the legality of a Community act on the basis of a rule of customary international law only a marginal appreciation test should apply, whereas this is not the case in reviewing the legality on the basis of a treaty provision.

Secondly, it should be noted that the task of the Court of Justice is to ensure that 'in the interpretation and the application of this treaty the law is observed'.[97] One of the means of ensuring the interpretation and application of Community law (of which rules of customary international law are an integral part) is the instrument of a reference for a preliminary ruling (Article 234 EC).

The particularity of a court case is that there is a discussion between the parties on the facts or on a point of law. In this context, it does make some sense to say that some facts or a point of law is unclear and that it is up to the court to elucidate this.

Moreover, the instrument of a preliminary ruling has the particularity that it tends to involve questions that are rather complex and that could not or should not be solved by the competent national court or tribunal.

Reference could be made in this respect to the *Cilfit* case. According to Article 234, third paragraph, EC national courts and tribunals against whose decisions there is no judicial remedy have to refer any question of Community law raised, for a preliminary ruling to the European Court of Justice. Nevertheless, the Court held in the *Cilfit* case that these national courts and tribunals do not have to refer the question raised, when they believe that the answer is clear so that no reference is warranted.[98] Consequently, one can assert that a

---

of Germany v. *Iceland*), judgment of 2 February 1973, ICJ Rep. (1973), p. 49 et seq., at p. 63, para. 36; ICJ, *Case concerning the Gabčíkovo-Nagymaros Project* (*Hungary* v. *Slovakia*, as cited), at p. 38, para. 46, and at p. 64, para. 104.

[96] See *Racke*, paras. 53-59. Commentators have wondered why the Court of Justice did not rather base its reasoning on the 1986 Vienna Convention, which contains similar provisions, as this treaty, as stated above, governs the conclusion of treaties between international organizations and states. Leray & Potteau (1999) note, concerning 'l'hésitation, voire l'hostilité de la CJCE à se référer à la CV 86': 'Ne faudrait-il pas y voir la volonté d'être assimilé à un Etat ou le refus d'être considéré comme une 'vulgaire' organisation internationale?'. Nevertheless, the Court of Justice has already referred to the 1986 Vienna Convention: see the references above, in note 53.

[97] Article 220 EC.

[98] '[P]aragraph (3) of Article 177 of the EEC is to be interpreted as meaning that a court or tribunal against whose decision there is no judicial remedy under national law is required, where a question of Community law is raised before is, to comply with its obligation to bring the matter before the Court of Justice, unless it has established that the question raised is irrelevant or that the Community provision

reference for a preliminary ruling to the European Court of Justice encompasses a judgment of the national court or tribunal that the question raised is rather complex.

Therefore, the refusal to proceed with a full-fledged review of the legality of a Community act 'because of the complexity of the rules in question and the imprecision of some of the concepts to which they refer, (...) and in particular in the context of a preliminary reference (...)' makes no sense. Above all, taking this into consideration, the Court's refusal to proceed with a full-fledged review of legality amounts to a refusal to exercise its judicial powers and thus to an infringement of the right to an effective judicial remedy.[99]

Thirdly, the marginal appreciation test is incompatible with the rule of *rebus sic stantibus*. After all, the corollary of a court's decision to proceed with a marginal appreciation test, is the granting of a discretionary competence or a large margin of appreciation to the government body. However, the rule of *rebus sic stantibus* does not accord a large margin of appreciation to the government that wishes to invoke this provision.

First of all, *rebus sic stantibus* is an exception to the principle of *pacta sunt servanda*. As an exception to a general rule, it must obviously be interpreted restrictively and should therefore 'be applied only in exceptional cases', as the International Court of Justice stated in its *Gabcíkovo-Nagymaros* judgment,[100] quoted in paragraph 50 of *Racke*. Secondly, Article 62(1) of the 1969 Vienna Convention is deliberately worded negatively[101] and may only be invoked under strict and cumulative conditions.[102] Thirdly, one should not lose sight of the fact that the rule of *rebus sic stantibus* is an exception to a *fundamental* rule of international (treaty) law and that a broad interpretation could jeopardise the stability of international relations:

---

in question has already been interpreted by the Court or that the correct application of Community law is so obvious as to leave no scope for any reasonable doubt. The existence of such a possibility must be assessed in the light of the specific characteristics of Community law, the particular difficulties to which its interpretation gives rise and the risk of divergences in judicial decisions within the Community'; Case 283/81 *Cilfit* [1982] ECR 3415, para. 21.

[99] The Court of Justice accepted the right to an effective judicial remedy as enshrined in Articles 6 and 13 of the European Convention of Human Rights as a general principle of Community law. See e.g. Case 222/84 *Johnston* [1986] ECR 1651, paras. 18, 21 and 58; Case 222/86 *Heylens* [1987] ECR 4097, para. 14; Case C-97/91 *Borelli* [1992] ECR I-6313, paras. 13-15; Case T-111/96 *ITT Promedia* [1998] ECR II-2937, paras. 55, 60-61 and 72-73.

[100] As cited, at p. 65, para. 104.

[101] 'A fundamental change of circumstances (...) may not be invoked (...) unless: (...)': Article 62, paras. 1-2 1969 Vienna Convention and Article 62, paras. 1-2 1986 Vienna Convention.

[102] See Article 62(1) and (2) and Articles 65-67 1969 Vienna Convention.

'Article 62 of the Vienna Convention is one of its fundamental articles, because of the delicate balance *it achieves between respect for the binding force of treaties and the need to terminate or withdraw from treaties which have become inapplicable as a result of a radical change in circumstances which existed when they were concluded and which determined the States' consent'.*[103]

In the appreciation of such a strict and severe rule, which is the expression of a delicate balance so as to retain the stability of international relations, a large margin of appreciation is not acceptable.

Considering all these factors, one must respectfully question the Court of Justice's decision to accept the invocability of a rule of customary international law to review the legality of a Community act if the Court subsequently makes a wrong and unacceptable application of the customary rule at hand. As a matter of fact, in those circumstances the enforcement of customary international law would be better served if the Court had not accepted the invocability of the rule of customary international law at all. Indeed, the erroneous application of the customary rule at hand might create the false impression that the customary rule has not been infringed, thus considerably weakening the instruments of international relations for complying with international law.

Moreover, customary international law is the result of an informal and continuous law-making process in which judgments of the domestic courts also amount to practice relevant for the formation, application and modification of rules of customary international law.[104] Therefore, there are two sides to the coin that have to be considered.

On the one hand, the domestic court's erroneous *application* of the rule of customary international law gives rise to an infringement of international law, provoking the international responsibility of the State. Although there is, in principle, no obligation under international law to make the rules of international law invocable before domestic courts, once the invocability is accepted, the domestic court is under an international obligation to apply the rule of (customary) international law correctly.

---

[103] ILC, *Draft Articles on the Law of Treaties between States and International Organisations or between International Organisations*, UN Doc. CONF.129/16/Add.1, Official Records, II, 42 (emphasis added).

[104] 'The practice of the executive, legislative and judicial organs of the State is to be considered, according to the circumstances, as state practice'; ILA, "Statement of Principles Applicable to the Formation of General Customary International Law", *Report of the Sixty-Ninth Conference held in London* (2000), 728: 'But customary law is rather different. Practice is what creates it, and practice is how it is applied: so it may be hard to distinguish which aspect one is dealing with. Similarly, established customary rules are rarely abolished: they are normally replaced by other rules. The customary process is in fact a continuous one (...)'.

On the other hand, the judgment of the domestic court might contribute to State practice *modifying* the rule of customary international law: 'Even after the rule has 'emerged', every act of compliance will strengthen it, and every violation, if acquiesced in, will help to undermine it'.[105] An erroneous interpretation or application by a domestic court of a rule of customary international law that might seem favourable to that State in the particular case, might be rather undesirable when this erroneous interpretation or application (by initiating or strengthening the practice) becomes the new rule of customary international law. As such, the negative consequences of an erroneous judgment might, in the long term and if repeated, be vaster than one could imagine having regard to the particular case at hand.

3.3 An analysis of *Opel Austria*

The Court of First Instance took an entirely different approach in the *Opel Austria* case. It starts off by recalling that 'the principle of good faith is a rule of customary international law whose existence is recognized by the International Court of Justice (...) and is therefore binding on the Community'.[106] This does not help us that much since stating that a rule of customary international law is binding on a subject of international law, like the Community, is self-evident. Secondly, the Court of First Instance notes that this principle has been codified by Article 18 of the 1969 Vienna Convention.[107] As is known, the latter provision lays down the obligation not to defeat the object and purpose of a treaty prior to its entry into force.[108] Then, the Court makes

---

[105] Mendelson (1998), at p. 175.

[106] *Opel Austria*, para. 90.

[107] *Opel Austria*, para. 91. Article 18 provides as follows: 'A State is obliged to refrain from acts which would defeat the object and purpose of a treaty when:

(a) it has signed the treaty or has exchanged instruments constituting the treaty subject to ratification, acceptance or approval, or until it shall have made its intention clear not to become a party to the treaty; or

(b) it has expressed its consent to be bound by the treaty, pending the entry into force of the treaty and provided that such entry into force is not unduly delayed'.

[108] *Opel Austria* was confirmed at this juncture by the Court of First Instance in Joined Cases T-186/97, T-187/97, T-190-192/97, T-210/97, T-211/97, T-216/97, T-217/97, T-218/97, T-279/97, T-280/97, T-293/97 and T-147/99 *Kaufring* [2001] ECR II-1337, para. 237: 'Article 7 of the Association Agreement provides that the contracting parties are to take all appropriate measures, whether general or particular, to ensure the fulfilment of the obligations arising from the Agreement and to refrain from any measures liable to jeopardise the attainment of its objectives. The provision expresses the *pacta sunt servanda* principle and the principle of good faith which must govern the conduct of the parties to an agreement in public international law'.

a sudden leap. It replaces the principle of customary international law 'not to defeat the object and purpose of a treaty prior to its entry into force' by the Community law 'principle of legitimate expectations':

'the principle of good faith is the corollary in public international law of the principle of protection of legitimate expectations which, according to the case law, forms part of the Community legal order. Any economic operator to whom an institution has given justified hopes may rely on the principle of protection of legitimate expectations'.[109]

The Court proceeds on the basis of the Community principle of legitimate expectations. In analogy to what it had previously elaborated on with respect to the principle of customary international law 'not to defeat the object and purpose of a treaty prior to its entry into force', the Court holds that Community principle of legitimate expectations provides that:

'In a situation where the Communities have deposited their instruments of approval of an international agreement and the date of entry into force of that agreement is known, traders may rely on the principle of protection of legitimate expectations in order to challenge the adoption by the institutions, during the period preceding the entry into force of that agreement, of any measure contrary to the provisions of that agreement which will have direct effect on them after it has entered into force'.[110]

The Court subsequently holds that, first, the invoked provision of the EEA Agreement (i.e. the prohibition on levies equivalent to custom duties)[111] has direct effect after its entry into force,[112] and secondly, that the contested Regulation is incompatible with the invoked provision of the EEA Agreement.[113] It therefore comes to the conclusion that the Community principle of legitimate expectations has been infringed.[114]

As the Court proceeded on a principle of Community law it did not express itself on the invocability of rules of customary international law. Nevertheless, the course of reasoning adopted by the Court of First Instance is quite interesting and is inspired by the Court of Justice's case law on fundamental rights. In fact, several fundamental rights enshrined in the European Convention on

---

[109] *Opel Austria*, para. 93.

[110] *Opel Austria*, para. 94.

[111] Article 10 EEA Agreement.

[112] *Opel Austria*, paras. 100-102

[113] *Opel Austria*, paras. 96-99 and 103-122.

[114] *Opel Austria*, para. 123.

Human Rights have been accepted by the Court of Justice as 'fundamental rights which form an integral part of the general principles of Community law protected by the Court of Justice'.[115]

One should not lose sight of the fact that several of these fundamental rights enshrined in the European Convention on Human Rights can also be qualified as rules of regional, i.e. European, customary international law.[116] As far as these fundamental rights can be qualified as European customary international law, the European Community is bound by these rules on the international level irrespective of the fact of whether or not the Community is a party to the European Convention on Human Rights (which it is not).

Viewed from this perspective, it becomes clear that the European Court of Justice has already on several occasions accepted the invocability of rules of customary international law by means of transforming a rule of (regional) customary international law into a general principle of Community law. The European Court of First Instance adopted a similar approach in *Opel Austria*.

By means of this 'transformation approach' a rule of customary international law becomes a rule of Community law, thus possessing all the characteristics of Community law, amongst which 'direct effect' and primacy over conflicting rules of secondary EC legislation and over conflicting national rules. Hereby, the complex question of invocability of rules of customary international law is avoided.

---

[115] Case 11/70 *Internationale Handelsgesellschaft* [1970] ECR 1125, para. 4. Case C-299/95 *Kremzow* [1997] ECR I-2629, para. 14: 'It should first be noted that, as the Court has consistently held, fundamental rights form an integral part of the general principles of Community law whose observance the Court ensures. For that purpose, the Court draws inspiration from the constitutional traditions common to the Member States and from the guidelines supplied by international treaties for the protection of human rights on which the Member States have collaborated or of which they are signatories. The [European Convention for the Protection of Human Rights and Fundamental Freedoms] has special significance in that respect. As the Court has also held, it follows that measures are not acceptable in the Community which are incompatible with observance of the human rights thus recognised and guaranteed'. See also Case 44/79 *Hauer* [1979] ECR 3727, para. 15: '[F]undamental rights form an integral part of the general principles of the law, the observance of which it ensures; that in safeguarding those rights, the Court is bound to draw inspiration from constitutional traditions common to the Member States, so that measures which are incompatible with the fundamental rights recognised by the Constitutions of those States are unacceptable in the Community, and that similarly, international treaties for the protection of human rights on which the Member States have collaborated or of which they are signatories, can supply guidelines which should be followed within the framework of Community law. That conception was later recognised by the joint declaration of the European Parliament, the Council and the Commission of 5 April 1977, which, after recalling the case law of the Court, refers on the one hand to the European Convention for the Protection of Human Rights and Fundamental Freedoms of 4 November 1950'.

[116] Compare: 'Thus these rulings [of the European Court of Human Rights] create a general European Law as much as regulations of the European Union do': Schermers (2000).

However, one should also be conscious that through the 'transformation approach' the 'general principle of Community law' starts to lead its own life, separate from the rule of customary international law. Not only does it possess the characteristics of 'direct effect' and primacy, but also the formation, interpretation, modification and termination of this 'general principle of Community law' are governed by Community law. As such, the Court of Justice becomes the highest authority on the interpretation and the enforcement of the 'general principle of Community law'.[117]

However, this dichotomy between the rule of customary international law and the general principle of Community law does not seem to pose that many problems.

First, it does not present many problems in the practice of the Court of Justice. For this purpose we could look at the Community case law on fundamental rights as enshrined in the European Convention of Human Rights and which the Court has accepted as general principles of Community law. There are indeed instances in which the interpretation of one of these fundamental rights does differ between the Court of Justice and the European Court of Human Rights. However, in general, the Court of Justice is careful to ensure that its case law on fundamental rights conforms with the case law of the European Court of Human Rights.[118] Schermers thus concluded that:

'Notwithstanding the absence of any formal binding Treaty commitments, the Court of Justice in fact considered the Community bound by the Convention. For the interpretation of the Convention it takes the interpretation by the European Court of Human Rights into account, and in fact it follows its case law wherever possible'.[119]

The *Opel Austria* judgment leads us to a similar conclusion. The Court's interpretation of the Community law principle of legitimate expectations is largely inspired by the rule of customary international law 'not to defeat the object and purpose of a treaty prior to its entry into force' as enshrined in Article 18 of the 1969 Vienna Convention. But above all, it can be submitted that the Court would

---

[117] Article 220 EC.

[118] See recently, *inter alia*, Case C-270/99P *Z* v. *European Parliament* [2001] ECR I-9197, para. 24 (process within a reasonable period); Case C-274/99P *Connolly* v. *Commission* [2001] ECR I-1611, paras. 39, 41, 49 and 51 (freedom of expression); Case T-62/98 *Volkswagen* [2000] II-2707, para. 281 (presumption of innocence); Case C-7/98 *Krombach* [2000] ECR I-1935 para. 39 (right to be defended by a lawyer in criminal cases); Joined Cases C-174/98P and C-189/98P *Van der Wal* [2000] ECR I-1, para. 17 (right to a fair trial); Case C-249/96 *Grant* [1998] ECR I-621, para. 34 (Article 12 ECHR); Case C-368/95 *Vereinigte Familiapress* [1997] ECR I-3689, para. 26 (freedom of expression); Case C-185/95P *Baustahlgewebe* [1998] ECR I-8417, para. 29 (process within a reasonable time).

[119] Schermers (2000), at p. 206.

have come to the same conclusion if it had proceeded on the basis of the latter rule of international law.

Some authors contested the Court of First Instance's application of the rule of customary international law 'not to defeat the object and purpose of a treaty prior to its entry into force'. In their opinion this rule can not lead to the conclusion that the signatory must nevertheless comply with the treaty or at least do nothing inconsistent with its provisions. They contend that a subject of international law is only bound by the treaty once he is a party to the treaty. As in these circumstances, it is only by means of ratification that one becomes a party to the treaty, mere signature could not have a similar effect.[120]

It must be acknowledged that the rule 'not to defeat the object and purpose of a treaty prior to its entry into force' gives rise to complicated legal questions and that the extent of duties incumbent upon signatories is not entirely clear.[121] However, there seems to be substantial support to purport that Article 18 of the 1969 Vienna Convention reflects a rule of customary international law[122] and that this rule is an expression of the principle of good faith.[123] Moreover, there is also ample support to suggest that in certain circumstances this rule obliges a signatory to do nothing inconsistent with a particular provision of the treaty.[124]

---

[120] Kuijper (2002).

[121] Aust (2000), at p. 94; Charme (1991), at p. 73-74 and 104; McDade (1985), at p. 6; Nguyen Quoc Dinh, Dallier & Pellet (1999), at p. 134; Rogoff (1980), at p. 272 and 297.

[122] 'That *an obligation* of good faith to refrain from acts calculated to frustrate the object of the treaty attaches to a State which has signed a treaty subject to ratification *appears to be generally accepted*'; ILC, "Draft Articles on the Law of Treaties with Commentaries, adopted by the ILC at it eighteenth session" in *United Nations Conference on the Law of Treaties. Official Records*, UN Doc A/CONF.39/11/Add.2, p. 22 (emphasis added). A similar duty was already included in Article 9 of the Harvard Law School Research in International Law prepared by the Harvard Law School Research in International Law 1935: 'Unless otherwise provided in the treaty itself, a State on behalf of which a treaty has been signed is under no duty to perform the obligations stipulated, prior to the coming into force of the treaty with respect of that State; under some circumstances, however, good faith may require that pending the coming into force of the treaty the State shall, for a reasonable time after signature, refrain from taking action which would render performance by any party of the obligations stipulated impossible or more difficult'; "Harvard Law School Research in International Law", *American Journal of International Law* (1935), p. 651, at p. 778; see also the references on p. 783-786. See also Charme (1991), at p. 74-85; McDade (1985), p. 13, 25 and 28; Rogoff (1980), p. 271-288.

[123] Cot (1968), at p. 141; ILC, "Draft Articles on the Law of Treaties...", 22; Kolb (1998), at p. 709-712; McDade (1985), at p. 18, 20-21; Nguyen Quoc Dinh, Daillier & Pellet (1999), p. 134; Rogoff (1980), p. 288-296.

[124] 'Duties of good faith and standards of conduct with which parties must comply before international juridical institutions may produce effects which are indistinguishable from back-dating the ratification'; Schwarzenberger, cited in McDade (1985), p. 16; see also the numerous references referred to by the

Furthermore, the facts weigh strongly in favour that particular treaty provisions would have binding force on the signatories in these circumstances. One should not forget that the European Community was not only a signatory of the EEA Agreement, but that it had in the meantime approved the agreement (on 13 December 1993) and that it was to enter into force (on 1 January 1994) twelve days after the contested regulation had been adopted (on 20 December 1993).[125] Furthermore, the EEA Agreement involves a high degree of integration, with objectives that exceed those of a mere free trade agreement. The aim of the EEA Agreement is to promote a continuous and balanced strengthening of trade and economic relations between the Contracting Parties with equal conditions of competition, and the respect of the same rules, with a view to creating a homogeneous European Economic Area. To that end, the Contracting Parties decided to eliminate virtually all trade barriers, in conformity with the provi-

---

latter author at p. 15-18. Moreover one can also deduce such a conclusion out of the (hypothetical) examples given by the Harvard Law School Research in International Law and the ILC in which the rule 'not to defeat the object and purpose of a treaty prior to its entry into force' would apply: 'Examples of hypothetical cases wherein the obligation of good faith referred to in Article 9 might be regarded as being ignored are the following: (1) A treaty contains an undertaking on the part of a signatory that it will not fortify a particular place on its frontier or that it will demilitarize a designated zone in that region. Shortly thereafter, while ratification is still pending, it proceeds to erect the forbidden fortifications or to increase its armaments within the zone referred to. (2) A treaty binds one signatory to cede a portion of its public domain to another; during the interval between signature and ratification the former cedes a part of the territory promised to another State. (3) A treaty binds one signatory to make restitution of certain property to the other signatory from which it has been wrongfully taken, but, while ratification is still pending, it destroys or otherwise disposes of the property, so that in case the treaty is ratified restitution would be impossible. (4) A treaty concedes the right of the nationals of one signatory to navigate a river within the territory of the other, but the latter would render navigation of the river difficult or impossible. (5) By the terms of a treaty both or all signatories agree to lower their existing tariff rates, but while ratification of the treaty is pending one of them proceeds to raise its tariff duties. (6) A treaty provides that one of the signatories shall undertake to deliver to the other a certain quantity of the products of a forest or a mine, but while ratification is pending the signatory undertaking the engagement destroys the forest or the mine, or takes some action which results in such diminution of their output that performance of the obligation is no longer possible'; Harvard Law School Research in International Law, p. 781-782. 'A treaty provides for the return of art work taken from the territory of another state. Prior to ratification, the signatory either destroys or allows the destruction of the art work. A treaty provides for the cession of certain installations owned by a signatory in another State. The ceding State destroys the installations or allows their destruction'; ILC, *Summary Records of the 788th Meeting*, (1953) 92.

[125] See above 3.1 for the facts. See also ILC, "Draft Articles on the Law of Treaties...", 22: 'The obligation of a State which has committed itself to be bound by the treaty to refrain from such acts is obviously of particular cogency and importance'.

sions of GATT on establishing free trade areas.[126] Under these circumstances it is not difficult to accept that infringing the prohibition on levies equivalent to custom duties runs counter to the object and purpose of a the EEA Agreement.

Secondly, the dichotomy between the general principle of Community law and the rule of customary international law caused by the 'transformation approach' does not create that many problems at the conceptual level either. In interpreting the general principle of Community law, the Court is bound to interpret this rule *as far as possible* in the light of rules of customary international law. Since the general principles of Community law are mainly the result of the Court's 'law finding' and since a rule of customary international law presupposes a certain degree of uniformity in the practice of subjects of international law (and thus also of EU Member States), there are not that many obstacles to interpret Community law in conformity with a rule of customary international law.

Finally, one should not forget that this transformation approach has a number of advantages at the political level. Annulling a Community act is not a simple neutral act, rather it can have quite a major impact at the political level. It often requires co-operation from the EU institutions and/or Member States to remedy the illegality and the political and legal gap it created. Under these circumstances it can only be hoped that these EU institutions and/or Member States understand and accept the Court's judgment. This process might be facilitated by explaining that they have breached a general principle of Community law rather than an extraneous and mysterious (*sic*) rule of customary international law. Would it be coincidental that the *Opel Austria* case is the only case in which an act of the EU institutions[127] has been found illegal on the basis of a rule of customary international law?

In any event, a correct application of the rule of customary international law, though under the veil of a general principle of Community law (*Opel Austria* case), is preferable to an erroneous application of a rule of customary international law even when the latter is submerged beneath a plethora of statements of principle as to the invocability of customary international law in the Community legal order (*Racke* case).

---

[126] Article 1 EEA Agreement; see also: *Opel Austria*, paras. 107-109.

[127] However, there are several examples in which the Court held that a Member State's act was not in conformity with an international agreement concluded by the European Community, e.g.: Case C-61/94 *Commission v. Germany* [1996] ECR I-3989; Case C-469/93 *Chiquita Italia* [1995] ECR I-4533.

4   The invocability of international agreements *viz.* customary international law: consistent case law?

4.1   Introduction

In contrast with the case law on the invocability of customary international law, the Community case law on the invocability of international agreements to which the EC is a party is rather extensive. However, the Court's case law on the invocability of such treaties does not seem to be entirely uniform. The standard for invocability of treaty provisions appears to differ depending on whether or not they belong to the GATT and WTO agreements. We will therefore firstly consider the invocability of treaty provisions in general (4.2) and, secondly, the invocability of the GATT and WTO agreements in particular (4.3). Subsequently, we will compare the Community Courts' case law on the invocability of customary international law with the case law on the invocability of treaty provisions to review the legality of a Community act (4.4).

4.2   International agreements in general

In dealing with the question of the invocability of international agreements so as to challenge the legality of Community acts we are again confronted with three sub-questions. First, do the rules of an international agreement to which the EC is a party form part of the Community legal order? Second, are these rules invocable in order to contest the legality of a Community act? Third, are these rules ranked higher in the hierarchy vis-à-vis the contested Community act?

Regarding the first question on, whether international agreements to which the EC is a party form an integral part of the Community legal order, the Court of Justice has answered in the affirmative. Once such an international agreement has entered into force and is thus binding on the Community, it forms an integral part of the Community legal order.[128] The Court of Justice thereto relies on Article 300 (ex 228) (7) EC, pursuant to which agreements concluded between the Community and one or more States or international organizations 'shall be binding on the institutions of the Community and on Member States'. It follows from this provision that Member States are bound

---

[128] See e.g. Case 181/73 *Haegeman* [1974] ECR 449, para. 5; Ruling 1/78 *Draft Convention of the IAEA* [1978] ECR 2151, para. 36; *Kupferberg*, paras. 11-13; Case 12/86 *Demirel* [1987] ECR 3719, para. 7; Case 30/88 *Greece* v. *Commission* [1989] ECR 3711, para. 12; Case C-192/89 *Sevince* [1990] ECR I-3461, para. 8. See Lenaerts & Van Nuffel (1999), p. 551, who add: 'This is in accordance with the monist approach: agreements concluded by the Community form part of the Community legal order without there being any necessity to transpose them into internal provisions of Community law'.

to ensure compliance with an international agreement concluded by the EC irrespective whether they are themselves a party to it. As in those cases Member States are not bound by reason of being a party to the said agreement, they must be bound by it as it became part of Community law.

Since international agreements binding on the Community are an integral part of the Community legal order, Member States (and the EU institutions) are required to comply with the obligation arising out of the treaty not only in relation to the contracting parties (in case they are a party to the treaty) but also and above all in relation to the Community that has assumed responsibility for the due performance of the agreement.[129]

The second question is whether the provisions of these international agreements are invocable before the Court of Justice. As indicated above (2.4), in *International Fruit* the Court of Justice held that an individual claimant can challenge the validity of a Community act based on a provision of an international agreement before the national courts if 'that provision of international law [is] capable of conferring rights on citizens (...) which they can invoke before the courts'.[130] The Court thus required that a provision of an international agreement has 'direct effect' in order to be invoked by an individual claimant.

What does the notion of 'direct effect', which has originally been developed by the Court of Justice as a principle applying to 'domestic' Community law, mean in its application to international agreements to which the EC is a party? It is useful to recall the *Kupferberg* judgment in this respect, since it provides probably the clearest and most elaborated examination of the direct effect of a treaty provision binding the European Community. In this case, a German importer contested the legality of a decision levying a customs duty on the import of Port wine from Portugal by invoking a provision of a Free Trade Agreement concluded between the (then) European Economic Community and Portugal.[131]

First, the Court of Justice examined whether the Parties to the free trade agreement intended to give the provision of that agreement direct effect:

'In conformity with the principles of public international law Community institutions which have power to negotiate and conclude an agreement with a non-member country are free to agree with that country what effect the provisions of the agreement are to have in the internal legal order of the contracting parties. Only if that question has not been settled by the agreement does it fall for decision by the courts having jurisdiction in the matter, and in particular by the Court of Justice within the framework of its jurisdiction under the treaty'.[132]

---

[129] *Haegeman*, paras. 4-5; *Kupferberg*, paras. 11-14.

[130] *International Fruit*, para. 8.

[131] *Kupferberg*, paras. 2-7.

[132] *Kupferberg*, para. 17.

The Court of Justice was unwilling to infer from the subject matter and purpose of the treaty that the parties had intended to preclude the direct effect of its provisions. Neither the lack of reciprocity on the implementation of the agreement (read: the fact that Portuguese courts would refuse to give direct effect to the treaty provisions), nor the presence of safeguard clauses, nor the existence of an institutional framework for the administration and implementation of the treaty obligations, could convince the Court to conclude that there was an implied intention by the parties to preclude direct effect.[133]

When the Court of Justice concluded that the parties to the treaty did not have an express or implied intention as to the direct effect of the treaty, it then continued by examining whether the invoked provision of the free trade agreement was unconditional and sufficiently precise to have direct effect. It therefore analysed the provision's words in the light of the context, the object and purpose of the agreement. In so doing, it concluded that this provision had direct effect.[134]

From *Kupferberg* it can be inferred that, while the Court of Justice does examine the subjective component, it does not accept the intention of the parties not to give direct effect to a treaty provision lightly. The examination of the objective component is, as a result, clearly predominant. When examining the objective component, it first examines the nature, object and purpose of the treaty in general and secondly it examines whether the wording of the invoked provision itself is clear, precise and unconditional. This two-tier approach and particularly the equal weight of the examination of the nature, object and purpose of the treaty in general in analysing the objective element is peculiar[135] for the invocability of international agreements provisions.[136] Later on, the Court's case law crystallized into the following formula:

'a provision in an agreement concluded by the Community with non-member countries must be regarded as being directly applicable when, regard being had to its wording and the purpose and nature of the agreement itself, the provision contains a clear and precise obligation which is not subject, in its implementation or effects, to the adoption of any subsequent measure'.[137]

---

[133] *Kupferberg*, paras. 18-22.

[134] *Kupferberg*, paras. 23-26.

[135] When examining direct effect of internal Community acts, the examination of the nature, object and purpose of the provision in question is rather limited and in any event subordinated to the examination of the clear, precise and unconditional character of the wording of the invoked provision.

[136] E.g. *Anastasiou*, paras. 23-27; *Demirel*, paras. 14-25; Case 17/81 *Pabst & Richarz* [1982] ECR 1331, paras. 25-27; Opinion of AG Darmon in *Demirel*.

[137] *Demirel*, para. 14; *Sevince*, para. 15 (the quotation stems from this judgment); Case C-18/90 *Kziber* [1991] ECR I-199, para. 15; *Anastasiou*, para. 23; *El-Yassini*, para. 25; Case C-262/96 *Sürül* [1999] ECR I-2685, para. 60; Case C-37/98 *Savas* [2000] ECR I-2927, para. 39; *Gloszczuk*, para. 30; *Kondova*, para. 31; *Barkoci*, para. 31; Judgment of 29 January 2002 in Case C-162/00 *Pokrzeptowicz-Meyer*, nyr, para. 19.

However, in some cases the Court of Justice does not even require direct effect for the invocability of a treaty provision. This is the case in two instances: first, when a Community act is intended to implement a particular obligation arising from the international agreement (the *Nakajima* exception)[138] and second, when a Community act expressly refers to a specific provision of an international agreement which is thus to be used as a touchstone when interpreting the act (the *Fediol* exception).[139]

These exceptions are plausible if one sees the implementing or referring to a treaty provision for interpretation as acts of incorporating the treaty provision into the underlying Community act and hence into the Community legal order. Or, one could even put it differently. By implementing a treaty provision or referring to it, EU institutions used their discretion as to the means of complying with the treaty obligation. Once this discretion is used, it is up to the Court to guarantee that the implementation and interpretation was done correctly.

Another exception can be found in the Court's well established case law where acts within the Community legal order are to be interpreted as far as possible in the light of the wording and the purpose of international agreements. There is no condition for invoking international agreements as a yardstick for the interpretation of Community acts, and acts of Member States within the Community legal order (the *Hermès* exception).[140]

In the *Bananas* case (*Germany* v. *Council*) the Court of Justice upheld direct effect as a condition for invocability of a treaty provision in the context of reviewing the legality of a Community act. However, in contrast to the *International Fruit* case, the question of legality of the Community act was not raised in the context of a preliminary ruling concerning the validity of that act. Rather, the case concerned a direct challenge of the legality of a Community act,[141] introduced by a privileged claimant (i.e. a Member State).[142] This puzzled quite a few commentators[143] since, firstly, direct effect is not one of the conditions for introducing an application for annulment,[144] and, secondly, the concept of

---

[138] *Nakajima*, para. 31.

[139] Case 70/87 *Fediol* [1989] ECR 1781, paras. 19-22.

[140] Case C-53/96 *Hermès* [1998] ECR I-3603, para. 35; Joined Cases C-300/98 and C-392/98 *Dior* [2000] ECR I-11307, para. 47; Case 61/94 *Commission* v. *Germany* (as cited), para. 52; Case C-70/94 *Werner* [1995] ECR I-3189, para. 23; Case C-83/94 *Leifer* [1995] ECR I-3231, para. 24.

[141] I.e. an application for annulment directed against the act of the EU institution concluding the international agreement, *in casu* a Council Decision. The EU institution concluding an international agreement is normally the Council and in exceptional cases the Commission (Article 300 EC).

[142] Case C-280/93 *Germany* v. *Council* (*bananas*) [1994] ECR I-4973, para. 109.

[143] See e.g. the Opinion of AG Saggio in *Portugal* v. *Council*, point 18; Berrod (2000), at p. 421 and 433; Lenaerts & De Smijter (1999-2000), at p. 108; Hahn & Schuster (1995), at p. 371-372.

[144] Article 230 EC.

direct effect has always been intrinsically linked to rights created for individuals and/or the right of the individual to invoke Community law before a national court for the purpose of challenging the conformity of a national measure with Community law. In fact the concept of direct effect had been developed by the Court of Justice to protect the rights of *individuals*, as a minimum guarantee of judicial protection.[145] But direct effect was never used as a condition for invoking an 'internal' Community act in an application for annulment introduced by a privileged claimant before the Court of Justice. This confusion is, to a certain extent, caused by the fact that no distinction is made between 'direct effect' as a concept in the relationship between the Community legal order and the Member States' legal orders on the one hand, and 'direct effect' as a condition for the invocability of international agreements in the Community legal order on the other.

Once the Court decides that a treaty concluded by the Community is invocable, we are confronted with a third question: do international agreements concluded by the Community possess a higher hierarchical order than secondary Community acts and Member States acts, which are part of the Community legal order? Out of its case law it becomes evident that the Court's answer is in the affirmative.[146]

4.3   GATT and WTO

Now we have outlined what the conditions are for the invocability of international agreement provisions in general, the question arises how the Court of Justice applies these principles to the provisions of the GATT and WTO agreements in particular ('GATT/WTO').

The main feature of the Court's case law on these agreements is that it has, until now, never accepted their direct effect.[147] As a result, it never considered

---

[145] See *Brasserie du Pêcheur* (as cited), para. 20, where the Court observes in this respect: 'the right of individuals to rely on the directly effective provisions of the Treaty before national courts is only a minimum guarantee and is not sufficient in itself to ensure the full and complete implementation of the Treaty (...) The purpose of that right is to ensure that provisions of Community law prevail over national provisions. It cannot, in every case, secure for individuals the benefit of the rights conferred on them by Community law and, in particular, avoid their sustaining damage as a result of a breach of Community law attributable to a Member State'.

[146] E.g. *International Fruit*, para. 6 and *Kupferberg*, para. 14.

[147] E.g. *International Fruit*, paras. 19-27; Case 9/73 *Schlüter* [1973] ECR 1135, paras. 27-30; Case 266/81 *SIOT* [1983] ECR 731, para. 30; Case 267/81 *SPI and SAMI* [1983] ECR 801, paras. 23-24; *Germany v. Council (bananas)*, paras. 106-110; *Chiquita Italia*, paras. 26-29; *Portugal v. Council*, paras. 34-52; *Dior*, para. 44; Case C-307/99 *Fruchthandelsgesellschaft* [2001] ECR I-3159, paras. 24-26; Case T-3/99 *Banatrading* [2001] ECR II-2123, para. 43; Case C-89/99 *Schieving-Nijstad* [2001] ECR I-5851, paras. 53-55.

these provisions to be invocable except in the cases where direct effect was not a condition for invocability: i.e. to review the legality of a Community act implementing a GATT/WTO provision,[148] to review the legality of a Community act expressly referring to a provision of GATT/WTO for its interpretation[149] and to interpret a Community act in conformity with the provisions of GATT/WTO.[150]

The Court's reasoning for denying direct effect to the provisions of GATT 1947 can be summarized as follows. Its point of departure is that to determine whether the invoked provisions have direct effect, it has to explore 'the purpose, the spirit and the general scheme and the terms (...)'.[151]

The Court then proceeds by examining the characteristics of GATT 1947:

'(...), which according to its preamble is based on the principle of negotiations undertaken on the basis of "reciprocal and mutually advantageous arrangements", is characterized by the great flexibility of its provisions, in particular those conferring the possibility of derogation, the measures to be taken when confronted with exceptional difficulties and the settlement of conflicts between the contracting parties'.[152]

After further elaborating these elements of *great flexibility* the Court concludes that

'[t]he special features noted above show that the GATT (1947) rules are not unconditional and that an obligation to recognize them as rules of international law that are directly applicable in the domestic legal systems of the contracting parties cannot be based on the spirit, general scheme or terms of GATT (1947)'.[153]

The Court thereby confirms the two-tier test for examining the direct effect of international agreement provisions in its case law on GATT 1947. However, from this point on the examination of the direct effect of GATT 1947 provisions significantly differ from that of other international agreements. In fact, the Court falls short of examining the nature of the invoked provision itself and solely relies on the general characteristics of GATT 1947.

As we have seen earlier (above 4.2), for other international agreements the Court relies on the context, object and purpose of the agreement concerned to interpret and clarify the invoked provisions *(in the light of)* and its final test is based on the clear, precise and unconditional wording of the provisions

---

[148] *Nakajima*, para. 31; *Portugal* v. *Council*, paras. 27 and 49; *Fruchthandelsgesellschaft*, para. 27.

[149] *Fediol*, paras. 19-22; *Portugal* v. *Council*, paras. 27 and 49; *Fruchthandelsgesellschaft*, para. 27.

[150] *Hermès*, para. 35; *Dior*, para. 47; *Schieving-Nijstad*, para. 35 and paras. 54-55.

[151] *International Fruit*, para. 20; *Germany* v. *Council (bananas)*, para. 105.

[152] *Germany* v. *Council (bananas)*, para. 106.

[153] *Germany* v. *Council (bananas)*, para. 110 (text between brackets added).

themselves. In contrast, the Court exclusively relies on general characteristics of GATT 1947, derived from not invoked provisions, in order to refuse direct effect to the entire GATT 1947. The Court clearly shifts away from the objective component of direct effect with regard to GATT 1947. In fact, one may say that it uses a different test for the invocability of GATT 1947 provisions.[154]

The incoherence and the propitiation of this case law has been criticized severely.[155] Its incoherence becomes even more apparent when one notes that the characteristics attributed to GATT 1947 do not differ that much from other international agreements to which provisions the Court attributed direct effect. It suffices to recall the above-mentioned *Kupferberg* case, where the lack of reciprocity on the implementation of the agreement, the presence of safeguard clauses and the presence of an institutional framework for the administration and implementation of the treaty obligations, did not keep the Court from granting direct effect to the provision concerned of the Free Trade Agreement.

Despite the criticism, refusing direct effect of GATT 1947 in general terms had thus become settled case law. Nevertheless, in the meantime, the Uruguay Round had come to an end and GATT 1947 along with the institutional framework was modified by virtue of the WTO agreements. Regarding the 'defects' attributed by the Court of Justice to the GATT 1947, in order to refuse its direct effect, the changes made by means of the WTO agreements are remarkable. The system's tremendous flexibility because of the extensive possibility of invoking derogations and measures for exceptional difficulties, etc., had changed considerably so as to make the system much stricter. The dispute settlement system had altered even more radically, making the system 'quasi-judicial'.[156]

These major changes to GATT's structure and nature made the Court of Justice's review of its previous case law unavoidable in the face of the issue of the WTO agreements' invocability. Either the Court of Justice would have to accept the direct effect of several provisions of the WTO agreements or it would have to change its motivation for refusing direct effect. Advocate General Tesauro and Advocate General Saggio took the view that the WTO agreements should be given direct effect, since the defects of GATT 1947 were resolved.[157]

---

[154] See also the Opinion of AG Tesauro in *Hermès*, para. 27; Vanhamme (2001a), p. 200-209.

[155] See e.g. the Opinions of AG Gulmann in *Germany* v. *Council (bananas)*, para. 141; AG Tesauro in *Hermès*, para. 27; AG Saggio in *Portugal* v. *Council*, para. 18; Berrod (2000), p. 420-422; Hahn & Schuster (1995), p. 381; Mengozzi (1994); Petersmann (1986); Petersmann (1983); Vanhamme (2001a), p. 209-212; Waelbroeck (1974), at p. 623.

[156] On the WTO Agreements, see e.g.: Jackson (1997); Jackson (1998); Trebilcock & Howse (1999); Voitocich (1995); Palmeter & Mavroidis (1999).

[157] Opinion of AG Tesauro in *Hermès*, paras. 28-30 (although AG Tesauro was of the opinion that WTO and GATT 1947 rules should be granted direct effect on substantive grounds, and as such criticized the Court's case law, he nevertheless concluded that the Court should refuse direct effect on the ground of lack of reciprocity: see paras. 31-35); Opinion of AG Saggio in *Portugal* v. *Council*, paras. 19-24.

In *Portugal* v. *Council*[158] the Court of Justice expressed itself for the first time on the question of invocability of WTO agreements for the review of the legality of Community law. While the Court admitted that the WTO agreements differ significantly from the provisions of GATT 1947 ' in particular by reason of the strengthening of the system of safeguards and the mechanism for resolving disputes', it underscored that the WTO framework still accords considerable importance to the negotiation between the parties.[159] The Court supported this by referring to the dispute settlement procedure. The Court more particularly referred to the fact that in case a WTO Member fails to bring the measure found to be inconsistent with the WTO agreements into compliance with the recommendations or rulings of the Dispute Settlement Body, the parties must enter into negotiations with a view to finding mutually acceptable compensation.[160]

The fact that the dispute settlement mechanism's primary purpose is to secure withdrawal of inconsistent measures and the fact that compensation can only be granted in certain circumstances and on an interim basis pending the withdrawal of the inconsistent measure, is not relevant for the Court of Justice. According to the Court, 'to require the judicial organs to refrain from applying the rules of domestic law which are inconsistent with the WTO agreements would have the consequence of depriving the legislative or executive organs of the contracting parties of the possibility afforded by Article 22 of that memorandum of entering into negotiated agreements even on a temporary basis'.[161]

The Court concluded from this that the WTO agreements do not determine the legal effect that its provisions are to have in the internal legal order. But as it had recalled from the outset, it was still up to the Court to decide on the effect of the provisions of the WTO agreements within the Community legal order.

Accordingly, it introduced a second and decisive argument based on the principle of reciprocity. As the judiciaries of the most important contracting parties had refused to consider the WTO rules invocable as a norm for reviewing the legality of internal acts, acceptance of this invocability by the Court of Justice would lead to a disuniform application of the WTO rules. Furthermore, it would deprive the legislative or executive organs of the Community of the scope for manoeuvre enjoyed by the other WTO members during the negotiations. The Court of Justice therefore concluded that the WTO agreements are not, in principle, amongst the rules in the light of which the Court is to review the legality of the measures adopted by EU institutions.[162]

---

[158] As cited.

[159] *Portugal* v. *Council*, para. 36.

[160] Articles 3 (7), 22 (1) and 22 (2) Understanding of Rules and Procedures governing the Settlement of Disputes, Annex II to the Agreement establishing the World Trade Organization.

[161] *Portugal* v. *Council*, para. 40.

[162] *Portugal* v. *Council*, paras. 42-48.

However, the Court recalled that there are two exceptions to this principle, where it is up to the Court to review the legality of Community acts in the light of the WTO rules, i.e. where the Community intended to implement a particular obligation assumed in the context of the WTO (the *Nakajima* exception), and where the Community measure refers expressly to the precise provision of the WTO agreements (the *Fediol* exception).[163]

This case law has subsequently been confirmed. In *Dior*, before a national court, an individual had invoked a provision of the Agreement on Trade-Related Aspects of Intellectual Property Rights ('TRIPs'), which is one of the WTO's multilateral agreements, in order to derive rights out of it. The Court confirmed that in these circumstances as well its *Portugal* v. *Council* case law applies: 'the provisions of TRIPs, an annex to the WTO Agreement, are not such as to create rights upon which individuals may rely directly before the courts by virtue of Community law'.[164] However, the Court continued that this 'does not fully resolve the problem' and held that in a field to which the TRIPs Agreement applies and in respect of which the Community has already legislated,[165] the judicial authorities of the Member States are required by virtue of Community law, when called upon to apply national rules, to do so as far as possible in the light of the wording and purpose of the TRIPs Agreement.[166] The Court furthermore confirmed this case law still more recently in *Fruchthandelsgesellschaft*.[167]

4.4   Comparing the case law on the invocability of international agreements *viz.* of customary international law

An international agreement concluded by the EC must in first instance have entered into force vis-à-vis the Community for it to be invocable in the Community legal order. Once the treaty has entered into force, a treaty provision can be invoked in order to interpret a Community act as far as possible

---

[163] *Portugal* v. *Council*, paras. 49-52.

[164] *Dior*, paras. 43-44.

[165] In these circumstances the Court of Justice considered that it had jurisdiction to interpret Article 50 TRIPs (*Dior*, paras. 32-40; *Hermès*, paras. 22-33; *Schieving-Nijstad*, paras. 30-35). The corollary of this is, that under these circumstances, the provisions of TRIPs are part of the Community legal order.

[166] *Dior*, para. 47; *Hermès*, para. 28; *Schieving-Nijstad*, para. 35 and paras. 54-55.

[167] *Fruchthandelsgesellschaft* (as cited). On the question of an individual to review the legality of a Community regulation as incompatible with a GATT 1994 provision, the Court held that the answer was clear from the existing case law and that it therefore would suffice to answer the preliminary question by means of a reasoned order: 'The answer to that question may be clearly deduced from existing case law, so that it is appropriate for the Court, in accordance with Article 104(3) of the Rules of Procedure, to give its decision by reasoned order' (para. 23). Thereafter the Court in essence referred to its *Portugal* v. *Council* and *Dior* case law (paras. 23-28).

in the light of the wording and purpose of this treaty provision. Moreover, a treaty provision that has entered into force can be invoked in order to review the legality of a Community act implementing this treaty provision or to review the legality of a Community act expressly referring to this treaty provision.

However, in other circumstances, the Court of Justice seems to require that the invoked treaty provision has direct effect in order for an individual to derive rights out of it or in order to rely on it to review the legality of a Community act. One should note that the Court of Justice's concept of direct effect differs according to whether the norm at hand is an 'internal' Community act, an international agreement not being a GATT/WTO agreement, or a GATT/WTO agreement.

Similarly, the Court does not require that any specific condition be fulfilled for it to accept the invocability of rules of customary international law binding on the Community with a view to interpreting a Community act as far a possible in the light of the wording and purpose of a rule of customary international law.

However, in contrast, the Court did not require 'direct effect' for the invocability of a norm of customary international law to review the legality of a Community act in *Racke*.

On the one hand, as we have indicated above (3.2), there is some room to reconcile the Court's case law in arguing that the *Racke* case is, in fact, an example of the *Nakajima* case law applied to rules of customary international law. If this turns out to be the case, the possibility of invoking rules of customary international law in order to review the legality of Community acts would be very restricted. This is an extra condition which we would rather not advocate. As we have seen, the Court of Justice already placed ample and broadly defined locks and escape routes on its case law for the invocability of customary international law. We can hardly imagine that it would need a further one.

On the other hand, it is rather the requirement of direct effect for the invocability of an international agreement as a prerequisite for the review of the legality of a Community act that is problematic. The main problem with the requirement of 'direct effect' is that it gives rise to much confusion and that it conceals different realities.

First, as we have outlined, the concept of direct effect used in the Community case law on the GATT/WTO treaties is quite different from the concept of direct effect used for other international agreements concluded by the Communities and, *a fortiori*, from the concept of direct effect used for 'internal' Community law. The two latter notions primarily concern the question of whether the invoked provision is justiciable:[168] i.e. is the particular treaty (provision) clear,

---

[168] See also the Opinion of AG Van Gerven in Case C-128/92 *Banks* [1994] ECR I-1237, para. 27, according to whom the test is whether the norm is 'sufficiently operational in itself to be applied by a court'. See also De Witte (1999), at p. 188.

precise and unconditional (objective component).[169] In contrast, the first concept predominantly concerns a policy question: i.e. whether the parties intended the treaty to be directly effective or whether the Court judges it right to confer direct effect to the treaty provision (subjective component). Nevertheless, the problem is that the Court persisted in pretending that it used the same concept of direct effect for GATT treaties: e.g. 'the special features noted above show that the GATT rules are not *unconditional*'.[170]

Secondly, in as far as the relevant concept of direct effect focuses on the objective component (clear, precise and unconditional), one could question what the point is of requiring direct effect as a condition for the invocability of a provision of an international agreement in the review of legality of a Community act. As has been seen above, direct effect is not a requirement for the invocability of 'internal' Community acts in the context of the review of legality. Moreover, the intrinsic qualities of the provision concerned (clear, precise and unconditional) will in any event be taken into consideration in the legality test itself.

For these reasons it would be altogether better to discard the use of direct effect as a requirement for the invocability of a treaty provision in the context of the review of legality of a Community act. If the concept of direct effect focuses on the objective component, there is no point in requiring direct effect; in as far as the concept of direct effect refers to the subjective component, it merely blurs reality and gives rise to confusion.

Moreover, the incoherence between the Court of Justice's case law on the invocability of international agreements and customary international law is rather awkward if one considers that the Community might be bound by one and the same international obligation both by means of an international agreement and by means of a rule of customary international law.[171]

This approach seems to be supported by the recent judgments of the Court of Justice. The terminology in the *Portugal* v. *Council* case in fact marks a change in the Court's case law. Despite the continuing reference to *Kupferberg*,[172] the

---

[169] Although, as we have seen earlier (above 4.2), there is also a difference between the concept of direct effect for 'internal' Community acts on the one hand and the concept of direct effect of international agreements concluded by the European Community not being a GATT/WTO agreement on the other, this difference is minor in comparison with the concept of direct effect of a GATT/WTO agreement.

[170] *Germany* v. *Council (bananas)*, para. 110 (emphasis added).

[171] The most famous example in this respect is the *Nicaragua* case of the International Court of Justice. The ICJ ruled that the United States was bound by the principle of non use of force and of non-intervention on the basis both of treaty law (UN Charter) and of customary international law (ICJ, *Case concerning Military and Paramilitary Activities in and against Nicaragua*, judgment of 27 June 1986, ICJ Rep. (1986) p. 14 et seq.). The Court of Justice has acknowledged this principle by accepting that several treaty provisions of the Montego Bay Convention on the Law of the Sea (1982), to which the EC is a party, are also binding on the European Community as rules of customary international law.

[172] *Portugal* v. *Council*, paras. 34, 35, 42 and 44.

Court is careful not to refer to the concept of direct effect. The term is avoided, just as is the standard terminology traditionally used to define or explain the concept of direct effect. Moreover, in the Court's arguments for the refusal of the invocability of the WTO agreements, it becomes clear what the questions of invocability and direct effect in the end are: they are questions of a constitutional order. They concern the issue of the proper division of powers in the execution and enforcement of the obligations of the state between, on the one hand, the legislature and the executive and, on the other, the judiciary. Therefore, at the end of the day, the argument of whether or not to accept the invocability or the direct effectiveness of a legal rule is political and not legal. This becomes quite clear when one reads the following considerations in *Portugal v. Council*:

> '[T]o require the judicial organs to refrain from applying the rules of domestic law which are inconsistent with the WTO agreements would have the consequence of depriving the legislative or executive organs of the contracting parties of the possibility afforded by Article 22 of that memorandum of entering into negotiated arrangements even on a temporary basis. (...)

> To accept that the role of ensuring that those rules comply with Community law devolves directly on the Community judicature would deprive the legislative or executive organs of the Community of the scope for manoeuvre enjoyed by their counterparts in the Community's trading partners'.[173]

It thus becomes apparent that the invocability of a treaty provision will, in the first place, depend on whether the Court of Justice thinks it fit that a certain treaty having regard for its nature and structure *should* be invocable in the internal legal order:

> 'It follows from all those considerations that, having regard to their nature and structure, the WTO agreements are not, in principle, among the rules in the light of which the Court is to review the legality of measures adopted by the Community institutions'.[174]

This reference to the *nature and structure* of a treaty seems to resemble closely the requirement in *Racke* that a rule of customary international law should be *fundamental* to be invocable. The *Opel Austria* and the *Racke* case both appear to confirm that the Community Courts will proceed with an assessment of whether the nature of a certain category of rules of customary international law is apt to be invocable to review the legality of Community acts. Or would it be pure

---

[173] *Portugal v. Council*, para. 40 and para. 46.

[174] *Portugal v. Council*, para. 47.

coincidence that both cases concerned the law of treaties and more particularly an expression of the *pacta sunt servanda* rule?

All in all, it seems that behind the apparent incoherence of the Court's case law on the invocability of treaty provisions and rules of customary international law, is hidden a basic similarity. This assumption has been confirmed in the recent *Biotechnological inventions* case.[175] In this latter case, the Netherlands contended that the obligations for Member States created by the Directive on the legal protection of biotechnological inventions[176] are incompatible with their obligations under international agreements. In particular, the Directive would, amongst others, breach provisions of TRIPs, the Agreement on Technical Barriers to Trade ('TBT') and the Convention on Biological Diversity ('CBD').[177]

The Council and the European Parliament in their defence contended that these treaties could not be invoked to review the legality of the Directive since they lacked direct effect.[178]

First, in referring to *Portugal* v. *Council* the Court of Justice confirmed that like the WTO Agreement, the TRIPs and TBT agreements, which are part of it, 'are not in principle, having regard to their nature and structure, amongst the rules in the light of which the Court is to review the lawfulness [in the lights of instruments of international law] of measures adopted by the Community institutions'.[179] However, this does not apply to the CBD since the latter is not strictly based on reciprocal and mutually advantageous arrangements.[180]

Secondly, the Court continues, even if the CBD contained provisions that do not have 'direct effect', this would not preclude the invocability of its provisions to review the legality of the Directive:

> '*Even if, as the Council maintains, the CBD contains provisions which do not have direct effect, in the sense that they do not create rights which individuals can rely on directly before the courts, that fact does not preclude review by the courts of compliance with the* obligations incumbent on the Community as a party to that agreement *(Case C-162/96 Racke [1998] ECR I-3655, paragraphs 45, 47 and 51)*'.[181]

Thirdly, the Court held that in any event the plea was admissible as it 'should be understood as being directed, not so much at a direct breach by the Community

---

[175] Judgment of 9 October 2001 in Case C-377/98 *Biotechnological inventions* [2001] ECR I-7079.

[176] Directive 98/44/EC of the European Parliament and the Council of 6 July 1998 on the Legal Protection of biotechnological inventions, OJ 1998, L 213/13.

[177] *Biotechnological inventions*, para. 50.

[178] *Biotechnological inventions*, para. 51.

[179] *Biotechnological inventions*, para. 52.

[180] *Biotechnological inventions*, para. 53.

[181] *Biotechnological inventions*, para. 54 (emphasis added).

of its international obligations, as at an obligation imposed on the Member States by the Directive to breach their own obligations under international law, while the Directive itself claims not to affect those obligations'.[182] As the plea was admissible the Court subsequently reviewed the legality of the Directive in the light of the provisions of the TRIPs, TBT and CBD agreements.[183]

Several conclusions can be drawn from this landmark case. First, direct effect is not a condition for the invocability of a rule of international law to review the legality of a Community act.

Second, the invocability of a rule of international law to review the legality of an international act depends on whether the Court is of the opinion that having regard to the nature and structure of the rule, it should be invocable.

Thirdly, a rule of customary international law is invocable to review the legality of a Community act under the same conditions as a treaty provision. The Court makes this clear by expressly providing that, on the one hand, *Portugal* v. *Council* is not only on treaties but on 'instruments of international law' in general,[184] and on the other, the considerations in *Racke* are not only pertinent for rules of customary international law but also for agreements to which the Community is a party.[185]

Fourthly, the Court confirmed that in some circumstances an instrument of international law that is, in principle, not invocable to review the legality of a Community act, will nevertheless be invocable. As has been seen, under the Court's well established case law, this was the situation when the contested Community act intended to implement the invoked international agreement (the *Nakajima* exception) or when the Community act expressly referred to the precise provisions of the international agreement (the *Fediol* exception). Of course, in the light of the *Biotechnological inventions* case, 'international agreement' should be read as 'instrument of international law'.

However, one should observe two things. On the one hand, in contrast with its previous judgments, the Court does not make reference to the *Nakajima*, or to the *Fediol* case. On the other, the case at hand does not seem to fall under either of these exceptions.

Instead of concluding that the *Biothechnological inventions* case is a new exception to, in principle, uninvocable international law instruments, we would argue that the *Biotechnological inventions* case is another example of one and the same situation in which in principle uninvocable international law instruments become invocable: i.e. where the EU institutions made clear that they used up their discretion as to the means for complying with the international obligations

---

[182] *Biotechnological inventions*, para. 55.

[183] *Biotechnological inventions*, paras. 57-68.

[184] *Biotechnological inventions*, para. 52.

[185] *Biotechnological inventions*, para. 54.

at hand. In fact, in stating that the Directive 'shall be without prejudice to the obligations of the Member States pursuant to international agreements, and in particular the TRIPs Agreement and the Convention on Biological Diversity',[186] the EU institutions were clear that they intended that this Directive would comply with their international obligations. As a result, concerning the subject matter of the Directive they have used up their discretion of how to comply with these international obligations.

5   By way of conclusion: the nature of customary international law and its invocability

5.1   The nature of customary international law

Beneath the surface, much of the hesitation which one finds in national and Community case law concerning the precise legal position of customary international law in the internal (i.e. national or Community) legal order has to do with certain features of this source of international law. As our survey of the Community case law has made clear, there is a broad willingness to take customary international law into account for considering the limits of State or EC jurisdiction and powers, for providing rules of interpretation and for the purpose of filling certain gaps in the internal legal order. Such indirect use of customary international law, through a method of consistent interpretation, does not seem to cause major problems. The complications arise when an individual relies on a rule of customary international law to challenge the validity of a Community act. The *Opel Austria* and *Racke* judgments each show different ways in which the hesitation to deal therewith can be overcome; we will come back to this below (5.2).

What is striking, though, especially in *Racke*, is the more or less biased manner in which the Court of Justice has considered the rule of customary international law at hand. One will remember that the Court limited the scope of its judicial review to manifest errors of assessment of the EU institution concerned 'because of the complexity of the rules in question and the imprecision of some of the concepts to which they refer'.[187]

Isn't this an indication of the rather patronizing way in which 'domestic' courts deal with customary international law and doesn't the Community case law on the invocability of international agreements (except for GATT/WTO) not show us how the Court of Justice feels much less constrained to accept the reliance on the latter in order to challenge Community acts?

---

[186] Article 1(2) Directive 98/44/EC (as cited).

[187] *Racke*, para. 52.

We believe we should warn for such attitudes. It has for a long time been a commonplace that, in contrast to international agreements, it is difficult to determine the existence of rules of customary international law and that such rules are vague and uncertain as to the precise scope and content. Often this is linked to the belief that the customary law-making process does not live up to the expectations of global participation in a world of growing interdependence between States. Treaties, so it is heralded, are superior instruments of law-making in the international legal order, and will therefore gradually displace customary international law.[188]

This assertion is clearly an oversimplification of reality. First, the contention that treaties are superior to custom in terms of being more precise simply as a result of the deliberate manner in which general rules are formulated, is based on the problematic assumption that the written word would be superior in terms of its capacity for instruction when compared to instruction provided through example or ostension.[189] To put it differently, the application of a (general) treaty provision to a (specific) case is seldom a straightforward exercise, which is done in one single stroke. Hence, we can refer to the sometimes elaborated legal and policy argumentation that a court needs to apply a certain treaty provision, which is moreover often topped by arguments leading to concurring or dissenting opinions, or arguments from authors annotating the case at hand.[190]

Secondly, the thesis that the treaty law-making process is by far better suited for our age of co-operation and globalization than the customary law-making process clearly needs some qualification. Against the view that the customary law-making process is (too) slow, one may outline that the conclusion, the entry into force and the widespread (let alone universal) ratification of international agreements can also be quite slow,[191] whereas there are examples of a quick and vivid formation of rules of customary international law.[192] The argument that

---

[188] See the points of view mentioned by Mendelson (1998), p. 168-169.

[189] See Lim & Elias (1997), at p. 4, quoting from Hart's *Concept of Law*: 'Much of the jurisprudence of this century has consisted of the progressive realisation (and sometimes the exaggeration) of the important fact that the distinction between the uncertainties of communication by authoritative example (precedent), and the certainties of communication by authoritative general language (legislation) is far less firm than this naive contrast suggests... In all fields of experience, not only that of rules, there is a limit, inherent in the nature of language, to guidance which general language can provide'.

[190] E.g. the *Gabcíkovo-Nagymaros Project* case (as cited), which concerned in essence the application of a bilateral treaty between (Tsjecho)Slovakia and Hungary.

[191] E.g. the time that elapsed before the entry into force of the 1969 Vienna Convention (signed: 23 May 1969, entered into force: 27 January 1980) and of the 1982 Law of the Sea Convention (signed: 10 December 1982; entered into force: 16 November 1994).

[192] In several cases the customary international law law-making process is clearly quicker than the treaty law-making process. One can again take the example of the 1982 Law of the Sea Convention. As such

treaties are at the origin of clearer and less ambiguous rules should also be taken *cum grano salis*: reality shows that, in the treaty-making process too, there is an inherent tension between the aim to reach the widest possible participation (which necessarily leads to some watering down) and the aim of reaching precise rules which are immune from arbitrary interpretations.[193] In addition, sometimes even the precision of treaties can be a disadvantage as States may be reluctant to sign up to too specific commitments.[194] That treaties are at the basis of more legal certainty and more legal cohesion will also depend on a number of factors, including the question as to whether parties have not opted out of certain obligations by making a reservation. Finally, one can have some critical thoughts on the process of multilateral treaty-making in terms of participation and co-operation between States: often there remains a clear gap between the participation in the negotiations and the creation of a resulting obligation (i.e. on the basis of consent).[195]

Of course, this does not preclude that in *certain* circumstances customary international law (just as international agreements in some other circumstances) is imprecise, clumsy and not able to live up to the expectations of an international community moving towards growing interdependence. However, these are by no means specific characteristics of customary international law in general.

While we do not see a compelling intrinsic reason to treat customary international law differently from international agreements, we acknowledge that there are more practical considerations which explain the relative scarcity of case law of national courts applying customary international law. Among other factors, lawyers and judges in our modern domestic legal systems are only rudimentarily trained in and are not familiar with international law on the one hand and with sources of law that are the result of informal law-making, such as customary international law, on the other. It is therefore no surprise that they do not tend

---

the Third Conference on the Law of the Sea had amongst others been convened in order to recognise the concept of the Exclusive Economic Zone. The Conference, however, had to conclude that this concept had in the meantime become a rule of customary international law: Nguyen Quoc Dinh, Daillier & Pellet (1999), p. 338.

[193] See further, contrasting the strive for precision and the strive for participation, Lim & Elias (1997), p. 17-19.

[194] Mendelson (1998), p. 169.

[195] Compare e.g. the active and dominant role the European Community played at the United Nations Conference on the Law of Treaties between States and International Organisations or between International Organisations, Vienna, 18-21 March 1986 on the one hand and the EC's refusal to become a party to the subsequent treaty on the other (Official Records of the United Nations Conference on the Law of Treaties between States and International Organisations or between International Organisations, Vienna, 18-21 March 1986, II, A/CONF.129/16).

to invoke and apply rules of customary international law.[196] It is also no surprise that comparative studies indicate that there is more case law on the invocability of customary international law in domestic legal orders that provide for a kind of 'reference for a preliminary ruling' to a superior court for questions as to the identification of rules of customary international law.[197]

5.2 The invocability of customary international law

A reflection on the relationship between Community law and international law is usually done by means of the terminology of the monist-dualist dichotomy. Although this dichotomy might have some didactical advantages, we believe that the terminology does more to conceal and confuse than to elucidate the complex question of the relationship between the Community and international legal order.

As early as 1957 Fitzmaurice clearly established that the monist-dualist dichotomy is from a practical point of view contradictory since even a monist system is the result of a pragmatic dualism.[198] As a matter of fact, in examining whether a rule of international law is invocable in the domestic legal order and whether it has primacy over rules of domestic law (depending on the answer to this question the domestic legal order is categorized as monist or dualist) one has to investigate what the domestic constitution, the domestic laws and/or the domestic courts provide in this respect.

Furthermore, the relationship between the international and the domestic legal order is much more complex than the monist-dualist dichotomy suggests. For example, when one concludes that international law is part of the domestic legal order, does this also mean that the international norm transforms and

---

[196] See also Dominicé & Voeffrey (1996), p. 55-58; Mendelson (1998), p. 172-173.

[197] See Dominicé & Voeffrey (1996), p. 58, who observe: 'Il est significatif à cet égard de constater que la jurisprudence en matière de droit international coutumier ne paraît véritablement abondante qu'en Allemagne et en Grèce, où l'identification de la coutume est facilitée par l'existence d'une procédure de 'renvoi', qui permet au juge de s'adresser à une juridiction supérieure (Tribunal constitutionnel en Allemagne, Tribunal supérieur spécial en Grèce) pour l'interroger sur l'état du droit coutumier'. See also the findings of Stirling-Zanda (2000), p. 277; Nguyen Quoc Dinh, Daillier & Pellet (1999), p. 341-342.

[198] Fitzmaurice (1957), II, p. 68-74. On the basis of an extensive comparative research Erades (1993), p. 945, came to a similar conclusion. Furthermore, this also holds in the context of the relationship between the Community and Member States' legal orders: 'It follows that the evolutionary nature of the doctrine of supremacy is necessary bi-dimensional. One dimension is the elaboration of the parameters of the doctrine by the European Court. But its full reception, the second dimension, depends on its incorporation into the constitutional orders of the Member States and its affirmation by their supreme courts'; Weiler (1981), at p. 275.

takes up the characteristics of a domestic legal norm? Moreover, the latter contention that international law is part of the domestic legal order does not say anything about what really matters: i.e. under what circumstances the international norm is invocable before domestic courts.

The much-heralded statement of principle in *Racke* that rules of customary international law are part of the Community legal order, does not tell that much. Such a statement remains to a large extent within the sphere of rhetoric if the Court of Justice does not subsequently accept a large degree of invocability of rules of customary international law. So one has to look *au-delà des apparences* in order to assess the real content of this assertion.

Our analysis of the Community case law indicates that the Court of Justice broadly accepts the invocability of customary international law as a *rule of interpretation*, i.e. in order to interpret Community acts in conformity with customary international law. The scope of this rule is rather wide ('as far as possible') and should be seen as the main and primary tool for the enforcement of customary international law in the Community legal order.

The possibility of invoking a rule of customary international law in order to *review the legality* of a Community act has been explicitly recognized, as a matter of principle, by the Court of Justice in the *Racke* case. However, seen in the light of the Court's case law as to the invocability of international agreements to review the legality of Community acts, and more in particular in view of the recent *Biotechnological inventions* case, the invocability seems to depend on the category of rules of customary international law and whether the Court is of the opinion that these are 'in principle, having regard to their nature and structure amongst the rules in the light of which the Court is to review the lawfulness of measures adopted by the Community institutions'.[199] Or, as it was put in the *Racke* case, whether these rules are 'fundamental rules of customary international law'.[200] Both the *Opel Austria* and the *Racke* case seem to suggest that rules of treaty law belong to these 'fundamental rules of customary international law'.

In any event, one should cast doubt on the Court's statement of principle on the invocability of customary international law if it subsequently makes an erroneous application of the rule of customary international law at hand.

The Court's case law did not, as of yet, have the opportunity to express itself on the possibility for private individuals to invoke a rule of customary international law in order to *derive (directly) a right from it*. This is not really surprising as customary international law in most cases is not in the first instance directed towards private individuals. Of course one has to nuance the aforementioned as in case an individual can invoke a rule of customary

---

[199] *Biotechnological inventions*, para. 52.

[200] *Racke*, para. 48.

international law to review the legality of a Community act, then the corollary of the duty for the EU institutions or the Member States (stemming out of the benchmark rule), is a right for the individual to see that the EU institutions or the Member State comply with this rule.

In any event, the rules of customary international law retain their nature and characteristics as a rule of international law when invoked in the Community legal order. Their formation, interpretation, suspension etc. remain governed by the relevant rules of international law. The 'transformation approach' adopted in the *Opel Austria* case and in the Court's case law on fundamental rights is an exception to this principle. Through the latter approach a rule of customary international law is transformed into a rule of Community law. It thus obtains all the characterics of Community acts, amongst which their large invocability through the concept of direct effect.

In contrast, the Court does not confer unconditionally the characteristics of Community law to the other rules of customary international law (and treaty law). As such, they are refused one of the most salient features of Community law: i.e. their large invocability through the concept of direct effect. The Court is only willing to accord them a similar invocability on a case-by-case basis having regard to the nature of the rule of customary international law at hand.

Finally, we return to our question as to the coherence between the Court's case law on the invocability of customary international law on the one hand and the Court's case law on the invocability of international agreements on the other. The comparison between both categories of cases revealed a rather striking difference. However, one could perceive a first step of mutual permeation between both lines in the Court of Justice's case law in *Portugal* v. *Council*, through the abandonment of the requirement that a treaty provision should have 'direct effect' for it to be invocable in order to review the legality of a Community act. In the recent *Biotechnological inventions* case the Court of Justice even went a step further in the co-ordination of both lines in the case law: i.e. the Court made clear that there is only one and the same rule as to the invocability of rules of international law in order to review the legality of Community law. Of course, with this statement of principle not all problems and not all our questions are resolved. In any event, as we have learned from our survey of the Community case law, it is safer to remain cautious as to statements of principle and to await the subsequent - as may be expected, pragmatic[201] - case law on the matter.

---

[201] See, with emphasis on the same dose of pragmatism, Ott (2001).

CHAPTER IX

Direct Effect, the Test and the Terms

In Praise of a Capital Doctrine of EU Law

prof. dr. Tom Eijsbouts

1 Introduction

Direct effect is legal relevance, in domestic situations, of Member States' obligations under EC law. Such relevance may take a variety of forms and it may affect a variety of situations or relations, leading to various consequences. On top of that, whether a provision is given such relevance may depend on EC legal or on national tests or procedures or on both. All this is amply demonstrated by Prechal in chapter II of the present volume.

The *doctrine* of direct effect is the ambition in the face of this widening variety of forms, situations and consequences, to consider all such domestic relevance of EC obligations on the Member States as a single intelligible field. About this Prechal is, to say the least, hesitant.

In the present author's view there are four reasons to maintain this ambition and keep attending to the doctrine. The first is practical: it is the need of coherence between different forms, situations, and the consequences of such relations which may be relevant in turn.

The second is conceptual. To drop the doctrine is to deny the need of opposing some countervailing intelligence to the increasing variety of forms, situations and consequences. One proof of such is Judge Edward's contribution in chapter I to the present volume. Related to this is a didactic argument. It would be a disservice to deny newcomers (students and incoming Member States' colleagues) a chapter and a platform well developed to study a related set of problems and answers.

Third: direct effect is a meeting place, a common ground, between legal traditions widely differing as to relationships between individuals and state authority, as to that between substantive right and remedy, as to that between subjective and objective normative situations. No wonder that its logic should be fuzzy. Rather than to discard it, this is a good reason to keep it.

Most important, however, is that direct effect is a constitutional founding stone of the EC and the Union which is still at the heart of the special relationship between EC law and the laws of Member States. Its claim is not, as orthodoxy has it, simply to have EC law supersede that of the Members. The claim is that it provides an agency crucial to the evolution of relationships between entities and traditions of public law involved in the Union. A *single* agency, it is present not only in the *foundation*, but also in the *evolution* of this constitutional relationship.

It is at this last point that the present piece intends mainly to draw attention. It is proposed, however, first to tackle the present preoccupation (and resulting frustration) with the search of some single touchstone to test any variety of Community provisions. Perhaps the leading misunderstanding is that direct effect revolves essentially around tests. This contribution has as its basic contention that there is much more to the doctrine than the *test* of direct effect. Allow it to call in some situational imagery ancillary to the argument.

2   Logic, limit, law

The location of the Conference inspiring this volume was *Kloveniersburgwal*, a street name referring to a part of the Amsterdam former city fortifications. These consisted of a moat, which is still there, and a wall, which is gone.[1] The moat and the wall at some stage defined the town and defended it. Before this wall there had been one closer to the heart of the old town and later the city's circumference would be shifted outward, to mark its growth. Presently there is no wall left; what you see are remains in the forms of towers. Somehow the town's definition by way of walls was no longer necessary. Did this also mean the town stopped to matter or to need definition?

A legal test such as the one active in direct effect is a sort of town wall.[2] Prechal began her argument from a confession.[3] Let me, likewise, cast my argument in this form but to confess, conversely, how from a critic I became a convert, from a sceptic a believer in direct effect. *CIA Security*[4] and its aftermath provided the turning point. This judgment at first seemed to confirm suspicions of the doctrine over-reaching. A formal shortcoming of the Belgian national bureaucracy, its failure to report a technical standard to the EC offices in Brussels, was made to affect the standard's validity. This was due to the direct effect of the (failed) obligation to report. Slot's commentary made this out to be a matter of simple logic: 'from the point of view of legal doctrine this part of the judgment is nothing new. It applies the standard test'.[5]

True, it did apply the standard test. One might wonder, however, is the test all there is to the doctrine? In due course Lemmens' case was to push the test to its logical limit. The man sought impunity from drunken driving by faulting the exhaler which proved him drunk. Indeed, the Dutch government had failed to report the device's specifications to Brussels as it should have. Direct effect of the failed obligation, Lemmens claimed, flawed the device's standards, hence its use and hence the proof at the basis of his indictment and hence the case against him. A cascading series of normative repercussions could lead from a failed government obligation to an individual's unrighteous profiting from this. Here was the critical situation. The standard test was in Lemmens' favour, but

---

[1]   In local parlance a *wal* is not a wall but a moat.

[2]   The analogy of law and city is not mine, it is the Greek philosopher Heraclitus', who left a fragment: *We should defend the law as we defend the town wall.* His time is past, however; we have come to understand and defend the city (and its boundaries) without the walls. It is noteworthy that medieval towns often in their first beginnings had no walls but used symbols representing walls among the instruments to set the town off as a free-hold from the surrounding country.

[3]   Prechal (2000).

[4]   Case C-194/94 *CIA Security* [1996] ECR I-2201.

[5]   Slot (1996), p. 1042.

the result would be legally and otherwise absurd. How was the ECJ to block the logic of direct effect from leading to the devil by letting Lemmens off the hook? Surely the Court stopped short of the absurd, yet in a reasoning thinly hiding its embarrassment. Lemmens could not invoke the authorities' failure because, the ECJ said:

'*The use of the product by the public authorities, in a case such as this, is not liable to create an obstacle to trade which could have been avoided if the notification procedure had been followed*'.[6]

This argument was understandably treated to wide criticism. Its way of limiting direct effect's repercussions saved the Court's day, but look what it had to do: to test the *use* of a product instead of the *standards* controlling this, and then test this use not against a (higher) *rule* but against the latter's *purpose*. One who seeks to be nasty may call this downgrading a normative regime to a raw conflict between crude fact and wide ambition.

There were no doubt other ways for the ECJ to apply the brakes in this case. One of them would have been to adopt the German principle of normative relativism (*Schutznorm*). This holds that an individual can only claim protection from a norm intended to protect his interests in question. Why it did not use this way out is an interesting question, to be elucidated in passing below. Whatever the answer, the judgment is problematic both as to the test's logic and as to how to keep its effects from getting out of control. Paradoxically, however, my own conversion matured as the case law seemed more awkward. There must be more to the doctrine, I surmised, than the mere test.[7] What the judgments did show was, first, that operating the doctrine is not a matter of logic or system but of practical judgment and makeshift criteria, second, that this will always involve, as a central ingredient, to apply limits to its own logic.

One might go further: it is not the logic but the limit which is the most interesting element of the test. And this is not a defensive angle. A limit is a meeting place and may become part of a common ground.

3 The test and its saving flaws

The original test seemed simple. To pass it, an EC provision had to be clear and unconditional *to the letter* and readable thus as to protect a tangible private interest, making this a 'right'. If it did, interested (private) par-

---

[6] C-226/97 *Lemmens* [1998] ECR I-3711, para. 36. For ample criticism of the judgment; Prechal (2000), p. 1056: 'particularly obscure on this point' and further opinions quoted by her under footnote 48.

[7] This is following the famous motto: *Credo quia ineptum* (Tertullian).

ties could avail themselves of the provision in a domestic tribunal to challenge a government measure and, under certain conditions, an act of other private parties. It involved a technique to enlist private parties in the supervision of their government's compliance by entitling them to invoke EC law directly.

This entitlement was then made into the key-stone by doctrine. Winter's 1972 and Judge Pescatore's equally well known 1983 articles were essential. Winter saw direct effect as compacted into a relationship of two elements: precision and the creation of individual rights. If a provision is sufficiently unambiguous (to the letter) and could be read as protecting a right, then direct effect is the result.

This compact no longer holds. Direct effect has emancipated on the one hand from the requirement of precision and on the other from the link of individual entitlement, as is explained by Judge Edward in the *Mancini liber,* to prove a matter of *obligation* of the governments.[8] The old test has obviously lost its bearings. Tribunals are presently asked and eager under cover of the ECJ to apply Community Law provisions even a) if these are in no way clear and unconditional; b) for other purposes than to protect private interests; c) of their own motion, without a right or rule invoked.

More significant, however, is the way Pescatore's theory was disproved by the same evolution. Pescatore even recoils from the very idea of a limit on direct effect, especially if this is a mere *technical* one. According to him 'direct effect is the normal state of health of the law; it is only the absence of direct effect which causes concern...'.[9] The key to Pescatore's theory is its ultimate denial of limits in the doctrine, limits other than those natural to the judicial function. In *Costanzo* the ECJ found that the obligations inherent in direct effect cover not only judicial, but administrative action as well.[10] Taken to its logical extreme, this would impose on any administrative authority the obligation to test national legislation against directives, even implemented, for conformity. And this without (as in the case of judicial testing) recourse to the ECJ for counsel. Again, then, the question is: up to what point do you oblige domestic authorities?

There have been conditions, controls, to the operation of direct effect from the start and there always will be. They have evolved with the doctrine. The requirement of precision was a limit, as was the requirement of individual rights; judicial application was a limiting condition. When the doctrine evolved to allow direct effect for directives, a new condition was added: not horizontally. When, from there, direct effect spread to legality review (*Kraaijeveld*), to construction (*Marleasing*) limits were called in to condition these outlays: legal

---

[8] Edward (1998).

[9] Winter (1972), at p. 438, Pescatore (1983), at p. 155.

[10] Case 103/88 *Fratelli Costanzo* [1989] ECR 1839.

certainty and, more generally, principles of Community law (*Kolpinghuis*).[11] The *Francovich* outlay generated its own limits, as *Brasserie* and *Dillenkofer* made clear.[12] Each time there is extension followed by a new limitation. Is this not analogous to the way a city develops?[13]

Instead of sighing at the break down of the original test and at the resulting fuzziness I think it is good to see the original test not as matter of logic or system, but as a *compact* of several distinct component legal traditions, one centred on *right* (let us say Germany), one on *result* (let us say France), one on *remedy* (let us say England). Naturally this triad is as simplistic as it is emblematic; it has less the ambition to reflect the compact's real composition, which in reality is much richer, than to point at an irreducible plurality. This test was like the old town wall, protecting a great diversity of social structure and interest. Legal development made this particular test break open at the seams and lose definition. This was, however, less a proof of its original weakness than of the success of the idea behind the test.

Each time, then, new ground is won and subsequently conditioned. Old walls go: domestic courts are told by the ECJ to apply Community law provisions which are not clear and to do so for other purposes than to protect private interests; if needed, *ex officio*. This evolution is not bringing on Pescatore's empire of the courts 'willing to carry the operation of the rules of Community law up to the limits of what appears to be feasible, considering the nature of their judicial function'.[14] Instead it keeps raising new questions and proposed solutions concerning, especially, the way to condition the operation of the rules of community law. Entrusting these limits to some 'nature of the judicial function' may give some but not full relief.

As is shown by Jans and Prinssen in this volume,[15] to an important extent the doctrine may come to rely, for its conditions, on national procedural constraints (*Comet*).[16] This line of thinking is promising in several respects. It accounts for the involvement of the national authorities (judicial, legislative, administrative) in the operation of direct effect not as passive recipients only, but as full participants. Does this then mean that the full weight of restraint may be asked

---

[11] Case C-72/95 *Kraaijeveld* [1996] ECR I-5403; Case C-106/89 *Marleasing* [1990] ECR I-4135; Case 80/86 *Kolpinghuis* [1987] ECR 3969.

[12] Joined Cases C-6/90 and C-9/90 *Francovich* [1991] ECR I-5357; Joined Cases C-46/93 and C-48/93 *Brasserie du Pêcheur* [1996] ECR I-1029; Joined Cases C-178/94, C-179/94 and C-188-190/94 *Dillenkofer* [1996] ECR I-4845.

[13] Interestingly it is the reverse of the way territory is claimed from the water in Holland: there first the limitation (the dyke) is created to encircle a prospective piece of land, then the water is evacuated.

[14] Pescatore (1983), p. 177.

[15] In chapter V.

[16] Case 45/76 *Comet* [1976] ECR 2043.

of domestic courts and procedure? This is probably a few steps too far. The Court presently *balances* requirements of Community uniformity and effectiveness against those of national procedural variety and autonomy. Prechal rightly terms this development one towards a 'procedural rule of reason'.[17]

Whatever the distribution of work between EC and domestic levels, however, this situation argues clearly in favour of drawing the domestic conditioning factors (in turn controlled by the *Rewe*[18] and *Comet* case law) into the operation of direct effect. Which suffices, incidentally, to prove that at the level of the test there is no finality or singularity to be expected.

To conclude from this that direct effect is lost to singularity and clarity is, however, to confound the doctrine and the test. What more than the test, than the *letter*, is there to the doctrine?

4 The spirit

Let us revert to the origins. Direct effect from its inception was given a two stage launch. *Van Gend en Loos*[19] bases it first at the level of the Treaty as a whole, depending on the latter's *spirit* (primarily). The Court in its famous formula leading up to direct effect resorted to the Treaty's 'spirit' as an aid to interpreting it as a new form of treaty:

> 'To ascertain whether the provisions of an international treaty extend so far in their effects [as to have direct effect] it is necessary to consider [the treaty's] spirit, general scheme and wording'. (French: d'en considérer l'esprit, l'économie et les termes)

In invoking the 'spirit' and according lowest rank to the wording, the Court distanced itself from classical treaty interpretation canons as laid down in the Vienna Convention on the Law of Treaties (Article 31). This, however, it did concerning the Treaty as such and as a whole: 'the spirit' is invoked to raise this from pedestrian status of an 'agreement which merely creates obligations between the contracting states', to that of an act creative of a 'new legal order of international law'.[20] What counts in our context is to know that all this was done

---

[17] Prechal (1998), at p. 690. Similarly Craig & De Búrca (1998), p. 235.

[18] Case 33/76 *Rewe* [1976] ECR 1989.

[19] Case 26/62 *Van Gend en Loos* [1963] ECR 1.

[20] The triad of 'spirit, general scheme and wording' is subtle and telling. Its downranking the letter in favour of the spirit echoes St Paul's famous letter to the Corinthians where he claims that the new testament should be read as to the spirit, since 'the letter kills while the spirit brings life'. In between spirit and letter in *Van Gend en Loos* we find in French the concept *l'économie*, rendering something

on the way to creating a new legal situation and that in turn direct effect is part and parcel of that new situation. The import of this is for the Court to establish a proper basis for its own authority from which to operate the doctrine, to some extent away from the Member States' authorities.[21]

Only after this founding act for the Treaty as a whole, and beyond that: of the legal order, raising it to authority on its own account, the step to follow was to mint the exact *test* of direct effect. This concerns individual provisions and, being a derivation, needed bring no great novelty. Nor did it. Direct effect was held to depend, quite in keeping with the canon of public international law prevalent since the 1928 PCIJ *Danzig* advisory opinion, on the justiciability of the provision, its legal readiness, i.e. its *wording*.[22]

The novelty of direct effect was less in the test than in the claim to authority, reflected in the two stage character of the Court's reasoning. This empowered first the Treaty, only then the individual provisions.

Unfortunately the span between spirit and letter here introduced has not always been understood let alone heeded. This may have had to do with a fault occurring in the English 1963 (unauthorized) translation of *Van Gend en Loos*. This blurred the distinction between the Treaty as a whole and individual provision, between spirit and wording, to read:

> '... it is necessary to consider the spirit, the general scheme and the wording [not of the Treaty but] of those provisions' (emphasis added).

As if the spirit were a matter of individual provisions also and, worse, as if there were nothing to direct effect but the provisions and their test.

This error has never been duly repaired by scholarship. In most English language textbooks the faulty translation subsists. No damage needed have been done, had the Court itself spotted the linguistic virus. Instead, however, the original triad (spirit, scheme, wording) was turned into a plastic mantra of changing terms, easily mixing up questions on the *status of the instrument* and

---

like 'the household' or 'internal structure' of the Treaty and referring to the possibility of systematic interpretation. What is meant by 'spirit' is left without explanation, but a) it does *not* refer to the (internal) Treaty structure; b) it may confidently be related to the idea of the EC Treaty as a new covenant.

[21] This is often misunderstood. Take Spiermann, who has devoted a doctoral thesis to debunking the originality of direct effect. To him the orthodoxy to be combated runs thus: 'because the treaty had direct effect, it constituted a new legal order'. Yet in actual reality, the Court's claim reads the other way: direct effect in its authoritative aspect follows upon and is part of the proclamation of a new legal order. And the novelty of that legal order is in turn based on the spirit of the Treaty; Spiermann (1999) at p. 765-6.

[22] *Danzig* PCIJ, Ser. B, No 15 (1928).

on the *effects of a single individual provision*. It suffices to quote from *Van Duyn*, whose version of the mantra features a standard sloppy use of language:

'*It is necessary to examine, in every case, whether* the nature, general scheme and wording of the provision in question *are capable of having direct effects on the relations between Member States and individuals*'.[23]

What *could be* the nature and general scheme of a (single) *provision?* Also, literally this passage would read that it is the nature, general scheme etc. of the provision which *has* direct effect. The nature might *cause*, or *confer* it.[24]

It was no doubt due only in part to the above terminological erosion that scholarship left to the spirit (later: nature) the role of a relict, to concentrate exclusively on the technical department, the *test* in isolation. The other factor is its close relationship with legal practice, naturally focusing on the aspect of individual entitlement and consequently on the element of (subjective) *right* in the test of direct effect.

5 From rights to obligations

In his aforementioned contribution to the *liber-Mancini* Judge Edward has tried to move the debate and the doctrine from one centring on *rights of private parties* to one revolving around *obligations of the state*: 'Direct effect is about the separation of powers and specifically about the extent of the judicial power to enforce the obligations of the state'.[25]

Switching from rights to obligations is not merely a matter of turning up the other side of the same coin, as one may be inclined to react. It is a smart move allowing or even imposing a fresh reading of *Van Gend en Loos*, thus as to land thinking on direct effect in a different world. This is one of *relationships*, even 'constitutional' relationships. Edward distinguishes three:

---

[23] Case 41/74 *Van Duyn* [1974] ECR 1337, para. 12; emphasis added.

[24] In *International Fruit* the Court resorted to the classic formula 'spirit, general scheme and wording' concerning a treaty, not to *grant* but to ward off direct effect for the GATT, compounding status of the instrument and effects of its provisions. 'For this purpose, *the spirit*, the general scheme and the terms of the General Agreement must be considered', Joined Cases 21-24/72 *International Fruit* [1972] ECR 1219, para. 20. In *Demirel* for the purpose of interpreting an association-agreement between the Community and a third country, it used a mix in which the two stages are recognizeable: 'that a provision in an agreement must be regarded as directly applicable when, *regard being had to its wording and the purpose and nature* of the agreement itself, the provision contains a clear and precise obligation...'; Case 12/86 *Demirel* [1987] ECR 3719.

[25] Edward (1998), p. 424 and 425

'- the contractual, obligation-creating relationships between the Member States, and between them and the Community, arising out of the Treaty;

- the consequent relationship between treaty law and domestic law; and

- the consequent modification of the relationship between the Member States and their subjects'.[26]

The telling case in support of this move is, significantly, *Grosskrotzenburg*, a case brought against Germany by the Commission for failure to implement the Environmental Impact Assessment Directive.[27] Germany emblematically built its defence on the argument that no individual's rights against the State were involved. The Court answered in the clearest terms:

'The question which arises is thus whether the directive is to be construed as imposing that obligation. That question is quite separate from the question whether individuals may rely as against the State on provisions of an unimplemented directive...'.[28]

Does not this passage, incidentally, also answer the question posed above (under paragraph 2) why the Court in *Lemmens* refused the escape offered by the relativity principle (*Schutznorm*) to limit repercussions of its own test? The principle is rooted too exclusively in a tradition focusing on (subjective) rights to be further acceptable.

Edward does not go much beyond operating the turn from right to obligation and does not need to. Asked to stamp his theory into legal change and answer the question *when* must courts enforce the obligation on the state and when not, he leaves the ground to others:

'What underlies the reasoning in all the cases is the identification of an obligation flowing from the directive which the Member State is bound to fulfil and once crystallized the courts are not only entitled but bound to enforce... When the obligation crystallizes remains, in some respects, open...'.[29]

Answers will come from practice, not from doctrine, and they come in the form of increments, not of finished reasonings. Doctrine may now turn to what is involved at the constitutional level.

---

[26] Ibid.

[27] Council Directive 85/337/EEC on the assessment of the effects of certain public and private projects on the environment; OJ 1985, L 175/40, amended by Council Directive 97/11/EC, OJ 1997, L 73/5.

[28] C-431/92 *Grosskrotzenburg* [1995] ECR I- 2189, para. 26.

[29] Edward (1998), p. 433 including a part of the note; emphasis added.

As we have seen, the test must be understood as part of a set: its counterpart is the acknowledgement of the Treaty's spirit. While the *test* of direct effect is about individual provisions, the *spirit* of direct effect is part of the (political) *terms* or *conditions* of the establishment of the Community/Union.

6 The terms

Let us revert to *Van Gend en Loos*, the ground-breaking judgment. As noted, this was not basically about the test; it was no less than a claim to authority. Introducing direct effect on its own authority is best seen as an act of bluff for the Court. And the bluff has worked. It might not have; the Member States (and the circumstances) might have let EC wither. All that is part of the game. If the bluff has been successful, this means that it has been accepted by others, notably the Member States (and that the circumstances have been gracious).

This means, however, that there was an unpaid bill underlying the Court's launch of direct effect. This is no problem (practical nor theoretical) as it is typical for a new venture to start off from a debt. But it must be acknowledged and so the Court does. It tacitly and logically acknowledges its actions to be under basic terms, which may be made explicit to some degree and which may themselves evolve.

It is consequently necessary to dig up the conditions, the terms of its success. These are not in the hands of the Court alone.

Direct effect is part of the development of a regime to which Member States are not only subjected but from which they profit. They have learned to read this case law as salutary, have accepted the terms and reap the fruits. The terms (drawn from the 'spirit') should consequently be remade part of the doctrine. This is a delicate exercise, as it is in the nature of these terms to be implicit and to lack the precision of legal criteria. But when the walls go, it becomes necessary to understand the city without them; likewise, when the lines lose definition, one is bound to look up to see what they intended to define.

a) Acknowledgement of the terms as such

The first step is inherent in the very *idea* of terms: it is to understand these as elements of an ongoing relationship. What this does is no less than to bring the Member States back into the picture as agents in the system's development. The Court's bluff in *Van Gend en Loos* was addressed at them; it is they who went along with it and still do. It is no use to put them out of existence inside the Community context and to read the doctrine as one created by the Court in splendid isolation or under the sole dictates of justice or Community interests. True, the Member States are not in control individually.

But when united or compounded to a critical mass, they will not be overruled. This is testified e.g. by the *Dori*[30] judgment in which all but one of the Members to make submissions pronounced themselves squarely against horizontal effect of directives, blocking the Court from taking that relatively simple and logical extra step.

There are two ways to look at this. The dominant line of legal doctrine seems to be to regret Member States' involvement and/or see it as a passing evil. Indeed, acknowledging the Member States' presence (not only as intervenients but as agents) in the evolution of EC legal doctrine is anathema to EC legal orthodoxy.[31] The other one is to appreciate their presence as part of the original deal and part of the constraints under which the Court has set out to operate. This is the line adopted in the present argument. While lacking the perspective of ease and logic which is so seductive in EC legal orthodoxy, it has some non negligible strong points. For one thing it allows to conceive *evolution*, which is never a matter of logic but one of time.

b) The exceptional nature

Paramount among the terms, one even directly flowing from their very idea, is the exceptional nature of the regime of direct effect. This is a denial of direct effect making Community law in a sense 'the law of the land' as Prechal wishes to consider it.[32] Being exceptional does not mean for direct effect to be minimized. It does, however, mean two things. First, that there will always need to be tests, however clumsy or makeshift these may be, to control the realm of the regime. The tests are in a sense the static controls. Second, more interestingly, it means that every *extension* needs to be argued and circumscribed. This is what forces the Court of Justice to its piecemeal action, of which the confusion (= lack of apparent logic) is but the most direct manifestation.

Is this a situation harmful to the development of EC Law or European integration, as it is implied by EC legal orthodoxy? I would argue to the contrary. If direct effect were part of the normal state of affairs, in the way of direct applicability, the doctrine would not be a vital agent in the *development* of the EU legal and political order and its significance would only have been temporary, an 'infant disease' in the famous expression of Pescatore.[33] Instead, direct effect has allowed (or led) EC Law to spread into undreamt-of new developments by refusing any single logic or natural state.[34]

---

[30] Case C-91/92 *Faccini Dori* [1994] ECR I-3325.

[31] Regrets: Craig & De Búrca (1998), p. 211, to name a few.

[32] See Prechal (2000) and chapter II, paragraph 4 of this volume.

[33] Pescatore (1983), p. 155.

[34] The denial of direct effect to framework decisions under Art. 34 EU is both proof that direct effect is not only a Community Law but an EU-law-at-large doctrine and a confirmation of its limited and conditional nature.

c) Stability

Once the presence of Member States acknowledged, it is but a step to realize that there is a requirement for the doctrine not to destabilize the Member States' legal systems, particularly the relationships between their nationals as under private law. Unqualified recognition of what in terms of tests is called 'horizontal direct effect' for directives might do precisely this; blocking it has been an acknowledgement of the Members' justified interest. This, incidentally, will be why the requirement to publish directives, while lifting the rule of law-objection, has not brought the Court to lift the ban.

d) Balancing between the Union and third states

This is the counterpart of the previous condition: direct effect may not affect the authority of the Union in the world nor put it or its members at a disadvantage in dealing with third states. This concerns direct effect in external relations.

e) Balancing among member states and their legal traditions

By far the most interesting conditional field is the one concerning the different Member States' legal traditions. As we noted at the end of paragraph 3 the original test could be considered, apart from other things, a compact between different traditions, simplified into a triad of 'right, of result and of remedy'. When this compact came apart under the pressures of time and effectiveness, it allowed or brought on at least three distinct developments, outgrowths of the original doctrine. Effectiveness through the tradition of *right* ushered in the *Francovich* lineage; through that of *remedy*: *Factortame*; through that of *result*: *Marleasing*.[35]

This is a crude and modest tri-partition without any claim to ultimate validity. It may serve to discover and respect the inherent and creative plurality inside the concept of direct effect. It would imply crediting for the evolution of Community Law under direct effect *and* of direct effect itself not uniformity nor the autonomy of the Community Legal Order but the interplay between the original variety of legal traditions and the increasing *political* solidarity of the Member States.

---

[35] *Francovich* (as cited); Case C-213/89 *Factortame* [1990] ECR I-2433; *Marleasing* (as cited).

7 Conclusion

Now to sum up the argument:

Direct effect is a capital doctrine of Union Law, covering the ways in which EU law breaks through the traditional divides between international law and domestic law. It must be seen, in the terms of modern physics, as a 'unified field'; in terms of the historian: a single intelligible field of study. In terms of common sense, including *legal* sense: a single field of practical and doctrinal intelligence. It may also be seen as a place of learning and of communication.

Van Gend en Loos was a bluff; its success is proof that the other players have gone along with it. We need to discover who they are. They are not only or even primarily the private parties, nor the judiciaries, but also the Member States. It is they who are understanding the Court's case law as challenging but advantageous. We need to re-chart the active presence of the Member States in the process, as factors of containment and of inspiration.

Direct effect is ever unfinished. It is not a doctrine seeking perfection but one seeking to inspire and channel evolution.

The Court of Justice administers justice not in its own name nor in that of its legal order, but in the name of European Union as a political community. This is inchoate and at any rate far from perfect. EC law, its evolution and its doctrine do not stand in isolation, but are conditioned by this political community. This means direct effect is not an EC legal doctrine but one of Union law at large.

CHAPTER X

Epilogue: Symbiosis?

prof. dr. Pieter-Jan Kuijper

1 Introduction

This book is the result of a Conference that aimed to set out and analyse the different aspects of direct effect. It concerns the Community law doctrine of direct effect as applied by the Community Courts (the European Court of Justice and the Court of First Instance). It connects this with the direct effect of international law within the Community legal order. Furthermore, it deals with the direct effect of Community law within the national legal orders of the Member States, in particular the direct effect of directives and a number of related phenomena, such as the 'State liability' for (non-implemented) directives. This epilogue seeks to recall, first of all, in summary fashion, the basic concepts of self-executingness or direct effect in international law and the results of those concepts in so-called monist and dualist States respectively. In addition, it devotes a few paragraphs to State responsibility under international law and State torts in national law, since the Conference under the broad cover of 'direct effect' of directives discussed many issues which are better linked to these concepts than to direct effect as such, although they are connected to the latter.[1]

Secondly, the epilogue then seeks to discuss the various aspects of direct effect which were discussed at the Conference and to determine where these aspects are straightforwardly borrowed from international law and where they have acquired, or flow from, uniquely Community law traits. Finally, the various contributions to the book are situated within this framework.

2 International law background to direct effect

Under international law direct effect, or the self-executing character of treaties (and even of customary international law), is linked to a number of underlying factors.

The first of these is whether or not international and national law are seen as being part of one overarching system of law: in other words, the notion of monism v. dualism. Even in monist systems, as we will see, there is some line drawn between international and national systems of law.[2] In dualist systems, however, the line is so important that it can only be crossed by an act of

---

[1]   It is to be noted that Prechal (in this volume's chapter II, paragraph 2.1) does consider that, at least the relationship between EC law and international law is not helpful for the understanding of EC direct effect. See also the conclusion (paragraph 5) of this contribution. But it is still my view that it is useful to look at the international law roots of the doctrine for inspiration. This does not imply that I do not recognize the force of her arguments on the changing nature of the Community legislative system, which in her view should entail changes in, or elimination of the concept of direct effect.

[2]   This is what Nollkaemper calls 'second order dualism'; see this volume's chapter VII, paragraph 5.

transformation of the norm concerned from international law into national law, usually performed by national parliament.

Second, questions of direct effect are closely linked to the balance between the different arms of government: the legislature, the judiciary and the executive.[3] Even in a system where parliament is not endowed with transformatory power of international law into national law, it may still have the power to set aside earlier legislation. Since an act of transformation of international law is not seen as an act of parliament endowed with special authority, later acts of parliament may set aside such acts of transformation (normal application of the later-in-time rule).

This is where there is a link with the notion of hierarchy within the universal legal system: the supremacy of international law. Basically there is a frontal clash between the full sovereignty of Parliament and full supremacy of international law. Conceptually and in reality a monist approach to the relationship between international and national law can co-exist with full sovereignty of Parliament, but it may lead to odd results in that it considerably increases the risk of State responsibility for breach of a rule of international law.[4]

It is here that we touch upon a third factor underlying direct effect, namely the role of judges, not only in mitigating the international responsibility of States, but also in respecting the internal constitutional balance and division of powers with the legislature and the executive. The courts have a natural tendency (or perhaps we should say: *should* have a natural tendency) to avoid placing the State in a position where it could be found to have infringed an international obligation, in particular treaty obligations. Hence the courts should normally not give interpretations of national law or regulations, which lead to open conflict with treaty obligations. As we will see below, there are different ways of doing this, including applying the doctrine of direct effect.

The courts also naturally respect the division of powers with the executive and with parliament. The respect of parliament and the executive is inherent in the notion of self-executingness and direct effect. If parliament or the executive needs to intervene in order to make a law or a regulation, with a view to 'execute', or to give 'effect' to an international norm, the judiciary should stay its hand; the international norm obviously does not 'execute itself' or is not directly effective, or - as the ECJ has put it - 'may [not] be applied by a court'.[5]

The kind of norm that may most easily be applied by a court is, of course, a straightforward individual right or obligation. In such a situation it is quite

---

[3] This seems now to have been fairly generally accepted about direct effect in Community law, see the contributions of Edward, Prechal and Eijsbouts to this volume's chapters I, II and IX. It is, however, originally just as true in international law and national constitutional law. See for instance the very perceptive writings of Vazquez (1992) on self-executingness in the US.

[4] See on State responsibility below paragraph 2.2.

[5] Case 104/81 *Kupferberg* [1982] ECR 3641, para. 26.

possible that the creation of such individual rights and/or obligations was the very intention of the contracting parties to the treaty. This was recognized very early by the Permanent Court of International Justice[6] and was recently confirmed by the International Court of Justice.[7] The PCIJ also added that such rights and obligations may be enforceable by national courts. All this can be detected by applying the normal rules of treaty interpretation.

2.1 Direct effect in monist and dualist systems

If we attempt to translate these factors underlying direct effect to monist and dualist systems of law respectively, the following picture emerges.

In monist States international law is the law of the land, whilst in dualist States this is not so and transformation of international law into national law is required in order to *make* it into the law of the land. It follows that in monist States international law, in principle, can be applied as such by the courts, but in dualist States only after it has become national law through transformation.

However, as we saw above, the deference courts normally grant to the other arms of government, leads the courts not to apply all international law directly in the national legal order, but only those provisions of international law which by their nature lend themselves to being applied by the courts, i.e. can be considered to be self-executing or having direct effect. Therefore, though in principle all international law could be applied in a monist system, in reality it is not and in this way at least some *de facto* boundary remains between international and national law.

In dualist States a phenomenon like direct effect is inherently impossible; it is literally 'unthinkable'. However, the 'natural tendency' of courts to avoid placing their States in a position of international responsibility leads, in dualist states, to a great reliance by the judiciary on so-called 'harmonious interpretation': the international (treaty) norm is not resorted to in order to set aside the national norm (as in the case of direct effect) but is used as a tool of interpretation of the national laws and/or regulations concerned so as to make the latter's interpretation conform to that of the former. This is an interpretative technique which may (and is) also applied by the courts in a monist system, insofar as the relevant norms of international law are not considered to be self-executing in such a system.

In monist systems, finally, a distinction may be made based on whether or not the system accepts full supremacy of international law. If international law merely becomes law of the land on the same basis as national law, rules such as the later-in-time rules and the *lex specialis* rule will apply to international law as

---

[6]   *Danzig*, PCIJ, Ser. B, No. 15 (1928), p. 17-18.

[7]   *LaGrand* case (*Germany v. United States*), judgment of 27 June 2001, [2001] 40 ILM 1069.

they do to national law. In the case of full supremacy, international law norms always take precedence over national law rules.

2.2 State responsibility

Looking at some of the issues discussed at the Conference from the perspective of State responsibility under international law and government responsibility under national law, broadly the following remarks can be made.

State responsibility for breach of a treaty (or part of a treaty)[8] may give rise to commensurate suspension of treaty rights or obligations on the part of other treaty partners. This results in a 'rebalancing' of treaty obligations between the treaty partners.

A breach of a customary rule of international law or the committing of an international tort, ideally ends in *restitutio in integrum*, but in reality most often gives rise to liability for damages, i.e. to monetary compensation.

Acts by all arms of government, including the judiciary, may give rise to international responsibility of the State. Hence the signalled tendency of the courts avoiding State responsibility for breach of treaty or any other norm of international law.

Insofar as breach of a treaty by national authorities leads to 'damages' for individuals, the normal national rules on government liability for tortuous government acts apply. Insofar as the damage caused to private interests by breach of a treaty is attributable to legislative activity, the possibilities for a remedy under most national legal systems are circumscribed by many onerous conditions and thus very limited. In principle, the possible direct effect of the treaty provision or customary rule of international law breached is of no importance for the remedy of damages for torts committed by the government. Unless the doctrine of government torts requires what the Germans call a *Schutznorm*, a norm protecting the complaining party. In practice, directly effective treaty norms or customary rules[9] are likely to operate as a *Schutznorm*.

---

[8] Vienna Convention, Article 60.

[9] In the case of customary rules direct effect may be difficult to ascertain because the precise scope of a customary rule may be difficult to determine. In this connection, it is quite significant that in the cases dealing with customary international law, the Court has often sought support in provisions of Conventions codifying international law, which were said by the International Court of Justice to constitute customary international law, see Kuijper (2002).

3 International law, Community law and direct effect

The European Court of Justice, as Nollkaemper has rightly pointed out,[10] plays a double role where direct effect is involved. On the one hand, it acts like any national court may act, by opening up the Community legal order to international law, insofar as it applies the doctrine of direct effect to treaties concluded by the Community or to customary rules of international law. On the other hand, it acts like a constitutional Court, imposing the supremacy of Community law, including that of directives, on the national courts and the national legal order of the Member States. Finally, just like in the international law approach, there is the aspect of State responsibility both on the level of Community law and on the level of national law.

3.1 Opening up the Community legal order to international law

To some, the notion of opening up the Community legal order to international law is a tautology, since Community law in their view is part of international law; international law permeates Community law and still applies, insofar as the Community has not contracted out of international law, between the Member States.[11] It would flow naturally from such a perspective that the Community legal system is monist and that Community law and international law, belonging to the same legal system, are at the same level.

However, such a perspective seems to take insufficiently into account that the Community also participates in the international legal order as a separate actor by concluding treaties, acting autonomously etc. The ECJ seems to have been ambivalent about its approach to the matter, speaking in *Van Gend en Loos*[12] about a legal order of its own within international law and leaving the last three words out in *Costa/ENEL*.[13] The latter perspective has prevailed as appears from the Court's later case law, for instance, on the differences between the EC legal order and the EEA Treaty,[14] which led the Court to conclude that the EC Treaty was different from ordinary international treaties.[15] It also appears from the early cases on the direct effect of treaties within the Community legal order and later of the position of customary international law in relation to Community law. The perspective that the Community legal order is separate from international law

---

[10] See his contribution to this volume's chapter VII.

[11] See Vanhamme (2001a) *passim*.

[12] Case 26/62 *Van Gend en Loos* [1963] ECR 1.

[13] Case 6/64 *Costa/ENEL* [1964] ECR 585.

[14] See Opinion 1/91 [1991] ECR I-6079 and Opinion 1/92 [1992] ECR I-2821.

[15] See Kuijper (1998).

clearly prevails: it is the Community legal order which opens itself up (through the case law of the Court) to international law and accepts monism. It is not the Community legal order being part of general international law so that the former is *ipso facto* permeated by the latter, a bit like Community law is supposed to permeate national law.

However, direct effect is applied to limit the consequences of monism and in order to keep the Court to its proper role and not permit it to impinge on the powers of the Commission as executive or the Council and the Parliament, as Community legislature. In doing so the Court of Justice and the Court of First Instance clearly follow not so much of an individual rights approach, but rather an approach based on the criterion whether the treaty provision concerned, or, especially where the GATT and WTO Agreements are concerned, the treaty as a whole are of a nature so as to be able to be applied by a Court. In order to determine whether this is the case, the international law norms for the interpretation of treaties are applied. This is best illustrated by the case law on the GATT and the WTO, where the analysis of object and purpose of the Agreement (or of the general scheme of the agreement as the Court also calls it) leads to the conclusion that the Court cannot be called upon to apply it 'directly', whether in favour of individuals or in favour of a Member State. It is the latter situation which is most illustrative for the position of the Court. In both *Germany* v. *Council*[16] on the old GATT 1947 and in *Portugal* v. *Council*[17] on the new WTO, the Court comes to the conclusion that the general characteristics of the treaty[18] make it just as impossible for Member States to invoke provisions of the treaty in a direct action for annulment of Community rules as for individuals to have the Court set aside provisions of Community law for reasons of incompatibility of the Agreement. In *Germany* v. *Council* it was not said explicitly, but the Court knew that the Commission was still negotiating with several Latin American countries about the sharing out of banana quotas and may have felt that any hard and fast pronouncements on its part would have undercut these efforts. In *Portugal* v. *Council* it was explicitly articulated by the Court that accepting the WTO Agreement as standard of review in an action for annulment would rob the Community of certain flexibilities in negotiating compensation, a negotiation which would be carried out by the Commission under instruction of the Council.

As to the 'openness' of the Community to customary international law, it is there that the 'harmonious' interpretation was first used by the Court without being called by its name. As I have pointed out elsewhere[19] and as Wouters also

---

[16] Case C-280/93 *Germany* v. *Council* [1994] ECR I-4973.

[17] Case C-149/96 *Portugal* v. *Council* [1999] ECR I-8395.

[18] Of which is it recognized in *Germany* v. *Council* that they are the same as those which make it impossible for individuals to invoke provisions of the treaty directly.

[19] Kuijper (2002).

lets shine through,[20] the first application of customary international law actually
occurred already very early on in respect of questions of jurisdiction in the field
of anti-trust law. It is after all almost 'natural' for a Court to determine the
jurisdictional limits of actions of the Executive (e.g. the Commission acting in
international anti-trust cases) or the limits of its own competence in terms of
'jurisdiction', and hence in terms of which limits are set by international law on
such jurisdiction. This is the line of case law that started with *Dyestuffs* in 1972[21]
and found its provisional culmination in *Gencor*[22] a few years ago. The so-called
'harmonious' interpretation goes rather far in these cases, because in the end
the customary international law of jurisdiction is seen as a true boundary
for the exercise of jurisdiction by the Commission in anti-trust cases. When
national authorities are called upon to apply Community law in international
situations, e.g. international fisheries,[23] they are similarly limited by the international legal rules of jurisdiction. Even where it concerns the private law relationships between individuals, the jurisdictional reach of Community law can have
'horizontal effects', but there the limits applied by the Court of Justice are more
of a private international law nature, namely whether there are sufficient points
of attachment with the Community.[24]

The Community Courts have been at pains to avoid the impression that in
certain situations they were giving direct effect to customary international law.
In the two cases where this arguably might have been the case, *Opel Austria*[25]
and *Racke*,[26] the Court emphasized very much that the persons concerned had
been denied the possibility to invoke a directly effective treaty right because of
certain intervening measures by the Council.[27]

Following the approach applied by the Courts in dualist countries, the
method of interpreting Community law in 'harmony' with international (treaty)
law, the Court has also, in response to preliminary questions, instructed
national courts to interpret Community law and national law in harmonious
fashion with Community Treaties which have been deemed by it, not to be
self-executing or having direct effect. This is the case in particular now for the
WTO Agreement and its annexes. The results can be quite far-reaching. Witness
the Court's interpretation of Article 50 of the TRIPs Agreement in *Schieving-
Nystad*.[28] This interpretation will now become the '*Schranke*', the outer limit,

---

[20] See his contribution to this volume's chapter VIII.

[21] Case 48/69, *Imperial Chemical Industries* v. *Commission* [1972] ECR 619 (Dyestuffs).

[22] Case T-102/96 *Gencor* [1999] ECR II-753.

[23] Cf. Case C-286/90 *Poulsen* [1992] ECR I-6019.

[24] Case 36/74 *Walrave & Koch* 1974 ECR 1405; Case 237/83 *Prodest* [1984] ECR 3153.

[25] Case T-115/94 *Opel Austria* [1997] ECR II-39.

[26] Case C-162/96 *Racke* [1998] ECR I-3655.

[27] See Wouters in chapter VIII.

[28] Case C-89/99 *Schieving-Nijstad* [2001] ECR I-5851.

for the application of the *'Kort geding'* procedure in the Netherlands (a special kind of speeded-up or provisional measures procedure, equipped with an equally speedy appeals procedure, which in the Netherlands is often used to settle civil cases, including intellectual property cases, definitively). Seen in this way, the situation resembles very much the way in which the international law of jurisdiction serves as guidance to national courts in interpreting and applying the territorial reach of Community law.[29] To speak in terms of Judge Edward's contribution to this volume, the Courts have no real choice whether to apply the procedural rules of TRIPs or not, just as they have no choice whether to apply the customary rules of jurisdiction.[30]

In following such a harmonious interpretation and instructing national courts to do so, the Community Courts, as was pointed out in paragraph 2, undoubtedly contribute to reducing the chances of international responsibility being incurred by the Community.

3.2 Imposing supremacy and direct effect as a constitutional court

3.2.1 The Treaty itself and regulations

There can be no doubt about the supremacy of Community law; it has clearly been imposed by the Court.[31] The Community Treaties and the regulations based thereon are the law of the land in all Member States. Nevertheless, here the Court of Justice has kept to the international law model and restricted itself to second order dualism: national courts are not bound to apply Community treaty provisions just like that, only those which are self-executing. Again the Court of Justice and the courts of the Member States can only give effect directly to those Treaty provisions which are of a kind as *can* be applied by the courts. In other words: the Court of Justice does not want to encourage Member States' courts to trot on the toes of their national executive authorities[32] which for certain Treaty provisions may have to take implementing action.

3.2.2 Directives

Most of the problems surrounding the direct effect of Community law arise in connection with, and the largest part of the Conference was devoted to, directives. Directives are different from the Community Treaties

---

[29] See *Poulsen* (as cited).

[30] See Edward in chapter I.

[31] *Costa/ENEL* (as cited); Case 106/77 *Simmenthal* [1978] ECR 629.

[32] National parliaments do not enter the picture as they have nothing to do with the EC Treaties.

and regulations; they are not automatically the law of the land, they are first in need of implementation. Directives are in form and in substance a bit like international treaties, in particular what are called nowadays legislative treaties, which attempt to harmonize segments of international law, such as, for instance, the intellectual property treaties managed by WIPO. The main difference with such treaties is that directives have a clear and obligatory date of entry into force (date of implementation) for *all* Member States.[33] We will see later on what special consequences flow from that particular difference.

However, if directives are indeed a bit like treaties, then there is no reason to assume that they cannot contain directly effective provisions as treaties can. The fact that directives require implementation is strictly speaking irrelevant; 'normal' international agreements mostly also require implementation *and* are found, after application of the normal rules of treaty interpretation, to contain directly effective provisions 'which the Courts may apply'. It is scarcely necessary, though from a Community law viewpoint perhaps desirable, to lay much emphasis on the fact that directives are binding under Article 249 (ex 189) of the EC Treaty.[34] In this respect, implemented directives do not differ from implemented treaties which have entered into force and, therefore, the Court's ruling that they may contain provisions which must be given direct effect should not be seen as surprising, if one takes the international law model as a benchmark.

The Court of Justice is not itself impinging upon, and is not instructing the national courts to impinge upon, the constitutional prerogatives of legislative and executive powers, if it restricts itself to declaring directly effective only those treaty provisions which give direct rights to individuals or enterprises or are, in any case, of a nature so as to permit their application by the courts.

Moreover, if directives are comparable with treaties, then it is also unsurprising to apply the approach of harmonious interpretation to those provisions of implemented directives which are not deemed to have direct effect. It is only logical that national courts should interpret the national provisions which have been adopted pursuant to a directive, in the light of the relevant clauses of that directive.[35] This contributes in the same way to avoiding State responsibility under Article 226 EC Treaty as such interpretation of treaty provisions contributes to limiting the chances a State runs to be exposed to responsibility under international law.

Where it concerns 'State responsibility', just as national authorities can be challenged before their own Courts for having caused damages in tort to the citizens or enterprises for having failed to properly implement an (even

---

[33] With the exception of special flexibility in certain situations.

[34] Case 41/74 *Van Duyn* [1974] ECR 1337, para. 12.

[35] E.g. Case 14/83 *Von Colson and Kamann* [1984] ECR 1891.

non-self-executing) provision of an international agreement, the Court of Justice can point out to national courts that the same is the case for the improper implementation of provisions of directives, even when these have no direct effect, but serve at least as some kind of *Schutznorm* for the individuals or companies concerned.

All these different aspects of direct effect, harmonious interpretation, or even damages in the absence of direct effect, of Community directives are not at all surprising or new, when one compares them with what would be considered normal in the case of international treaties in most of the Member States.

4 The doctrine of 'direct effect of directives'

However, an extra twist is added, if one considers a number of typical Community characteristics which in my view play a role - either explicitly or implicitly - in the doctrine of 'direct effect of directives' and its attendant aspects, as discussed at the Conference.

The first one of these is that though the parallel between directives and normal international treaties is valid enough, it is valid only as far as its goes. And directives clearly transcend normal treaty-making techniques, even in international organizations such as the ILO, where there is an obligation to put the treaty text before the national authorities for ratification, in that the date of full entry into force and implementation is laid down beforehand in binding fashion for all parties, i.e. the Member States. It is as if parties to a treaty lay down, at the moment of signature, of the adoption of the treaty test, the date of ratification, implementation and entry into force of the treaty, all in one date. It is thus known, at the date of adoption of the directive, when all Member States must be in conformity with it.

Moreover, according to the classical case law, such as *Van Gend en Loos*,[36] the Community Treaties were intended from the beginning to create rights and obligations for individuals as much as for the Member States.

In addition, State responsibility under the Community system is extra strong: the duty of implementation of directives is owed to the Community, for whom the Commission acts, if necessary with the help of the Court of Justice, as enforcer. Recourse to the *exceptio non adimpleti contractus* by other Member States is not tolerated in the Community system; a Member State cannot pay for its delinquency in not implementing a directive by having to suffer non-application of the directives by the other Member States.[37] The only possible result is full conformity, which is all the more important because direc-

---

[36] As cited.

[37] Joined Cases 90/63 and 91/63 *Commission v. Belgium/Luxembourg* [1964] ECR 1279 (dairy products).

tives, like the whole Community legal system, create rights and obligations for individuals and enterprises.

Since the duty to be in conformity is owed to the Community and to the Community citizens, there is great interest in ensuring that rights and obligations resulting from a directive are equally strong everywhere: requiring uniform interpretation (Article 234 EC) and enforcement, including comparable remedies, everywhere throughout the Community.

In order to achieve all this, there is a duty of cooperation incumbent on Member States and their national authorities, both executive and judicial authorities (Article 10 EC) on which the Court of Justice has assiduously built a whole super-structure of case law, ranging from cooperation between Member State courts and itself on judicial matters and between Member States and the Commission in the field of external relations where these fall within the area of mixed competence. These typical Community characteristics are responsible for the following additional, and typically Community, aspects of direct effect and State responsibility.

4.1 Non-implemented directives

First of all, the obligation to be in conformity with a directive at a certain date, has led the Court of Justice to accept direct effect for appropriate provisions of non-implemented directives.[38] The underlying logic is obviously that the Member State which has not implemented the directive at the required date, contrary to its obligation under Community law should not be allowed to get away with this. This is all the more true, since provisions of the directive which are capable of being applied by the Courts are obviously of the kind whereby the Community Treaty intended to create rights and obligations, not merely for the Member States, but also for the Community citizens. Moreover, since the Court, recognizing direct effect for non-implemented directive provisions, is supposed to reprimand the State's delinquency, it is proper that the granting of such direct effect should be limited to 'vertical cases', i.e. in situations where the individual or enterprise must be protected against the State, in this case the State's delinquency.

The perspective that the Member State must not be allowed to profit from its own fault in not implementing a directive at the expense of the rights individuals derive vis-à-vis the Member State from the Community system, may also lead to new and expansive ways of interpreting direct effect.[39] One particular

---

[38] Case 80/86 *Kolpinghuis* [1987] ECR 3969.

[39] Edward (in this volume's chapter I) uses a different tool of analysis to explain some of these phenomena and one which, with the benefit of hindsight, may well be more powerful than mine, namely whether the directive contains an obligation of result incumbent on the State.

evolution that direct effect has gone through in Community law is that not merely provisions granting rights to individuals, but also provisions imposing unconditional obligations on Member States are deemed to have direct effect. They are obviously equally capable of being applied by the Courts, without letting them impinge on the domains of the legislator and the executive. However, even when a directive leaves Member States a certain margin of discretion within which the Member States' authorities must operate and one would normally be inclined to assume that courts should not wish to sit in the chair of the Members' executives, an extensive interpretation of direct effect can nevertheless bestow upon the national courts the function to police the *limits* to this discretion, at least as long as they are clear and unambiguous. Although this approach to direct effect was developed in the *Kraaijeveld* case,[40] a case concerning an *implemented* directive,[41] there is no inherent reason it could not also be applied in the case of non-implemented directives.

If one considers that it is only perhaps a small step from this extensive interpretation of judicial direct effect by way of the duty of cooperation incumbent on national executives to imposing a direct obligation of 'direct effect' on the national executive to respect the limits of the discretion imposed in a directive.[42] Then, one may indeed ask oneself why that should still be called direct effect and not simply supremacy. Such provisions of directives which would have so-called 'direct effect' for national executive authorities would in reality be regulations.

4.2 Directives and individuals

The restriction of direct effect of directives to situations between the citizen and the Member State (vertical direct effect) is a typical Community law restriction which is mitigated by two other Community law approaches to such situations. The one is that, if implementation on the stated date of directives is so important and Member States are not allowed to draw advantage from their failure to implement, harmonious interpretation of non-implemented directives should also be possible. Betlem has usefully documented in his contribution[43] how far the Court can go in prescribing the results of such harmonious interpretation and hence coming very close to the same results as direct effect would have had, even in relations of a horizontal nature, both in respect of implemented and non-implemented directives. Nevertheless, Betlem is fairly critical of some of the results of such 'disguised direct effect' as a result of harmonious interpretation. However, the cases that

---

[40] Case C-72/95 *Kraaijeveld* [1996] ECR I-5403.

[41] Though perhaps an incorrectly implemented directive.

[42] *Kraaijeveld* (as cited), para. 50 et seq.

[43] In this volume's chapter IV.

he mentions in this connection are primarily cases about jurisdiction.[44] Here he seems to lose sight of the rather special position that jurisdictional cases (whether of a public law nature, such as in competition law, or of a quasi private law nature, such as in cases concerning contracts or social security)[45] naturally have for any court. A court cannot but react in such cases and is inevitably bound to consider its own or the executive's power to act or to rule in the light of the interpretation of the Community clauses concerned, seen through the prism of public or private international law rules on jurisdiction. This is the domain of consistent interpretation *'par excellence'*, as we saw above.

The second Community law approach mitigating the consequences of vertical direct effect *only* for provisions from directives, is found in the 'incidental'[46] or 'disguised' vertical direct effect of certain directives.[47] Both Betlem and Dougan seem to regard the cases that are normally mentioned under this heading as somewhat special and difficult to explain.[48] Of the two, Betlem seems to have the most satisfactory explanation by showing that the result in the cases most commonly discussed under this heading (*CIA Security, Unilever Italia* and *Ruiz Bernáldez*)[49] can most easily be explained by the fact that the tortious or contractual liability in issue was a question of national law alone.

4.3   Uniform application and remedies

Finally, the need to achieve equal application of directives throughout the Community, leads to a certain obsession with 'remedies' and their equal application throughout the Community and with equal application of the notion of direct effect itself. All these issues are almost inevitable coloured, when applied by national courts, by the national idiosyncrasies where 'direct effect' is concerned. This was well demonstrated by Besselink, who managed to show that the Community notion of direct effect was strongly influenced by the Dutch discussions about this problem during the successive constitutional reforms of the 1950s, in which Judge Donner of the ECJ played such an important role.[50] That the Community notion of direct effect, having been derived at least in part from Dutch constitutional debates, obtains specific 'national'

---

[44]   Ibid.

[45]   See old case law, such as *Walrave & Koch* and *Prodest*, as cited

[46]   See Betlem's chapter IV in this volume.

[47]   See Dougan (2000).

[48]   See Betlem in chapter IV and Dougan (2000).

[49]   Case C-194/94 *CIA Security* [1996] ECR I-2201; Case C-443/98 *Unilever Italia* [2000] ECR I-7535; Case C-129/94 *Ruiz Bernáldez* [1996] ECR I-1829.

[50]   At the Conference on 'Direct Effect' which preceded the present volume. See also Edward in this volume's chapter I.

character traits is convincingly shown by Gerkrath, who compares the situation in France and in Germany, only to come to the conclusion that the different national approaches in the end are difficult to suppress and persist in spite of the fact that the German and French constitutions have found highly comparable solutions to the EC problem.[51] Although what the constitutions say is largely the same, what judges say that the constitution says is still steeped in national tradition and inevitably influenced by the distinction between the traditionally monist and the traditionally dualist State.

Ward points out how the notion of direct effect and supremacy inexorably lead to concern with the question of 'sufficient and effective sanctions' and 'adequate remedies' in order to enforce directly effective Community law.[52] As was noted above, in my view an extra dimension is added to this problem by the concern about equal enforcement throughout the Community. But questions of remedies and sanctions are by nature steeped in national legal (and social) traditions. A certain tolerance for diversity would, therefore, seem to be neces- sary if the Community is to maintain its unique character. Ward also points out what an important role the 'rights' perspective of direct effect has played in the judicial drive for 'effective sanctions' (at least on an equal level in different Member States) in the Community.

She seems to plead for some restraint with respect to this, in her view almost excessive, role that the emphasis on 'individual rights' plays in the drive for direct effect and its ramifications on the interpretation and application of directives. She rightly asserts that this leads to confusion, when in the case of so-called 'horizontal directives' the right of one stands opposed to the right of the other. A somewhat more modest view as direct effect also contributing to the respect for the separation of powers might be of some assistance here.

Contrary to the view expressed above that there must be some tolerance for diversity in the rather unique Community system, Jans and Prinssen are very wary of differences in the case law of national courts with respect to the direct effect of provisions of directives and their horizontal side-effects.[53] It must be admitted that they have amassed some interesting national case law, demonstrat- ing some considerable divergences. They then attempt to draw a line between the 'acceptable' differences and 'unacceptable' deviations. Differences concern- ing the 'modalities' of the doctrine of directives do not worry them. However, none of the cases they have discovered, seems to fall in this category. They all seem to fall in the category of cases which concern the conditions, the scope and the content of the direct effect doctrine. The remedies for these problems are fairly simple: both sides should fully shoulder their responsibilities: the

---

[51] See his contribution to this volume's chapter VI.

[52] See chapter III of this volume.

[53] See their contribution to this volume's chapter V.

Court of Justice in developing the doctrine more and the national courts in raising more properly preliminary questions, when necessary. Although the material presented is interesting enough, the final result of the analysis is rather conventional, but perhaps inevitably so. The remedies to the travails of the human race are normally not shocking in their newness.

5 Concluding remarks

All the above may equally sound rather simple and straightforward. In reality it was not. The harmonious interpretation was developed by the Court, first for directives and only later for treaties, although the other way round might have been more systematic. Actually, the Court seems to have 'borrowed' from international law practice and doctrine for developing its case law on the direct effect and harmonious interpretation of directives, before actually applying some of this in the domain of the relationship between international law - both customary and treaty law - and Community law. This leads to an interesting kind of cross-fertilization, where notions which originally developed in international law gain as it were an extra twist because they have undergone the influence of the Community system, before being applied to the domain of international law again. In my view, there can be little doubt that notions such as direct effect and harmonious interpretation are now applied with added stringency in the international/national law relationship, even by some Member States' courts, because they have 'passed through' Community law. But to have this hypothesis fully confirmed further research and a new Conference may well be necessary.

Bibliography

ADINOLFI (1998)

A. Adinolfi, "The Judicial Application of Community Law in Italy (1981-1997)", *CMLRev.* 1998, p. 1313-1369.

ALBORS-LLORENS (1998)

A. Albors-Llorens, "Changes in the Jurisdiction of the Court of Justice Under the Amsterdam Treaty", *CMLRev.* 1998, p. 1273-1294.

ALLAND (1997)

D. Alland, "La coutume internationale devant le Conseil d'État: l'existence sans la primauté", *RGDIP* 1997, p. 1053-1067.

ALLAND (1998)

D. Alland, "L'applicabilité directe du droit international du point de vue de l'office du juge: des habits neufs pour une vieille dame ?", *RGDIP* 1998, p. 203-244.

ALLAND (2000)

D. Alland (ed.), *Droit international public* (Paris 2000).

ALSTYNE (1969)

W. Van Alstyne, "A Critical Guide to *Marbury v. Madison*", *Duke Law Journal* 1969, p. 1-47.

AMADOR (1974)

G. Amador e.a. (eds.), *Recent Codification of the Law of State Responsibility for Injuries to Aliens* (New York 1974).

ANDENAS (2000)

M. Andenas, "Liability for Supervisors and Depositors Rights – The BCCI and the Bank of England in the House of Lords", *Euredia* 2000, p. 388-409.

ARNULL (1988)

A. Arnull, Annotation of *Kolpinghuis*, *ELRev.* 1988, p. 42-45.

ARNULL (2000)

A. Arnull a.o., *Wyatt and Dashwood's European Union Law* (London 2000).

ARNULL (2001)

A. Arnull, "Private Applicants and the Action for Annulment Since *Codorníu*", *CMLRev.* 2001, p. 7-52.

AUST (2000)

A. Aust, *Modern Treaty Law and Practice* (Cambridge 2000).

AUTEXIER (1997).

C. Autexier, *Introduction au droit public allemand* (Paris 1997).

BAMFORTH (1999)

N. Bamforth, "The Application of the Human Rights Act 1998 to Public Authorities and Private Bodies", *CLJ* 1999, p. 159-170.

BARBERO (1998)

J.R. Barbero, "La cosumbre internacional, la cláusula *rebus sic stantibus* y el derecho comunitario", *Revista española de derecho internacional* 1998/2, p. 9-34.

BASEDOW (2000)

J. Basedow, "The communitarization of the conflict of laws after the Treaty of Amsterdam", *CMLRev.* 2000, p. 687-708.

BEAUD (1999)

O. Beaud (ed.), *Une science juridique allemande?* (Baden-Baden 1999).

BELOFF (1999)

M. Beloff, "'What Does it All Mean?' Interpreting the Human Rights Act 1998", in: L. Betten (ed.), *The Human Rights Act 1998. What it Means* (The Hague etc. 1999), p. 11-56.

BERRAMDANE (1999)

A. Berramdane, "L'application de la coutume internationale dans l'ordre juridique communautaire", *Cahiers de droit européen* 1999, p. 253-279.

BERROD (2000)

F. Berrod, "La Cour de justice refuse l'invocabilité des accords OMC: essai de régulation de la mondialisation", *RTDE* 2000, p. 419-450.

BETLEM (1993)

G. Betlem, *Civil Liability for Transfrontier Pollution* (London etc. 1993).

BETLEM (1995)

G. Betlem, "The Principle of Indirect Effect of Community Law", *ERPL* 1995, p. 1-19.

BIEBER (1988)

R. Bieber, "On the Mutual Completion of Overlapping Legal Systems: the Case of the European Comunities and the National Legal Orders", *ELRev.* 1988, p. 147-158.

BIONDI (1999)

A. Biondi, "The European Court of Justice and Certain National Procedural Limitations: Not Such a Tough Relationship", *CMLRev.* 1999, p. 1271-1287.

BLECKMANN (1975)

A. Bleckmann, "Die Position des Völkerrechts im inneren Rechtsraum der Europäischen Gemeinschaften. Monismus oder Dualismus der Rechtsordnungen?", *Jahrbuch für Internationales Recht* 1975, p. 300-319.

BLECKMANN (1977)

A. Bleckmann, "Zur Verbindlichkeit des allgemeinen Völkerrechts für internationale Organisationen", *Zeitschrift für ausländisches und öffentliches Recht* 1977, p. 107-121.

BLECKMANN (1981)

A. Bleckmann, "Self-executing Treaty Provisions", in: Bernhardt (ed.), *Encyclopedia of Public International Law* 1981, Installment 1, p. 374-377.

BODANKSY & BRUNNÉE (1998)

D. Bodanksy & J. Brunnée, "The Role of National Courts in the Field of International Environmental Law", *Review of European Community & International Environmental Law* 1998, p. 11-20.

BRAUNSCHWEIG & DE GOUTTES (1995)

A. Braunschweig & R. de Gouttes, "Note à propos des arrêts de 1993 de la 1ère chambre civile de la Cour de cassation sur la convention des Nations Unies relative aux droits de l'enfant", *Gaz. Pal.* 1995, p. 878-879.

BRIDGE (1984)

J. Bridge, "Procedural Aspects of the Enforcement of European Community Law Through the Legal Systems of the Member States", *ELRev.* 1984, p. 28-42.

BROWNLIE (1998)

I. Brownlie, *Principles of Public International Law,* 5th ed. (Oxford 1998).

BUERGENTHAL (1992)

T. Buergenthal, "Self-Executing and Non-Self-Executing Treaties in National and International Law", *Recueil des Cours* 1992, p. 303-400.

CASSESE (1985)

A. Cassese, "Modern Constitutions and International Law", *Recueil des Cours* 1985, p. 394-412.

CASSESE (2001)

A. Cassese, *International Law* (Oxford 2001).

CELS (1997)

CELS, "EC Treaty Project", *ELRev.* 1997, p. 395-516.

CHARME (1991)

J.S. Charme, "The Interim Obligation of Article 18 of the Vienna Convention on the Law of Treaties: Making Sense of an Enigma", *George Washington Journal of International Law & Economics* 1991, p. 71-114.

COMBACAU & SUR (2001)

J. Combacau & S. Sur, *Droit international public* (Paris 2001).

CONFORTI & LABELLA (1990)

B. Conforti & A. Labella, "Invalidity and termination of treaties: the role of national courts", *EJIL* 1990, p. 44-66.

CONFORTI (1993)

B. Conforti, *International Law and the Role of Domestic Legal Systems* (Dordrecht etc. 1993).

CONSEIL D'ETAT (2000)

Conseil d'Etat, *La norme internationale en droit français* (Paris 2000).

COPPEL (1994)

J. Coppel, "Rights, Duties, and the End of Marshall", *MLR* 1994, p. 859-879.

COT (1968)

J.-P. Cot, "La bonne foi et la conclusion des traités", *Revue belge de droit international* 1968, p. 140-159.

COTTIER & SCHEFER (1998)

Th. Cottier & K. N. Schefer, "The Relationship between World Trade Organization Law, National and Regional Law", *Journal of International Economic Law* 1998, p. 83-122.

CRAIG (1997)

P. Craig, "Directives: Direct Effect, Indirect Effect and the Construction of National Legislation", *ELRev.* 1997, p. 519-538.

CRAIG (1998)

P.P. Craig, "Indirect Effect of Directives in the Application of National Legislation", in: M. Andenas & F. Jacobs (eds.), *European Community Law in the English Courts* (Oxford 1998), p. 37-55.

CRAIG & DE BURCA (1998)

P. Craig & G. De Búrca, *EU Law. Text, Cases and Materials*, 2nd ed. (Oxford 1998).

CURTIN (1990)

D. Curtin, "Directives: the Effectiveness of Judicial Protection of Individual Rights", *CMLRev.* 1990, p. 709-739.

DAILLIER (1998)

P. Daillier, "Monisme et dualisme: un débat dépassé?", in: R. Ben Achour & S. Laghmani (eds.), *Droit international et droits internes, développements récents* (Paris 1998), p. 9-21.

DASHWOOD & JOHNSTON (2001)

A. Dashwood & A. Johnston, *The Future of the European Judicial System* (Oxford 2001).

DAVID (1999)

E. David, "Le droit international applicable aux organisations internationales", in: *Mélanges en hommage à Michel Waelbroeck*, I (Brussels 1999), p. 3-22.

DÍETZ-HOCHLEITNER (1998)

J. Díetz-Hochleitner, "Rapport espagnol", in: *Les Directives Communautaires: effets, efficacité, justiciabilité*, Stockholm XVIII FIDE-congress 1998 (I), p. 185-214.

VAN DIJK & VAN HOOF (1998)

P. van Dijk & G.H.J. van Hoof, *Theory and Practice of the European Convention on Human Rights*, 3rd ed. (The Hague 1998).

DOMINICÉ & VOEFFREY (1996)

C. Dominicé & F. Voeffrey, "L'application du droit international général dans l'ordre juridique interne", in: P.M. Eisemann (ed.), *The Integration of International and European Community Law into the National Legal Order. A Study of the Practice in Europe* (The Hague 1996), p. 51-62.

DOMMERING-VAN RONGEN (1991)

L. Dommering-van Rongen, *Produktenaansprakelijkheid* (1991).

DOUGAN (1999)

M. Dougan, "Cutting Your losses in the Enforcement Deficit: A Community Right to the Recovery of Unlawfully Levied Charges", *Cambridge Yearbook of European Legal Studies* 1999, p. 233-268.

DOUGAN (2000)

M. Dougan, "The 'Disguised' Vertical Direct Effect of Directives?", *CLJ* 2000, p. 586-612.

DOUGAN (2002)

M. Dougan, "Enforcing the Single Market. The Judicial Harmonisation of National Remedies and Procedural Rules", forthcoming.in: C. Barnard & S. Scott, *The Law of the Single European Market* (Oxford 2002).

DOYLE & CARNEY (1999)

A. Doyle & T. Carney, "Precaution and Prevention: Giving Effect to Article 130r Without Direct Effect", *European Environmental Law Review* 1999, p. 44-47.

DUPUY (2000)

P.-M. Dupuy, *Droit international public* (Paris 2000).

EDWARD (1998)

D. A.O. Edward, "Direct Effect, the Separation of Powers and the Judicial Enforcement of Obligations", in: *Scritti in onore di Giuseppe Federico Mancini* (Vol. II, Giuffrè 1998), p. 423-443.

EDWARDS (2000)

R.A. Edwards, "Reading Down Legislation under the Human Rights Act", *Legal Studies* 2000, p. 353-371.

EHRICKE (1999)

U. Ehricke, "Die richtlinienkonforme Auslegung nationalen Rechts vor Ende der Umsetzungsfrist einer Richtlinie", *EuZW* 1999, p. 553-559.

EISEMANN (1996)

P.M. Eisemann (ed.), *The Integration of International and European Community Law into the National Legal Order. A Study of the Practice in Europe* (The Hague 1996).

ELIAS (2000)

O. Elias, "General International Law in the European Court of Justice: from Hypothesis to Reality?", *Netherlands Yearbook of International Law* 2000, p. 3-34.

ELIASSON, ABRAHAMSSON & MATTSSON (1998)

D. Eliasson, O. Abrahamsson & D. Mattsson, "Rapport suédois", in: *Les Directives Communautaires: effets, efficacité, justiciabilité*, Stockholm XVIII FIDE-congress 1998 (I), p. 391-402.

EPINEY (1999)

A. Epiney, "Zur Stellung des Völkerrechts in der EU", *EuZW* 1999, p. 5-11.

ERADES (1980)

L. Erades, "International Law in the Netherlands Legal Order", in: H.F. van Panhuys e.a. (eds.), *International Law in the Netherlands* 1980, p. 376-432.

ERADES (1993)

L. Erades, *Interactions between International and Municipal Law. A Comparative-law Study* (The Hague 1993).

FAVOREU (1993)

L. Favoreu, "Le contrôle de la constitutionnalité du traité de Maastricht et le développement du «droit constitutionnel international»", *RGDIP* 1993, p. 39-64.

FISCHER (1998)

P. Fischer, Annotation Case T-115/94, *CMLRev.* 1998, p. 765-781.

FITZMAURICE (1958)

G. Fitzmaurice ,"The General Principles of International Law – Considered from the Standpoint of the Rule of Law", *Recueil des Cours* 1957 II, Vol. 92. (1958), p. 1-227.

FITZMAURICE (1986)

G. Fitzmaurice, *The Law and Procedure of the International Court of Justice* (Cambridge 1986).

FLAUSS (2001)

J.-F. Flauss, "Rapport français", in: J. Schwarze (ed.), *The birth of a European constitutional order, The interaction of national and European constitutional law* (Baden-Baden 2001), p. 25-107.

FOX, GARDNER & WICKREMASINGHE (1996)

H. Fox, P. Gardner & C. Wickremasinghe, "The Reception of European Community Law into Domestic Law", in: P.M. Eisemann (ed.), *The Integration of International and European Community Law into the National Legal Order. A Study of the Practice in Europe* (The Hague 1996), p. 27-38.

FROWEIN (1993)

J.A. Frowein, "Incorporation of the Convention into Domestic Law", in: J. Gardner (ed.), *Aspects of Incorporation of the European Convention into Domestic Law*, The British Institute of International and Comparative Law and The British Institute of Human Rights (London 1993), p. 2-11.

FROWEIN & OELLERS-FRAHM (1996)

J.A. Frowein & K. Oellers-Frahm, "L'application des traités dans l'ordre juridique interne", in: P.M. Eisemann (ed.), *The Integration of International and European Community Law into the National Legal Order. A Study of the Practice in Europe* (The Hague 1996), p. 11-25

FURLAN (1999)

S. Furlan, "L'utilizzazione del mutamento di circostanze a fini sanzionatori da parte della Communità : riflessioni in margine alla sentenza *Racke*", *Il Diritto dell'Unione Europea* 1999, p. 315-335.

GAGLIARDI (1999)

A. F. Gagliardi, "The Right of Individuals to Invoke the Provisions of Mixed Agreements before the National Courts: A New Message from Luxembourg?", *ELRev.* 1999, p. 276-292.

GANSHOF VAN DER MEERSCH (1975)

W. Ganshof van der Meersch, "L'ordre juridique des Communautés européennes et le droit international", *Rec. Cours* 1975, Vol. V, 1, p. 148.

GARCIA DE ENTERRIA (1993)

E. Garcia de Enterria, "The Extension of the Jurisdiction of National Administrative Authorities by Community Law: the Judgment of the Court of Justice in *Borelli* and Article 5 of the EC Treaty", *YBEL* 1993, p. 19-37.

GAUTRON & GRARD (2000)

J.-C. Gautron &L. Grard, "Le droit international dans la construction de l'Union européenne", in: *Droit international et droit communautaire, perspective actuelles* (Paris 2000), p. 11 *et seq.*

GERKRATH (1995)

J. Gerkrath, L'arrêt du Bundesverfassungsgericht du 22 mars 1995 sur la directive « télévision sans frontières ». Les difficultés de la répartition des compétences entre trois niveaux de législation", *RTDE* 1995/3, p. 539-559.

GERKRATH (1997)

J. Gerkrath, *L'émergence d'un droit constitutionnel pour l'Europe* (Brussels 1997).

VAN GERVEN (1990)

W. van Gerven, "EC Jurisdiction in Antitrust Matters: the *Wood Pulp* Judgment", in: B. Hawk (ed.), *1992 and EEC/U.S. Competition and Trade Law* (New York 1990), p. 451-483.

VAN GERVEN (1995)

W. van Gerven, "Bridging the Community Gap Between Community and National Law: Towards a Principle of Homogeneity in the Field of Legal Remedies", *CMLRev.* 1995, p. 679-702.

VAN GERVEN (1998)

W. van Gerven, "Taking Article 215 Seriously", in: J. Beatson & T. Trimidas (eds.), *New Directions in European Public Law*, (Oxford 1998), p. 35-47.

VAN GERVEN (2000)

W. van Gerven, "Of Rights, Remedies and Procedures", *CMLRev.* 2000, p. 501-536.

VAN GERVEN (2001)

W. van Gerven, "Substantive Remedies for the Private Enforcement of EC Antitrust Rules Before National Courts", to appear in *European Competition Law Annual* 2001, temporarily available at http://www.iue.it/RSC/competition2001(papers).html.

GILLIAMS (2000)

H. Gilliams, "Horizontale werking van richtlijnen: dogma's en realiteit", in: H. Cousy e.a. (eds.), *Liber Amicorum Walter van Gerven* (Deurne 2000), p. 223-245.

GILLIAUX (1998)

P. Gilliaux, "Contribution des juges belges à l'application du droit communautaire en matière de protection de l'environnement", in: *Les juges et la protection de l'environnement* (Bruxelles 1998), p. 111-131.

GREAVES (1996)

R. Greaves, "The Nature and Binding Effect of Decisions under Article 189 EC", *ELRev.* 1996, p. 3-16.

GREWE & OBERDORFF (1999)

C. Grewe & H. Oberdorff, *Les constitutions des États de l'Union européenne, La documentation française* (Paris 1999).

GREWE & RUIZ FABRI (1995)

C. Grewe & H. Ruiz Fabri, *Droits constitutionnels européens* (Paris 1995).

GUNDEL (2001)

J. Gundel, "Neue Grenzlinien für die Direktwirkung nicht umgesetzter EG-Richtlinien ubter Privaten", *EuZW* 2001, p. 143-149.

HÄBERLE (1995)

P. Häberle, "Die europäische Verfassungsstaatlichkeit", *KritV* 3/1995, p. 298-312.

HAHN & SCHUSTER (1995)

M.J. Hahn & G. Schuster, "Le droit des Etats membres de se prévaloir en justice d'un accord liant la Communauté. L'invocabilité du GATT dans l'affaire République fédérale d'Allemagne contre Conseil de l'Union européenne", *RGDIP* 1995, p. 367-384.

HARHOFF (1996)

F. Harhoff, "Danemark", in: P.M. Eisemann (ed.), *The Integration of International and European Community Law into the National Legal Order. A Study of the Practice in Europe* (The Hague 1996), p. 151-182.

HARRIS, O'BOYLE & WARBRICK (1995)

D.J. Harris, M. O'Boyle & C. Warbrick, *Law of the European Convention on Human Rights* (London 1995).

HARTLEY (1994)

T.C. Hartley, *The Foundations of European Community Law*, 3rd ed. (Oxford 1994).

HARTLEY (1998)

T.C. Hartley, *The Foundations of European Community Law*, 4th ed. (Oxford 1998).

HEUKELS & MCDONNELL (1997)

T. Heukels & A. McDonnell, *The Action for Damages in Community Law* (The Hague etc. 1997).

HIGGINS (2000)

R. Higgins, "Dualism in the Face of a Changing Legal Culture", in: M. Andenas & D. Fairgrieve, *Judicial Review in International Perspective, Liber Amicorum in Honour of Lord Slynn of Hadley* (Vol. II, The Hague 2000), p. 9-22.

HILSON & DOWNES (1999)

C. Hilson & T. Downes, "Making Sense of Rights: Community Rights in EC Law", *ELRev.* 1999, p. 121-138.

VAN HOEK (2001)

A.A.H. van Hoek, Casenote on *Ingmar*, *SEW* 2001, p. 195-197.

HOFFMEISTER (1998)

F. Hoffmeister, "Die Bindung der Europäischen Gemeinschaft and das Völkergewohnheitsrecht der Verträge", *Europäisches Wirtschafts- und Steuerrecht* 1998, p. 365-371.

HOSKINS (1996)

M. Hoskins, "Tilting the Balance: Supremacy and National Procedural Rules", *ELRev.* 1996, p. 365-377.

HUNT 1998

M. Hunt, *Using Human Rights Law in English Courts* (Oxford 1998).

IWASAWA (1986)

Y. Iwasawa, "The Doctrine of Self-executing Treaties in the United States: A Critical Analysis", *Virginia Journal of International Law* 1986, p. 627-692.

IWASAWA (1997)

Y. Iwasawa, "International Human Rights Adjudication in Japan", in: B. Conforti & F. Francioni (eds.), *Enforcing International Human Rights in Domestic Courts* (The Hague 1997), p. 223-293.

JACKSON (1997)

J.H. Jackson, *The World Trading System. Law and Policy of International Economic Relations*, 2nd ed. (Cambridge 1997).

JACKSON (1998)

J.H. Jackson, *The World Trade Organisation. Constitution and Jurisprudence* (London 1998).

JANIS, KAY & BRADLEY (1978)

M. A. Janis, R. Kay & A. Bradley, *European Human Rights Law Text and Materials*, 2nd ed. (Oxford 2000).

JANS (1994)

J.H. Jans, "Rechterlijke uitleg als implementatie-instrument van EG-richtlijnen: spanning tussen instrument en rechtszekerheid", in: T. Hoogenboom & L.J.A. Damen (eds.), *In de sfeer van administratief recht*, Konijnenbelt bundel (Utrecht 1994).

JANS E.A. (1999)

J.H. Jans, R. de Lange, S. Prechal & R.J.G.M. Widdershoven, *Inleiding tot het Europees bestuursrecht* (Nijmegen 1999).

JANS (2000)

J.H. Jans, *European Environmental Law* (Groningen 2000).

JANS & DE JONG (1999)

J.H. Jans & M. de Jong, "Interne harmonisatie van rechtsbeschermingsclausules in het secudaire gemeenschapsrecht?", *RegelMaat* 1999, p. 73-83.

JANS & DE JONG (2002)

J.H. Jans & M. de Jong, "Somewhere between Direct Effect and Rewe/ Comet", in: K.-H. Ladeur (ed.), *The Europeanisation of Administrative Law: Transforming National Decision-Making Procedures* (Aldershot 2002), p. 68-92.

JARASS (1994)

H. D. Jarass, *Grundfragen der innerstaatlichen Bedeutung des EG-Rechts* (Köln 1994).

JOHNSTON (2001)

A. Johnston, "Judicial Reform and the Treaty of Nice", *CMLRev.* 2001, p. 499-523.

JOLIET (1983)

R. Joliet, *Le droit institutionnel des Communautés européennes. Les institutions - Les sources - Les rapports entres ordres juridiques* (Liège 1983).

KAHIL (1998)

B. Kahil, Annotation Case T-115/94, *EuZW* 1998, p. 671-672.

KAPTEYN & VERLOREN VAN THEMAAT (1998)

P.J.G Kapteyn & P. VerLoren van Themaat, *Introduction to the Law of the European Communities*, 3rd ed. (London 1998).

KIRCHHOF (1994)

P. Kirchhof, "Das Maastricht-Urteil des Bundesverfassungsgerichts", in: Mommelhoff & Kirchhof (eds.), *Der Staatenverbund der Europäischen Union* (Heidelberg 1994), p. 11-24.

KLABBERS (1999A)

J. Klabbers, Annotation Case C-162/96, *CMLRev.* 1999, p. 179-189.

KLABBERS (1999B)

J. Klabbers, "Re-inventing the Law of Treaties: the Contribution of the EC Courts", *Netherlands Yearbook of International Law* 1999, p. 45-74.

KLEIN (1988)

E. Klein, *Unmittelbare Geltung, Anwendbarkeit und Wirkung von Europäischem Gemeinschaftsrecht*, Vorträge, Reden und Berichte am Europa Institut no. 119 (Saarbrücken 1988).

KNOP (2000)

K. Knop, "Here and there: international law in domestic courts", *New York University journal of international law and politics* 2000, p. 501-535.

KOH (1991)

H.H. Koh, "Transnational Public Law Litigation", *Yale Law Journal* 1991, p. 2347-2402.

KOKOTT (1996)

J. Kokott, "German constitutional jurisprudence and European integration", *EPL* 1996, p. 237-269 and 413-436.

KOKOTT & HOFFMEISTER (1999)

J. Kokott & F. Hoffmeister, Annotation Case C-162/96, *American Journal of International Law* 1999, p. 205-209.

KOLB (1998)

R. Kolb, "La bonne foi en droit international public", *Revue belge de droit international* 1998, p. 661-732.

KUIJPER (1998)

P.J. Kuijper, "The Court and the Tribunal of the EC and the Vienna Convention on the Law of Treaties 1969", *LIEI* 1998, p. 1-23.

KUIJPER (1999)

P.J. Kuijper, Annotation Case T-115/94 and Case C-162/96, *SEW* 1999, 65-67.

KUIJPER (2002)

P.J. Kuijper, "From Dyestuffs to Kosovo wine: From avoidance to acceptance by the Community Courts of Customary International Law as Limit to Community Action", *Liber in memoriam Herman Meyers*, forthcoming.

KVJATKOVSKI (1997)

V. Kvjatkovski, "What is an 'Emanation of the State'? An Educated Guess", *EPL* 1997, p. 329-338.

LACKHOFF & HAROLD NYSSENS (1998)
> K. Lackhoff & H. Nyssens, "Direct Effect of Directives in Triangular Situations", *ELRev.* 1998, p. 397-413.

LAUTERPACHT (1978)
> H. Lauterpacht, *International Law. Being the Collected Papers of Hersch Lauterpacht*, E. Lauterpacht (ed.), (Vol. II, Cambridge etc. 1978).

LAUWAARS & TIMMERMANS (1997)
> R.H. Lauwaars & C.W.A. Timmermans, *Europees gemeenschapsrecht in kort bestek* (Deventer 1997).

LEBEN (1998)
> C. Leben, "Hans Kelsen and the Advancement of International Law", *EJIL* 1998, p. 287-305.

LEIGH & LUSTGARTEN (1999)
> I. Leigh & L. Lustgarten, "Making Rights Real: the Courts, Remedies, and the Human rights Act", *CLJ* 1999, p. 509-545.

LENAERTS E.A. (1999)
> K. Lenaerts e.a., *Procedural Law of the European Union* (London 1999).

LENAERTS & VAN NUFFEL (1999)
> K. Lenaerts & P. Van Nuffel, *Constitutional Law of the European Union* (London 1999).

LENAERTS & DE SMIJTER (1999-2000)
> K. Lenaerts & E. De Smijter, "The European Union as an Actor under International Law", *YBEL* 1999-2000, p. 95-138.

LENZ E.A. (2000)
> M. Lenz e.a., "Horizontal What? Back to basics", *ELRev.* 2000, p. 509-522.

LERAY & POTTEAU (1999)
> E. Leray & A. Potteau, "Le droit coutumier international et l'ordre juridique communautaire", *La Semaine Juridique (édition générale)* 1999, II 10022, p. 276-281.

LHERNOULD (1999)
> J.-Ph. Lhernould, "Un employeur peut-il s'opposer à la demande d'une de ses salariées de travailler la nuit?", *Droit Social* 1999, p. 129-132.

LIM & ELIAS (1997)
> C. Lim & O. Elias, "The Role of Treaties in the Contemporary International Legal Order", *Nordic Journal of International Law* 1997, p. 1-22.

LINDELL (2000)
> G. Lindell, "Invalidity, Disapplication and the Construction of Acts of Parliament: Their Relationship with Parliamentary Sovereignty in the Light of the European Communities Act and the Human Rights Act", in: A. Dashwood & A. Ward (eds.), *The Cambridge Yearbook of European Legal Studies*, 1999 (Vol. 2, Oxford 2000), p. 399-415.

LOWE (1998)

V. Lowe, "Can the European Community Bind the Member States on Questions of Customary International Law?", in: M. Koskenniemi (ed.), *International Law Aspects of the European Union* (The Hague 1998), p.149-168.

LOUIS (1990)

J.-V. Louis, *The Community Legal Order*, 2 nd ed. (Luxembourg 1990).

MANCINI (1989)

G.F. Mancini, "The Making of a Constitution for Europe", *CMLRev.* 1989, p. 595-614.

MANIN (1987)

Ph. Manin, "The European Communities and the Vienna Convention on the Law of Treaties between States and International Organisations or between International Organisations", *CMLRev.* 1987, p. 457-481.

MARTENS (2000)

S.K. Martens, "De grenzen van de rechtsvormende taak van de rechter", *Nederlands Juristenblad* 2000, p. 747-758.

MCDADE (1985)

P. McDade, "The Interim Obligation between Signature and Ratification of a Treaty", *Netherlands International Law Review* 1985, p. 5-47.

MCDOUGAL (1977)

M. McDougal, "The Impact of International Law upon National Law: a Policy-oriented Perspective", in: *Studies in World Public Order* (New Haven 1987), p. 157-236.

MEESSEN (1976)

K.M. Meessen, "The Application of Rules of Public International Law within Community Law", *CMLRev.* 1976, p. 485-501.

MEHDI (1999)

R. Mehdi, Annotation Case C-162/96, *Journal du droit international* 1999, p. 527-530.

MENDELSON (1998)

M.H. Mendelson, "The Formation of Customary International Law", 272 *Rec.Cours* 1998, p. 155-410.

MENGOZZI (1995)

P. Mengozzi, "Les droits des citoyens de l'Union européenne des accords de Marrakech", *Revue du marché unique européen* 1994, p. 165-174.

MENGOZZI (1997)

P. Mengozzi, "Evolution de la méthode suivie par la jurisprudence communautaire en matière de protection de la confiance légitime", *Revue du marché unique européen* 4/1997, p. 13-29.

MIRKINE-GUETZÉVITCH (1933)

B. Mirkine-Guetzévitch, *Le droit constitutionnel international* (Paris 1933).

MORGENSTERN (1950)

F. Morgenstern, "Judicial Practice and the Supremacy of International Law", *BYIL* 1950, p. 42-92.

MORRIS (1991)

P. E. Morris, "EEC Directives and the State", *European Business Law Review* 1991, p. 34-45.

NGUYEN QUOC DINH, DALLIER & PELLET (1999)

Nguyen Quoc Dinh, P. Dallier & A. Pellet, *Droit International Public,* 6th ed. (Paris 1999).

N.N. (1998)

N.N., La coopération franco-allemande en Europe à l'aube du XXIème siècle (Aix-en-Provence 1998).

NOGUERES & BARBERO (1993)

L. Nogueres & R. Barbero, "Community law in Spain", *CMLRev.* 1993, p. 1135-1154.

NÖLL (1986)

H.-H. Nöll, *Die Völkerrechtssubjektivität der Europäischen Gemeinschaften und deren Bindung an das allgemeine Völkerrecht* (Baden-Baden 1986), p. 60-64.

OJANEN (2000)

T. Ojanen, "The Changing Concept of Direct Effect of European Community Law", *European Review of Public Law* 2000, p. 1253-1255.

OTT (2001)

A. Ott, "Thirty Years of Case-law by the European Court of Justice on International Law: A Pragmatic Approach Towards its Integration", in: V. Kronenberger (ed.), *The EU and the International Legal Order: Discord or Harmony?* (The Hague 2001), p. 95-140.

PALMETER & MAVROIDIS (1999)

D. Palmeter & P.C. Mavroidis, *Dispute Settlement in the World Trade Organization: Practice and Procedure* (The Hague 1999).

VAN PANHUYS (1964)

H.F. Van Panhuys, "Relations and interactions between international and national scenes of law", *Recueil des Cours* 1964, p. 1-89.

VAN PANHUYS (1965-66)

H.F. van Panhuys, "Conflicts between the Law of the European Communities and Other Rules of International Law", *CMLRev.* 1965-66, p. 420-449.

PERNICE (1999)

I. Pernice, "Multilevel Constitutionalism and the Treaty of Amsterdam: European Constitution-Making Revisited?", *CMLRev.* 1999, p. 703-750.

PESCATORE (1983)

P. Pescatore, "The Doctrine of 'Direct Effect': An Infant Disease of Community Law", *ELRev.* 1983, p. 155-177.

PETERS (1997)

A. Peters, "The Position of International Law Within the European Community Legal Order", *German Yearbook of International Law* 1997, p. 9-77.

PETERSMANN (1983)

E.-U. Petersmann, "Application of GATT by the Court of Justice of the European Communities", *CMLRev.* 1983, p. 397-437.

PETERSMANN (1986)

E.-U. Petersmann, "The EEC as a GATT Member – Legal Conflicts Between GATT Law and European Community Law", in: M. Hilf, F.G. Jacobs and E.-U. Petersmann (eds.), *The European Community and GATT* (Deventer 1986), p. 23-71.

PETIT (1999)

Y. Petit, "La Cour de Justice des Communautés européennes et les rapports droit international/droit communautaire", *Recueil Dalloz* 1999, Chron., p. 184-188.

PISILLO-MAZZESCHI (1999)

R. Pisillo-Mazzeschi, "International Obligations to Provide for Reparation Claims?", in: A. Randelzhofer & C. Tomuschat (eds.), *State Responsibility and the Individual. Reparation in Instances of Grave Violations of Human Rights* (The Hague 1999), p. 149-172.

PLÖTNER (1998)

J. Plötner, "Report on France", in: A.-M. Slaughter, A. Stone Sweet & J.H.H. Weiler (Eds.), *The European Court and National Courts – Doctrine and Jurisprudence* (Oxford 1998), p. 41-75.

PRECHAL (1995)

S. Prechal, *Directives in European Community Law* (Oxford 1995).

PRECHAL (1998)

S. Prechal, "Community law in National Courts: The Lessons from Van Schijndel", *CMLRev* 1998, p. 681-706.

PRECHAL (2000)

S. Prechal, "Does Direct Effect Still Matter?", *CMLRev.* 2000, p. 1047-1069.

PRECHAL (2001)

S. Prechal, "Judge-made Harmonisation of National Procedural Rules: a Bridging Perspective", in: J. Wouters & J. Stuyck (eds.), *Principles of Proper Conduct for Supranational, State and Private Actors in the European Union: Towards a Ius Commune. Essays in honour of Walter van Gerven* (Antwerpen 2001), p. 39-58.

PRECHAL & HANCHER (2002)

S. Prechal & L. Hancher, "Individual Environmental Rights: a Conceptual Pollution in EU Environmental Law", *Oxford Yearbook of European Environmental Law* 2002, p. 89-115.

PUISSOCHET (1998)

J.-P. Puissochet, "La place du droit international dans la jurisprudence de la Cour de Justice des Communautés européennes", in: *Scritti in onore di Giuseppe Frederico Mancini* (Vol II, Giuffrè 1998), p. 779-807.

PUISSOCHET (2000)

J.-P. Puissochet, "La Cour de justice des Communautés européennes et la Constitution des États membres", in: *La constitution face à l'Europe* (Paris 2000), p. 77-89.

RIESEFELD (1980)

S. A. Riesefeld, "The Doctrine of Self-Executing Treaties and US v. Postal: Win at any Price?", *American Journal of International Law* 1980, p. 892-904.

ROGOFF (1980)

M.A. Rogoff, "The International Legal Obligations of Signatories to an Unratified Treaty", *Maine Law Review* 1980, p. 263-299.

ROUSSEAU (1993)

D. Rousseau, *Droit du contentieux constitutionnel* (Paris 1993).

RUFFERT (1996)

M. Ruffert, *Subjektive Rechte im Umweltrecht der Europäischen Gemeinschaft* (Heidelberg 1996).

SAURON (2000)

J.-L. Sauron, *L'application du droit de l'Union européenne en France* (Paris 2000).

SCHERMERS (1975)

H.G. Schermers, "Community Law and International Law", *CMLRev.* 1975, p. 77-90.

SCHERMERS (2000)

H.G. Schermers, "European Remedies in the Field of Human Rights" in: C. Kilpatrick, T. Novitz and P. Skidmore (eds.), *The Future of Remedies in Europe* (Oxford 2000), p. 205-211.

SCHREUER (1974)

C. Schreuer, "The Authority of International Judicial Practice in Domestic Courts", *ICLQ* 1974, p. 681-708.

SCHWARZE (1983)

J. Schwarze, "Das allgemeine Völkerrecht in den innergemeinschaftlichen Rechtsbeziehungen", *Europarecht* 1983, p. 1-39.

SHAW (1997)

M. N. Shaw, *International Law*, 4th ed. (Cambridge 1997).

SIMMA E.A. (1997)

B. Simma e.a., "The Role of German Courts in the Enforcement of International Human Rights", in: B. Conforti & F. Francioni (eds.), *Enforcing International Human Rights in Domestic Courts*, The Hague 1997, p. 71-109.

SIMMONDS (1975)

K. Simmonds, "*Van Duyn* v *Home Office*: the Direct Effectiveness of Directives", *ICLQ* 1975, p. 419-437.

SLOT (1994)

P.J. Slot, Comment on case C-286/90 *Poulsen* and *Diva Navigation*, *CMLRev.* 1994, p. 147-153.

SLOT (1996)

P.J. Slot, "Comment on case C-194/94, *Cia Security*", *CMLRev* 1996, p. 1035-1050.

SORENSEN (1968)

M. Sorensen (ed.), *Manual of Public International Law* (New York 1968).

SPIERMANN (1999)

O. Spiermann, "The Other Side of the Story: an Unpopular Essay on the Making of the European Community Legal Order", *European Journal of International Law* 1999, p. 763-789.

STARMER (2001)

K. Starmer, *Blackstone's Human Rights Digest* (London 2001).

STEIN (1981)

E. Stein, "Lawyers, Judges, and the Making of a Transnational Constitution", *AJIL* 1981, p. 1-27.

STEIN (1994)

E. Stein, "International Law in Internal Law: Toward Internationalization of Central-Eastern European Constitutions?", *AJIL* 1994, p. 427-450.

STIRLING (2000)

S. Stirling-Zanda, *L'application judiciaire du droit international coutumier. Etude comparée de la pratique européenne* (Zürich 2000).

TAMMES (1962)

A.J.P. Tammes, "The Obligation to Provide Local Remedies", in: *Volkenrechtelijke Opstellen aangeboden aan prof. dr. Gesina H.J. van der Molen* (Kampen 1962), p. 152-168.

TASH (1993)

A.P. Tash, "Remedies for European Community Claims in Member State Courts: Toward a European Standard", *Columbia Journal of Transnational Law* 1993, p. 377-401.

TIMMERMANS (1979)

C.W.A. Timmermans, "Directives: Their Effect within National Legal Systems", *CMLRev.* 1979, p. 533-555.

TIMMERMANS (1999)

C. Timmermans, "The EU and Public International Law", *European Foreign Affairs Review* 1999, p. 181-194.

TRAVERS (1998)

N. Travers, "Community Directives: Effects, Efficiency, Justiciability", *Irish Journal of European Law* 1998, p. 165-230.

TREBILCOCK & HOWSE (1999)

M.J. Trebilcock. & R. Howse, *The Regulation of International Trade*, 2nd ed. (New York 1999).

TRIDIMAS (1999)

T. Tridimas, *The General Principles of EC Law* (Oxford 1999).

TRIDIMAS (2001)

T. Tridimas, "Liability for Breach of Community Law: Growing up and Mellowing Down?", *CMLRev.* 2001, p. 301-332.

VANDAMME & REESTMAN (2001)

T. Vandamme & J.-H. Reestman (eds.), *Ambiguity in the Rule of Law, The interface between national and international legal systems* (Groningen 2001).

VANHAMME (2001A)

J. Vanhamme, *Volkenrechtelijke Beginselen in het Europees Recht* (Groningen 2001).

VANHAMME (2001B)

J. Vanhamme, "Inroepbaarheid van verdragen en volkenrechtelijke beginselen voor de Europese rechter: stand van zaken", *SEW* 2001, p. 247-256.

VÁZQUEZ (1992)

C.M. Vázquez, "Treaty-based Rights and Remedies of Individuals", *Columbia Law Review* 1992, p. 1082-1163.

VERESHCHETIN (1996)

V. S. Vereshchetin, "New Constitutions and the Old Problem of the Relationship between International Law and National Law", *EJIL* 1996, p. 29-41.

VERHOEVEN (1997)

J. Verhoeven, "Abus, fraude ou habilité? A propos de l'arrêt *Poulsen* (CJCE)", in: *La loyauté. Mélanges offerts à Etienne Cerexhe* (Brussel, Larcier, 1997), p. 407-425.

VERHOEVEN (2000)

A. Verhoeven, "The Application in Belgium of the Duties of Loyalty and Co-operation" (Fide report), *SEW* 2000, p. 328-340.

DE VISSCHER (1952)

P. de Visscher, "Les tendances internationales des Constitutions modernes", *RCADI* 1952-I (Vol. 80), p. 515-578.

VITZTHUM (1998)

W.G. Vitzthum, "Gemeinschaftsgericht und Verfassungsgericht – rechtsvergleichende Aspekte", *JZ* 1998, p. 161-167.

VOITOCICH (1995)

S.A. Voitocich, *International Economic Organisations in the International Legal Process* (Dordrecht 1995).

WAELBROECK (1974)

M. Waelbroeck, "Effect of GATT within the Legal Order of the EEC", *Journal of World Trade* 1974, p. 614-623.

WARD (2000A)

A. Ward, *Judicial Review of the Rights of Private Parties in EC Law* (Oxford 2000).

WARD (2000B)

A. Ward, "The Limits of the Uniform Application of Community Law and Effective Judicial Review: A Look Post-Amsterdam" in: C. Kilpatrick e.a. (eds.), *The Future of Remedies in Europe* (Oxford 2000).

WEATHERILL (1996)

S. Weatherill, "Compulsory Notification of Draft Technical Regulations: the Contribution of Directive 83/189 to the Management of the Internal Market", *YBEL* 1996, p. 129-204.

WEATHERILL (2001)

S. Weatherill, "Breach of Directives and Breach of Contract", *ELRev.* 2001, p. 177-186.

WEIL (1992)

P. Weil, "Le droit international en quête de son identité. Cours général de droit international public", *Recueil des Cours* 1992, p. 220-223.

WEILER (1981)

J. Weiler, "The Community Legal System: the Dual Character of Supranationalism", *YBEL* 1981, p.267-306.

WINTER (1972)

J.A. Winter, "Direct Applicability and Direct Effect. Two Distinct and Different Concepts in Community Law", *CMLRev.* 1972, p. 425-438.

WISSINK (2001)

M.H. Wissink, *Richtlijnconforme interpretatie van burgerlijk recht* (Deventer 2001).

WISSINK (2002)

M.H. Wissink, "Staatsaansprakelijkheid voor falend banktoezicht; het oordeel van de House of Lords in de Three Rivers-zaak", *SEW* 2002, p. 93-97.

DE WITTE (1995)

B. De Witte, "Sovereignty and European Integration: The Weight of Legal Tradition", *MJ* 1995, p. 145-173.

DE WITTE (1999)

B. de Witte, "Direct Effect, Supremacy, and the Nature of the Legal Order", in: P. Craig and G. De Búrca (eds.), *The Evolution of EU Law* (Oxford 1999), p. 178-213.

WOUTERS (2002)

J. Wouters, "De Europese Unie als internationale actor na het Verdrag van Nice", *Nederlands Tijdschrift voor Europees Recht* 2002, p. 62-69.

WYATT (1983)

D. Wyatt, "The Direct Effect of Community Social Law – Not Forgetting Directives", *ELRev.* 1983, p. 241-248.

ZIMMER (2001)

W. Zimmer, "De nouvelles bases pour la coopération entre la Cour constitutionnelle fédérale et la Cour de justice de Luxembourg?", *Europe*, March 2001, p. 3-6.

European Court of Justice

Case 8/55 *Fedechar* [1956] ECR 245   5, 6

Case 6/60 *Humblet* [1960] ECR 559   5

Case 10/61 *Commission* v. *Italy* [1962] ECR 1   193

Case 26/62 *Van Gend en Loos*
   [1963] ECR 1   6, 7, 25, 26, 50, 108, 129, 132, 171, 185, 242, 257, 262

Joined Cases 29/63, 31/63, 36/63, 39-47/63 and 50/63
   Usines de la Providence v. *High Authority* [1965] ECR 911   69

Joined Cases 90/63 and 91/63 *Commission* v. *Belgium/Luxemburg* [1964]
   ECR 1279   262

Case 6/64 *Costa/ENEL* [1964] ECR 585   6, 26, 159, 166, 185, 257, 260

Case 57/65 *Lütticke* [1966] ECR 205   145

Case 28/67 *Mölkerei-Zentrale* [1968] ECR 585   108

Case 34/67 *Lück* [1968] ECR 346   35

Case 48/69 *Imperial Chemical Industries* v. *Commission*
   [1972] ECR 619   185, 259

Case 11/70 *Internationale Handelsgesellschaft* [1970] ECR 1125   210

Case 5/71 *Schöppenstedt* [1971] ECR 975   53, 56

Joined Cases 21-24/72 *International Fruit*
   [1972] ECR 1219   7, 197-198, 216, 219, 244

Joined Cases 6/73 and 7/73 *Istituto Chemioterapico Italiano*
   and *Commercial Solvents* v. *Commission* [1974] ECR 223   185

Case 9/73 *Schlüter* [1973] ECR 1135   219

Case 181/73 *Haegeman* [1974] ECR 449   8, 215-216

Case 26/74 *Roquette Frères* [1976] ECR 677   70

Case 36/74 *Walrave & Koch* [1974] ECR 1405   259, 265

Case 41/74 *Van Duyn* [1974] ECR 1337   9, 45, 51, 186-187, 244, 261

Case 43/75 *Defrenne II* [1976] ECR 455   68, 123

Joined Cases 3/76, 4/76 and 6/76 *Kramer* [1976] ECR 1279   186-187

Case 33/76 *Rewe* [1976] ECR 1989   48, 50, 54, 73, 120, 242

Case 45/76 *Comet* [1976] ECR 2043   24, 25, 48, 50, 54, 73, 120, 241

Case 61/77 *Commission* v. *Ireland* [1978] ECR 417   187

Joined Cases 83/76, 94/76, 4/77, 15/77 and 40/77 *HNL*
   [1978] ECR 1209   53, 56, 58

Case 106/77 *Simmenthal* [1978] ECR 629   34, 108, 260

Ruling 1/78 *Draft Convention of the IAEA* [1978] ECR 2151   215

Case 148/78 *Ratti* [1979] ECR 1629   85

Case 238/78 *Ireks-Arkady* [1979] ECR 2955   58, 71

Case 265/78 *Ferwerda* [1980] ECR 716   120

Case 44/79 *Hauer* [1979] ECR 3727   210

Case 130/79 *Express Dairy Foods* [1980] ECR 1887   70

Case 812/79 *Attorney General* v. *Burgoa* [1980] ECR 2787   193

Case 244/80 *Foglia* v. *Novello* [1981] ECR 3045   *186*

Case 270/80 *Polydor* [1982] ECR 329   *8*

Case 8/81 *Becker* [1982] ECR 53   *45, 107, 111-112, 162*

Case 17/81 *Pabst & Richarz* [1982] ECR 1331   *217*

Case 60/81 *IBM* [1981] ECR 2639   *199*

Case 104/81 *Kupferberg* [1982] ECR 3641   *8, 185-186, 193, 215-217, 219, 254*

Joined Cases 115/81 and 116/81 *Adoui and Cornuaille* [1982] ECR 1665   *187*

Case 266/81 *SIOT* [1983] ECR 731   *219*

Case 267/81 *SPI and SAMI* [1983] ECR 801   *219*

Case 283/81 *Cilfit* [1982] ECR 3415   *114, 206*

Case 199/82 *San Giorgio* [1983] ECR 3595   *50*

Case 14/83 *Von Colson and Kamann* [1984] ECR 1891   *21, 47, 50, 59, 82, 261*

Case 79/83 *Harz* [1984] ECR 1921   *82*

Case 145/83 *Adams* [1985] ECR 3539   *56*

Case 237/83 *Prodest* [1984] ECR 3153   *259, 265*

Case 152/84 *Marshall I* [1986] ECR 723   *19, 45, 86*

Case 222/84 *Johnston* [1986] ECR 1651   *48, 65, 206*

Joined Cases 89, 104, 114, 116, 117 and 125-129/85, *Woodpulp*
     [1988] ECR 5193   *186-188, 199*

Case 314/85 *Foto-Frost* [1987] ECR 4199   *62, 114*

Case 12/86 *Demirel* [1987] ECR 3719   *8, 215, 217, 244*

Case 14/86 *Pretore di Salò* v. *X* [1987] ECR 2545   *96-97*

Case 80/86 *Kolpinghuis* [1987] ECR 3969   *47, 85, 96-97, 124, 241, 263*

Case 121/86 *Epicheirision Metalleftikon* [1989] ECR 3919   *57*

Case 222/86 *Heylens* [1987] ECR 4097   *206*

Case 286/86 *Deserbais* [1988] ECR 4907   *186*

Case 70/87 *Fediol* [1989] ECR 1781   *218*

Case 165/87 *Commission* v. *Council* [1988] 5557   *192*

Case 380/87 *Enichem* [1989] ECR 2491   *32*

Case 30/88 *Greece* v. *Commission* [1989] ECR 3711   *215*

Case 103/88 *Fratelli Costanzo* [1989] ECR 1839   *116, 240*

Case 142/88 *Hoesch and Germany* [1989] ECR 3413   *192*

Joined Cases C-143/88 and C-92/89 *Zuckerfabrik* [1991] ECR I-415   *36, 66-67*

Case C-152/88 *Sofrimport* [1990] ECR I-2477   *56*

Case C-177/88 *Dekker* [1990] ECR I-3941   *74, 81, 83, 98*

Joined Cases C-206/88 and C-207/88 *Zanetti* [1990] ECR I-1461   *90*

Case C-221/88 *Busseni* [1990] ECR I-495   *116*

Case C-262/88 *Barber* [1990] ECR I-1889   *123*

Case C-331/88 *Fedesa* [1990] ECR I-4023   *30*

Case C-359/88 *Zanetti II* [1990] ECR I-1509   *90*

Case C-9/89 *Spain* v. *Council* [1990] ECR I-1401   *185, 188*

Case C-63/89 *Assurances du Crédit* [1991] ECR I-1799   *61*

Case C-69/89 *Nakajima* [1991] ECR I-2069   *203, 218, 220*

Case C-104/89 and C-37/90 *Mulder II* [1992] ECR I-3061   *58*

Case C-106/89 *Marleasing* [1990] ECR I-4135   *25, 47, 82-84, 241, 248*

Case C-146/89 *Commission v. United Kingdom* [1991] ECR I-3533   *185, 196*

Case C-188/89 *Foster* [1990] ECR I-3313   *45*

Case C-192/89 *Sevince* [1990] ECR I-3461   *215, 217*

Case C-213/89 *Factortame* [1990] ECR I-2433   *36*

Case C-221/89 *Factortame II* [1991] ECR I-3905   *185, 194-195*

Case C-246/89 *Commission v. United Kingdom* [1991] ECR I-4585   *185, 194*

Case C-258/89 *Commission v. Spain* [1991] ECR I-3977   *187*

Case C-280/89 *Commission v. Ireland* [1992] ECR I-6185   *195*

Case C-298/89 *Gibraltar* [1993] ECR I-3605   *58*

Case C-309/89 *Codorniu* [1994] ECR I-1853   *58*

Case C-369/89 *Piageme I* [1991] ECR I-2971   *36, 38*

Joined Cases C-6/90 and C-9/90 *Francovich*
[1991] ECR I-5357   *24, 25, 36, 46, 52, 64, 101, 112-113, 241, 248*

Case C-18/90 *Kziber* [1991] ECR I-199   *217*

Case C-87-89/90 *Verholen* [1991] ECR I-3757   *85*

Case C-208/90 *Emmott* [1991] ECR I-4269   *122*

Case C-286/90 *Poulsen* [1992] ECR I-6019   *188-190, 195, 197, 201, 259-260*

Case C-369/90 *Micheletti* [1992] I-4239   *186, 195*

Opinion 1/91 *EEA I* [1991] ECR I-6079   *26, 193, 257*

Case C-97/91 *Borelli* [1992] ECR I-6313   *60, 206*

Case C-101/91 *Ten Oever* [1993] ECR I-4879   *34*

Case C-156/91 *Mundt* [1992] ECR I-5567   *47, 85*

Case C-158/91 *Levy* [1993] ECR I-4287   *29, 186, 192-194*

Case C-271/91 *Marshall II* [1993] ECR I-4367   *21, 70-71, 97*

Case C-312/91 *Metalsa* [1993] ECR I-3751   *193*

Case C-327/91 *France v. Commission* [1994] ECR I-3641   *192*

Opinion 1/92 *EEA II* [1992] ECR I-2821   *257*

Case C-90/92 *Dr Tretter* [1993] ECR I-3569   *80*

Case C-91/92 *Faccini Dori* [1994] ECR I-3325   *10, 19, 47, 86, 96, 101, 114, 247*

Joined Cases C-92/92 and C-326/92 *Phil Collins* [1993] ECR I-5145   *30, 31*

Case C-128/92 *Banks* [1994] ECR I-1237   *224*

Case C-236/92 *Comitato* [1994] ECR I-438   *21*

Case C-334/92 *Wagner Miret* [1993] ECR I-6911   *84*

Case C-405/92 *Etablissements Armand Mondiet v. Armement Islais*
[1993] ECR I-6133   *187*

Case C-421/92 *Habermann-Beltermann* [1994] ECR I-1657   *47, 82*

Case C-431/92 *Grosskrotzenburg* [1995] ECR I-2189   *11, 12, 245*

Case C-432/92 *Anastasiou* [1994] ECR I-3087   *192-193, 217*

Joined Cases C-46/93 and C-48/93 *Brasserie du Pêcheur*
[1996] ECR I-1029   *46, 52, 55, 70, 102, 113, 122, 186, 219, 241*

Case C-135/93 *Spain v. Commission* [1995] ECR I-1651   *80*

Case C-280/93 *Germany v. Council (bananas)*

     [1994] ECR I-4973   *218-221, 225, 258*

Case C-312/93 *Peterbroeck* [1995] ECR I-4599   *69-70, 176*

Case C-316/93 *Vaneetveld* [1994] ECR I-763   *84, 97*

Case C-324/93 *Evans Medical* [1995] ECR I-563   *186*

Case C-392/93 *British Telecommunications* [1996] ECR I-1631   *46, 53*

Joined Cases C-430/93 and C-431/93 *Van Schijndel*

     [1995] ECR I-4705   *69, 122*

Case C-441/93 *Pafites* [1996] ECR I-1347   *92*

Case C-465/93 *Atlanta* [1995] ECR I-3761   *66-67*

Case C-469/93 *Chiquita Italia* [1995] ECR I-4533   *214, 219*

Case C-5/94 *Hedley Lomas* [1996] ECR I-2553   *46, 54, 67*

Case C-25/94 *Commission v. Council* [1996] ECR I-1469   *187, 190, 192*

Case C-61/94 *Commission v. Germany* [1996] ECR I-3989   *80, 188, 193, 214*

Case C-70/94 *Werner* [1995] ECR I-3189   *80, 218*

Case C-83/94 *Leifer* [1995] ECR I-3231   *80, 218*

Case C-85/94 *Piageme II* [1995] ECR I-2955   *36, 116*

Case C-129/94 *Ruiz Bernáldez* [1996] ECR I-1829   *92, 96, 265*

Joined Cases C-178/94, C-179/94 and C-188-190/94 *Dillenkofer*

     [1996] ECR I-4845   *24, 46, 52, 53, 112, 241*

Case C-192/94 *El Corte Inglés* [1996] ECR I-1281   *38, 114*

Case C-194/94 *CIA Security*

     [1996] ECR I-2201   *11, 25, 29, 34, 38, 48, 92-94, 116, 238, 265*

Case C-212/94 *FMC* [1996] ECR I-389   *53, 61, 74*

Case C-268/94 *Portugal v. Council* [1996] ECR I-6177   *192*

Joined Cases C-283/94 and C-291-292/94 *Denkavit* [1996] ECR I-5063   *46*

Joined Cases C-304/94, C-330/94, C-342/94 and C-224/95 *Tombesi*

     [1997] ECR I-3561   *96*

Case C-10/95 *Asocarne* [1995] ECR I-4149   *58*

Joined Cases C-65/95 and C-111/95 *Shingara and Radiom*

     [1997] ECR I-3343   *187*

Case C-66/95 *Sutton* [1997] ECR I-2163   *70*

Case C-72/95 *Kraaijeveld* [1996] ECR I-5403   *11, 12, 18, 19, 46, 109-110, 116, 118, 161,*

     241, 264

Joined Cases C-74/95 and C-129/95 *Procura della Republica v. X*

     [1996] ECR I-6609   *89, 125*

Case C-124/95 *Centro-Com* [1997] ECR I-8   *186*

Case C-127/95 *Norbrook Laboratories* [1998] ECR I-1531   *46*

Case C-168/95 *Arcaro* [1996] ECR I-4705   *47, 88*

Case C-180/95 *Draehmpaehl* [1997] ECR I-2195   *72, 74, 83, 98*

Case C-185/95P *Baustahlgewebe* [1998] ECR I-8417   *211*

Case C-188/95 *Fantask* [1997] ECR I-6783   68

Joined Cases C-192-218/95 *Comateb* [1997] ECR I-165   36, 72

Case C-222/95 *Parodi* [1997] ECR I-3899   113

Case C-235/95 *Dumon* [1998] ECR I-4531   32

Case C-242/95 *GT-Link* [1997] ECR I-4453   24

Case C-284/95 *Safety Hi-Tec* [1998] ECR I-4301   80, 188

Case C-299/95 *Kremzow* [1997] ECR I-2   210

Case C-300/95 *Commission v. UK* [1997] ECR I-2649   81, 87

Case C-321/95P *Greenpeace* [1998] ECR I-1651   61

Case C-341/95 *Bettati* [1998] ECR I-43   188

Case C-352/95 *Phytheron* [1997] ECR I-1729   80

Joined Cases C-364/95 and C-365/95 *T-Port* [1998] ECR I-1023   186, 194

Case C-368/95 *Vereinigte Familiapress* [1997] ECR I-3689   211

Case C-27/96 *Danisco Sugar* [1997] ECR I-6653   192

Case C-53/96 *Hermès* [1998] ECR I-3606   9, 218, 220-221, 223

Case C-62/96 *Commission v. Greece* [1997] I-6730   189, 194

Case C-129/96 *Inter-Environnement Wallonie* [1997] ECR I-7411   11

Case C-149/96 *Portugal v. Council*

  [1999] ECR I-8395   8, 193, 203, 218-223, 225-226, 258

Case C-162/96 *Racke* [1998] ECR I-3655   160, 184, 188, 200-208, 229, 233, 259

Case C-171/96 *Pereira Roque* [1998] ECR I-4607   187, 195

Case C-177/96 *Belgian State v. Banque Indosuez and others*

  [1997] ECR I-5659   186

Case C-228/96 *Aprile* [1998] ECR I-7141   72

Case C-231/96 *Edis* [1998] ECR I-4951   72

Case C-249/96 *Grant* [1998] ECR I-621   211

Case C-260/96 *Spac* [1998] ECR I-4997   72

Case C-262/96 *Sürül* [1999] ECR I-2685   217

Joined Cases C-279-281/96 *Ansaldo Energia* [1998] ECR I-5025   72

Case C-319/96 *Brinkmann I* [1998] ECR I-5255   46

Case C-326/96 *Levez* [1998] ECR I-7835   72

Case C-336/96 *Gilly* [1998] ECR I-2812   199

Case C-343/96 *Dilexport* [1999] ECR I-5025   72

Case C-348/96 *Calfa* [1999] ECR I-11   187

Case C-350/96 *Clean Car* [1998] ECR I-2521   28

Case C-386/96P *Dreyfus* [1998] ECR I-2309   58

Case C-391/96P *Compagnie Continentale* [1998] ECR I-2377   58

Case C-403/96P *Glencore Grain* [1998] ECR I-2405   58

Case C-404/96P *Glencore Grain* [1998] ECR I-2435   58

Case C-416/96 *El-Yassini* [1999] ECR I-1209   187, 193, 217

Case C-2/97 *IP* [1998] ECR I-8597   89

Joined Cases C-10-22/97 *IN.CO.GE* [1998] ECR I-6307   35

Case C-77/97 *Österreichische Unilever* [1999] ECR I-431   94-95

Case C-120/97 *Upjohn* [1999] ECR I-223   36, 65, 120

Case C-126/97 *Eco Swiss* [1999] ECR I-3055   70

Case C-131/97 *Carbonari* [1999] ECR I-1103   32

Case C-140/97 *Rechberger* [1999] ECR I-3499   46

Case C-179/97 *Spain v. Commission* [1999] ECR I-1251   192

Case C-185/97 *Coote* [1998] ECR I-5199   47, 74

Case C-215/97 *Bellone* [1998] ECR I-2191   34, 83, 86

Case C-224/97 *Ciola* [1999] ECR I-2517   34

Case C-226/97 *Lemmens* [1998] ECR I-3711   48, 95, 239

Case C-262/97 *Engelbrecht* [2000] ECR I-7321   34

Joined Cases C-270/97 and C-271/97 *Sievers* and *Schrage*
    [2000] ECR I-929   123

Case C-302/97 *Konle* [1999] ECR I-3099   46

Case C-321/97 *Andersson* [1999] ECR I-3551   46

Case C-365/97 *Commission v. Italy* [1999] ECR I-7773   22

Case C-373/97 *Diamantis* [2000] ECR I-1705   39

Case C-378/97 *Wijsenbeek* [1999] ECR I-6207   33

Case C-424/97 *Haim II* [2000] ECR I-5125   46

Case C-435/97 *World Wildlife Fund (WWF)* [1999] ECR I-5613   46, 116, 118

Case C-7/98 *Krombach* [2000] ECR I-1935   211

Case C-17/98 *Emesa Sugar* [2000] ECR I-675   67

Case C-37/98 *Savas* [2000] ECR I-2927   217

Cases C-62/98 and C-84/98 *Commission v. Portugal*
    [2000] ECR I-5171   185-186, 192-193

Case C-65/98 *Eyüp* [2000] ECR I-4747   17

Case C-78/98 *Preston* [2000] ECR I-3201   54, 72-73

Case C-165/98 *Mazzoleni* [2001] ECR I-2189   88

Joined Cases C-174/98P and C-189/98P *Van der Wal* [2000] ECR I-1   211

Case C-179/98 *Mesbah* [1999] ECR I-7955   195

Case C-219/98 *Anastasiou II* [2000] ECR I-5241   199

Case C-228/98 *Kharalambos Dounias* [2000] ECR I-577   54, 60, 73, 167

Joined Cases C-240-244/98 *Océano* [2000] ECR I-4941   38, 47, 86, 122

Case C-281/98 *Angonese* [2000] ECR I-4139   26, 28, 31, 37

Case C-287/98 *Linster* [2000] ECR I-6917   13, 22, 46

Joined Cases C-300/98 and C-392/98 *Dior*
    [2000] ECR I-11307   9, 123, 218-220, 223

Case C-344/98 *Masterfoods* [2000] ECR I-11369   62

Case C-348/98 *Mendes Ferreira* [2000] ECR I-671   85-86, 92

Case C-352/98P *Bergaderm* [2000] ECR I-5291   55

Case C-365/98 *Brinkmann II* [2000] ECR I-4619   47, 82

Case C-377/98 *Biotechnological inventions* [2001] ECR I-7079   163, 227-228, 233

Case C-381/98 *Ingmar* [2000] ECR I-9305   47, 90, 199
Joined Cases C-397/98 and C-410/98 *Metallgesellschaft*
   [2001] ECR I-1727   70-71, 79, 102
Case C-411/98 *Ferlini* [2000] ECR I-8081   26
Joined Cases C-441/98 and C-442/98 *Kapniki Mikhailidis*
   [2000] ECR I-7145   61, 72
Case C-443/98 *Unilever Italia*
   [2000] ECR I-7535   11, 19, 20, 29, 34, 48, 94, 96, 116, 118, 265
Case C-448/98 *Guimont* [2000] ECR I-10663   37
Case C-456/98 *Centrosteel* [2000] ECR I-6007   34, 47, 82, 86-89, 98
Joined Cases C-52/99 and C-53/99 *Camarotto and Vignone*
   [2001] ECR I-1395   54, 72
Case C-63/99 *Gloszczuk* [2001] ECR I-6369   187, 217
Case C-74/99 *Imperial Tobacco* [2000] ECR I-8599   30
Case C-89/99 *Schieving-Nijstad* [2001] ECR I-5851   9, 47, 80, 219-220, 223, 259
Case C-109/99 *Association Basco-Béarnaise des Opticiens I*
   ndépendants [2000] ECR I-7247   34
Case C-150/99 *Stockholm Lindöpark* [2001] ECR I-493   46, 108
Case C-192/99 *Kaur* [2001] ECR I-1237   195
Case C-235/99 *Kondova* [2001] ECR I-6427   187, 217
Case C-257/99 *Barkoci and Malik* [2001] ECR I-6557   187, 217
Case C-268/99 *Jany* [2001] ECR I-8615   193
Case C-270/99P *Z v. European Parliament* [2001] ECR I-9197   211
Case C-274/99P *Connolly v. Commission* [2001] ECR I-1611   211
Case C-307/99 *Fruchthandelsgesellschaft* [2001] ECR I-3159   219-220, 223
Case C-413/99 *Baumbast*, pending   26
Case C-453/99 *Courage* [2001] ECR I-6279   46
Case C-481/99 *Heininger* [2001] ECR I-9945   34
Case C-500/99P *Conserve Italia Soc. Coop. v. Commission*,
   judgment of 24 January 2002, nyr   192
Case C-37/00 *Weber*, judgment of 27 February 2002, nyr   186, 195
Case C-50/00P *UPA* judgment of 25 July, 2002, nyr   60-63
Case C-162/00 *Pokrzeptowicz-Meyer*, judgment of 29 January 2002, nyr   217
Case C-380/01 *Schneider*, pending   36

European Court of First Instance
Joined Cases T-24/93, T-25/93, T-26/93 and T-28/93 *Compagnie maritime*
   belge [1996] ECR II-1201   199
Case T-468/93 *Frinil-Frio Naval* [1994] ECR II-33   59
Case T-115/94 *Opel Austria* [1997] ECR II-39   183, 200-201, 208-214, 259
Case T-167/94 *Nölle* [1995] ECR II-2589   57
Case T-390/94 *Schröder* [1997] ECR II-501   56

Joined Cases T-198/95, T-171/96, T-230/97, T-174/98 and T-225/99
    Comafrica [2001] ECR II-1975   *56*
Case T-102/96 *Gencor* [1999] ECR II-753   *188, 259*
Case T-111/96 *ITT Promedia* [1998] ECR II-2937   *206*
Case T-135/96 *UEAPME* [1998] ECR II-2335   *58*
Joined Cases T-125/97 and T-127/97 *Coca Cola* [2000] ECR II-1733   *58*
Joined Cases T-186/97, T-187/97, T-190-192/97, T-210/97, T-211/97,
    T-216/97, T-217/97, T-218/97, T-279/97, T-280/97, T-293/97 and
    T-147/99 *Kaufring* [2001] ECR II-1337   *208*
Case T-14/98 *Hautala* [1999] ECR II-2489   *59*
Case T-62/98 *Volkswagen* [2000] II-2707   *211*
Joined Cases T-172/98 and T-175-177/98 *Salamander*
    [2000] ECR II-2487   *58, 60, 63*
Case T-178/98 *Freshmarine* [2000] ECR II-3331   *56, 57*
Case T-2/99 *T-Port* [2001] ECR II-2093   *192, 194*
Case T-3/99 *Banatrading* [2001] ECR II-2123   *219*
Case T-18/99 *Cordis* [2001] ECR II-913   *56*
Case T-30/99 *Bocchi* [2001] ECR II-943   *56*
Case T-52/99 *T-Port* [2001] ECR II-981   *56*
Case T-83/99 *Carlo Ripa di Meana* [2000] ECR II-3493   *58*
Case T-120/99 *Kik* [2001] ECR II-2235   *192*
Case T-123/99 *JT's Corporation* [2000] ECR II-3269   *59*
Case T-196/99 *Area Cova v. Council and Commission* [2001] ECR II-3597   *187*
Case T-26/00 *Lecureur* [2001] ECR II-2623   *59*
Case T-177/01 *Jégo-Quéré*, judgment of 3 May 2002, nyr   *63*

European Court of Human Rights
Ireland v. the United Kingdom, 18 January 1978, Appl. 5310/71,
    EHHR Ser. A, No. 25   *164*
Swedish Engine Drivers' Union v. Sweden, 6 February 1976,
    Appl. 5614/72, EHRR Ser. A, No. 20   *165*
The Holy Monasteries v. Greece, 9 December 1994, A.301-A   *165*
Auerbach v. the Netherlands, Admissibility Decision of 29 January 2002   *179*

International Court of Justice
Legal Consequences for States of the Continued Presence of South Africa in
    Namibia (South West Africa) Notwithstanding Security Council Resolution
    276 (1970), advisory opinion of 21 June 1971, ICJ Rep. (1971), p. 16   *191*
Interpretation of the Agreement of 25 March 1951 between the
    WHO and Egypt, 95-96   *192*
Fisheries Jurisdiction Case (United Kingdom v. Iceland), judgment of 2
    February 1973 (jurisdiction), ICJ Rep. (1973), p. 3   *192, 204*

Fisheries Jurisdiction Case (Federal Republic of Germany v. Iceland),
  judgment of 2 February 1973, ICJ Rep. (1973), p. 49   *204-205*
Interpretation of the Agreement of 25 March 1951 between the WHO and
  Egypt, advisory opinion of 20 December 1980, ICJ Rep. (1980), p. 73   *183*
Case concerning Military and Paramilitary Activities in and against
  Nicaragua, judgment of 27 June 1986, ICJ Rep. (1986), p. 1   *225*
Advisory Opinion on the Applicability of the obligation to Arbitrate under
  Section 21 of the United Nations Headquarters Agreement of 26
  June 1947, ICJ Rep. (1988), p. 12-35   *165*
Gabčíkovo-Nagymaros Project (Hungary v. Slovakia), judgment of 25
  September 1997, ICJ Rep. (1997), p. 7   *192, 205-206, 230*
Difference relating to immunity from legal process of a special rapporteur
  of the Commission on Human Rights, ICJ Rep. (1999), p. 62,
  [1999] ILM 873   *170, 180*
LaGrand (Germany v. United States), judgment of 27 June 2001,
  [2001] 40 ILM 1069   *157, 174, 255*

Permanent Court of International Justice
Danzig PCIJ, ser. B, No 15 (1928)   *132, 170, 243, 255*
Interpretation of the Memel Statute PCIJ, ser. A/B, No. 49   *165*

International Criminal Tribunal for the Former Yugoslavia
Case IT-94-1 *Presecutor* v. *Tadic.* Decision on the defence motion for
  interlocutory appeal on jurisdiction, 2 October 1995   *170*

National Courts

Denmark
Danish Supreme Court, case I 361/1997 *Carlsen a.o.* v. *Poul Rasmussen,* 6
  April 1998, *SEW* 1998, p. 398, *Ars Aequi* 1999, p. 121   *168*

France
Cassation Civile 1, 16 May 1961, [1961] Dalloz, p. 489
Cassation Civile 1, 10 March 1993, *Lejeune, RGDIP* 1993, p. 1051   *148*

Conseil constitutionnel, 16 July 1971, *Liberté d'association,*
  décision No. 71-44 DC, Rec. p. 29   *137*
Conseil constitutionnel, 15 January 1975, *Intérruption volontaire de grossesse,*
  décision No. 74-54 DC, Rec. p. 19   *147*
Conseil constitutionnel, 30 December 1976, *Assemblée européenne,* décision
  No. 76-71 DC, Rec. p. 15   *149*

Conseil constitutionnel, 30 December 1977, *Prélèvement isoglucose*,
    décision No. 77-89 DC and No. 77-90 DC, Rec. p. 46   146
Conseil constitutionnel, 25 July 1991, *Accord de Schengen*,
    décision No. 91-294 DC, Rec. p. 91   146, 150, 152-153
Conseil constitutionnel, 9 April1992, *Maastricht I / Traité sur l'Union
    européenne*, décision No. 92-308, Rec. p. 55   139, 149
Conseil constitutionnel, 2 September 1992, *Maastricht 2*, décision No.
    92-312, Rec. p. 76   139
Conseil constitutionnel, 23 September 1992, *Maastricht 3*, décision No.
    92-313, Rec. p. 94   139
Conseil constitutionnel, 18 December 1997, *Loi de financement de
    la sécurité sociale pour 1998*, décision No. 97-393 DC, Rec. p. 320   147
Conseil constitutionnel, 31 December 1997, *Traité d'Amsterdam*,
    décision No. 97-394 DC, Rec. p. 344   150
Conseil constitutionnel, 22 January 1999, *Traité portant statut de la Cour
    pénale internationale*, décision No. 99-408 DC, Rec. p. 29   149

Conseil d'Etat, 13 July 1965, *Société Navigator*, Rec. p. 423   147
Conseil d'Etat, 22 December 1978, *Cohn-Bendit*, Rec. p.524, English
    translation in [1980] 1 CMLR 543   109, 148
Conseil d'Etat, 21 September1993, *Reintjes*, Rec. No. 44.142   118
Conseil d'Etat, 29 July 1994, *Préfet de la Seine-Maritime c. Abdelmoula*,
    RGDIP 1995, p. 502   148
Conseil d'Etat, 10 March 1995, *Demirpence*, Rec. p. 610   148
Conseil d'Etat, 6 June 1997, *Aquarone*, Rec. p. 206   148
Conseil d'Etat, 18 December 1998, *Sarl du parc d'activité de Blotzheim*
    Rec. p. 483   147
Conseil d'Etat Ass., 9 April 1999, *Madame Chevrol-Benkeddach*
    Rec. p. 115   148

Germany
Bundesverwaltungsgericht, 25 January 1996, *DVBl.* 1996, p. 677-682,
    NJW 1997, p.144   118
Bundesverfassungsgericht, 18 October 1967, BVerfGE Vol. 22, p. 293   145
Bundesverfassungsgericht, 9 June 1971, *Lütticke*, BVerfGE Vol. 31, p. 174   145
Bundesverfassungsgericht, 29 May 1974, *Solange 1*,
    BVerfGE Vol. 37, p. 280   145
Bundesverfassungsgericht, 22 October 1986, *Solange 2*,
    BVerfGE Vol. 73, p. 375   146
Bundesvefassungsgericht, 8 April 1987, *Kloppenburg*,
    BVerfGE Vol. 75, p. 223   146, 151

Bundesverfassungesgericht, 12 October 1993, *Brunner*, BVerfGE Vol.
   89, p. 155, English translation in [1994] 1 CMLR 57 and
   [1994] ILM 388   *133, 150, 153, 168*
Bundesverfassungsgericht, 24 October 1996, *Brasserie du Pêcheur*,
   English translation in [1997] 1 *CMLR* 971   *55*
Bundesverfassungsgericht, 7 June 2000, *Bananenmarktordnung*,
   BVerfGE Vol. 102, p. 147   *150*

Ireland

Irish High Court, 17 June 1997, *SIAC Construction* v. *Mayo
   Country Council*   *117*

Italy

Corte di Cassazione, 3 February 1995, No. 1271, *Dir. Lav.* 1995, II, 8   *115*
Corte di Cassazione, 27 February 1995, No. 2275,
   *Riv. dir. internaz.*1995, 448   *115*

Netherlands

Hoge Raad, 30 May 1986, NJ 1986/688, reproduced in *Netherlands
   Yearbook of International Law* 1987, p. 392   *162, 173*
Hoge Raad, 16 May 1997, *Hansa Chemie* v. *Bechem Chemie* [1999]
   Netherlands Yearbook of International Law, Vol.30   *173*
Hoge Raad, 5 September 1997, NJ 1998/686   *178*

Raad van State, 19 December 1991, *Aramide*, AB 1992/122   *117*
Raad van State, 10 May 2001, *HMG*, JB 2001/152   *24*

Hof 's Gravenhage, 2 August 2001, *Waterpakt*, M&R 2001/95   *35, 108*

Spain

Tribunal Constitucional 28/1991, 14 February 1991, and 64/1991,
   22 January 1991, BOE of 15 March 1991 and 24 April 1991   *110*

Tribunal Supremo, 30 November 1991, Rep.5371, reproduced in
   83 Noticias C.E.E. 1991, p. 121-124   *110*
Tribunal Supremo, 8 November 1996, RJA 1996/7954   *115*
Tribunal Supremo, 30 November 1996, RJA 1996/8457   *115*
Tribunal Supremo, 5 July 1997, RJA 1997/6152   *115*

Sweden

Supreme Administrative Court, 26 June 1996, Case RÅ 1996, Ref. 50   *117*

United Kingdom

High Court of Justice of England (Chancery Division), 14 February 1974,
  Van Duijn [1974] 1 WLR 1107 and [1974] 1 CMLR 347   10

The Queens Bench *Bourgoin SA and Others* v. *Ministry for Agriculture,*
  Fisheries and Food [1986] QB 716   64

House of Lords, *Duke* v. *Gec Reliance,* [1988] CMLR 719   115
House of Lords, *Webb* v. *EMO Air Cargo (UK) Ltd,* [1992] 4 All ER 929,
  [1993] 1 WLR 49   100
House of Lords, *Webb* v. *EMO Air Cargo (UK) Ltd,* [1996] 2 CMLR 990,
  [1995] 4 All ER 577, [1995] 1 WLR 1454   100
House of Lords, *Regina* v. *Secretary of State for Employment ex parte*
  Seymour Smith, [1997] 2 CMLR 904   94, 115-116
House of Lords, *Regina* v. *DDP ex parte Kebilene,* [1999] 3 WLR 972   99
House of Lords, *Regina* v. *Secretary of State for the Environment, Transport*
  and the Regions ex parte International Air Transport Association, [1999] 1
  CMLR 1287   62
House of Lords, *Ingmar GB* v. *Eaton Leonard Technologies,*
  [1999] *European Commercial Cases* 49   91
House of Lords, *Three Rivers District Council and Others* v. *Governor*
  and Company of the Bank of England, [2000] 2 WLR 1220   19, 52, 53, 111, 113
House of Lords, *Regina* v. *Secretary of State for Transport ex parte*
  Factortame Ltd and Others, [2000] EuLR 40   55
House of Lords, *Regina* v. *Secretary of State for Transport ex parte*
  Imperial Tobacco Ltd, [2000] EuLR 70   61
House of Lords, *Berkeley* v. *Secretary of State for the Environment and*
  Others, [2001] *Journal of Environmental Law,* p. 89-105   120-121
House of Lords, *White and the Motor Insurer's Bureau,* [2001] 2 CMLR 1   92
House of Lords, *British Horseracing Board* v. *William Hill,*
  [2001] 2 CMLR 12   81

Court of Appeal 15 May 1980, *Polydor,* [1980] 2 CMLR 413   8
Court of Appeal, 31 July 1998, *Ingmar GB* v. *Eaton Leonard Technologies,*
  [1999] *European Commercial Cases* 49 (C.A.)   91
Court of Appeal, 4 December 1998, *Three Rivers District Council*
  and Others v. *Governor and Company of the Bank of England,*
  [2000] 3 CMLR 1, 152   113
Court of Appeal, 8 March 2000, *Regina* v. *Durham Country Council and*
  Others ex parte Rodney Huddleston, [2000] 2 CMLR 313   92-93, 117
Court of Appeal, *Regina* v. *Bartle and the Commissionar of Police for the*
  Metropolis and Others ex parte Pinochet, [2000] 1 AC 147   80
Court of Appeal, *Regina* v. *Offen and Others,* [2001] 1 WLR 253   100

United States

Court of Appeals (Fourth Circuit), *Breard* v. *Pruett*, 134 F.3d 615 (1998)   175

Court of Appeals (Fourth Circuit), *Republic of Paraguay* v. *George F. Allen*,
    134 F.3d 622 (1998)   175

Court of Appeals (Ninth Circuit), 24 February 1999,
    Karl LaGrand v. *Stewart*, 170 F.3d 1158   157

Court of Appeals (Ninth Circuit), 16 January 1998,
    Karl LaGrand v. *Stewart*, 133 F.3d 1253   157

Court of Appeals (Ninth Circuit), 6 March 2000,
    USA v. *Lombera Carmorlinga*, 170 F.3d 1244   175

Court of Appeals (Fifth Circuit), 9 February 2001,
    Beazley v. *Johnson*, 242 F3d 248   177

Supreme Court, *Foster* v. *Neilson*, 27 US (Pet.) 253, 314 (1829)   4, 51, 162

Supreme Court, *Chae Chan Ping* v. *US*, 130 US 581 (1889)   165

Supreme Court, *Breard* v. *Greene*, Warden, 000 U.S. 97-8214 (1998)   175

District Court, E.D. Virginia, *Angel Breard, Petitioner* v. *JD Netherland*,
    Warden, Respondent, 949 F.Supp.1255 (1996)   175

District Court, E.D. Virginia, *Republic of Paraguay* v. *George Allen,*
    Governor of Virginia, et al., Defendants, 949 F.Supp. 1269 (1996)   175

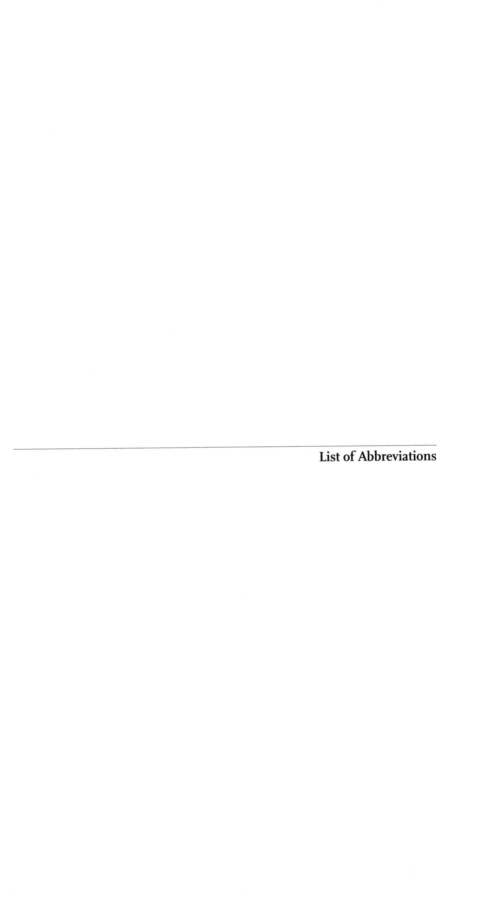

List of Abbreviations

AB	Administratiefrechtelijke Beslissingen
AC	Appeal Cases
AG	Advocate General
AJIL	American Journal of International Law
ALL ER	All England Reports
BB	Betriebsberater
BCCI	Bank of Credit and Commerce International S.A.
BL	Basic Law (Germany)
BOE	Boletin Oficial del Estado
BverfGE	Bundesverfassungsgericht
BYIL	British Yearbook of International Law
BW	Burgerlijk Wetboek (Dutch Civil Code)
CBD	Convention on Biological Diversity
CESCR	Committee on Economic, Social and Cultural Rights
CFI	European Court of First Instance
CLJ	Cambridge Law Journal
CMLR	Common Market Law Reports
CMLRev.	Common Market Law Review
DC	Décision portant déclaration de conformité à la Constitution
Dir.Lav.	Diritto di Lavoro
DVBl.	Deutsches Verwaltungsblatt
EC	European Community
ECHR	European Court of Human Rights
ECJ	European Court of Justice
ECR	European Court Reports
ECSC	European Coal and Steel Community
EEA	European Economic Area
EEC	European Economic Community
EHRR	European Human Rights Reports
EIA	Environmental Impact Assessment
EJIL	European Journal of International Law
ELRev.	European Law Review
EPL	European Public Law
ERPL	European Review of Private Law
EU	European Union
EuLR	European Law Reports
EuZW	Europäische Zeitschrift für Wirtschaftsrecht
FCC	Federal Constitutional Court (Germany)
FIDE	Fédération Internationale de Droit Européen
GATT	General Agreement on Tariffs and Trade
HMSO	Her Majesty's Stationery Office
HRA	Human Rights Act

HRC	Human Rights Committee
ICCPR	International Covenant on Civil and Political Rights
ICJ	International Court of Justice
ICLQ	International and Comparative Law Quarterly
IGC	Intergovernmental Conference
ILA	International Law Association
ILC	International Law Commission
ILM	International Legal Materials
ILO	International Labour Organization
JB	Jurisprudentie Bestuursrecht
JZ	Juristenzeitung
KritV.	Kritische Vierteljahreszeitschrift für Gesetzgebung und Rechtswissenschaft
LIEI	Legal Issues of European (since 2000 Economic) Integration
LJ	Lord Justice
MJ	Maastricht Journal of European and Comparative Law
MLR	Modern Law Review
M&R	Milieu en recht
NJ	Nederlandse Jurisprudentie
NJW	Neue Juristische Wochenschrift
nyr	not yet reported
OJ	Official Journal of the European Communities
PCIJ	Permanent Court of International Justice
QB	Queen's Bench Reports
RCADI	Recueil des Cours de l'Académie de Droit Internationale
RdeC	Recueil des Cours
Rec.	Recueil (des arrêts du Conseil d'Etat/ des décisions du Conseil constitutionnel)
Rep.	Repertorio
RFDA	Revue française de droit administratif
RGDIP	Revue generale de droit international public
Riv.dir.internaz.	Rivista del diritto internazionale
RJA	Revista de jurisprudencia Aranzadi
RJC	Recueil de jurisprudendence constitutionnelle 1959-1993 (Favoreu)
RTDE	Revue trimestrielle de droit européen
SDLRev.	San Diego Law Review
SEW	Sociaal Economische Wetgeving
TBT	Technical Barriers to Trade
TRIPs	Trade Related Intellectual Property Rights
UK	United Kingdom
UN	United Nations
UNTS	United Nations Treaty Series

US(A)	United States (of America)
WHO	World Health Organization
WIPO	World Intellectual Property Organization
WLR	Weekly Law Reports
WTO	World Trade Organization
YBEL	Yearbook of European Law

Index

Action for annulment   58-59, 218, 258
Administrative law
                109-10, 120, 130, 133
Advisory opinion   132
Agreement on international
humane trapping standards   171
Agreement on Technical
Barriers to Trade (TBT)   227-228
Amsterdam Treaty   141
Anti-dumping Regulation   57, 203
Anti-trust law   259
Application for annulment   218
Association Agreements   7-8
Alternativ-Normierung   21
Austria   134
Authoritiy/authorities   5
  -administrative   29, 110
  -Community   13, 110
  -domestic   145, 240
  -executive   260, 263-264
  -judicial   263
  -legislative   241
  -local   4
  -state   23, 28, 30, 237
Autonomy   24, 40, 179, 242
——
Belgium   5, 129, 202
Bilateral agreements   138
——
Civil law   4, 89-92, 98
Community interests   246
Community legal order 3, 6, 18, 20, 23,
123, 209, 248, 253, 257-258, 263
Compensation   21, 35-36, 55,
58, 102, 163, 256, 258
Competence(s)   126, 206, 259
  -judicial   3, 13, 110, 125
  -legislative   143
  -mixed   263
  -transfer of   139, 141, 149
Consistent interpretation (see also
harmonious interpretation/

sympathetic interpretation)24, 79-104,
133, 265
Constitution for Europe   130
Constitution of the United States   4
Constitutional charter   130
Constitutional heritage   130
Constitutional law
  -domestic 129, 131, 133-134, 139, 145, 149
  -Dutch   129
  -French   128-154
  -German   128-154
  -national   26, 114-115, 122, 124-125,
  129-130, 134, 137-138, 254
Constitutional restraints   146
Constitutional requirements   133
Constitutionality of EC law   130
Constitutive structures   150
Contra legem   47
Convention for the Conservation of
Salmon in the North Atlantic   190
Convention on Biological Diversity
                                   163
Convention on Consular Relations
                           157, 173-175
Convention on the law applicable to
contractual obligations   91
Convention on the Privileges and
Immunities of the United Nations
                                   170
Co-operation Agreement of 2 April
1980   201
Council of Europe
Criminal law   36-37, 89, 97, 100, 124
Customary international law 138, 148,
183-234, 253, 256-260, 267
——
Damages   46, 48, 51-55,
58, 62, 62, 70, 73, 75, 84, 102-103, 111-113,
123, 256, 261-262
Declaration of 1789   137
Democratic legitimation   151
Democratic principles   150, 152

Differentiation   131
Direct applicability   4, 6-8, 45, 75, 115,
131-134, 145-146, 163, 178-179
Direct concern   58
Direct effect
    -absence of   82-83, 86, 240, 262
    -concept of   17, 22, 25, 27, 158-160, 163,
    179, 219, 224-226, 234, 253
    -conditional nature of   164, 247
    -condition(s) for 21-22, 33, 114, 122, 133
    -conditions: unconditional and
    sufficiently precise   25, 107, 111-113
    -consequences of   179
    -disguised (indirect)   90
    -disguised (vertical)   24, 116, 265
    -extensive interpretation of   264
    -horizontal   10-11, 17, 26, 29-30, 37,
    114-118, 124, 244, 266
    -in international law   253
    -incidental   92, 265
    -inverse vertical   96, 124
    -logic of   239
    -manifestations of   179
    -national perceptions of   20
    -nature of   164-167
    -notion of   161, 172, 265-266
    -plea against   18
    -objective   161-162, 173, 176-177
    -of a rule of international law
                                 158, 168
    -of directives
    7, 9-10, 17, 26, 115-117, 123, 146, 148, 253,
    257, 262, 262
    -of international agreements   7, 17
    -of international law   130, 168,
    173-174, 177, 253
    -of treaty provisions   133, 148
    -operation of   240-242
    -principle of   151, 160, 164
    -subjective   161, 163, 173
    -test of   237, 243-244, 246
    -vertical   116-117, 125, 264-265

Direct validity   151
Directive(s)
    -application of   265
    -direct effect of (see also direct
    effect)7, 9-10, 17, 26, 51, 82, 115-117, 123,
    146, 148, 253, 262, 264
    -horizontal   30, 37, 51, 96-97, 114, 118
    -horizontal effect of   247
    -non-implemented   111-112, 253,
    263-264
    -unimplemented 12, 47, 51, 74, 110, 245
    -64/221   9-10
    -65/65   65
    -69/335   68
    -72/166   86
    -75/363   32
    -75/442   21
    -76/207   21, 29, 33-34
    -76/768   56
    -77/388   146
    -77/780   111, 113
    -80/987   52
    -82/76   32
    -83/189   11, 19-20, 29-30
    -85/203   30
    -85/337   12, 19, 117, 245
    -85/374   87
    -85/577   10, 28
    -86/653   86
    -90/232   86
    -90/314   52
    -90/531   53
    -91/676   108
    -92/13   117
    -92/25   147
    -92/43   21
    -93/13   34, 115
    -94/10   11
    -97/11   12, 19, 117, 245
    -2000/35   34
    -2001/23   81
Disapplication   38

Divergence
39-40, 107-126, 169, 206, 266

Dualism   134-136, 148, 153, 173,
180, 232, 253, 260

——

EC Treaty

-Article 10   5-6, 23-24, 61,
64, 115, 121, 125, 263

-Article 12   6, 26, 30-31

-Article 18   26

-Article 25   6

-Article 28   8, 37

-Article 39   28, 37, 186

-Article 65   91

-Article 81   34-35, 187, 199

-Article 88   34

-Article 90   145

-Article 141   68, 73, 123

-Article 174   26

-Article 181   59

-Article 203   143

-Article 220   205, 211

-Article 226   34, 119, 173, 261

-Article 230   58-64, 218

-Article 234   60-61, 66-67, 151, 169,
173, 197, 205, 263

-Article 242   67

-Article 243   67

-Article 249   8, 45, 51,
82, 131, 145-146, 261

-Article 288   48, 53-54, 57-58, 62, 64

-Article 300   218

-Article 307   193

-Article 308   126

EEA Agreement/Treaty   200, 209,
213-214, 257

Effective judicial protection   54

Effective legal protection   107, 119, 121

Effet utile   90, 196

EIA   19, 46, 117-118, 120-121

Enforcement

-of community law (EC law)   23, 50,
59, 64, 111, 120

-of directives   51, 64

-procedure   119

Equal pay   68, 72, 73, 123

Equal treatment   10, 29, 123, 147

Estoppel   10, 98

EU Treaty

-Article 34   124

European Convention (Human
Rights, ECHR)   63, 89, 100, 165,
171, 177-178, 210-211

European integration   18, 23, 138

Excusable error   68

External relations   135, 248, 263

——

France   5, 109, 127-154

Federal

-legislation   137

-principles   140

-statute   137, 142

Federation   135-143

Free movement of workers   168

French Constitution   134-135, 137-143,
146, 148, 153

——

GATT   21, 192, 194, 198, 203, 214-215,
219-225, 229, 244, 258

GATT Anti-Dumping Code   203

General principles   88-90, 97,
124-125, 210-211, 214

General scheme   132, 220, 242-244, 258

German Basic Law (BL)   134-137, 140,
142, 145-146, 150-154

Germany   127-154

——

Harmonious interpretation (see also
consistent interpretation/
sympathetic interpretation)   255,
260-264, 267

Hierarchy of norms   54, 75, 166, 186

Horizontal effects   118, 259

Human Rights Act (HRA)   98-101

——

ILO   194, 262

Individual concern   58
Incidental effect(s)   48, 51,
74, 92-96, 104
Incompatibility 18, 29, 31, 34, 36, 39-40,
116, 132, 176, 178, 198, 258
Indirect effect   30, 80-81, 88-90, 96,
115, 119, 124, 158, 197
Individual rights   12, 35, 49,
54, 108, 112-113, 119, 125, 132, 144, 157, 170,
173-175, 240, 255, 258, 266
Interface between international and
national law   159
Intergovernmental
  -institutions   135, 145
  -organ   151
Interim relief   66
Internal
  -effect   6, 26, 167
  -procedures   171
  -situation   37
Infringement56-57, 87, 108, 111, 173, 207
International constitutional law
137-138
International customary law (see
customary international law)
International environmental law 161
International law
  -direct effect of   130, 168,
  173-174, 177, 253
  -domestic effect of   135, 153
  -supremacy of   165, 254-255
  -transformation of   254-255
International responsibility   254-256,
260
International tort   256
Invocabilité de substitution   21, 83
Invocability   133, 161, 215, 223, 229, 232
Italy   5, 168

Judicial
  -adjudication   120
  -application   22, 27, 33, 51
  -competence   3, 13

-control   146-147, 153
-protection   23, 48, 53, 58, 63, 65, 219
-remedy   56, 60, 75, 205-206
-review   4, 36, 48,
58, 60, 63, 65, 109-110., 117, 120, 146,
152, 204, 229
-self-restraint   144, 179
Judiciary   3, 7, 12, 22, 161, 172,
178, 202, 226, 254-256
Justiciability   162, 243

Länder   135, 142-143
Legal
  -certainty   49, 62, 74, 88-90,
  96-98, 103, 123-125, 231
  -change   245
  -consequences   27, 34, 38-39,
  103, 157, 190-191
  -development   241
  -personality   149, 183
  -relationship   27, 116, 161
  -review   37-38
  -traditions   20, 63, 131, 237, 241, 248
Legality review   240
Liability
  -civil   83, 89
  -criminal   124
  -contractual   265
  -damages   256
  -of Community institutions   54-57
  -State (see State liability)
  -tortious   256, 265
Locus standi   58-60, 121, 126

Maastricht Treaty   143, 148
Minimum harmonization 70, 122-124
Mitigation of loss   102-103
Monism   134-136, 153, 253, 258
Multilevel constitutionalism   131
National constitutions 26, 114-115, 122,
124-125, 129-130, 180, 254
National differences   107, 119-122,
124-125

National law
-application of   *116, 123*
-(in)compatibility of   *110*
-interpretation of   *124, 158*
-review of   *36*
-setting aside of   *34-36, 163*
National provisions
-review of legality of   *21-22*
Nemo auditur (see also *estoppel*) *98*
Netherlands   *5-6, 121,*
129, 172, 178-179, 260
Notification (procedure)   *19, 29-30,*
51, 94-96, 239
Nulla poena sine lege   *89, 97*
Nullity   *58*

——

Obligation(s)
-contractual   *6*
-directly effective   *113*
-for/on individuals *19-20, 50-51, 86,*
88, 125, 170, 262-263
-for/on private parties
-individual
-on Member States

——

Pacta sunt servanda *192, 204, 206, 227*
Parallelism
-between direct effect and
  consistent interpretation   *79, 85,*
  87, 101
-between directives and
  regulations   *10*
Payment of interest   *70-71*
Plea of illegality   *31, 36-37*
Portugal   *8, 134*
Precision   *7, 22, 32-33, 53, 162, 240*
Preliminary
-inquiry   *22, 25*
-question(s)   *87-88, 151, 189, 195,*
204, 223, 259, 267
-ruling(s)   *60-61, 65, 81, 125-126, 132,*
146, 154, 173, 201, 205-206, 218, 232

Primacy   *5-6, 39, 45, 102, 172, 188,*
195-196, 202, 210-211
Principle
-of effectiveness   *64, 70, 102-103, 120*
-of equal treatment *62, 70, 83, 123, 194*
-of equivalence (see also principle
  of non-discrimination) *69, 71-73, 120*
-of good faith   *208, 212*
-of legitimate expectations *209, 211*
-of non-discrimination   *69, 71-73*
-of non-interference   *199*
-of reciprocity   *222*
Private international law *90, 259, 265*
Procedural
-autonomy   *24, 40, 242*
-defect   *34, 38, 94, 96*
-rules   *39, 48-49, 53-54, 59, 61, 64, 66,*
  70-75, 120-121, 126
Public policy exception   *186*

——

Raising of new arguments *69-70, 176*
Rebus sic stantibus   *200-206*
Remedies   *35-36, 40, 48-50, 53-54, 59,*
61-62, 64-66, 70-75, 102-103, 120-121, 163,
172, 174, 177, 263-267
Reparation   *5, 112-113*
Right(s)
-citizens'   *145, 153*
-creation of *18-20, 136, 154, 163, 170,*
174, 227, 240, 262-263
-enforceable   *4, 31, 175*
-fundamental   *130, 140, 149-152*
-human   *98, 101, 161, 164, 169,*
172, 178, 206, 210
-individual *12, 35, 49, 54, 108, 111-113,*
125, 132, 144, 157, 170, 173-174, 240, 255,
258, 264, 266
-of man   *137*
-of private parties   *244*
-parameters on   *19, 49*
-subjective   *245*
-substantive   *237*

-suspension of 256
Rule of law 63, 140, 248
Rules of procedure of the Court of
Justice
-Article 42 69

———

Sanctions 35, 54, 266
Schengen 146, 150, 152-153
Schutznorm 256, 262
Self-executing(ness) 3, 50-51, 122,
132, 161-162, 166, 171-172, 175-177, 253-255,
259-262
Separation of powers 3, 8, 22, 35, 266
Side-effect 36, 116-118, 266
Social security 72, 121, 126, 147, 265
Sovereignty 134-140, 149-150, 254
Spain 110, 115
Standing 35, 161
State Immunity Act (of 1978) 80
State liability 54, 112, 114,
119, 122-123, 133, 253
State responsibility 253-254, 256-257,
261-263
Subsidiarity 122, 140
Sufficiently precise (see precision)
22, 33, 107, 111-113
Supranational(ism) 49
Supremacy 39, 50-51,
81, 103, 119, 159-160, 164-168, 173, 180, 232,
254-260, 264, 266
Sympathetic interpretation (see
consistent interpretation/
harmonious interpretation) 46-47, 51,
74
Sweden 117, 168

———

Tax 37, 68, 102, 121, 126
Technical standard(s) 11, 19, 30, 238
Territoriality principle 187, 199
Third States 248
Time limits 35
Transposition period 85

Treaties
-accession 139, 191
-amendment of 51, 139
-commercial 138
-direct effect of 257, 259
-founding 139
-peace 138
-self-executing 253, 259
-suspension 160
-termination of 160, 162
Treaty interpretation 173, 193,
242, 255, 261
TRIPs 9, 223, 227-229, 259-260

———

UK 20, 96, 99, 102, 111, 115, 121
Unconditional(ity) 22, 25, 53, 107,
111-113, 133, 162, 239-240, 264
Uniformity 39-40, 122, 167, 179, 242, 248
Uniform application 67, 107-108, 265

———

Validity of Community acts 60, 152,
160
Vienna Convention on the Law of
Treaties 191-194, 205, 207, 242, 256

———

WTO 8-9, 80, 84, 194, 198,
215, 219-229, 258-259

Contributors

Contributors

David Edward
David Edward was Judge at the Court of First Instance from 25 September 1989 to 9 March 1992. Since then he is Judge at the European Court of Justice. He also is Honorary Professor at the University of Edinburgh.

Sacha Prechal
Sacha Prechal is Professor of European law at Tilburg University (The Netherlands). Her special interests lie in the interaction between European and national law in the broad sense of the term.

Angela Ward
Angela Ward is Reader in Law at the University of Essex and barrister at Middle Temple. She is one of the founding editors of the Cambridge Yearbook of European Legal Studies, and author of *Judicial Review and the Rights of Private Parties in EC Law* (Oxford 2000).

Gerrit Betlem
Gerrit Betlem LL.M. (Groningen, the Netherlands), Ph.D. (Utrecht, the Netherlands) is Senior Lecturer at the University of Exeter Law School (UK). He teaches EU law and international business law courses. His research interests focus on European private (international) law, including the private enforcement of Community law and *Francovich* liability (website URL: www.eel.nl/dossier/francovi.htm) as well as on comparative tort law, in particular environmental liability.

Jan Jans
Jan Jans is Professor of European Union Law and head of the department of International Law at the University of Amsterdam. Prior to this he worked at the University of Groningen and the University of Edinburgh (visiting Leverhulme Fellow). He has published on Public Law, Constitutional Law, Environmental Law, European Law, European Public Law and European Environmental Law. His *European Environmental Law* (second edition Europa Law Publishing, 2000) is generally regarded as one of the leading publications on the issue.

Jolande Prinssen
Jolande Prinssen LL.M. is Research Associate and lecturer in European Law at the University of Amsterdam. She prepares a thesis on the relationship between the mechanisms for enforcing EC law in national courts. Her research interests include European administrative law, more in particular the interaction between European law and national law.

Jörg Gerkrath

Jörg Gerkrath is Professor of International and EC Law at the University of Avignon (France). His research concentrates on European Constitutional Law. He wrote his thesis, *L'émergence d'un droit constitutionnel européen. Modes de formation et sources d'inspiration de la Constitution de l'Union européenne*, at the Université Robert Schuman, Strasbourg.

André Nollkaemper

André Nollkaemper is Professor of Public International Law at the University of Amsterdam and Director of the Amsterdam Centre for International Law. He is counsel at 'Van den Biesen Prakken Böhler', attorneys-at-law in Amsterdam and editor of the Netherlands Yearbook of International Law.

Jan Wouters

Jan Wouters is Professor of International Law and the Law of International Organisations at the University of Leuven and of Banking and Financial Law at the University of Maastricht. He is counsel at 'De Bandt, Van Hecke, Lagae & Loesch – Linklaters & Alliance', attorneys-at-law in Brussels.

Dries Van Eeckhoutte

Dries Van Eeckhoutte LL.B. (KULeuven), Dipl. (KCL-London) is a researcher at the Institute for International Law, Law Faculty, University of Leuven. He is working on a project for the Fund for Scientific Research-Flanders (Belgium) concerning the The Belgian and Flemish Treaty Practice in an International, Constitutional and Comparative Perspective

Tom Eijsbouts

Tom Eijsbouts is Professor of European Constitutional law and its History at the University of Amsterdam and holds a Jean Monnet chair. He also is Director of the G.K. van Hogendorp Centre for European Constitutional Studies and chairman of the editorial board of *Legal Issues of Economic Integration*.

Pieter Jan Kuijper

Pieter Jan Kuijper is presently Director in the Legal Service of the European Commission, responsible for external relations. From 1999 until 2002 he was Director of the Legal Affairs Division of the World Trade Organization (WTO). He also is Professor of European Community Law, in particular the external relations law of the Community, at the University of Amsterdam.